The Compleat

BRAHMS

JOHANNES BRAHMS
oil painting by Hermann Torggler
(Ackermanns Kunstverlag, Munich)

The Compleat

BRAHMS

*A Guide to
the Musical Works of
Johannes Brahms*

Edited by

LEON BOTSTEIN

W. W. NORTON & COMPANY
New York · London

The text of this book is composed in ITC Legacy Serif Book, with
the display set in Bernhard Tango and Charlemagne.
Composition by the Haddon Craftsmen, Inc.
Manufacturing by Courier Companies, Inc.
Book design by Charlotte Staub

Library of Congress Cataloging-in-Publication Data

The compleat Brahms : a guide to the musical works of Johannes Brahms
／ edited by Leon Botstein.
    p. cm.
    Includes bibliographical references (p.   ) and index.
    ISBN 0-393-04708-3
    1. Brahms, Johannes, 1833–1897—Criticism and interpretation.
I. Botstein, Leon.   II. Title: Compleat Brahms.
ML410.B8C64   1999
780′.92—dc21

                                                    98-43968
                                                    CIP
                                                    MN

W. W. Norton & Company, Inc., 500 Fifth Avenue, New York, N.Y. 10110
http://www.wwnorton.com

W. W. Norton & Company, Inc., 10 Coptic Street, London WC1A 1PU

1 2 3 4 5 6 7 8 9 0

CONTENTS

PREFACE

The *Compleat Brahms* was initially intended to appear during the centennial year of Brahms's death, 1997. But as fate would have it, that was not to be. What at first glance seemed a missed opportunity, however, has turned out to be fortuitous. As the bibliography included in this volume indicates, the editor and all of the authors have benefited from the explosion in new scholarship and commentary that accompanied the centenary celebrations between 1996 and early 1998. Therefore *The Compleat Brahms*—a survey of Brahms's music—marks the beginning of a second century of posthumous preoccupation with Brahms.

Why, after the outpouring of newly published writing on Brahms in 1997, is another book on Brahms needed? The justification lies in the special character and design of this volume. *The Compleat Brahms* is the first and only annotated catalog of Brahms's music in English. The closest German-language equivalent is Christian Martin Schmidt's fine *Musikführer* published in 1994. There are currently many excellent specialized as well as popular writings concerning Brahms available to readers in English, from Walter Frisch's monograph on the four Brahms symphonies and David Brodbeck's study of the First Symphony, both published in 1997, to Jan Swafford's recent biography. But there are few volumes meant to illuminate Brahms's music that address themselves to both the specialist and the general music enthusiast. *The Compleat Brahms* seeks to be of value to scholars, professional and amateur musicians, and listeners. It is a handbook and work of reference in the best sense. Practically all the works of Brahms are touched on. Every opus number has its own entry; the works without opus numbers are discussed collectively at the end of the volume.

The book is organized by genre rather than chronology. For each piece of music, basic information has been included so that English-speaking readers, or those who do not own Margit McCorkle's indispensable *Thematisch-bibliographisches Werkverzeichnis* (1984), will not be at a disadvantage. At the same time there is no effort to duplicate the wealth of scholarly detail in McCorkle's catalog. In *The Compleat Brahms,* the essential information on individual works is contextualized in brief, freestanding essays written by thirty different scholars, performers, and composers. The result is a wide-ranging though systematic source book on Brahms's music that is also a geography of current attitudes toward Brahms and toward the larger question of how we now write and think about music.

The Compleat Brahms represents what leading scholars at the end of the twentieth century think is important about the music of Brahms. The interpretive strategy deemed appropriate to each piece was chosen by the author responsible for that piece, so that no two entries will have exactly the same balance in their coverage of musical form, structure, history, biography, and affect. But while the book offers no single point of view about the composer and his works, readers will find that the essays, taken as a whole, present a remarkably well-rounded picture that no single author could provide. Eclecticism in point of view and interpretive perspective, then, are the strengths of this volume. Some entries will please while others may infuriate. The only concern about consistency has been that the volume be as useful to those who are just beginning their exploration of Brahms's music as to those who would like to extend their knowledge. The entries, by some of the world's foremost experts, can serve as introductions, as guides for listening, or as commentaries on works already familiar to the reader. For the most ambitious, comparisons between the analyses offered herein and the scores should prove rewarding. *The Compleat Brahms* hopes to inspire both active listening and reflection on the memory of what one has heard.

It was determined from the start that music examples be avoided, so that readers with no music training would nevertheless be able to follow the discussions. Among the difficult decisions that had to be made in the planning and editing of this volume, the most prominent was to omit any reference to recordings. It has become increasingly fashionable in musicology and music journalism to study and use recordings. No doubt the contemporary audience for "classical" music is no longer made up of amateurs and music lovers whose reference point is a score, but is weighted toward listeners whose attachment to music is inspired and sustained by recordings. In the current state of so-called classical music in our culture, the role of live performance is a diminished one. At any concert performance of a Brahms symphony, for example, those in the audience familiar with the work owe their acquaintance to the long-playing record and the CD, whether directly or through radio broadcast. During the first decades of the twentieth century, recording was contingent on concert life; today concert life is dependent on recordings.

As a consequence, we now find close comparisons of recordings in scholarly accounts and analyses of musical works. The vast library of recorded literature has spawned a new scholarly industry: the study of interpretation and twentieth-century performance practice using recordings as source material. The decision to omit any reference to recordings resulted from a strong—if conservative—conviction that for Brahms and all of nineteenth-century music, the printed score remains the only legitimate source of reference, particularly if the objective is to educate a new generation of listeners. The score must retain its function as a bulwark against the inherent, and welcome, transience of performance practice fashions. Contemporary performers suffer enough from a species of music criticism based mainly on comparisons with recordings, and, therefore, on interpretative tastes fashioned by recorded performances rather than by judgments based on readings of the score. Insofar as *The Compleat Brahms* is valuable to listeners and to individuals who play and sing, it is so because it legitimates divergent ways to perform and therefore interpret Brahms's music.

Of course, great music lends itself to multiple modes of sonic realization, despite the claims of some diehards who believe that there is a single "right" way to interpret a score. The music of Brahms, in part because of the composer's own terrifying penchant for self-criticism, is unusual in that much or even most of it can make a claim to "greatness" (whatever that might mean). All of it deserves a place in the standard repertory. Not surprisingly, therefore, as in the cases of Shakespeare and Goethe, one person's Brahms is not another's. A recorded performance from the 1940s may sound painfully exaggerated to some listeners, just as a recent period-instrument studio recording might sound bland, clinical, and emotionally distant to others. So, we have decided to forgo such judgments in this book.

Surely all contributors to this volume share the hope that decades from now there will be many new performances and recordings of Brahms's music. It is one thing to create a canon of musical compositions; however, the creation of a canon of CDs seems destructive to the enterprise of music. Brahms wrote for an audience that played and listened to music as acts of public and private communication—as modes of interaction among living contemporaries that demanded remembrance and repetition. Any piece exists only in the moment of its realization, whether in the mind of a person able to read or remember the music or in the hearing of those who play or listen to someone else turn the printed notation into sound. *The Compleat Brahms* seeks to honor the character of musical life that Brahms himself experienced. We would be rightly horrified if the texts of Shakespeare were no longer available or referred to, but permanently replaced by video discs of theatrical performances. Although there is no reasonable expectation that the active musical literacy within the literate public of Brahms's day will experience a resurgence, there is also no reason to believe that singers and instrumentalists of the future will not continue to recreate Brahms's music for their contemporaries, using the musical text as their starting point.

The freezing of any moment of musical performance by today's technology of both visual and auditory documentation will, despite the power of reproduction, always be an incomplete account of the musical experience. A studio recording by definition possesses no public in the ordinary sense at the moment of its creation. A live recording removes the musical event from its temporal context. In Brahms's era, the notion of music was rooted in the expectation of a response to live sounds at a discrete moment and in a particular place. That amalgam of sound and experience would then be inscribed in the memory of the listener. The listener's age, the conditions of that person's life when a particular moment of listening occurred, the individual's capacity to remember and compare past hearings from other times and places, were integral components to understanding music as a temporal and social event in the late nineteenth century. It is hard for today's readers to appreciate how rare live performances by professionals were in Brahms's day, and how much musical culture depended on reading, playing music oneself, and memory. Brahms heard Beethoven's Ninth Symphony for the first time as a young adult, even though the music was already familiar to him. The impact on him of the live performance was staggering in a way nearly inconceivable to us today. The collective biography of prominent musicians in the nineteenth century reveals how the auditory experience of professional live performances created a sequence of memories that contributed decisively to each individual's self-invention as an artist.

Recordings may, indeed, function today in an analogous way and assist in the process of self-invention among lay listeners and musicians. So one purpose of this volume is to suggest an experience of music outside of recordings—to posit for the reader the existence of a musical entity at the intersection of all interpretations. Defining that entity is an elusive task, but it can be aided by reading about music—which is why in the nineteenth century and also in the twentieth, accounts in words of musical works were indispensable allies in the appreciation of music. One hopes that given this perspective, readers of this book will find their own way through the increasing flood of available recordings of Brahms's music, and make their own critical assessments of performance practices and achievements on the basis of their reading, their experience of live performances, and their investigation of printed music.

This brings us to what may be the most daunting of challenges that lie beneath an enterprise such as *The Compleat Brahms*. How can we understand the possibilities and uses in modern life of writing about music? How does the way we talk about music, describe it, analyze it, and comment on it influence and define our habits of listening? How does it affect the formation of our emotional attachments to and preferences for works and styles? Despite the over-argued affinity between Brahms and the mid-nineteenth-century ideology of "absolute music," for Brahms and his audience music was never merely about itself: there was always more to the experience of music than a response to self-contained formalism. Just as it is today, the making of music and listening to music in Brahms's time was an effort in the creation of meaning which must necessarily refer to other modes of expression. Therefore, probably no such category as the "extramusical" exists when we think about music. Inevitably, even the most hardened formalist makes an indispensable appeal to ordinary language. Conversely, as the examples of Liszt and Wagner amply demonstrate, the capacity of music to communicate an extramusical program or meaning was dependent on the composer's command of forms and the craft of composition defined strictly within the realm of music. This accounts for the dominant role techniques of musical transformation associated with sonata form played even in the music of Brahms's antagonists, the proponents of a new music for the future. *The Compleat Brahms* therefore is an effort to present the wide varieties of meaning past and present engendered by Brahms's music.

That said, a dilemma bequeathed by nineteenth-century controversies concerning the most reasonable and useful ways to speak and write about music remains. How can language supplement and even act as a surrogate for the direct experience of music? During the eighteenth century and well into the early nineteenth, philosophers and musicians sought, with considerable enthusiasm and enjoyment, ways to describe and explain musical beauty and communication. With the advent of a large industry of music journalism during the mid-nineteenth century, philosophical speculation gave way to a more modern pattern of regular reportage and criticism, much of it on a less elevated plane than we find in the musings of Shaftesbury, Schopenhauer, Heinrich von Kleist, or Jean Paul Richter. (One trait shared by Brahms and Richard Wagner— Brahms's presumed arch-rival but also an object of his admiration—was a certain mistrust of music journalism. Their reaction to it was decidedly ambivalent, since Wagner used his own polemical skills much to his advantage, and Brahms, despite recurring doubts about Eduard Hanslick's judgment, never distanced himself from Hanslick's vociferous advocacy.) By the turn of the century, in the context of aestheticism's growing popularity, skepticism about the capacity of language to add to or illuminate the function of music became widespread. In the present, when access to recorded sound is so ubiquitous, the circumstances that led to the explosion of music journalism in the nineteenth century—represented by daily reports, weekly music magazines, guidebooks, encyclopedias, and book-length commentaries—seem to have disappeared. Since, a century ago, access to professional performances of music was rare even in large urban centers, the only way enthusiasts could keep up with developments in music was to read about concerts and new music, just as one would read about political events in distant locales. But today, when we can hear everything we want to hear at will, what is the function of writing and reading about music?

This volume mirrors some of the different and manifold alternatives that modern criticism and scholarship can offer. Some of the entries utilize very particular descriptive approaches to form and structure in a piece of music. Their language aims at analytic precision and assumes, in the act of revealing an underlying structure, coherences beyond the surface of events to which our ear naturally gravitates. This form of analysis can often point out important dimensions in a work of music that we might not otherwise notice. The knowledge of how we might understand a work to be organized gives us insight not only into its structure but into how we may respond to the work's apparent magic: its adaptations of musical conventions. This insight is particularly appropriate for Brahms, who never put pen to paper without being keenly aware of historical precedents to his own work. Several of the contributors have properly stressed the materials Brahms used—the specific instrumental practices and textures that are integral components to understanding the structure of his music.

Many entries seek to place Brahms's musical accomplishment within a biographical narrative in order to explain the origin and circumstances surrounding a work's genesis. This inherently fascinating approach has traditionally had pitfalls, not the least of which is the tendency to view Brahms's way of life and personality judgmentally or even polemically, particularly on the shadowy issues of interpersonal relations and sexuality. However, as nearly all of the modern biographers suggest, Brahms was a contradictory, complex person about whom, in the end, we know less than we would like. Even recent biographies persist in perpetuating fictions about Brahms's relationships with women. With a personality shrouded from view by so many permanent secrets and indelible myths, the use of biography becomes hazardous. Nevertheless, appeals to character and personality may assist us in understanding individual works, just as the works may even tell us something about the man. However fascinating this approach may be, it is by no means essential. The turn of the third millennium is an age obsessed with revealing the private lives of the famous. For many musicians and artists, however, an ideal circumstance might be a concert in which the names of the composers are not identified, just as the labels on paintings hanging in a museum might be best removed from view. Musicians could well be encouraged to maintain the premise that a work of music is interesting as an experience without reference to the biography or personality of its creators or re-creators.

Yet another current pattern in writing about music that is reflected in this collection is the effort by many authors to link Brahms's achievement to music history. That Brahms was profoundly aware of this history and his debt to it is not a recent discovery. Furthermore, Brahms had very strong views about the place of his generation within a trajectory in the development of music and culture. Whether they liked it or not, he and his contemporaries were heirs to a great tradition. Brahms considered himself within a generation of followers (Wagner's conceits notwithstanding) rather than one of innovators who created fundamentally new ways of writing music. His relationship to Bach, Handel, Mozart, Haydn, Beethoven, and Schumann is touched on repeatedly in these essays. Given Arnold Schoenberg's seminal twentieth-century reassessment of

Brahms's place in music history, this volume also bears witness to the current standing of Brahms from the vantage of a particular conception of music history *since* Brahms. Were nineteenth-century commentators sympathetic to Richard Wagner and Hugo Wolf alive today, they would be surprised at the prestige and popularity of Brahms's music a century later. For instance, Brahms's popularity as an orchestral composer reached its peak in the twentieth century. Possible explanations for this phenomenon can be gleaned from the pages of this book. Foremost among them may be the rise and fall of the prestige of modernism in this century. Brahms managed posthumously to please most of the contentious factions (with the possible exception of Stravinsky and his followers) surrounding modern music in our time.

Perhaps the most novel dimension in today's writing about music that is evident in this volume is the effort—as it were—to place a work within a larger construct of the history of nineteenth-century culture and society. Our contributors reflect the gradual evolution of musicology, or music history, as a humanistic discipline. When Brahms died one hundred years ago, the scholarly discipline of music history was in its infancy. Brahms's own view of the past and his efforts to preserve it contributed to the advance and position of music history as an intellectual pursuit on a par with the history of art and literature. Among Brahms's friends and protégés were Philipp Spitta and Eusebius Mandyczewski, who in turn trained a large number of important scholars. Since World War II, research in music history has extended not only chronologically to include the nineteenth century as well as the Middle Ages, the Renaissance, the Baroque, and the Classical era, but across disciplinary boundaries. The range of concerns today includes the reciprocal influences between music and literature and painting, and the connections between music and politics and social change. This volume assumes that readers will be interested in Brahms as part of the intellectual and social character of late-nineteenth-century Europe. A comparable book written fifty years ago would scarcely have touched on such issues.

All this still does not mitigate the difficulties we encounter when we try to convey our impression of music through language. Deeply aware of the philosophical and aesthetic problems attendant on describing, explaining, and appreciating music through language, writers today have all but abandoned the kind of straightforward descriptive writing we find in concert guidebooks of a century ago. When *The Compleat Brahms* was originally conceived, some thought had been given to reprinting important analyses of Brahms's music written during the last hundred years by, for instance, Hermann Kretzschmar and Donald Tovey. Further reflection led to a decision to exclude critical writings from the past, which, though historically fascinating, would make for a very different kind of book. Each generation must craft its own language of assessment and description, just as each generation of musicians must fashion its own interpretations. The late nineteenth century was fond of imposing so-called extramusical programs and emotional narratives onto instrumental music. Furthermore, writers of a century ago construed the interaction between gender, sexuality, and music quite differently. And the way earlier writers located and interpreted the expression of desire, fulfillment, and loss often bears little resemblance to the way contemporaries locate comparable experiences and connect them to music. To reprint articles on Brahms in which witnesses from the past read human sentiments onto the music is to legitimate those readings ahistorically. Insofar as contemporary listeners wish to find in Brahms's music responses to human experiences and emotions such as love, grief, and faith, they do so quite differently. Very few modern writers have the inclination (or perhaps the audacity) to assert the link between life and music in quite the way our predecessors were prone to do. Today the only tolerated field of such speculation is the biographical mode in which one tries to find Brahms's personal views of these dimensions of life in his own music. *The Compleat Brahms,* therefore, documents the current reticence or lack of confidence in connecting music normatively to internalized experience per se.

If readers, after examining this volume and reflecting on it as a tribute to the profound impact Brahms has had on the history of music, on the writing about music, and on his individual listeners (as represented by the engrossing interests, insights, and manifest enthusiasm of each of our contributors), walk away with only one impression, it should be the confirmation of two pithy observations about Brahms penned by the philosopher Ludwig Wittgenstein. In the early 1930s Wittgenstein jotted down in his notebooks two phrases: "the *strength of the thoughts* in Brahms's music" and "Brahms's overwhelming *ability.*" In two simple lines, the spirit and substance of this book's many pages are stated with brevity and eloquence.

Every preface is an occasion to give thanks. The entire project would not have come to fruition without the dedication and editorial supervision provided by Lynne Meloccaro, formerly a faculty member of the English department at the University of Rochester and currently general manager and artistic administrator of the American Symphony Orchestra. I would like to thank all of the contributors to this volume for their excellent work and for their assistance and patience. I am deeply grateful to Michael Ochs, the music editor at Norton, who first had the idea for such a volume and supported this project patiently from its inception. My thanks also to Neal Zaslaw and Walter Frisch for their support and counsel, and Irene Zedlacher for assistance in matters of translation. Finally, I thank Dorothy Miller at Bard College, whose outstanding and devoted work with me over nearly twenty years has, unfortunately for me, come to an untimely and premature end owing to her retirement. This is the last large undertaking completed with her, and it would have been impossible without her. I am still trying to imagine how I will manage in the years ahead.

Leon Botstein

The Compleat
BRAHMS

INTRODUCTION

I.

Friedrich Nietzsche in his 1874 essay "On the Use and Abuse of History" put forth a trenchant challenge to his contemporaries, claiming that they were living in an age already saturated with history. An obsessive preoccupation with history seemed to him "dangerous to life" because it "implanted the belief, harmful at any time in the old age of mankind, that one is a latecomer and epigone; it leads an age into a dangerous mood of irony in regard to itself and subsequently an even more dangerous mood of cynicism." It is perhaps ironic to introduce the work and life of Johannes Brahms through the words of Nietzsche—given the extremes of Nietzsche's initial enthusiasm for and subsequent rejection of Brahms's antipode Richard Wagner, as well as Nietzsche's lifelong doubts about Brahms's greatness. Yet Nietzsche's concern with the nineteenth century's obsession with history aptly frames the intellectual and artistic climate in which Brahms worked and against which he struggled. Brahms's achievement and character contained a central contradiction. On the one hand, there was the composer's legendary arrogance about his own understanding of tradition and the standards of musical greatness. On the other, there was Brahms's equally renowned penchant for lacerating doubt and self-criticism. The same individual could startle a young composer like Josef Suk with the laconic remark that no one, including Brahms himself, had been able to write a great quintet since Mozart, yet at the same time display an unabashed and enduring respect for a few select but not comparable contemporaries such as Antonín Dvořák and Robert Fuchs. Despite an overridingly harsh view of himself and his contemporaries, Brahms continued to struggle along well-trodden paths over which the shadow of history was relentlessly visible. He respected the German composer Max Bruch as an ally whose aesthetic ambitions paralleled Brahms's own, yet he was absolutely certain that the music of his self-styled enemy Richard Wagner far excelled anything Bruch had written or could write. Perhaps Brahms even secretly envied Wagner's overt capacity to claim that he had transcended history. Whatever his private introspections, however, Brahms's public confidence in the value and propriety of a contemporary musical aesthetic explicitly indebted to traditional models was unyielding.

Despite such contradictions, one finds ample proof of Nietzsche's observations in the case of Brahms. Brahms indeed was obsessed by the "lateness" of his day and he anguished with his contemporaries about history and historicity. Like Mendelssohn, he was an avid student of musical tradition, and he treasured his collection of autograph manuscripts, especially the music of Mozart and Schubert. Mendelssohn's famous rediscovery of Bach in 1829 marked not only the beginning of a Bach revival but of a nineteenth-century movement that invented the narrative of music history now widely familiar to us. The reemergence of the Baroque as an important era in music history and the codification of the musical Classicism of the late eighteenth and early nineteenth centuries as an ideal, normative realization of musical beauty set the stage for the definition of Romanticism, that unique movement pioneered by the first generation of composers after Beethoven. Therefore, for Mendelssohn, the search backward in time represented an effort to use history against itself, as an antidote for a generation obsessed primarily with the figure of Beethoven and the models and strategies of Beethovenian composition. By turning to Bach, Mendelssohn found a novel historical model that could circumvent Beethoven and yet offer an inspiration within history for the music of a new era. Mendelssohn's generation—also the generation of Chopin, Schumann, Liszt—entered a dialogue with the history of music that was clearly in the service of doing something new and original: in this case, the development of the Romantic movement in music.

Like the philosophical, literary, and architectural reaction to the eighteenth century during the first decades of the nineteenth (by, for example, Hegel, Novalis, Byron, Scott, Pugin), the composers who came directly after Beethoven challenged the eighteenth-century Enlightenment's facile belief in historical progress. While their contemporaries outside of music reinvented the Middle Ages, thereby defying the primacy of the rationalist, neo-Classicist Moderns, composers in the early nineteenth century began to reach beyond Classicism to the Baroque and ultimately the Renaissance. For Brahms, however, the previous generation of Schumann and Mendelssohn was itself part of the musical past with which *he* had to contend. His view of history was far less sanguine than Mendelssohn's and was, as Nietzsche's comment suggests, ironic, pessimistic, and verging on the cynical. Brahms perceived himself as someone working within an already established nineteenth-century framework defined by Beethoven and Schumann.

Therefore, his ambitions were to extend and perfect the models not only of Classicism but of early Romanticism. He saw himself as a leading creative figure in a mature, if not declining, musical culture. The bittersweet and melancholy aspects so frequently commented upon in Brahms's music are thus not surprising. With the exception of the stormy, powerful, and ecstatic works of his youth—particularly the D-minor Piano Concerto—much of Brahms's work has an inward turn, away from the theatrical and dramatic. It is what Nietzsche might have called "subjective"—that is, not directed toward the invention of a novel, outward, public culture, but rather toward self-reflection, introspection, and intimacy.

But Brahms did not fall entirely into the category of an epigone as Nietzsche defined it, for in addition to the fecundity of his musical mind and the extraordinary talent, imagination, and ingenuity he displayed, Brahms possessed something to which Nietzsche was entirely tone-deaf: a profound, simple, and unassuming religiosity. Alongside Brahms's pessimism, self-criticism, and historical anxiety a fundamental belief in the grace of God, a sustaining faith, co-existed. Although, ironically, this faith increased Brahms's dismay at the spiritual trajectory of the nineteenth century, he remained a loyal Protestant who believed that our essential fallen nature made work guided by faith an absolute necessity for any individual seeking to achieve something of value in the world. The struggle to achieve goodness and beauty was a noble but involuntary, God-given task that demanded—of the individual whose calling was art—modesty, frugality, self-discipline, inflexible standards, and above all awe for God's creations, humanity and nature. Artistic narcissism was for Brahms the enemy of artistic production. Therefore, nothing could have been more distasteful and destructive to true art and beauty than the mannerisms and decadent aestheticism of Richard Wagner and late-nineteenth-century music's inclination toward the grandiose, lavish, megalomaniac, and grotesque.

Brahms displayed the characteristics of great genius while retaining the traits of his simple, hardworking, lower middle-class background; throughout his life he remained a man of humble pretensions and tastes. An autodidact who felt somewhat defensive about his lack of formal education, he embraced uncritically the nineteenth century's voracious appetite and enthusiasm for *Bildung*—culture and learning. He once confided to Gisela von Arnim that as a young man, he spent every penny he had on books. Later in life, he became an avid student of ancient history who loved classical antiquity. He was truly impressed once to have witnessed, during a vacation in Italy, the admiration expressed by the ordinary public for Theodor Mommsen, the great German historian of Rome. Despite his pessimistic outlook, Brahms was fascinated with philosophy, science, and the progress of knowledge. He was delighted by new gadgets and inventions such as Edison's phonograph (for which he made a cameo recording speaking and playing one of his *Hungarian* rhapsodies). Brahms enjoyed the friendship of a diverse group of Viennese intellectuals, including the classicist Theodor Gomperz and Theodor Billroth, a leading pioneer in thoracic and abdominal surgery. For Brahms, the progress of modernity centered on the enterprise of science and scholarship, and therefore on professionals who acknowledged their indebtedness to the past, even if that explicit indebtedness forced the transcending of the established boundaries of knowledge. If art could be construed as being analogous to science and scholarship, it becomes clear why Brahms never flirted with the illusions indulged in by Richard Wagner, who like Swift's famous spider dreamed of spinning a world and culture anew entirely from himself. One can understand Brahms as implicitly sympathetic with the position articulated by Matthew Arnold in his classic of nineteenth-century cultural criticism, *Culture and Anarchy* (1869). From our current perspective at the end of the twentieth century, we recognize in Brahms a profound philosophical insight: that the pretensions of Wagner and his followers (as Nietzsche later came to realize) were self-delusive; the ostentatious assertion of a break with the past and the confident claim to have reinvented art actually manifested the worst aspects of the nineteenth century's obsession with history.

What finally endures from Wagner's ambitious project is what Brahms credited Wagner with from the start: an utterly remarkable command of musical discourse and a staggering degree of musical invention, all of which made Wagner's philosophical and poetic apparatus, if not plausible, at least tolerable.

Perhaps because of Brahms's outspoken apprehensions concerning the cultural trends toward debased standards of musical taste and connoisseurship, Brahms was unfairly cast during his lifetime as the standard-bearer of a conservative movement in musical aesthetics. He was both hailed and pilloried as a champion of the tradition of Schumann and Mendelssohn. His close friendship with the preeminent Viennese music critic Eduard Hanslick led to a facile association between Brahms and the mid-nineteenth-century theory of "absolute" music articulated by Hanslick in his famous 1854 book *On the Beautiful in Music.* According to Hanslick's theory, which became widely popular, music was an essentially formalist art, self-referential, autonomous in its means, and incapable of representing emotions, ordinary meanings, and narratives. Brahms's introspective style and the non-theatrical use of musical language, as well as the traditional compositional forms he favored, fostered the prevailing perception of a reductive opposition between him and the innovative, progressive, and modern in music, represented by the New German School—initially by Liszt and Wagner, and later during the 1890s by Richard Strauss and Gustav Mahler. Mahler himself is reputed to have considered Brahms a melancholy genius obsessed by the past rather than the possibilities of the present. Mahler's contemporary Hugo Wolf, embittered by what he imagined to be Brahms's disrespect for the talents of a new generation (particularly his own), relentlessly harried Brahms in the 1880s as an empty, vacuous imitator who rehashed the past.

A significant reversal in this view was sparked during the first half of the twentieth century by the intervention of Arnold Schoenberg. Schoenberg's renowned essay "Brahms the Progressive," written in 1933 and revised in 1947, sought to rectify the older perception of Brahms as a conservative. By 1909, Schoenberg was well on his way in his own struggle to break free from the legacy of Wagner. Like Mendelssohn's appropriation of Bach, Schoenberg's turn to the unlikely source of Brahms as the legitimizing model of history for the radical innovations of twentieth-century modernism was startling. Brahms the previous

generation's conservative now became Brahms the forerunner of a new
approach to musical composition which favored thematic transformation without excessive repetition, smaller instrumental ensembles, an
avoidance of Brucknerian scale, and an abandonment of extramusical
programs for instrumental music. For all his pretensions to innovation,
Schoenberg was keenly aware that the path for the early twentieth century that he championed after 1920 was itself an explicit rejection of
late-nineteenth-century enthusiasms and a return to the very models
that Brahms himself had admired: Mozart and Haydn. Insofar as
Beethoven was invoked, it was Brahms's Beethoven, not Wagner's—the
romanticizing Classicist, not Classicism's great dramatist and harbinger
of the music drama—that became the paradigm for musical modernism.
The sea change vis-à-vis Brahms that Schoenberg occasioned has itself
now become the subject of criticism, just as the modernism he championed has receded from prominence as exclusively emblematic of
twentieth-century music. Schoenberg's perspective was too rooted in debunking the late-nineteenth-century conservative image of Brahms. In
his attempt to revise his contemporaries' understanding of Brahms,
Schoenberg accepted too uncritically the idea that Brahms was an adherent of formalist aesthetics. Although Brahms believed in the autonomy of music and cherished its unique capacity for abstraction as well as
its apparent independence from words and pictures, Brahms was closer
to Schumann and Mendelssohn than Schoenberg believed. Brahms
shared with Wagner a crucial aspect of nineteenth-century expectations:
that music engage the listener's emotions and visual imagination.
Schoenberg's image of Brahms the progressive as a kind of neo-Classicist
and as the master of developing variation was not so much inaccurate as
incomplete.

It is a unique synthesis of musical Classicism and nineteenth-century
expressiveness that makes Brahms so compelling to listeners at the turn
of the twenty-first century. If one considers the surface appeal of
Brahms's music for non-musicians as well as the deeper formal subtleties
in which professional musicians delight, one encounters the protean
character of his music, its resistance to facile categorization, and its capacity to sound forever new and vibrant. Brahms's music has the intensity and emotional immediacy we associate with late Romanticism, as
well as the grace, clarity, symmetry, and interior invention we associate
with Classicism. Brahms's music, though in a form utterly different from

Wagner's, was in the end designed for much the same task as Wagner's: to communicate to the listener genuine insight into the human predicament and human soul. If one sets aside the interpretive tyranny generated by Hanslick's dichotomy, it is clear that Brahms's ambition was most reminiscent of two of his idols, Mozart and Schubert. As with these composers, there is certainly nothing dry about Brahms, though at the same time few composers have managed to produce so much music that is as flawless in its economy as it is unerring in its command of structure and time. As an artist, Brahms managed to elude the destiny suggested by Nietzsche. Brahms transcended a preoccupation with the past by creating music rooted in history that is still capable of engaging subsequent generations of listeners whose connections to the past are at best severely attenuated.

II.

When we consider the life of this extraordinary individual, we immediately find ourselves embroiled in another historical legacy, for it was during the nineteenth century that biography assumed its dominant and pervasive status as the primary form of music history. The cult of the heroic innovator, inherited from Romanticism, fostered by the larger-than-life antics of celebrated personalities and clothed in biography, is still an active force in our own perceptions of history. Furthermore, Freud's construct of personality as an interpretable narrative still influences the way we think about history and art, despite the precipitous decline in respect for his methods in the science of psychology and the practice of medicine. Psychology, particularly in music history, remains a favored route for those in search of interpretation and explanation for the unnerving differences between those possessing artistic genius and ourselves. Our abiding concern with a composer's interpersonal relationships is a kind of intellectual residue of the nineteenth century's excessive investment in the artist as a deviant personality. Beethoven was glorified in the years after his death as a freestanding, rebellious genius, whose rough mannerisms and defiance of bourgeois expectations also resulted in a life presumably condemned to unrequited love and sexual disappointment. Schumann may have led an overtly mundane domestic life with his wife and children. But his wife was Clara Wieck, and the difference in their ages caused something of a scandal.

And of course, Schumann performed the ultimate Romantic feat of going insane. Chopin's relationship with George Sand has become the cultural archetype of the ambivalent passion of the artist, and Berlioz's life and memoirs did much to secure his image as a romantically obsessed, near-mad genius. In the category of self-conscious legend-making, Paganini and Liszt equaled the rock stars of the present; theirs were lives marked by seemingly endless trails of orchestrated conquests and infatuations. Following their lead, Wagner surpassed all of them. The nineteenth-century cult of personality provided Wagner with a platform for a spectacular self-fashioning in which the division between personal and public was intentionally obscured and ordinary rules of behavior discarded.

For those composers who did not help themselves in this respect, twentieth-century scholarship has provided insight into their inner isolation, eccentricities, and genius. Mahler's relationship with Alma has offered a limitless resource for pseudo-biographical, psychological explanations for his music. Schubert's alleged bisexuality (with particular emphasis on his homosexual attachments) has not only determined much of the recent critical work on his music but has been used to promote CD sales. Tchaikovsky's homosexuality has become a favorite starting point for contemporary interpretations of his works. Would Beethoven be surprised to learn that his purported kissing of the young Liszt on the forehead would become the subject of an entire volume on music, culture, and history? By way of contrast, when composers whose domestic and sexual lives were relatively unremarkable are subjected without much success to biographical elaboration and criticism, our perception of their artistic achievement becomes colored. For example, despite halting attempts to inject mystery into Felix Mendelssohn's close relation with his sister Fanny and to speculate on Richard Strauss's marriage to a philistine and obnoxious woman, the reputations of both of these composers remain dogged by charges of superficiality, as though a stable lifestyle translates into an absence of artistic depth.

Within this kaleidoscope of nineteenth- and twentieth-century constructs of composers' lives and romantic attachments, Brahms's life has been quite resistant to convincing interpretation and characterization. This does not mean, however, that since his death Brahms's life and activities have not been subject to constant and penetrating scrutiny. His first biographer, Max Kalbeck, the Viennese critic and writer, had been a loyal friend who deeply admired Brahms. When Kalbeck produced his four-volume, nearly hagiographic biography (1904–14), he presented Brahms's daily life as the subject of interest and defined the outlines of biographical interpretation. All subsequent biographers have had to contend with expanding and debunking Kalbeck's account.

From Kalbeck's initial effort to the most recent contributions in the 1990s (see the Bibliography), the recurring focus of fascination in Brahms's biography has been his personal relations, his sexuality, and the influence of his apparent psychological isolation from others on his creative output. He was born in 1833 in Hamburg to a twenty-seven-year-old local musician and his wife, a seamstress who was forty-four. Johanna Brahms was at an extremely advanced age for childbirth for that era, but that did not stop her two years later from giving birth to yet another child, Brahms's brother Fritz. Like so many other famous composers, such as Mozart and Beethoven, Brahms, the son of a musician, took his first music lessons from his father. At the age of eight, Brahms began piano lessons with Otto F. W. Cossel, who quickly recognized his student's aptitude and persuaded the Brahms family to allow their eldest son to study with Eduard Marxsen, a prominent figure in Hamburg. With Marxsen, Brahms studied piano and composition in a purely Classical regimen. (Brahms's lifelong disaffection with some dominant attitudes of his time—such as anti-Semitism—is apparent in his loyalty to Marxsen, about whom Robert Schumann remarked upon meeting him, "His Jewish physiognomy disgusted me." Brahms's circle of friends consistently included many leading Jewish figures and prominent liberals.)

While in Hamburg, the fifteen-year-old Brahms heard the seventeen-year-old violin virtuoso Joseph Joachim (who was of Jewish birth) play the Beethoven Violin Concerto, a work that Joachim almost single-handedly reintroduced into the standard repertory. Over the next five years, Brahms earned a moderate reputation in Hamburg as a pianist and teacher. During his lifetime, performance and composition were still inextricably linked, and it was therefore natural that young Brahms should begin to compose. Brahms's performing skills led him to the major breakthrough in his career: a concert tour in 1853 with the Hungarian violinist Eduard Reményi. In the course of that tour, Brahms finally met the much admired Joachim in person, and was introduced to Robert and Clara Schumann. The young Hamburg composer suddenly found himself in a cosmopolitan circle of intellectuals and artists that utterly transformed his life and ambitions. His acceptance by Schumann was invaluable. In a landmark 1853 article, Schumann hailed Brahms as the new hope of the future of music. This approbation became Brahms's official passport of approval into the highest circles of musical culture; it also legitimated the heavy burden of scrutiny that would haunt the composer for many years.

Joseph Joachim (1831–1907) became Brahms's closest friend and colleague for most of his adult life. Despite a brief rift years later when Brahms sided with Amalie Weiss during the dissolution of Joachim's marriage to the singer, Joachim remained a faithful advocate of Brahms's music and proved especially helpful in establishing Brahms with English audiences. In the 1850s, Brahms and Joachim lived together in Joachim's room in Göttingen (Brahms's only student-life experience; he never attended university himself). They made concert tours together and, in 1856, began the mutual counterpoint studies that would have so great an effect on Brahms's music, particularly for chorus. However, it is Brahms's relationship with Clara Schumann that continues to engage biographers most intensely. Brahms corresponded with his friends regularly. The two volumes of letters between Clara and himself (as well as the correspondence with Joachim) remain the primary source for an understanding of Brahms's personality and creative process.

Clara Schumann was a renowned pianist and brilliant musician as well as an intense and compelling individual who, at age thirty-three, was still a young woman when she met the twenty-year-old Brahms. Brahms never married, even though throughout his life there were several women to whom he developed close attachments, including Schumann's daughter Julie, Agathe von Siebold, Elisabet von Herzogenberg, and Hermine Spies. But no other relationship with a woman ever rivaled Brahms's love for Clara during the 1850s. His attachment to Clara, compared to, for example, Tchaikovsky's relationship with his patroness Nadezhda von Meck, provides an illuminating illustration of the ambivalence inherent in biographical depictions of the composer as artist. Deviance and aberration of lifestyle are often cited to explain what distinguishes the artist from "average" people, but that deviance is just as often diffused in the presentation, especially if it is of a nature to diminish our exaltation of the artist. In the case of Tchaikovsky, many early-twentieth-century commentators have considered his close relationship with Madame von Meck (whom Tchaikovsky never met) as a kind of surrogate marriage, a safe and softening context for the composer's documented homosexuality. In the case of Brahms, one could say that after 1854, he was tied to Clara Schumann as to no one else, in a relationship that can be effectively compared to marriage (despite the geographical distance between them after 1861). There is every reason to suspect that Brahms and Clara Schumann were intimate with one another perhaps until 1858, though there is no conclusive documentation. Yet generations of scholars have produced complex rhetorical exercises to quell such an insinuation. Based on a spectrum of propriety including puritanical prejudices then, biographical traditions have imposed a psychologically "normalizing" relationship onto Tchaikovsky with extremely slim justification, and, despite considerable circumstantial evidence, have denied a "normal" consummated relationship to the unmarried Brahms and Clara Schumann. Clara died in 1896 at the age of seventy-seven. Brahms's last great work, *Vier ernste Gesänge*, Op. 121, was his valedictory expression of attachment to her. Apart from the personal dimension of their relationship, the extent to which each regarded the other as a professional equal and the degree to which the substantive discussions of music secured their intimacy are striking. Few composers of Brahms's stature in the history of music can be said to have had a relationship with another musician in which the personal and the professional were so profoundly intertwined.

The years of 1854 to 1862 represented a relatively peripatetic creative period in Brahms's life. He came into contact with leading musicians of the day, and his reputation as a composer continued to grow. He lived in Hamburg, Detmold, and Düsseldorf, teaching, playing, and conducting as well as composing. From 1862 to 1871 he lived in and out of Vienna, working as a choral conductor and teacher. When his mother died in 1865 (when Brahms was thirty-two), it occasioned a work that proved to be his greatest single public triumph, *Ein deutsches Requiem*. In 1871 Brahms moved into Karlsgasse 4 in Vienna, the home he would occupy until his death. The house stood near the city's most famous architectural landmark, the great Baroque Karlskirche designed by Fischer von Erlach. In the last twenty-five years of his life, Brahms played a decisive public role in the musical and cultural life of the Habsburg capital. From 1871 to 1875 he served as a director of the Gesellschaft der Musikfreunde, succeeding Anton Rubinstein, the Russian pianist and composer for whose music Brahms had limited respect. Brahms eventually became a member of the board of directors of the Society. After 1875, he did not teach in any formal capacity nor hold any institutional appointment—a significant acknowledgment of his success as a composer, which permitted him to live a comfortable life on the basis of royalties and income from concerts. In addition to writing music, he devoted his time to working as a music historian, participating in critical editions of Schumann, Schubert, and Bach, and collecting manuscripts. He would bequeath his remarkable collection of music manuscripts to the Gesellschaft der Musikfreunde. Brahms also traveled regularly every summer, vacationing in Austria, Switzerland, and Italy. His circle of musical friends in Vienna and Budapest included many composers and performers.

In this final quarter-century of his life, Brahms achieved the stature of a leading public figure, an important voice in culture and music. This standing was a responsibility he took seriously. He was helpful to his extensive circle of devoted friends, including the composers Karl Goldmark, Robert Fuchs, and Johann Strauss, Jr., the pianists Julius Epstein, Ignaz Brüll, and Anton Door, and the critic Eduard Hanslick. He also found himself involved in factious disagreements, some of which were imposed more by the critical establishment than by any action on his part. His well-known rivalry with Wagner, symbolized by the *Tannhäuser* manuscript that Wagner gave to Brahms and later demanded back, was exacerbated by Wagner's triumphant return visit to Vienna in 1875 and the rising spell of Wagnerism. In response to this acclaim, Brahms turned his compositional attention to large-scale orchestral works, revitalizing a tradition that Wagner had pronounced dead. Tension then developed between Brahms and Anton Bruckner, a devoted Wagnerian and symphonic composer who also settled in Vienna in the 1860s. Although Bruckner taught at the Conservatory where Brahms served on the board, the social and artistic divide between them was never bridged. When Bruckner died, however, Brahms attended his funeral.

As a public figure, Brahms was much more interested in fostering young talent than he was in defending himself against rivals. In the 1880s, his music found an influential champion in the great conductor Hans von Bülow. Brahms and Bülow embarked on an unprecedented tour with Bülow's fabled Meiningen orchestra—one of the first orchestras to tour throughout Europe. After 1875, he became particularly attached to Dvořák and energetically advocated his music. When Dvořák was in America in the 1890s, Brahms personally helped copy-edit Dvořák's manuscripts for publication. By that time, Brahms was a revered and popular figure in Vienna. The young, handsome composer of the 1850s, beardless and angelic looking, had gradually transformed himself into a portly, bearded, cigar-smoking, avuncular presence, renowned for his outspoken views, sharp tongue, dry wit, and childlike playfulness. He enjoyed life as a highly prized guest and acquaintance of the financial and social elite of the city, and even indulged in a final infatuation with Alice Barbi, a soprano he met in 1890. In 1891, Brahms, approaching sixty, began to think that his career as a composer was nearing its end. It is an enduring loss to the musical world that the older composer was allowed to pass judgment on the work of his younger self. Brahms carefully sifted through manuscripts and destroyed numerous works to ensure that after his death nothing would remain that did not meet his present standard.

The sorrows of 1894 serve as a counterbalance to the glories of 1853 in Brahms's life. His melancholy nature had been reinforced by the death of many friends, old and young, including Elisabet von Herzogenberg, Theodor Billroth, Hans von Bülow, and the Bach scholar Philipp Spitta. Although Brahms took pleasure in the younger talents who admired him, including Richard Strauss, Eugen d'Albert, Josef Suk, and Ernst von Dohnányi, Brahms's loneliness became an increasingly dominant feature of his disposition. By 1896, the year both Bruckner and Clara Schumann died, Brahms was already visibly ill with cancer. In his final year he was surrounded by friends and devotees, including Kalbeck and Brahms's amanuensis, the composer and critic Richard Heuberger. His health deteriorated rapidly through the autumn of 1896. His last public appearances in Vienna included attendance at a performance of his Fourth Symphony by the Vienna Philharmonic and the premiere of his friend Johann Strauss, Jr.'s *The Goddess of Reason.*

Looking back over Brahms's life, we can divide it into a reductive but useful scheme of four distinct periods. The first (1833–53) comprises his youth and early development. The second (1853–62) includes the crucial years of early fame and maturation. The earlier phase of his years in Vienna (1862–75) are years of clarification during which Brahms reinvented himself as a composer, decided to settle in Vienna and develop a new persona quite distinct from the young man who had burst upon the scene in 1853. The final phase (1875–97) encompasses the years of the mature Viennese Brahms. These phases roughly mirror the range of genres in which Brahms worked, from solo piano pieces to music for voice and chorus and the great symphonic masterpieces of the late 1870s and 1880s. These years also span a range of social change from the pre-1848 European world to the thoroughly modern industrialized late-nineteenth-century civilization of the 1890s. In Brahms as in few other composers, we have a musical mirror of nineteenth-century Europe extending from the work of the early Romantics to the onset of modernism, from the early Nazarene painters to Arnold Böcklin and Max Klinger, from a world entranced by E.T.A. Hoffmann to one engaged with the writings of Theodor Fontane and the young Thomas Mann, from the world of Schumann to that of Mahler and the young Schoenberg.

If, rather than trying to understand the effects of such a wide historical canvas on Brahms's music, we wanted to learn what this great man thought about these developments, we might consider browsing through the library Brahms left behind when he died. There, the evolution from late-eighteenth-century Classicism to turn-of-the-nineteenth-century incipient modernity is represented in works of literature, philosophy, the visual arts, and science. The walls of his home were adorned with everything from a copy of Raphael to a Klinger etching of a landscape painting by Böcklin. Clearly, Brahms took enormous pains to understand the consequences of history and his place in it. Yet this massive musical, philosophical, and political context will always be only a partial guide and in the end illuminate only dimly the music which, as it is played and heard by readers of this volume, reinvents itself for the listener without the residue of the historical encounters that created it.

It is perhaps music's unique capacity as a performed art in time, independent of language, to shed its original, historical patina or identification and fit into a new cultural and social context—that of new listeners—with remarkable ease. But in order to achieve this cherished result, the music of the past must in some indescribable way defy predictability and triumph over repetition, convention, and facile description. When at the end of his life Brahms was compared to Bach and Beethoven, his contemporaries were acknowledging their belief that in the future, the act of rediscovery and reinvention that had been applied to Bach and Beethoven by subsequent generations would be possible in the case of Brahms. Steeped in the lessons of history, the composer was certainly aware of how easily a celebrated artist could vanish from memory. Perhaps he smiled at the apparent shortsightedness and disregard for history that his contemporaries' lavish praise implied. But could he have known how right they were to predict his enduring fame, his characteristic modesty would have made him the first to appreciate the irony that, despite his historical erudition, the most startling shortsightedness turned out to be his own.

1863

1865 *1866 (?)*

THE YOUNG BRAHMS

Part One

ORCHESTRAL MUSIC

INTRODUCTION

Brahms's posthumous reputation owes a great deal to his mastery of larger orchestral forms. The two piano concertos and the violin concerto are now essential components of the standard repertory, and the four symphonies are largely responsible for Brahms's inclusion in that most elite of triumvirates in the popular imagination, "the three B's." In the context of Brahms's career, this basis of recognition is somewhat ironic, for Brahms found the writing of orchestral music a particularly daunting prospect. His delay in composing his First Symphony is legendary and has long been considered traumatic, since the two Serenades and the First Piano Concerto initially met with mixed response. It was only later in his career—after he was securely established in Vienna and had achieved enough success as a composer to allow him finally to give up his desire for a permanent, salaried position—that Brahms was able to produce a steady stream of great orchestral music.

The initial (and constant) manifestation of Brahms's genius lies in his works for solo piano, chamber music, and choral music. This fact, perhaps more than any other, indicates the fine edge between two generations in which Brahms walked during his lifetime. In the 1850s, after his entrance into the circle of Robert and Clara Schumann, and particularly through his relationship with the great violinist and promising composer Joseph Joachim, Brahms became painfully aware of his own shortcomings in the technique of orchestration. It was Joachim, and not Brahms's teacher, the pianist Eduard Marxsen, who guided Brahms through the subtleties of orchestration. In many ways, Brahms's early career mirrored the requirements of musical culture in German-speaking Europe during the first part of the nineteenth century. Choral societies flourished, the middle-class market for chamber and piano music was well established, and the tradition of aristocratic patronage still held attractive opportunities for composers. As a young man, Brahms desired above all else to follow the same path as his idols of the previous generation and find the security of an appointment to a court or to an urban musical institution. His tenure at the court of Detmold as a conductor and piano teacher from 1857 to 1860 resulted in the Serenades and lay important groundwork for his concertos and for a great deal of chamber and piano music. His later appointment, in 1863, as conductor of the Vienna Singakademie produced some of his most memorable choral works for small ensemble. Brahms's professional positions at such institutions were a determining factor in the chamber music character of his compositions.

But during the twenty years between Robert Schumann's 1853 article "New Paths"—hailing Brahms as the hope of the future—and the appearance of the *Haydn* Variations and the First Symphony, the musical world had changed dramatically. The standard career path for composer-performers through patronage was rapidly becoming obsolete. In his article, Schumann already recognized that Brahms needed to "direct his magic wand where the powers of the masses of chorus and orchestra may lend him their forces." Brahms realized that his aesthetic and musical commitments could no longer be sustained within the confined realms of court circles or the patronage of connoisseurs. The new musical culture of mid-nineteenth-century Europe increasingly depended on large-scale public events held on the concert stage, reflecting the shift in the composer's social position to that of a public professional. Great orchestral works, particularly for a composer who did not write operas, oratorios, or Masses, had become especially crucial by the mid-1870s, when an open struggle for the musical soul, as it were, of the contemporary audience was under way. But despite Schumann's assertion that Brahms's piano sonatas were "veiled symphonies," all of Brahms's explicit attempts to write a symphony before the 1870s were unsuccessful. (See discussions of the First Piano Concerto and the Serenade Op. 11.) Brahms's difficulties have conventionally been ascribed to his struggle to answer the question that plagued his generation—namely, what to write after Beethoven.

The appearance of another larger-than-life figure may have helped Brahms to conquer this obstacle. Richard Wagner gave an urgency to Brahms's need to create large-scale orchestral works. If indeed the rivalry between Brahmsians and Wagnerians has a legitimate historical basis, it became manifest in the 1870s and 1880s, and Brahms sought to disprove through music rather than through polemic the Wagnerian claims about the future of music. Wagner argued that the symphony was a historically dated form, and the achievement of Beethoven logically led not to orchestral music but to music drama. Historians have persistently assumed that between the death of Schumann in 1856 and the first performance of Brahms's C-minor Symphony, there was a lull in the fortunes of the symphonic form. Actually, a large number of symphonies were performed and published, but the quality of these works was at best uneven and seemed to give credence to Wagner's claims that the symphony was an anachronistic form of musical expression whose moment had passed.

Wagner's success, therefore, may have had the ironic consequence of inspiring one of the greatest symphonic composers in history. Initially paralyzed by the towering precedent of Beethoven, Brahms came to the rescue of the Beethovenian legacy with his first symphony in 1875, the same year that Wagner conducted a memorable series of concerts in Vienna. Brahms's composition of the Second Piano Concerto, Op. 83, the Violin Concerto, Op. 77, and the Double Concerto, Op. 102, may also be understood as a response to the cultural politics and milieu of his own time—particularly to the Wagnerian challenge. In his orchestral works Brahms explicitly chose to render historical precedent relevant to his own day, rather than, like Bruckner, reinvent the symphony in the spirit of Wagner. Few would dispute that Brahms was entirely successful in his endeavor. The four symphonies and the later orchestral music not only became the edifice upon which Brahms's reputation was based, but his achievement reasserted the relevance of Classical models and set the stage for the revival of large instrumental forms without programs during the twentieth century.

1

SERENADES

SERENADE NO. 1 IN D MAJOR, OPUS 11
Composed 1857–60; published 1860

SCORING: 2 flutes, 2 oboes, 2 clarinets, 2 bassoons, 4 horns, 2 trumpets,
timpani, strings

MOVEMENTS: 1. Allegro molto; 2. Scherzo: Allegro non troppo. Trio: Poco
più moto; 3. Adagio non troppo; 4. Menuetto I, Menuetto II; 5. Scherzo:
Allegro; 6. Rondo: Allegro

The two Serenades Opp. 11 and 16 are closely associated with
Brahms's Detmold period (1857–60), when he taught and played piano
and had charge of the court choir during three winter seasons. His biographer Max Kalbeck and others have attributed the markedly Classical
stylistic features (in great contrast to the preceding, first orchestral work,
the Piano Concerto in D Minor, Op. 15) to his study of the orchestral
scores of Haydn and the wind serenades of Mozart, and to the fine playing of the winds of the court orchestra. However, the origin of Op. 11 suggests a broader provenance. The work was first composed as chamber
music, apparently for wind and strings, either first as an octet (as noted
by Brahms's Detmold colleague Karl Bargheer) or as a nonet for horn,
flute, two clarinets, bassoon, and strings (which Kalbeck notes as its scoring when first performed). This semiorchestral format, taken with the
number of movements, rather suggests such works as Beethoven's Septet
and Schubert's Octet, both for similar ensembles, though Brahms's
prominent use of the horn solo might be attributed to memories of the
eighteenth-century serenade and symphony. The score, from which
Joseph Joachim first conducted on March 28, 1859, at a special Philhar-

monic concert in the Wörmerscher Saal in Hamburg, "for small orchestra" (with augmented strings) has not survived, and neither have the parts; recent performances and recordings have been of "reconstructed" versions.

From its first reference, in the summer of 1858, the Serenade in D seems to have been known as a four-movement work, comprising the present outer movements, an Andante (apparently the present Adagio non troppo) and a "Trio," which was probably the first Minuet, in triple meter and three parts. In December followed "two new scherzos and a minuet" to make the six-movement work. But Brahms had long had doubts about the scoring—and Joachim had already pointed out the awkwardness of the violin writing in the sixth movement—eventually concluding that the work was of symphonic character. On December 8, 1859, Brahms asked Joachim to send music paper in full score for him to rework the Serenade as a "symphony," commenting that the work was not right, but a "hybrid." By this time, Joachim had come to know it as a "symphony serenade," and the manuscript temporarily bore this title, but it was later deleted. The work was first performed in the final version by Joachim conducting the court orchestra of Hanover on March 3, 1860. The score was sent to the publisher Breitkopf & Härtel in Leipzig on July 14, 1860 (now with the opus number 11 instead of 18), and published by the firm in December 1860 as Serenade in D Major "for full orchestra" with parts (to distinguish it from the Serenade in A "for small orchestra," published by Simrock in November 1860), and also in a four-hand arrangement by Brahms, which had been completed in May 1859.

Though Brahms remained attached to the earlier version of the work, Joachim was right in recognizing its symphonic character. Its powerful tuttis and broad ideas demand a full orchestra for achieving a full effect. But the title "Serenade" is still justified by the preponderance of typically outdoor ideas associated with the horn, clarinet, and flute solos, and the often dancelike character of the music, which even extends to the developmental passages. In providing two scherzos and paired minuets (the latter effectively functioning as a transition from slow movement to second scherzo), Brahms allies the multi-movement character of the Classical serenade to a range of styles that display features suggestive of Haydn, early Beethoven, and Schubert, while always suffused with his characteristic warmth of feeling, to make a very individual whole—for this work is no pastiche. Though its symphonic significance was short-lived (Brahms produced a genuine symphonic first movement, which begins like the Allegro of the First Symphony, by 1862), this Serenade laid a crucial foundation for the composer's mature style in its integrated yet idiomatic use of the orchestra, free of pianistic thinking.

In the chamber version, the wind instruments were used very idiomatically, tied stylistically to traditional associations. Thus, the use of duetting clarinets in sixths over an articulated pedal in the bassoon in Menuetto I; the bold solo horn theme in hunting style at the beginning of the work, and likewise that in the second Scherzo and its Trio; the scherzo theme and its counterpointing bass have been related respectively to the Scherzo in Beethoven's Symphony No. 2 and the Finale of Haydn's Symphony No. 104 (both also in D major). The revised version of the work hardly extends the characterization of the ideas at all, leading themes being given throughout to the flute, clarinets, horn, and bassoon, the additional instruments used rather to balance the full string group in the tuttis. A particular feature taken from the original in the first movement and especially in the third is the extensive woodwind writing in the codas, recalling the parallel point in the third movement of Beethoven's *Pastoral* Symphony, a movement already strongly hinted at in the string figuration in the transition passage to the second theme. Yet in formal terms, Brahms overweighed the serenade genre with the concentration of his ideas and their working. The first movement is longer than those of any of the symphonies: 574 measures without the repeat of the lengthy exposition, which has much repetition in the first thematic group and a weighty closing group. The ternary-form third movement is also symphonic in breadth, with a leisurely transition to the central section and a striking false reprise of the exposition, beginning in F♯ major before the predictable tonic, B♭. The sonata-rondo Finale is also expansive and plays a structural role in completing the whole, with a recomposed recapitulation that reverses the themes and leads to a reflective coda before the tutti conclusion. Even one of the minuets displays developmental features. Menuetto II functions not as a trio contrast but as a wistful commentary on the closing phrase of its companion, substituting minor for major and strings for winds. Only one movement is driven by a really Brahmsian idea: the first

Scherzo has a mysterious "unison" idea in the lower strings which realizes its contrapuntal implications when imitation occurs in the course of
a lengthy exposition, made more effective by the total contrast of a swing-
ing trio at a quicker tempo in the submediant major, B♭. The work was
not easily accepted in early performances; features to which modern listeners are accustomed—cross rhythms, intricate part-writing, subtleties
of blend and balance—presented entirely new challenges to players at
the time.

Michael Musgrave

SERENADE NO. 2 IN A MAJOR, OPUS 16
Composed 1858–60; published 1860

SCORING: piccolo, 2 flutes, 2 oboes, 2 clarinets, 2 bassoons, 2 horns, violas,
cellos, basses
MOVEMENTS: 1. Allegro moderato; 2. Scherzo: Vivace; 3. Adagio non
troppo; 4. Quasi Menuetto; 5. Rondo: Allegro

Unlike its predecessor, the Serenade in D, the Serenade in A was apparently conceived in its finished version from the start, and was completed more quickly. Its scoring is much closer to that of the Mozartean
serenade in its use of a full wind complement of doubled clarinets, flutes,
horns, and bassoons. Its twelve independent wind and brass parts create
a self-sufficient ensemble to which strings are added for contrast and
counterpoint rather than essential support. However, Brahms gives an
entirely original dimension to the concept by the use of a string body
without violins, thereby adding a mellow quality to the whole; the thematic lead is invariably given to the winds, with the violas and cellos
often doubled in thematic response rather than statement. Additionally,
Brahms includes a piccolo in the Finale to contribute to a celebratory
quality that almost suggests an outdoor band—perhaps an allusion to the
Detmold wind players.

Clara Schumann was most intimate to the origins of this serenade.
Brahms sent her the first movement in December 1858. She found the
ideas comparable to those of the First Serenade but the "working out
far more successful" and asked if there were any more movements.
Despite her requests, he did not reveal more until September 10, 1859,
sending the first, third, and fourth movements to her for her birth-

day, September 13, and requesting especially her reaction to the Adagio, to find whether "it is worth all the trouble I have taken with it." Her lengthy reply is very enthusiastic, and she particularly notes the Trio and the Adagio, writing of the intense pleasure given by the latter that it is "as if I were to gaze at each filament of a wondrous flower. It is most beautiful." She received the complete score on November 9, and the work was first performed on February 10, 1860, in Hamburg at a private Philharmonic concert, conducted by Brahms. Though he offered it to the publisher Breitkopf & Härtel at the same time that he sent its companion, it was not accepted (a sign of its less popular effect); it was, however, published at almost the same time as the Serenade in D (November 1860) by Simrock of Bonn, later his main publisher, with the subtitle "for small orchestra" since it lacks trumpets and timpani as well as violins. The piano four-hand version made by Brahms appeared at the same time. Brahms was exceptionally pleased with the result, commenting when he made the arrangement, "I have seldom written music with greater delight. It seemed to sound so beautiful that I was overjoyed," though adding with typical irony, "My pleasure was not increased by the knowledge that I was the composer." However, he later made numerous amendments to the markings and a completely revised edition, "New, revised by the Author," on which subsequent editions are based, appeared in 1875 or 1876. For performance around this time, Brahms indicated a desired performing body of eight violas, six cellos, and four basses.

The second Serenade is more formally balanced and stylistically integrated than its predecessor and anticipates even more closely features of Brahms's mature orchestral idiom, in which interchanging and soloistic wind and horn writing are characteristic. The predominance of winds and the less expansive style, though again with prominent dancelike elements, makes the title "Serenade" more appropriate for this work, which could almost be played out of doors. The integration of style elements is immediately apparent in the incorporation of triplets into the first subject, whereas they appear only as a means of contrast in the second subject in the Serenade in D. Also, his treatment of the dance movements shows more individuality. The outer movements are again in sonata form and sonata-rondo form, with a central Adagio non troppo in ternary form flanked now by two rather than three movements, one each of Scherzo and Trio and "Quasi-Menuetto" and Trio; the total structure displays much greater economy and ingenuity. There is a strong difference in the organization of the first movements, this one being notable for omitting the repetition of the exposition and, instead, prefacing the development with a brief statement of the first theme in the tonic with a modulating continuation into the development. But the form is not a rondo; its sonata spirit is apparent in the extensive and powerful later development of the first theme and the retransition back to it, though the themes themselves are succinct. The Rondo Finale is similarly economical, though with a development in the central section that makes particularly expressive use of the lyrical second theme in the oboe—the theme is now cast in the minor and is imitated by the cellos. The main theme recalls the Scherzo (notable for its ostinato rhythm and its continuously connected trio serving as a variation) in its use of a hunting-horn idiom, which includes the same opening interval of a rising fourth as a call to attention. The movement also includes a false reprise of the rondo theme in augmentation after the development, with a complete recomposition of the section. In form and ideas, the movement comes closer to its counterpart in the Serenade in D than do any other corresponding movements. The third movement now carries even more expressive weight, in view of its reflective and expansive character and its dramatic central section, with horn and wind writing that looks directly to the Second Symphony and the Violin Concerto. Clara's comment that "it might be eleison" perhaps alludes to the association with Baroque church music of the modulating ostinato bass, on which the first section of its ternary form is built; the wind melody above intensifies the sense of a contrapuntal structure, especially as it is treated in imitation. The central section comes closest to a fully orchestral idiom with its tremolo strings and dramatic horn writing, initiating an elaboration that yields to the recapitulation of the ostinato by gradual stages of theme and key.

The greater maturity of the work is especially clear in the adaptation of traditional idioms. The "quasi-Menuetto" transforms the triple meter into a larger duple meter of 6/4, the motivic idiom giving the whole a reflective and improvisatory quality, intensified when the second part begins in the mediant, F♯ major; the Trio is in the minor mode of this key and its even more elusive character led Clara to note a "floating" quality in the oboe melody. The ostinato rhythm of the Scherzo permits a reading of three groups of two beats in the two-measure idea, which is made more explicit in the tied hemiola effect at the final cadence, a feature that continues through the Trio. Subtleties such as these, combined with the unusual scoring and length—too long for an overture, not long enough for a symphony—have made the work difficult to program and denied it the popularity of its companion until the era of the CD, though it was at first better received.

Michael Musgrave

2

CONCERTOS

PIANO CONCERTO NO. 1 IN D MINOR, OPUS 15
Composed 1854–58; published 1861

SCORING: 2 flutes, 2 oboes, 2 clarinets, 2 bassoons, 4 horns, 2 trumpets, timpani, strings
MOVEMENTS: 1. Maestoso; 2. Adagio; 3. Rondo: Allegro non troppo

Listeners encountering this towering masterpiece for the first time will scarcely believe that its young composer struggled for some five years to get its shape right. The story begins in 1854, when Brahms embarked on a sonata in D minor for two pianos. By the summer of that year, he had recast it as a symphony. Three movements are known to have been drafted. During this period of gestation, Brahms sought advice from various friends: the violinist Joseph Joachim, the composer Julius Otto Grimm, his piano teacher Eduard Marxsen, and Clara Schumann. In due time, the second of these movements—a slow Scherzo—became the funeral march of *Ein deutsches Requiem*. The third was destroyed by the composer. Brahms continued to rework the first movement and added two new ones: an Adagio and a Rondo Finale.

The huge opening movement—in 6/4 time, D minor, marked Maestoso—is longer than Liszt's entire four-movement First Piano Concerto. Whatever Brahms's intention might have been to afford the pianist an opportunity to display keyboard virtuosity, the real subject of this movement is thematic transformation. The technique is usually associated with Liszt and Wagner, but Brahms showed himself even in this early work to be a master of causing heroic motives to become gentle and intimate and turning tender themes into aggressive and dramatic ones. To understand this process, it is helpful to tag the main thematic elements.

The concerto begins with an emphatic anchoring low D in the basses, violas, horns, and timpani. Above this we hear from violins and cellos an angry theme, which unexpectedly outlines the chord of B♭ major before bursting into a trill on A♭, a note not contained in the scale of either B♭ major or D minor. This bold use of a trill—not as a cadence or keyboard embellishment, but to give a fist-shaking character to the main theme—becomes a hallmark of the movement and is one of many original touches to be found in the work.

Two quiet themes follow; the first, over a barcarole accompaniment that finally establishes clearly the home key of D minor, features a long-short-long rhythm, and consists of upward skips that are filled in with downward scale motion. This is followed by a theme in B♭ minor, exhibiting a steady, flowing rhythm. The stormy first theme returns in canon, leading to yet more new material: a strident theme consisting of pairs of repeated notes followed by a more sustained motif that emphasizes the interval of the upward fourth.

After a simmering down, the piano enters with what appears to be a new theme, presented over the rocking accompaniment that the soloist's left hand takes over from the cellos, but is in fact a quiet variant of the earlier, strident theme that builds in intensity until the pianist breaks out into the first-theme trills. Using an idea reminiscent of the design found in the first movements of many Mozart piano concertos, Brahms causes the soloist to review the themes presented by the orchestra alone, adding coloristic keyboard figuration as embellishment. This procedure is followed in the two quiet themes.

In another Mozartean touch, the soloist—now playing alone—presents a theme not rendered previously by the orchestra. Its upward-fourth opening interval relates it clearly to the earlier theme that emphasizes the upward fourth, but its sustained lyricism is something new to the movement. This new theme flows smoothly into a dolce transformation of the earlier one, which is taken up by the orchestra. Finally, the strings get their chance at the piano's theme as the soloist provides accompanying figuration. The upward fourth becomes the basis for a showy passage in double octaves that signals the opening of the development section. Two remarkable transformations of the earlier B♭-minor theme—the first stormy and the second waltz-like—occur just before the buildup to the recapitulation.

At its first appearance, the main theme outlines a chord not of D minor but of B♭ major. At its return, played by the soloist over a low D sustained in the orchestra, the outlined chord is E major. Music theorists may be able to explain the principles on which both occurrences are based, but these moments remain surprising even after dozens of hearings. At the conclusion of the recapitulation, the piano enters with a quiet version of the stormy transfiguration—a transformation of a transformation—that soon reverts to its aggressive tone and leads a thunderous, virtuosic coda.

The Adagio movement begins with an extreme contrast of mood—serenity rather than turbulence—but Brahms is careful to include common elements to give a sense of connectedness. The meter remains the relatively unusual 6/4; the tonic is again D, although major rather than minor; and the movement begins with a sustained D pedal point. Above this, however, the music proceeds more smoothly in accord with the underlying bass note, in contrast to the clashes of the opening movement.

The piano's entry takes up the accompanimental figure of the orchestra, adding an expressive melody above it. The plan of this movement is to alternate piano and orchestra in a dialogue—not a contention, as in the second movement of Beethoven's Fourth Concerto, but rather a sharing of the same affect or mood. Certain of the piano's phrases, in fact, recall passages from the middle movement of Beethoven's *Emperor* Concerto. (Both Beethoven works were frequently performed by Brahms.) When the piano's opening returns, it is extended over a memorable pedal point on D (horns, cellos, and basses), a rapturous peroration for the soloist. This passage of heightened emotion is balanced by a restrained but equally eloquent passage marked *cadenza ad lib.* for the piano alone. The closing orchestral phrase includes a viola solo—a rarity in Brahms's orchestral writing—and timpani notes that seem oddly suspensive.

Brahms chooses as the refrain for his Rondo Finale a transformation of the piano's solo theme from the first movement; its new character is emphatic rather than autumnal, its rhythm syncopated rather than flowing, its mode minor rather than major. The manner in which this theme is presented, taken up by the orchestra against piano figuration, given a contrasting phrase, and then returned to via a brilliant pianistic flourish—all this resembles to an uncanny degree the Finale of Beethoven's Third Piano Concerto. Fugal passages, located at almost exactly the same point in each piece, strengthen the relationship between the two. Two short cadenzas mark structural points: the first leads to a change to major mode for the remaining quarter of the movement, the second leads to the exciting coda. Between the two, the tempo slows as bassoons and clarinets give the theme against a drone in the cellos and timpani. Scale figurations in the piano lead back brilliantly to the rapid tempo.

Brahms began work on this concerto a few months after meeting Clara and Robert Schumann, which is also to say at the time of Schumann's attempted suicide and committal to the asylum at Endenich. It has occurred to many commentators that the heightened emotions of this work—from the rage of the opening to the eloquent serenity of the second movement—may relate directly to Brahms's deep feelings about both of the Schumanns.

Richard Wilson

VIOLIN CONCERTO IN D, OPUS 77
Composed 1878; published 1879

SCORING: 2 flutes, 2 oboes, 2 clarinets, 2 bassoons, 4 horns, 2 trumpets, timpani, strings

MOVEMENTS: 1. Allegro non troppo; 2. Adagio; 3. Allegro giocoso, ma non troppo vivace

Unlike the composers to whom Brahms is most often compared in the popular imagination (for example, Bach and Beethoven), Brahms was unusual in that he never developed serious proficiency playing any instrument other than the piano. Mendelssohn, Mozart, Beethoven, and Bach all had extensive practical experience with string instruments; their music helped define what came to be understood in the nineteenth century as the "idiomatic" use of the violin. It is therefore remarkable that Brahms, through the three Violin Sonatas and most particularly the Violin Concerto, made a substantial contribution to our perception of the violin's capacity for expression. Nevertheless, as in the comparable cases of Chopin and Schumann, the piano remained the primary instrumental medium of Brahms's imagination, competing only with the voice in the compositional process of the formulation of musical ideas.

Brahms's encounter with the violin was first as an accompanist. His awareness of the genre of the violin concerto was heightened by his close friendship with Joachim, whose extensive concertizing actively promoted concertos from the eighteenth and early nineteenth centuries, particularly those of Viotti, Spohr, and Mozart. Joachim was responsible for the re-entry into the repertory of the Beethoven Violin Concerto. Until his advocacy of this work (including his composition of a great cadenza), the concerto was regarded as one of Beethoven's lesser accomplishments. The "historical" tendency in Joachim's tastes during the mid-century when he was active as a soloist can be understood as part of a campaign (linked closely with Schumann's aesthetic viewpoint) against Philistinism and the mere display of virtuosity. Joachim had worked as concertmaster in Weimar under Liszt. He subsequently took a stand against Liszt and became a convert to Schumann, in part because Joachim came to accept Schumann's distinction between pure musical values on one hand and the superficial display of technique and manipulation of theatricality in music on the other. However, as Joachim's own Violin Concerto in D minor, the "Hungarian," Op. 11 (written during the same time Brahms was writing his D-minor Piano Concerto) indicates, Joachim was himself unequaled as a virtuoso. His concerto still ranks among the most difficult and taxing in the repertory. But Joachim set out to do something with the violin quite different from what had been done by Paganini. He wanted to find a way to reconcile the most serious aspirations of instrumental music with the visceral power associated with the display of virtuosic technique.

It is therefore poignant that the greatest fulfillment of this ambition should have turned out to be Brahms's only Violin Concerto, written for and dedicated to his friend Joseph Joachim. Not surprisingly, Brahms delayed writing a concerto until it was quite clear that Joachim had given up composing. Brahms was a great admirer of Joachim's own concerto and the two close friends developed their careers in a way designed to diminish rivalry. Joachim, recognizing the superior gifts of his friend, ultimately relinquished his own compositional ambitions by the early 1860s.

Brahms wrote the Violin Concerto in the summer of 1878 at the Austrian resort of Pörtschach, exactly one year after and in the same place he completed the Second Symphony, also in D major. The process of composition involved a very close exchange of views with Joachim; Joachim's influence on the violin part was decisive. Brahms also consulted Pablo de Sarasate and Emile Sauret. But despite the advice of leading practitioners, Brahms's musical imagination broke with conventions associated with the violin. Indeed, Brahms's Concerto (together with Tchaikovsky's Violin Concerto, written coincidentally in the very same year) helped to transform expectations of what a violin can sound like in the concerto setting. Hence the well-known quip of Hans von Bülow that Max Bruch's more conventionally idiomatic G-minor Concerto was for the violin, but Brahms's was *against* it. Few concertos exploit the high register so magically and lyrically. In no previous concerto is the percussive and harmonic potential of the instrument so profoundly explored. The violin becomes the driving rhythmic force leading the orchestra forward. Joachim, who had worked with Brahms on the shaping of the violin part, was still taken aback and initially even somewhat ambivalent toward the soloist's part. The first performance took place on New Year's Day in Leipzig at the Gewandhaus with Brahms conducting and Joachim as soloist.

The Violin Concerto is in three movements. The first begins with a staggeringly dramatic tutti, the excitement of which is generated in part by the thematic material (which shows the same contrast of lyricism and intense drama that is evident in the opening of the Second Symphony) and Brahms's characteristic use of rhythmic displacement. Ninety measures into the work, the violin enters on the tonic D and quickly erupts into an assertive minor-key variant of the main theme. This initiates the intense dialogue with the orchestra that ultimately characterizes the entire movement. The violin's entrance is prepared by the full string section, which states a theme in the minor; this the violin reproduces all by itself later in the movement with comparable vigor. The close of the cadenza (which in most performances is the one written by Joachim) is the lyrical high point as the violin soars over the orchestra in what is surely one of the most transcendent moments in concerto literature. The first movement at times fleetingly suggests the model of the Beethoven Concerto, including references to C major against D major, a relationship already established in the ninth measure of the opening. Brahms ventures throughout the movement to even more remote keys, such as C minor.

The first movement is based on an extended sonata model with a development section and a recapitulation. The second movement is basically in song form *(A B A),* although it is heavily influenced by Brahms's use of variation and thematic transformation. As Donald Tovey points out, the subject of the second movement is remarkably long, a quality characteristic of the nineteenth century. It has the exterior appearance of simplicity, but it contains its own elaboration without being easily divisible. In this second movement, in F major, the oboe states the opening theme in a truly eloquent and affecting fashion. This opening is scored for horns and woodwinds without any strings, and demonstrates Brahms's deft employment of writing for wind choir. After an F♯-minor episode, the movement closes with an exchange between the French horn and the violin, followed by a return of the oboe solo, this time with the violin's accompaniment. The coda of the movement, which is dominated by the solo violin, comes to an end with a spare accompaniment including cellos and basses. In the closing F-major chord, the violin sustains a high F over the whole orchestra.

The last movement is in rondo form and once again in D major. Here the violin begins by stating the theme in thirds and broken chords. From the outset, a rhythmic tension between duple and triple figures is established. As the opening bars of this Finale indicate, Brahms uses double-stops to great effect (as he does throughout the Concerto). In Brahms's hands, double-stops show how the violin can become an instrument not only of melody but of harmony as well, beyond the natural harmonic relationships suggested by the tuning of the instrument. Brahms was inspired in his use of the violin in part by his close knowledge of Bach, whose solo Chaconne Brahms adapted for the piano left-hand. In addition to the initial and recurring subject of the movement, there is a lyric melody and a subordinate subject first stated by the violin in octaves, both of which are reminiscent in articulation and rhythm of material from the first two movements. Brahms, without explicitly recalling any themes from prior movements, offers the listener echoes of earlier events, so as to give the concerto an organic unity. The movement builds to a brief violin flourish supported and even surrounded by a pedal on the dominant. What follows then is a transformation of the opening material in which the violin takes on triplet figurations that shift the rhythmic emphasis and propulsion from what was heard at the opening of the movement. This coda (for which there are many precedents in concertos by Mozart and Beethoven) is faster than the rest of the movement, and includes variants of preceding material from the movement in new configurations. The Concerto ends forcefully but abruptly with almost Haydnesque surprise, after seven measures of an alluring diminuendo.

Leon Botstein

Piano Concerto No. 2 in B♭, Opus 83
Composed 1878–81; published 1882

Scoring: 2 flutes, 2 oboes, 2 clarinets, 2 bassoons, 4 horns, 2 trumpets, timpani, strings
Movements: 1. Allegro non troppo; 2. Allegro appassionato; 3. Andante; 4. Allegretto grazioso

Although only a few years separate the publication of the final version of Brahms's First Piano Concerto and the emergence of his Second, the pieces could hardly be more different. Whereas the opening movement dominates the earlier work, weight and interest are more evenly distributed among the four movements of the later one. (That there are four movements is itself unusual—making the B♭ Concerto resemble a symphony more than any concerto preceding it.) The First Concerto begins with a succession of themes, including an unforgettable one for the piano alone. The Second Concerto is more economical with thematic material and presents its two most memorable themes not in the piano solo but in the horn (at the outset of the first movement) and the solo cello (at the outset of the third movement). The lyrical, melody-dominated piano writing of the earlier work gives way in the later to figuration that seems to activate all registers of the instrument at once. Melodic material is indeed present but is often embedded in a complex accompanimental texture. Perhaps to celebrate the greater range of the more modern piano, the Second Concerto begins on a note lower than any appearing in the first; in the course of the work, the soloist makes frequent sweeps from one keyboard extreme to the other.

Beginning a massive work such as this with a single horn playing alone is already a daring touch. But even more notably, Brahms avoids clichés associated with the hunting horn and instead gives the instrument a quiet, stepwise theme that first seems to ask and then, in its second phrase, to answer some unknowable question. The piano responds with ruminative comment that echoes the horn's cadential turn. Only then does the piano take command, with abrupt and almost fierce gestures. This cadenza-like solo passage renders a variant of the horn's theme (in the left hand) before ushering in with great force (as well as some ingenious rhythmic displacements) the full orchestra's sonorous, richly harmonized version of that same theme. The ensuing orchestral exposition will present additional themes, but none will engage the ear or linger in the memory as effectively as this opening melody and its many variations and transformations.

Music similar to the opening occurs at two later points of formal articulation: the development begins with the horn giving its melody in minor against ominous tremolos in the violins; the piano responds much as it did at the start. Later, the recapitulation begins with the piano engaging in coloristic, if not ethereal, figuration in its upper register, against which the horn—supported by clarinets, bassoons, and strings—renders its melody in the original major mode.

The movement's coda yields another remarkably coloristic piano texture consisting of trills low in the left hand and a spidery, chromatic arrangement of broken octaves in the right—all of it pianissimo. This is followed by the piano's most thunderous version of the horn's gentle melody.

The "added" movement, the second, recalls the First Concerto in that it is in D minor and projects a *Sturm und Drang* character that stands in contrast to the largely autumnal feeling of the other three movements. One of its very few scherzo-like features is the form: a main section, a middle or "trio" section, then a return to the main section which, in this case, has been reworked as to orchestration and the role of the solo piano. Going into the Trio, the orchestral interlude changes from minor to major as the tempo slows very slightly—causing one to hear three beats to the measure rather than one. Thus the tempo both slows and speeds up at the same time—a most remarkable, and strangely celebratory, effect. The piano responds with one of the most fearsome challenges in the literature—double octaves smoothly connected that skip and slither but must remain at a whisper. Countless pianists have been defeated by this diabolical passage. It is followed by an orchestral response exuding innocence or indifference—evidence of the composer's sly humor.

The slow movement begins with a cello solo, the melody of which closely resembles Brahms's love song *Immer leiser wird mein Schlummer.* (Only the melody is related; the harmonizations differ radically and the concerto's version adds an important metric subtlety.) The text of the song is about longing, and the tone of the cello's solo conveys the same sentiment. The piano's role in this movement is as commentator and embellisher; at no time does the soloist render the theme in its unadorned form. That job is left to the cello. Just before the cello returns with its theme, the piano engages in a colloquy with the clarinets and then continues against a background of sustained strings. Quoting directly from another Brahms song (*Todessehnen,* at the words "Vater in der Höhee"), it is a memorable passage, hushed and deeply expressive, in which a coherent melody seems to be trying to emerge but cannot find the means to do so. The cello then enters and shows the way.

Alone among the four movements, the Finale presents a clear succession of themes, which might be characterized as flirtatious, gypsy, serenade, and playful. But they all share a simple melodic figure: the neighboring tone. Each of the four features a principal note, the note just below it, and then the main note again. No matter how different in rhythm and tone, the themes are thus related to each other. Compared with, say, the Finale of the Quartet in G Minor, Op.25, the *alla zingarese* flavor of this movement is subtle. One notices it especially in the frequent guitarlike pizzicato accompaniments given by the strings to all the themes except the "gypsy," which elicits from the soloist staccato chords that seem imitative of plucked strings.

Beethoven's ghost seems to hover over this last movement. The refrain (the "flirtatious" theme) begins not on the tonic or the dominant chord, as might be expected, but rather on the subdominant (the fourth chord of the scale) exactly as does the Finale of Beethoven's Fourth Concerto. And following the model of Beethoven's Third Concerto Finale, the movement progresses toward a speeding up of the tempo that also includes a change of meter from 2/4 to 6/8; at this point the refrain is transformed correspondingly by the addition of decorating notes. The section that begins there serves as a coda and builds to a grand conclusion in which the solo piano seems finally to be swallowed up in the luxuriance of the orchestral sound.

Richard Wilson

CONCERTO IN A MINOR FOR VIOLIN AND VIOLONCELLO [DOUBLE CONCERTO], OPUS 102
Composed 1887; published 1888

SCORING: 2 flutes, 2 oboes, 2 clarinets, 2 bassoons, 4 horns, 2 trumpets, timpani, strings
MOVEMENTS: 1. Allegro; 2. Andante; 3. Vivace non troppo

The Double Concerto displays a historical view of concerto form, seen through the filter of Brahms's imagination. The Classical era saw a presentation problem with the concerto that demanded structural solution—namely, how the solo artist, representing but one element of the soloist/orchestra duality, might at the outset of the work be formally introduced. The solution was a double opening section of the first movement (its exposition), the initial part presenting the orchestra as purveyor of main themes in the work, the "second exposition" presenting the soloist, who would deal with these or yet newer themes. A solo cadenza, with its opportunity for improvisatory and pyrotechnical brilliance, would arrive later in the movement.

In writing a concerto for two instruments, Brahms upped the structural ante, for here a pair of soloists must be presented in a formalized manner. How this was done reveals not only Brahms's regard for tradition but his unique reworking, indeed inversion, of the presentational procedure. The soloists are introduced at the outset of the movement, each with an extended cadenza. To be sure, the cadenza as opening gambit had been explored earlier—by Beethoven in his last two piano concertos, and by Brahms, six years before the Double, in the Second Piano Concerto. Presenting two soloists was yet another matter.

Some violinists have bemoaned their role in this work. How, they ask, can they hope to equal the sound, the character, the sheer power of the cello, so richly presented only four measures into the work? But Brahms not only deals with form and tradition at this juncture; he further establishes musical personalities for the solo instruments themselves—a critical feature that has consequences throughout the work. The cello, by its physical nature, easily achieves the force of character and depth of sonority mentioned above. The violin, in its opening notes some minutes later, is a counterpart, if not counterfoil—a soulful, lyrical voice, qualities inherent in its higher range. As the two instruments collaborate throughout their joint cadenza, these differences are enlarged, to such an extent that even the duet, which sees the same musical lines played in octaves as the phrases press toward the orchestral return, highlights their unique musical properties.

This concern with musical character carries over to the second movement. Heard at the outset are two phrases, each a mere two notes long, each spanning a four-note interval (thus: A–D, spanning A–B–C♯–D; and E–A, spanning E–F♯–G♯–A). The horns carry the first phrase, their low register, dark color, and somewhat broad articulation redolent (despite their garb as wind instruments) of the solo cello in its first-movement cadenza. The winds, notably the high flutes and clarinets, carry the second phrase. Again there is a familial connection: the singing tones, with their expressive swells and their upper register, are reminiscent of the solo violin in its initial entrance in the prior movement.

This moment is more than one of character portrayal alone. These long, isolated two-note phrases, with their swells and their separation by notable pauses, are thus disguised, removed from their true function. It becomes clear from the following measures that the four notes comprise the opening steps of the songful theme that is the main transport of the second movement. Transformation is thus the means by which identity, character, and function are affected and altered—means typical of Brahms's melding of craft, art, and expressive detail.

Brahms forecasts in this movement a side of himself that becomes ever more prominent in the decade to follow—his last years, characterized by increasing loneliness. The closing phrases of the slow movement show a different kind of character transformation. As the solo instruments trade passages back and forth, the accompaniment of strings and winds descends to ever lower registers, ever darker colors, indeed to music of ever grayer character. It is a preview, a glimpse, of qualities found in the Clarinet Quintet, Op. 115, that quintessential statement of Brahms's late years, and the subsequent piano pieces of Opp. 116, 117, 118, and 119. Like Beethoven before him, also isolated in spirit and social context in late life, Brahms turned to particular media into which his reflective music was cast—chamber ensembles and the piano.

The details of this remarkable concerto are innumerable. One is the subtle play with rhythm and motive in the folklike third movement, done with such artistry that the "oom" and the "pah" elements of the dance-like tune permeating the movement are often unclear—deliberately so. As a consequence, we are not always sure where the strong pulse in the melody may lie. Ambiguity pervades the texture. Like transformation, it is a prime feature of the Brahmsian vocabulary.

Last but hardly least is the cohering role of the tempo. Typical of his procedures, Brahms gives nothing but general indications of pacing for all the movements in this work. No metronome markings convey precise concepts; naught is provided but Allegro, Andante, and Vivace non troppo, the Vivace all the more ambiguous by its suggestive, if vague, qualifier. The lack of precision in tempos is not the signpost of an unclear mind. The reality of tempo lies deeper within the musical fabric than mere words or numbers can suggest. The movements convey their tempos through the musical qualities that shape their character.

It is striking in this respect that the entire concerto shares a common pulse, one that underlies in various ways the complexities of this multifarious music. This pulse is felt if we hum the music or hear it in our minds. The quarter note, by which the first movement moves with such power, is essentially doubled in duration to form the prevalent beat of the second movement. Brahms's concern with character is effected here by articulation: the phrases of the middle movement flow in such legato manner—so much in contrast with the opening movement—as to disguise the connection in pace.

By yet another means of contrast (read: transformation), the closing movement, with its folklike qualities, shares a pulse equal in duration to the first movement. Again, the alteration in character is so great as to mask this kinship in pace. Singing the opening bars of each movement, even experimenting to find the "right" tempo in each case, tends to make these connections of pacing evident. Indeed, one sees a virtual *evolution* of tempos, of pulse in its manifest roles, as the music progresses from movement to movement.

A Darwinian notion of tempo? Evolution relevant to music—in its organic sense of growth, in its developmental complexity, guided by the "genetic" materials of the work? Was yet another nineteenth-century concept, miles removed from Brahms in purview as well as geography, reflected in the web of musical interconnections fostered by this intellectually sophisticated artist? It is a striking thought to pursue.

David Epstein

3

SYMPHONIES

SYMPHONY NO. 1 IN C MINOR, OPUS 68
Composed 1862–76; published 1877

SCORING: 2 flutes, 2 oboes, 2 clarinets, 2 bassoons, contrabassoon,
4 horns, 2 trumpets, 3 trombones, timpani, strings
MOVEMENTS: 1. Un poco sostenuto. Allegro; 2. Andante sostenuto; 3. Un
poco Allegretto e grazioso; 4. Finale: Più Andante. Allegro non troppo,
ma con brio.

Brahms wrestled with the completion of his First Symphony over a
period of about fourteen years. The score was finally finished in September 1876, the first and last movements preceding the second and
third. (The four-hand arrangement, important for the distribution of
the symphony as music to be performed in the home, was prepared by
Brahms himself during the early summer of 1877.) The premiere took
place in Karlsruhe on November 4, 1876. Otto Dessoff conducted the
Großherzogliche Hofkapelle. A series of revisions continuing even until
after the first set of performances seems to indicate that Brahms still experienced a notion of insecurity, in particular about the form of the slow
movement and the formal relationship of both inner movements to the
Finale. The main revision took place in May 1877, directly before the en-
graving of the score. The entire second movement was restructured and
formally altered, from a rondo to a three-part Liedform, as Roger Pascall
notes. No other Brahms symphony underwent such significant changes
at such a late date.

Paul Bekker, the influential German critic of the early twentieth century, saw the historical significance of the "Viennese" symphony since
Beethoven in its social character, its ability to shape and form society.

And Theodor W. Adorno called Beethoven's symphonies public orations addressing mankind. Brahms's First Symphony belongs in this tradition. The striking power of its orchestral writing and the forcefulness of its teleological form, however, are complemented by an extreme sophistication in the thematic working and formal conceptualization. Sociologically this double face is characteristic of Brahms. His symphonies certainly speak to the "masses" in the emphatic Beethovenian sense. But their complicated structural and formal design require expert knowledge to be fully understood and thus they are more directed toward the individual connoisseur, the single person among the listening crowd. Within this general designation, the First Symphony is closest to the Beethovenian model; more, it is a musical essay *about* the historical validity of this symphonic intent in the late nineteenth century.

The early reception of the First Symphony was not altogether enthusiastic, though it was favorable in general. Almost unanimously, the Finale was seen as the most powerful piece of music Brahms had written so far. But the most important discussion concerned the historical place that the symphony pointedly assigned to itself. For the music historian Friedrich Chrysander, the "act of referring to Beethoven, the connection with the . . . Ninth Symphony of that master," was a conscious measure. Chrysander saw the historical significance of Brahms's First in its answer to the question of "how to create a counterpart to the last sections of the Ninth Symphony that would achieve the same effect in nature and intensity, without resorting to song." Thus Brahms's critical relation to Beethoven is marked by the "return of the symphony that combines playing and singing to the purely instrumental symphony." Certainly, Brahms is here taking up a Beethovenian matrix, that "plot archetype," as Anthony Newcomb calls it, of nineteenth-century symphonic music which might be paraphrased as the resolution of a conflict of ideas through an inner formal process aimed toward a liberating ending—in short, the "positive" overcoming of a "negative" principle. And indeed, Brahms does not use the human voice.

The symphony's train of thoughts is laid out exclusively in the two outer movements. Both Allegros are preceded by large-scale slow introductions and their monumental tone originates in the spirit of the sonata. The two lighter inner movements do not participate in, but also do not interrupt, the course of ideas. Character and brevity place them together as the middle part of what is actually a three-part design for the four-movement symphony. Eduard Hanslick, among others, found fault with these proportions in both Brahms's First and Third Symphonies: "Their two middle movements appear, in their content and breadth, somewhat too light compared to the mighty pieces of music surrounding them."

The slow introduction to the first movement sets the tone and the dimension. The listener enters a monumental building through a huge portal. The repeated ternary strokes of the timpani immediately evoke the *topos* of a tragic world. The following Allegro adheres to the Classical scheme of sonata form, with the exposition repeated. And the themes also follow established patterns: an energetic first subject in the fortissimo strings, a lyrical second theme played by the solo oboe, and a rhythmically forceful epilogue using the full orchestra. But there are unconventional divergences from the sonata scheme. First, the chromatic line that already determines the majestic opening also precedes the main Allegro theme, syntactically like an emphatic colon; it functions as a motto and occurs throughout the first movement. Second, the main subject is not a melody but a complex configuration, compounded from the short motives exposed in the slow introduction. Third, all thematic *Gestalten,* all the textures in this movement, are derived from these motives or from the motto. And fourth, the technique of universal motivic integration is displayed for all three sections of the sonata form. Though the traditional thematic characters are discernible, there is in principle no distinction between expositional and developmental passages. As a consequence, the borders between the formal sections are obscured: the exposition is developmental from the beginning; the thematic entrance of the second theme is delayed and separated from its harmonic entrance; the recapitulation appears as the climactic ending of the development and only *post festum* as the beginning of a new section; and the actual entrance of the coda is almost unrecognizable. Essentially, the movement becomes a sequence of motivically defined textures of different designs and densities.

Two contextually important points of attraction in the development and coda are connected to central moments of the Finale. The first of the two large-scale climactic waves that determine the form of the development culminates in the appearance of a chorale-like tune played by the full strings. This tune prefigures the chorale-like formula of the Finale. Its initial turn of the upper major second, which forms a motivic link between the two "chorales," is in the coda of the Finale an enchanting figure that grows out of the chorale formula and leads the symphony to a triumphant close. At another important point, the coda of the first movement introduces a change of the symphony's basic key. Together with a slowing down of the tempo the sound is brightened from C minor to C major and the movement calmly fades away. But the coda is short and has a double face: it also marks the return to the repeated strokes of the timpani from the slow introduction and thus recalls its tragic mood. Therefore the resolution is not quite complete at this point; it needs to continue in the Finale.

The second and the third movements are Romantic character pieces for orchestra. Both follow the ternary *A B A* Liedform, and both display a restrained expressivity: no grand, expansive Adagio but a moderately spirited Andante, no demonic Scherzo but a gracefully pulsating Intermezzo with a middle section more forceful than usual. Differing from the compound motivic configurations of the first movement, the themes of the second movement are real melodic lines, often sung by solo instruments (oboe, horn, solo violin), and it is the solo violin that brings the movement to a close.

The form of the Finale is singular in Brahms's output. First, there is the slow introduction, unusual for Brahms and extraordinary in its design. Certainly, in its first section the Adagio recalls the slow introduction to the first movement and the tragic conflict is represented by similar means (minor key, chromaticism, orchestral apparatus, timpani strokes, expressive character). But within the actual introduction, an opposite world suddenly appears. The sphere of the diminished-seventh chords is cut off, and pure C major emerges in the noble sound of the trombones (which are saved for this important point of attraction) along with string tremolos, all pianissimo—a previously unheard tone encases the central event of the Adagio, the great "Alphorn call" in the first horn. Within the context of the symphony it designates an epiphany. And the horn call is followed by another extraordinary moment: the chorale-like cadential formula solemnly intoned by dominating trombones. Only now, after the formulation of the opposite world, does the Allegro movement commence, with its communal song theme in C major that points so clearly to Beethoven's "Joy" melody.

The form of this Allegro is ambiguous. It has a rather conventional exposition (not repeated) with first and second themes, and with an epilogue. But the exposition ends in E minor instead of the expected G major, and the next section opens with the main theme in the tonic C major as if it were a repeat of the exposition or the second ritornello of a rondo (a good ear, however, will also realize the enhanced orchestration with added winds, horns, trumpets, and timpani). At first, thus, this statement does not confirm a reading of the passage as the start of a development. But the varied repeat of the main theme firmly leads into a genuine development of considerable length and dramatic intensity. The goal of this development, the entrance of the reprise (or assuming a rondo design: of the third ritornello), is, however, again obscured. Instead of the main Allegro theme (and, as Giselher Schubert has shown, brought about through a motivic transformation), the great horn call reappears, in an epiphanic mode similar to that within the Adagio. Here it has the power of a real "breakthrough" reprise entry. Then a normal reprise continues, with the second theme and the epilogue in the tonic. At the close of the Allegro (or in terms of a rondo, at the place for the fourth ritornello) another interpolation takes place: while the repeated head motive of the main subject in the basses seems to indicate the theme's final appearance, it remains, instead, reduced to an auxiliary role, becoming developmental material for a coda stretto, which finally culminates in the trombone chorale. Thus the main theme is twice substituted, first by the Alphorn call, representing "nature," and finally by the chorale intonation, representing "religion."

The world view of Brahms's First Symphony is evident if one takes the formal and structural designs as metaphors for its ideology. Through its allusion to the Finale of Beethoven's Ninth, the main theme recalls the ideas and hopes from the beginning of the bourgeois century, that is, the historical perspectives and political ideas of the French Revolution as Beethoven codified them in his Ninth. Thus Brahms's symphony includes these ideas as part of the "positive" resolution of the "symphonic problem." But through the two thematic substitutions, the Finale proclaims for its own "late" historical position a dissent with Beethoven's optimistic view of the historical development. Instead of "history" Brahms's symphony invokes "nature" (the Alphorn call) and "religion" (the imaginary chorale). Beethoven, at the beginning of the nineteenth century, was concretely relating his symphonic music to history, shaping a program of ideas that has precise structural analogies in the processive form of the music and its drive toward a goal—aiming at change, reformulation, and new foundations, and even postulating a utopia. The skeptical Brahms, at the end of that "historical" century, was relating the program of ideas in his—formally at first analogous—First Symphony to what is beyond history, unchanging, essentially at rest: to use a Nietzschean term, the "suprahistorical" forces of nature and religion.

Reinhold Brinkmann

SYMPHONY NO. 2 IN D, OPUS 73
Composed 1877; published 1878

SCORING: 2 flutes, 2 oboes, 2 clarinets, 2 bassoons, 4 horns, 2 trumpets, 3 trombones, tuba, timpani, strings

MOVEMENTS: 1. Allegro non troppo; 2. Adagio non troppo; 3. Allegretto grazioso (Quasi Andantino); 4. Allegro con spirito

Brahms composed his Second Symphony only one year after the completion of the First Symphony, within fewer than five months—between June and October 1877. The four-hand piano reduction was already prepared by Brahms himself in November 1877. The premiere took place on December 30, 1877, in the Vienna Musikverein with the Philharmonic Orchestra, Hans Richter conducting.

Chronologically as well as contextually, the four symphonies of Brahms are to be placed in pairs. Philipp Spitta remarked that the First and Second Symphonies "must be regarded as a pair that has sprung from the self-same, deeply hidden root." Recent studies have suggested that the First Symphony marks the point where Brahms finally achieved a self-detachment from his overly powerful symphonic inheritance, the Beethoven tradition. Thus the Second Symphony, after the First's act of liberation, begins at the point where the latter ended, with the Romantic nature-*topos* of the horns and winds and its seemingly undisguised pastoral tone. It thus represents Brahms's most personal position.

The early listeners heard and interpreted the music as displaying exactly this pastoral imagery. "It is all blue sky, babbling of streams, sunshine, and cool green shade," wrote Theodor Billroth. A Leipzig review rightly applied the concept of the idyllic to the work. However, Brahms's symphonic idyll is—in Schiller's terms—not "naïve" but "sentimental." Etched on this idyll is the historical consciousness of a late period which is excluded from the pure representation of an Arcadian state. The imagined promise of an "idyllic" harmony between man and life is met with skepticism. This broken idyll is the hallmark of Brahms's Second Symphony: the first two movements at least blend idyll and elegy, and there are meditative echoes in the third. Thus the natural tone at the beginning of the symphony has only the semblance of spontaneity. This main subject of the first movement—with its 3/4 time, the triadic arpeggiation as well as its rhythmic shape—clearly recalls the main subject of Beethoven's *Eroica* Symphony. And the two superimposed components of the contrapuntal thematic configuration—the "natural" horn/wind theme and the bass drone with its one-measure head-motive—are displaced against each other by one measure, forming a hypermetrical and harmonic conflict. Thus even the nature-idyll is determined reflectively; there is, in Brahms, no naïve immediacy that has escaped from the idea and obligation of history. In letters from the time of composing the symphony Brahms embarked on a cryptic game with opposing characterizations of the work, proclaiming it sometimes to be lightminded-serene ("a quite innocent, cheerful little thing") and at other times to be deeply elegiac ("it will be printed with a black border"). But in an important letter devoid of irony from August 1879, he referred to the state of melancholy as a signature of this music and its author.

The Second is the longest of Brahms's four symphonies. This is due in particular to the expansive first movement, which, as Tovey rightly remarked, "is one of the few perfectly constructed examples that can be compared in length to that of Beethoven's *Eroica.*" At the premiere the durations for the four movements were nineteen (with the exposition repeated), eleven, five, and eight minutes. The Second features the only Adagio in Brahms's symphonic output—with its expressive cantilena, imposing tone, and adherence to sonata form it is a demanding piece of music. Then, however, follows a much lighter, comparatively uncomplicated and relatively short third movement, a sequence of contrasting Bohemian dances. Finally there is a Haydnesque "last dance," Allegro con brio, with its brilliant ending of virtuoso trombone runs.

In the First Symphony the course of ideas gave all weight to and connected the two monumental outer movements. In the Second, however, the first two movements, with their grand tone, are bound together, and the last two, with their light character, are as well. Thus the entire symphony is divided into two polar "halves" of quite different expressive qualities and lengths: two "melancholic" movements (lasting about thirty minutes) are followed by two "serene" ones (of about thirteen minutes only). And the question is whether the latter are able to counterbalance the former, whether they can convincingly transform the melancholic state of mind into a serene view of the world.

The first movement is a large-scale sonata, without a slow introduction but with a repeat of the exposition. All the work's thematic formulations are derived from the initial material, a small stock of basic motivic elements given in the thematic configuration at the beginning of the symphony. There is scarcely a measure in the work which is not "thematic." According to the postulates of Goethean classicist aesthetics, the formal principles of "metamorphosis" and "repeated mirroring" serve to give a large, multisectional composition an inner unity, while at the same time permitting a rich diversity of *Gestalten* and characters.

The principle of "repeated mirroring" relates the opening thematic configuration to its reappearances at the beginnings of both reprise and coda. At the start of the symphony its two elements are, as mentioned, in structural disagreement. At the entrance of the reprise then, this configuration—its two elements still out of phase but the original horn theme now played by oboes—is combined with the violins' intensified variant of the horn theme (in the exposition following the dark trombone passage shortly after the start). The rhythmic acceleration gives this second appearance a new impetus forward, and as a consequence the trombone passage is cut to half in the reprise and integrated into the move. The beginning of the coda then brings the third appearance of the initial configuration. But now both elements are phased together and the metrical and harmonic ambiguity is resolved, as is the displacement of the superimposed phrases. And their now harmonious simultaneity is cast in a rich, warm, animated tone of expressive strings. A summoning horn monologue leads to this great event. It has the character of fulfillment. For a moment of reconciliation here seems to be the positive goal of the movement's narrative. But from the very beginning there is an effective counterstrategy to this affirmative evolution. Its concentrated center is the extraordinary moment of an almost complete halt of the symphony's unfolding after only a few measures. At this "negative" pole the somber trombones and tuba enter with dissonant diminished-seventh chords—an extreme darkening casts a long shadow ahead over the entire movement. In a letter to Vincenz Lachner, August 1878, Brahms himself commented on that striking moment:

> I very much wanted to manage in that first movement without using trombones, and I tried to. . . . But their first entrance, that's mine, and I can't get along without it and thus the trombones. Were I to defend the passage, I would have to be long-winded. I would have to confess that I am, by the by, a severely melancholic person, that black wings are constantly flapping

above us, and that in my output . . . that symphony is followed by a little essay about the great 'Why' (the *Job* motet, Op. 74).

Indeed, the trombone passage emphatically questions the pastoral world. The violins' animated variant of the pastoral theme has to reopen the movement, rescuing it from the virtual standstill. But later comes, again out of the melancholic box, the elegiac second theme in minor; then follow the harmonic and metrical tensions of the development section with extreme orchestral outbursts. Finally, a clouding over of the coda's emphatic beginning leads to the ambiguous ending of the movement, with its dissonant superimposition of the subdominant G minor and the dominant D major—again signposts for Brahms's skeptical view of the possibility of pure serenity.

The passionate Adagio song of the cello cantilena marks the main subject of the second movement's sonata form, the graceful animation of a contrasting passage in 12/8 time functioning as second theme; a brief epilogue concludes the exposition and at the same time introduces the developmental fugato model. The reprise drops the second subject and integrates figurations from the development. The coda's tone and meaning are defined by the kettledrum with its repeated triplets of dominant F♯ and tonic B—it can be heard quite indubitably as a distant echo of the First Symphony's tragic introduction.

The third movement lacks the low brass. Formally it is in five sections, with a double repetition of the initial section, symmetrically arranged so as to form the centerpiece and frame. This organization is outwardly reminiscent of the "great scherzo form" with its triple scherzo and two often not wholly identical trios. But in reality it is the opposite: a back-to-front Scherzo and Trio, so to speak, with a primary, twice-repeated trio-like section interrupted by two nonidentical scherzo-like contrasting sections, all dressed with artificial dance characters and their various guises (not excluding darker undertones). Drastic contrast (tempo, time, tone, character) and varied repetition of the stylized dances are the most obvious formal principles.

The fourth movement indeed is a "last dance," using all the resources available to round up the symphony in a fulminating drive forward. The intention of a euphoria let loose is audible from the unison main theme's collective "go ahead" through all the pertinent stages of a sonata layout to the blaring octave passages on the heavy brass toward the end. The development section, however, displays two formally "dissident" features:

the development begins—as in the Finale of the First Symphony—with the main theme on the tonic D major, and the last part of the development is a lyrically contrasting tranquillo couplet, in ternary *A B A* form and thus internally autonomous. These two formal elements can be explained best as rondo derivatives. Thus the sonata design is complicated by a partial superimposition with the rondo. Rondo-sonata would be an adequate label for the movement's form. Its last authoritative word rests with the three trombones (again, but in a different tone and spirit). Tovey calls this "blast of the trombones" the "most surprising effect of all in the coda," sanctioning the brilliant and triumphant close of the work.

Reinhold Brinkmann

Symphony No. 3 in F, Opus 90
Composed 1883; published 1884

Scoring: 2 flutes, 2 oboes, 2 clarinets, 2 bassoons, contrabassoon,
4 horns, 2 trumpets, 3 trombones, timpani, strings
Movements: 1. Allegro con brio; 2. Andante; 3. Poco Allegretto; 4. Allegro

Brahms's focus on orchestral compositions in 1880–85 (especially the Second Piano Concerto and the Third Symphony) was partly encouraged by his having at his disposal for private performances the excellent orchestra at the ducal court of Saxe-Meiningen after Hans von Bülow became its director. The adjustments to the scoring seen in the manuscript of the Third Symphony show Brahms's fascination with orchestration in a work that has been greatly admired for its timbral color. While sketching or drafting compositions, Brahms preferred the inspiration of natural beauty found in rural surroundings. The Third Symphony was composed near the Rhine, in the spa town of Wiesbaden, during the summer of 1883; indeed, the beginning echoes the exuberant opening melody of Robert Schumann's own Third Symphony, the *Rhenish.*

Although early commentators considered the Third Symphony "heroic," in the vein of Beethoven's Third Symphony, the *Eroica,* its adaptations of symphonic tradition deliberately undermine the monumentality that the nineteenth century came to associate with the genre of the symphony. The tonal structure of the entire work is based on the Classical key scheme for a single movement, tonic-dominant-tonic. The outer movements are in F major and F minor, and the inner movements in C major and C minor. The work's relative brevity, as the shortest of

Brahms's four symphonies, aids perception of this tonal compactness. And Brahms's avoidance of the dominant at the expected points in the outer movements—the second theme and the lead-in to the reprise—renders the dominant relationship between movements even more powerful. The anti-heroic stance of the Symphony is more immediately sensed in how its opening grand gestures dissipate, and in a second theme in the clarinet and bassoon that seems a melodic blossoming rather than inevitable logic. Here, the Classical procedure of repeating the exposition does not reinforce a conflict of theme groups, but renders more palpable the unwinding of tension. The confirming nature of symphonic music is further revoked in the development section, where each of the two main themes undergoes a radical transformation in character. Rather than working out motivic problems in the exposition's themes, the development takes an unexpected turn: the pastoral second subject is invigorated into an epic-heroic gesture, and the energetic first subject relaxes into a restrained, veiled, somewhat brooding passage just prior to the recapitulation.

With its prominent wind scoring, the second movement has struck commentators as a tranquil sublimation of folk song. Where a contrasting theme might introduce tension, Brahms retains placidity of mood by using the same poignant coloring for the second theme as for the first— clarinet and bassoon, then violins. The reprise is varied, with rich swirling figuration in the strings, but the coda reestablishes a sense of calm as it ends with the same scoring as the opening: the gentle turning motive from the first theme repeats above a warm, sustained cello sonority and bassoon in counterpoint, winding downward.

Casting off expectations for a scherzo, whether exuberant or mysterious, the third movement initially promises an eternal calm. The opening cello theme aspires to the infinite, with ever new extensions of its basic materials. Its slow, twelve-measure unfolding arrives at no breath of closure, but rather at gentle gestures upward: the theme ends inconclusively, with the expected tonic displaced up to an F, and this dissonance is resolved as the theme begins again in the higher register of the first violins. As if time stands still, the opening theme is repeated without change until its conclusion, where the anticipated tonic is finally heard. For earlier listeners the central A-major section, with its offbeat accents, major-minor shifts, and playful cello counterpoint, evoked gypsy mystery. But these gestures of the profane cannot be sustained: twice the gypsy music is interrupted by a more reflective string theme, bringing back intimations of the infinite.

Unlike the sustained rejoicing of Beethoven finales, which by the late nineteenth century had become the norm, Brahms's Finale achieves a symphonic victory as the result of a process. Each segment of the sonata-form scheme in the fourth movement thwarts grand gestures of closure. Brahms turns on its head what nineteenth-century critics often described as a gendered opposition in the exposition themes—an assertive "masculine" first theme followed by a gentle, lyrical "feminine" second theme. The movement opens much like the Finale of the Second Symphony, with a mysterious theme of running eighth notes in barren octaves. More like a second theme, this material exudes a lyrical warmth as the winds take over, with leggiero flourishes in the low strings and a pizzicato bass. And while a series of interruptions—above all, a dark A♭-major chorale—precludes any sustained buildup in the first group, the second begins assertively in the cello and horn, developing its strong triadic gestures continuously, more like a symphonic first group. The usual symphonic energy is curiously absent from the development as well. Brahms's fluid thematic treatment only builds tension after the first theme has twice dissipated into sweeter, calmer moments. Even this process of fragmentation first resists the drive to greater pressure so typical in development sections—the turn motive from the first theme group, though tightly wrought, is pitted against a calmer descending scale. But an intense conflict ensues between the turn motive and various ideas developed out of the scalar figure until finally, the chorale is reconstructed in the brass, heralding a victory marked by the recapitulation, traditionally the highest point of excitement in a sonata-form movement.

The famous transcendent coda has posed problems in the programming of the Symphony, with audience expectation of a victorious close as a reward for concentrated listening. But for the discerning ear, the unity offered by the Finale is more satisfying in its completion of procedures left undone in earlier movements. The ending to the first movement is a calming statement of the main theme that sinks down into the tonic, then dissipates into an ethereal cadence two octaves higher (ostensibly because the final low F is beyond the violin's register). This promise is fulfilled at the end of the Symphony, where the first movement's close is rescored so that F is reached first in the violins and then again in the lower strings, with a final ethereal cadence.

Even the standard device for symphonic unity—a majestic quotation from an earlier movement in the Finale—becomes a deeper structural matter for Brahms. The Finale quotes three times from the chorale-like second theme of the second movement, as if correcting an imbalance in the earlier movement, where that theme was missing in the recapitulation. Thus questioning the confirmatory symphonic experience preferred by the century of the bourgeoisie, Brahms anticipates the subjective, evanescent nature of "spiritual struggle" and "true victory" that Gustav Mahler articulated to Richard Strauss in justifying the bold course of symphonic writing he began in the 1880s, prefiguring developments of the next century.

Karen Painter

SYMPHONY NO. 4 IN E MINOR, OPUS 98
Composed 1884–85; published 1886

SCORING: piccolo, 2 flutes, 2 oboes, 2 clarinets, 2 bassoons, contrabassoon, 4 horns, 2 trumpets, 3 trombones, timpani, triangle, strings
MOVEMENTS: 1. Allegro non troppo; 2. Andante moderato; 3. Allegro giocoso; 4. Allegro energetico e passionato

Brahms's greatest and most severe instrumental work, the Fourth Symphony, was also virtually his last orchestral work (excepting the Double Concerto, Op. 102, whose freedom and lyricism show the composer taking a different path, after more than two decades of struggle with the symphonic genre). Its austerity is reflected in the choice of key areas: the dark E minor, highly unusual for a symphony, for the first and fourth movements; a raw, almost metallic C major for the brash third movement; and the dark Phrygian mode inflecting the Romantic key of E major of the second movement. While summering at Mürzzuschlag in the Styrian Alps (where the first two movements were composed in 1884 and the latter two in 1885), Brahms wrote the conductor Hans von Bülow that the new work "tastes of the climate here. The cherries are hardly sweet here; you wouldn't eat them!"

Brahms was nonetheless dismayed that friends initially rejected the Symphony, as Kalbeck notes, with such radical suggestions as abandoning the last two movements and publishing the Finale as a separate work. Brahms's fear that the work would be too stern for his contemporaries proved true, especially in Vienna, where not until near the very end of Brahms's life, at a concert in March 1897 attended by the gravely ill composer, did the work receive substantial acclaim.

The Fourth Symphony represents Brahms's most sustained, original response to his inheritance as a composer and music historian, especially his solution to the so-called finale problem (how to summarize earlier movements, impart unity, and establish closure). Faced with the opposed traditions of a lighter rondo form and a weighty sonata form, composers tended toward the latter, struggling to achieve a sonata form more conclusive than that of the opening movement. Brahms's deployment of a variation form, with the principles of sonata form helping to group the thirty variations, nods at a late-eighteenth-century tradition (especially the variation finale found in concertos), attaining gravity by a rigorous application of Baroque form.

The appeal such form had for Brahms appears as early as in a letter to Clara Schumann from 1877, accompanying his arrangement for piano left-hand of the D-minor Chaconne from J.S. Bach's second solo Violin Partita. The form enabled Bach to express "a whole world of the deepest thoughts and most powerful feelings," Brahms writes. "If I could picture myself writing, or even conceiving, such a piece, I am certain that the extreme excitement and emotional tension would have driven me mad. . . . The piece certainly inspires one to occupy oneself with it somehow." Five years later, Brahms discussed an idea for the theme of the Chaconne from Bach's Cantata 150, *Nach dir, Herr, verlanget mich,* a work which he had studied carefully. Brahms could elicit only restrained admiration from Bülow at a piano rendition of the Chaconne. To the latter's objection that the climax, with its adamantly intellectual conception, needed to be executed by vocal forces, Brahms suggested, "What would you think of a symphonic movement written on this theme someday? But it is too heavy, too straightforward. It would have to be chromatically altered in some way" (witnessed by Siegfried Ochs). Brahms's ultimate decision in the symphony Finale to intensify this theme's scalar ascent through a striking chromatic passing note A♯ was probably inspired by the E-minor Chaconne of Buxtehude, another composer he esteemed highly. Lacking the usual traits of symmetry or melodic fullness, the Bach subject is less a theme than a powerful invocation, especially with Brahms's scoring for trombones, absent in the three earlier movements.

Though steeped in musical influences, the Fourth Symphony repre-

sents Brahms's most profoundly innovative essay in the symphonic tradition. The conflict behind the first movement is not of the usual symphonic ethos, strengthening the heroic subject, but one where the subject
faces struggle without hope or self-confirmation. The listener is drawn
gradually into the bleak world of the Symphony, for the opening theme
offers a series of disjunct, yet caressing motions below which an arpeggio
motive strives urgently upward. Even the joint between the opening thematic statements offers no stability, as an oboe dissonance pierces
through the rich string texture. As in Beethoven's Fifth, a fanfare bridges
into the next theme group, but with Brahms the militaristic gestures
persist, such that the simple lyricism of the B-major theme in winds and
horn, almost too sweet, is quickly abandoned. For the first time in an
opening movement of his symphonies, Brahms avoids a repeated exposition so welcomed by listeners attempting to grasp a complex thematic
work. Instead, the movement pushes forward, inexorably leading to its
downfall, as the conductor Felix Weingartner wrote of the Finale. The
comfort of recognition is missing in the recapitulation as well. As in first
two symphonies, the opening theme's return is mysteriously veiled,
drawn out in empty octaves. The strain of austere thematic work, without sustained lyricism, led Eduard Hanslick to report of the first movement when Brahms and a friend played it on the piano: "I felt I was being
thrashed by two terribly clever men."

The striking instrumental colors in the second movement—solo horn,
pizzicato accompaniment—as well as the bold changes in mood, such as
the tender lyricism of the second theme and the powerful development
later in the movement, suggest the influence of Schubert, the complete
edition of whose works Brahms helped edit at the time. Otherwise the
music shows a defiance of the comfortably reflecting subject. The severe
opening horn call and successive entrances of the woodwinds in stark
unison stretto elicit melancholy through the archaic Phrygian mode on
E (a mode "expressing profound need and remorse," as noted in a passage
that Brahms highlighted in a book on the early Baroque composer Giovanni Gabrieli), achieved through flattening the second degree, F♯, in E
major. Even the melodic blossoming and rich accompaniment defy any
sense of motion, with the harmony hovering for almost four measures on
E major. The coda acts as a final revocation of the lush melody in the
reprise. As if time were suspended, the extended B in the bass, normally
the dominant preparing for the final assertion of E major, is harmonized
mysteriously with a subdued timpani roll, above which the famed clarinet

solo hovers with fragments of the melody. The movement closes with a return to the gravity of the opening—the horn melody in its modal coloring—abandoning any effort to create a lyrical whole.

The gentle evaporation of E major ending the second movement is brutally answered by the rough, almost blaring C-major opening of the third movement, as if Brahms reinforces the failure of symphonic music at proclaiming overarching truths. The assertive gestures of the movement, through its strange pattern of accents and pauses as well as its abrupt harmonic and thematic shifts, elicited divergent reactions. While Kalbeck's rejection of the movement presages more recent commentators' embarrassment over the ostentatious counterpoint and the triangle, Brahms's audiences evidently welcomed novelty and extremes in a scherzo movement, expressively the freest of all symphonic traditions: the third movement was the most popular, to the point of being repeated. This testifies to Brahms's brilliant solution to the formal problem of the genre, with the last two movements fulfilling the finale expectations. (Indeed, as was his practice, Brahms composed the two movements out of order, completing the Finale before writing the third movement.) Action-filled, unreflective, and ultimately celebratory with its raw C-major power, the Scherzo is evocative of the older symphonic finale tradition, leaving the last movement open to a more somber, original kind of development.

Karen Painter

4

VARIATIONS AND OVERTURES

Variations on a Theme by Haydn in B♭, Opus 56
Composed 1873; published 1874

Scoring: piccolo, 2 flutes, 2 oboes, 2 clarinets, 2 bassoons, contrabassoon, 4 horns, 2 trumpets, timpani, triangle, strings

One approach to musical composition views it as something vaguely Talmudic, a discussion among sages. Certainly much of Brahms seems to comment on and amplify salient points in the works of Beethoven, Mozart and Bach, and, of course, Haydn. This is especially true of the *Variations on a Theme by Haydn,* originally composed for two pianos in 1873 and orchestrated and premiered later that same year.

Although it is most often performed in its orchestral arrangement (Op. 56a), the two-piano version (Op. 56b) of the *Variations* is splendid. While the orchestral color is, of course, lost, the contrapuntal lines are more clearly heard, the argument of the composition is easier to follow, and the conclusion is more effective.

The first thing to catch our attention is the jaunty and jagged little theme itself (originally titled *Chorale St. Antoni;* it was probably not composed by Haydn). Featuring a pair of five-measure phrases at the beginning, it is almost a miniature sonata movement, complete with its own small coda. Composers have worked with many kinds of variations, from the bass variations of the late Renaissance and Baroque to the melodic variations of Mozart and the virtuoso variations of the early nineteenth century (these had become so commonplace that Mendelssohn had to call his own set *Serious Variations* in order to distinguish them from others). Brahms made several important choices in putting this set together. Although motivic ideas are preserved from variation to variation, the piece is, in effect, a variation on everything except the structure and the basic harmonic patterns, which remain inviolate in all variations except the last.

A brief diagram of the structure of the theme might look like this:

Basic form	A	A1	B	A	Coda
Subdivisions	a + a1 +	a + a2 +	b + b1 +	a + a2 +	c + c + d

It is this pattern that is repeated and preserved, though nearly everything else changes, especially the character of each variation.

Variations posed a special problem for the nineteenth-century composer. The laws of the genre are quite simple: there can be no movement to a distant key, the only change of mode permitted is from major to minor and vice versa, and some aspect of the theme must be preserved. The leading formal principle of the late eighteenth and nineteenth centuries, that of the sonata, uses thematic contrast and long-range harmonic motion as a means of creating that illusion of tension and forward motion we sometimes call drama. How, though, can one create analogous drama if one must stick to a single theme (or structure) and remain in the same key throughout?

Brahms solves the problem in several ways. First, he chooses an engaging, formally interesting theme. Second, he treats each variation as a separate character piece, with a complementary series of affects. Third, by pairing groups of variations and featuring a very long, slow variation (Variation VII), he creates some of the sense of a multi-movement work. Finally, by carefully controlling the elements of motion, and by fragmenting and subsequently reintroducing thematic materials, he creates analogies with the general notion of development and recapitulation. Indeed, the patterns used are traditional: the theme is marked Andante, and the acceleration commences directly as both of the first two variations have the word "più" in them, to ensure an increase in speed. The third variation is perhaps neutral in terms of acceleration, while the fourth represents a decrease in speed. As the piece progresses, the differences in tempo between variations become more extreme in order to heighten the effect of acceleration: Vivace–Grazioso–Presto. Variation VIII reaches the high point in terms of both speed and fragmentation.

A real clue to the identity of the work is supplied by the last super-variation, itself a compendium of nineteen variations. Leading us back to the early eighteenth century and before, it is based on the first five measures of the theme and comprises a series of bass variations—not unlike the chaconne and passacaglia but for its being in common time instead of triple meter. This most venerable of variation principles is a microcosm of the whole, for in it Brahms must keep the listener's attention by creating illusions of varying speed and intensity—thickening and thinning the texture, moving the theme from the bass to the treble, and turning the material from major to minor and back again.

But he does more than that in order to provide an aspect of the sonata to the work. Toward the end of the last variation, we gradually hear the theme reassert itself, like a phoenix emerging out of its own ashes, but with a difference: the charming little theme from the opening has vanished and though almost exactly the same, it now carries with it a sense of triumph and grandeur.

It is impossible to overestimate the various ways in this work that Brahms was linking himself to a previous, essentially German tradition of composition. His theme suggests a connection not only with Haydn but with the idea of a chorale as well; at the same time, his manner of treatment, though modern on the surface, finds its inspiration in the earliest years of the North German organ school, when composers from Sweelinck onward struggled with the process of creating music designed as intellectual refreshment (in the words of Georg Muffat) rather than something more functional. Yet it is not merely this careful planning and precise sense of order and pacing that make the *Haydn* Variations such an effective piece—it is that all of the variations strike perfectly contemporary poses: though they may refer in structure and technique to earlier times, they are in no way antiquarian in nature.

Even though music historians make distinctions between the German composers and nationalists such as Grieg, Smetana, and Musorgsky, it is hard to see how Brahms differs from many of these figures in the way he used history. All of these composers seem to have striven to uncover and revive historical elements, yet focus them in such a way as to ensure their passage into the future.

Michael Beckerman

Academic Festival Overture in C Minor, Opus 80
Composed 1880; published 1881

Scoring: piccolo, 2 flutes, 2 oboes, 2 clarinets, 2 bassoons, contrabassoon, 4 horns, 3 trumpets, 3 trombones, tuba, timpani, bass drum and cymbals, triangle, strings

Single Movement: Allegro. L'istesso tempo. Un poco maestoso. Animato. Maestoso.

The Overture was completed by August 1880 in Bad Ischl, Upper Austria. It owes its origins to the conferring upon Brahms of an honorary Doctor of Philosophy degree by the University of Breslau on March 11, 1879; the diploma described him as "Artis musicae severioris in Germania nunc principi" ("the most famous living German composer of serious music"). The conductor of the Orchesterverein of Breslau, his friend, the composer Bernhard Scholz, had hoped that Brahms would write a symphony or at least a festal ode in acknowledgment. But Brahms chose rather to respond to the honor with a work partly inspired by its context, using student songs well known to an academic audience, thus adding an extramusical dimension otherwise unusual in his instrumental work. The Overture was given its first performance by the Breslau Orchesterverein under Brahms's direction on January 4, 1881, from manuscript. (Publication was delayed by Brahms's wish to rehearse it, as well as the *Tragic Overture*, Op. 81, with the orchestra of the Hochschule für Musik in Berlin, made available by the director, Joseph Joachim.) It was published with its companion in July 1881 by Simrock of Berlin (the piano-duet version by Brahms had appeared the preceding March). The composer supplied the unusual title, though he was not satisfied with it and initially invited alternative suggestions, once referring to it as his "Janissary Overture" on account of its use of "Turkish" instruments—bass drums, cymbals, and triangle.

In a conversation with Kalbeck, Brahms referred to the Overture as being "a pretty medley of songs à la Suppé." This is probably a reference to von Suppé's overture to *Flotte Bursche*, which utilizes student songs, including one used by Brahms. This understatement masks a movement of far greater formal interest: the songs are integrated into an unusual sonata-form structure that still enables each song to fully reveal its character. Thus Brahms honors the gravity of the distinction he had received while offering an appropriately public and sometimes witty acknowledgment, in which he could employ his proven skill in the elaboration of traditional melodies. In the many reflective moments of this movement of widely contrasting moods one might also sense Brahms's nostalgia for his youthful acquaintance with student festivities at Göttingen through his friendship with Joachim, though he was never himself a university student.

The formal structure is that of a sonata form in the major key with an introduction in the minor; its notable features are a two-stage tonal treatment of the second theme, a disguised recapitulation, and an independent coda in contrasting triple time. The borrowed melodies are "Wir hatten gebauet ein staatliches Haus" in the introduction, the *Landesvater* ("Hört ich sing") at the opening of the second theme, the *Fuchslied* ("Was kommt dort von der Höh") for the closing group, and the *Gaudeamus Igitur* for the coda. Additionally, the opening orchestral figure is strikingly akin to the opening motive of the *Rákóczi March*, while the exposition includes clear reference to a prominent figure from Brahms's own Serenade for solo voice and piano, Op. 106/1, which appeared later, its text referring to the "pipe and drum and zither" in student revels. But the art of the movement lies in the disguising rather than prediction of these themes until the grandiose conclusion. The developmental character and minor key of the introductory motive, and the following apparently original chorale-like phrase led by violas, suggest rather a serious sonata movement. Only with the appearance of "Wir hatten gebauet" as a bright major-key chorale on trumpets in chorus does a clue to the thematic material appear. But the working of the structure is sustained by the elaboration of the introductory material, the opening figure reworked to make an insistent first subject. The second subject, given to suave first and second violins, appears first in the major mediant key, E major, before the expected dominant G, and is followed by the Serenade motive (which is already a part of it) as a foil to the *Fuchslied*, now given a humorous setting for two bassoons and offbeat pizzicato strings before the full outburst of the orchestra reinforces the point. This passage serves for the development until the introductory material is reworked to herald a completely recomposed recapitulation up to the second subject. The coda resumes from the point at which development began with the Brahmsian equivalent of a grand opera overture, which clothes the *Gaudeamus* chorale in rushing string scales and extra percussion support (triangle, bass drum) in the largest orchestra Brahms ever used, including contrabassoon, trombones, tuba, and piccolo. The bluntness of the conclusion is offset in the main movement by constant changes of texture and color, which include, at the quietest point of development, the use of stopped notes *piano* in the horns. The Overture was frequently performed after the premiere and quickly established itself as his most accessible orchestral work.

Michael Musgrave

Tragic Overture in D Minor, Opus 81
Composed 1880; published 1881

Scoring: piccolo, 2 flutes, 2 oboes, 2 clarinets, 2 bassoons, 4 horns,
   2 trumpets, 3 trombones, tuba, timpani, strings
Allegro ma non troppo. Molto più moderato. Tempo primo

The Overture was composed during the same period as Op. 80, the summer of 1880 at Ischl. However, the ideas may go back further as sketches for the closing group material are included in a sketchbook with earlier works, the *Alto Rhapsody,* Op. 53, and the *Liebeslieder Walzer,* Op. 52. The first reference to the Overture is to Theodor Billroth on August 28, 1880, when Brahms comments that "the *Academic* has led me to a second overture which I can only entitle the *Dramatic,* which does not please me"; and then to Bernhard Scholz on September 17, "You may include a 'dramatic' or 'tragic,' or 'Tragedy Overture' in your program for January 6; I cannot find a proper title for it." To the publisher Fritz Simrock he had written on September 6 of the *Academic Festival Overture* with its " 'Gaudeamus' and all manner of other things" that "I could not refrain from writing a Tragedy Overture as well," and also commenting to Karl Reinecke that "one weeps while the other laughs." The Overture was first performed on December 26, 1880, by the Vienna Philharmonic Orchestra conducted by Hans Richter, and then, in addition to Op. 80, by Brahms with Scholz's Breslau Orchesterverein on January 4, 1881. It was published at the same time as Op. 80 in July 1881 by Simrock of Berlin, the four-hand version by Brahms appearing, like that of Op. 80, in March 1881.

In addition to simply providing a companion work to the *Academic Festival Overture,* it is possible that this overture also arose from external causes, which would explain why Brahms employed the genre of the concert overture, with its usual requirement of a title and program, otherwise absent from his instrumental compositions. Max Kalbeck suggests that the music originated for a dramatic production, noting that Brahms had been interested in a request by the head of the Vienna Burgtheater to compose music for both parts of Goethe's *Faust*. He claims that this overture and the inner movements of the Third Symphony were intended for *Faust*, though Brahms denied having any particular tragedy in mind. The idea of his acquiring inspiration from specific dramatic subjects stems from the character of the main themes and the unusual form of the whole. Both first and second subjects are self-contained eight-measure structures, unlike the themes of sonata forms, which are usually irregular and designed for their role within a continuous and developmental structure. This self-contained quality arises additionally from their inherently dramatic and contrasted qualities. The first attracts attention to itself with two introductory *ff* chords (taken from the theme itself), which focus attention on its quieter, brooding character (partly arising from its opening harmonic ambivalence), and it is then repeated *ff* for further emphasis. The second does likewise through the different means of the continuous reshaping and growth of its opening phrase. The fact that both themes are developed extensively thereafter to create lengthy but still discrete sections, rather than transitions to new ideas or development within the sonata structure, suggests treatment born of a dramatic rather than instrumental purpose. This results in a sectional structure which further distances the form from instrumental works. The first thematic complex ends decidedly in the tonic, the long transition appearing as almost a separate, atmospheric section, the lack of development in which seems designed to focus attention on the coming second theme by the lengthiest of means, just as the first subject was presented with the briefest. The development proper is designed as an entirely separate section, an expressive transformation of the second part of the first subject at half the speed, marked *dolce*; it appears as a response to the first part of this subject already given in extended form in the tonic, where it replaces the conventional repeat of the exposition that would be impossible in this design. After this "development," the second theme follows at the original tempo in the tonic to complete the recapitulation. A dramatic model such as *Faust* is possible for a movement with a brooding and volatile first theme and lyrical and reflective second theme, though the characters could also relate to other subjects, just as the arresting *ff* chords of the opening can be related to previous dramatic overtures, notably Schumann's *Manfred* and Beethoven's *Coriolan*. But the drama might equally be thought of in purely musical terms as the exploration and contrast of particularly characterful themes, the "tragedy" perhaps lying in the failure of the structure to transform the inexorable course of the first subject, despite its striking transformation in the "development." For at the point where this section could have recurred as coda, perhaps in a newly transformed working in the major key, the first subject generates fresh energy to reaffirm its unchangeable character and relentless impetus.

Despite several early repetitions after the first performance, the reception was cold and the work was very slow to gain favor, remaining among the least performed of his orchestral works, though it is one of his most powerful and individual movements.

Michael Musgrave

*Brahms and the violinist
Joseph Joachim in 1867.*

Part Two

CHAMBER MUSIC

INTRODUCTION

If Schumann recognized the symphonic character of Brahms's early chamber music, others have perceived the chamber music-like quality of Brahms's symphonic works. That is hardly surprising, since Brahms's chamber music was a continuous, integral part of his artistic expression throughout his career—a primary medium for the development of his compositional technique. Consequently Brahms's chamber music represents one of the great achievements of nineteenth-century European music. As critics from Paul Bekker to Reinhold Brinkmann have pointed out, Brahms felt that a mastery of chamber music forms was necessary as preparation for symphonic endeavors. However, his chamber music should by no means be seen as something preliminary, but rather as close to the heart of all of Brahms's accomplishment. In terms of its critical reception, it was the most consistently highly prized dimension of Brahms's music during his lifetime.

Brahms's models for chamber music were the masters of Viennese Classicism: Haydn, Mozart, and Beethoven. The string quartet constituted an indispensable benchmark for the genre of chamber music. For Johann Wolfgang von Goethe, the quartet was the idealized "conversation," a sustained narrative and philosophical experience transmitted purely musically. In the hands of Haydn and Mozart it became the elite genre of musical composition, and its prestige was further enhanced by Beethoven's contribution, particularly in the late quartets. In Brahms's day, these late quartets were just beginning to be widely appreciated. Like much late Beethoven, they had initially been viewed as eccentric if not wildly experimental. Beyond Beethoven, the other quartet and chamber music literature that Brahms admired included the work of Schubert, Schumann, and Mendelssohn.

During Brahms's lifetime, quartet playing and other forms of instrumental chamber music made a gradual but steady migration from the salon and living room to the concert stage. The leading protagonists in this development included the violinist Joseph Hellmesberger (with whom Brahms made his debut in 1861 in Vienna), whose quartet helped bring late Beethoven into prominence, and the quartet formed later by Brahms's oldest friend, Joseph Joachim. By the 1890s, the last years of Brahms's life, Europe boasted many significant professional quartets. Among the most prominent of these was the quartet led by the concertmaster of the Vienna Philharmonic, Arnold Rosé, Mahler's future brother-in-law, whose ensemble was responsible for premiering much new quartet music at the turn of the century.

Brahms's friends from the 1850s on included many amateur and professional instrumentalists, including Joachim, cellist David Popper, clarinetist Richard Mühlfeld, and many others whose knowledge of the chamber music repertory was intimate. Their evaluation of Brahms's chamber music reflected the standards of high connoisseurship associated with the genre. Brahms was writing not only in the shadow of great historic achievements but also in the context of the opinions of his contemporaries, who held chamber music to exacting and somewhat conservative standards. This explains in part Brahms's extraordinary self-criticism (apparently Brahms destroyed dozens of quartets he had composed before publishing the Op. 51 quartets) and his serious consideration of the judgments of close friends such as Elisabet von Herzogenberg and Clara Schumann.

Predictably, many of the chamber music forms in which Brahms excelled often involved the piano. The three piano trios are nearly unequaled masterpieces of the form; although Brahms would have shuddered at the comparison, it has been said that his achievements here exceed those of Beethoven, Schubert, and Mozart. Similarly, the sonatas for violin and piano and cello and piano are sturdy pillars of the canon and required repertory for every violinist and cellist. Violists and clarinetists are in Brahms's debt for the sonatas and other music for clarinet and strings, and the larger ensemble forms, the quintets and the sextets, continue to be heard regularly in modern chamber concert programs.

This impressive range of accomplishment made Brahms's music a frequent presence among the most sophisticated groups of connoisseurs as listeners and players in both Europe and America (the Op. 8 Trio in B Major was premiered in Boston by Theodore Thomas). But the real source of his endearment to the culture of nineteenth-century chamber music was the fact that, despite the professionalization of chamber music playing, Brahms never forgot the gifted amateur as his primary consumer. The Op. 51 quartets are dedicated to Brahms's friend Theodor Billroth, the surgeon and an avid violist. Brahms was one of the first composers in modern times to maintain a suitable living from the royalties of his compositions; his income was derived, however, not so much from the royalties from public performance as from the purchase of sheet music by the bedrock of active amateurs. Brahms was one of the few composers able to maintain the highest standards of musical literacy and craftsmanship—to an aesthetic lineage begun by Haydn in his chamber music that was characterized by complexity, formal brilliance, and excellence—in a manner that appealed to professional and non-professional players alike. Brahms's chamber music is outstanding not only for its capacity to satisfy the intellect of the sophisticated music enthusiast but also for its accessibility, the beauty of its melodic invention, its variety, wit, and excitement. Brahms's chamber music is the proper place in which to discover the full range of Brahms's compositional genius, and to witness the development of his trademark characteristics of ruthless clarity, economy, invention, emotional intensity without sentimentality, and unerring sense of proportion.

5

SONATAS

SONATA NO. 1 FOR PIANO AND CELLO IN E MINOR, OPUS 38

Composed 1862–65; published 1866

MOVEMENTS: 1. Allegro non troppo; 2. Allegretto quasi Menuetto. Trio; 3. Allegro

Few composers are as distinctly recognizable by their "tone of voice" as Brahms. This stylistic characteristic combines registral preferences with chord voicings and timbral combinations. Brahms perfected an enriched musical texture that gave extra weight to the lower-middle registers and that is already apparent in his earliest known solo piano music. It seems no accident that during the period 1859–65, when this characteristic "tone of voice" was being explored in a series of chamber works, Schubert's Quintet with two cellos provided an important textural model. That Brahms's first published duo was a cello sonata reflects this exploration.

Three movements of the Sonata in E Minor were composed in 1862, including an unused Adagio affettuoso, but the Finale was added only in 1865. For this work, Brahms seems to have turned to several sources, each offering support for a different side of its character. On the one hand, motivic and formal links to Bach's *Art of Fugue* speak to the gravity and rigor with which Brahms sought to imbue the dialogue. These allusions are sometimes overt, as in the subject and fugal development of the third movement, and sometimes disguised, as in the outline of the theme of the first movement. Along with Brahms's choice of a minuet for the second movement, they create an atmosphere of retrospection; the work lives partly in the past and partly in the present.

On the other hand, this sonata displays certain resemblances to an earlier sonata by the cellist-composer Bernhard Romberg, his Op. 38/1 in E Minor, an example of craftsmanship rather than inspiration. Never one to despise solid and inventive craftsmanship, Brahms may have used some idiomatic materials from this work as starting points; its first movement, Allegro non troppo, foreshadows not only specific thematic shapes but overall mood and sonority for Brahms's first movement, which shares that tempo marking. In any case, Brahms has thoroughly transformed these materials; his ingeniously varied sequence of textures give body to ideas that might otherwise have remained somewhat abstract.

The Sonata was apparently planned to have the usual four movements. (The unused Adagio affettuoso reappeared twenty-one years later with a new key signature as the second movement of the Cello Sonata No. 2.) This change of plan would have resulted from a judgment that the slow movement had too great a weight to be placed alongside the already weighty outer movements of the E-minor Sonata; Max Kalbeck commented that with it, the sonata would have been "too stuffed with music." The Sonata as it stands has a unique shape, in which the gravity of the opening Allegro non troppo is perfectly offset by the old-fashioned elegance of the Minuet and the remarkable power and momentum of the fugal Finale. It may be that the three-year delay in its completion was due to the formal dilemma posed by the Adagio and brilliantly solved by its omission and the composition of the Finale.

The challenge of a texture in which a low-pitched instrument has the leading melodic role inspired Brahms to develop varied, versatile relationships between the instruments, maintaining the piano as equal partner. This approach can be seen immediately as the melody rises from the soloist's lowest string under the piano's inexorable offbeat chords. The textural interplay between the two instruments shows the utmost ingenuity, with the cello moving below the piano without sacrificing its melodic role, or moving seamlessly from a melodic to a bass-line function. The cello line retains a strongly motivic profile even when it assumes a subordinate role, as it does in the transition, where the piano takes over the continuation of the first theme in C major. Although the cello can occupy the more usual position between the right- and left-hand registers of the piano, and even briefly sound above the entire accompaniment, its tessitura remains low throughout the Sonata. The balance in the fugal Finale is notorious for the disadvantage suffered by the cello; according to legend, a struggling cellist reading the Finale with the composer complained, "I can't hear myself," to which Brahms replied, "You're lucky!"

Each movement is distinguished by inventive form and harmony. The first possesses a strong sense of continuity, with a discourse of motifs and harmonies continuously flowing from one theme to the next across the sectional boundaries of sonata form. The first theme expressively emphasizes the motive C–B, or 6–5, which plays an expanded role throughout the Sonata. The more urgent-sounding second theme was singled out by Schoenberg as a textbook example of "developing variation," a process of melodic growth characteristic of Brahms's mature works whereby melodies evolve out of varying motivic fragments. The closing theme of the exposition, a lyrical procession of great stillness unfolded over a reiterated pedal, is expanded into a radiant coda in the tonic major, a transformation that allows the opening theme to discover its true consequent in ample, flowing phrases, to which nothing could be added in the way of songfulness or sense of fulfillment.

That being the case, the Allegretto quasi Menuetto and Finale offer bracing contrasts. Beneath piano figuration that always reminds us of the 6–5 motto, the cello dances its minuet with the piano a little stiffly, pausing a bit to catch its breath. The form is expanded binary, with an extra grazioso episode that adds warmth to the antique elegance. The Trio, in strict binary form, is a much more flowing dance, with piano and cello sharing the melody in octaves most of the time. This is the only section of the Sonata in which the cello sings the melody throughout. Its flexibility and spontaneity provide welcome contrast within the movement.

An altogether more radical contrast is provided by the Finale, whose fugue subject refers to motivic material from the first movement. The powerful, objective mood of the fugal exposition generates rhythmic momentum; a motif from the first theme is transformed into the exposition's second theme, in the relative major. Despite its lyrical warmth, the contrapuntal texture and harmonic instability insure that this lyric moment will not rob the music of its forward impulse.

The inversion of the theme appears along with the second countersubject as part of an exhaustive development, and in yet another inventive reinterpretation, Brahms begins his compressed recapitulation in the piano, on the dominant, with the answering version of the fugue subject as originally heard in the cello. This condensing adds further momentum to the dialogue, and instead of bringing back his second theme, Brahms moves straight to the coda, più presto. If nowhere else, it is here that beleaguered cellists must fight to remain in the picture (especially if they are faced with inconsiderate accompanists who are encouraged by the composer's own example). But any suspicions that may have been aroused that the composer was stuck in the past are surely put to rest by the absolute balance between virtuosity and rigor that brings this work to the firmest of conclusions.

Laurence Wallach

SONATA NO. 1 FOR PIANO AND VIOLIN IN G MAJOR, OPUS 78

Composed 1878–79; published 1880

MOVEMENTS: 1. Vivace ma non troppo; 2. Adagio; 3. Allegro molto moderato

Brahms's *Regen* (Rain) Sonata was composed during the summers of 1878 and 1879 in the idyllic surroundings of the resort town of Pörtschach, and much has been written about the relationship between the music and its place of origin. But while Brahms wrote many pieces in summer resorts, the atmosphere of this work remains unique. In it, Brahms creates a combination of lyrical sweetness and subdued emotional urgency, matched by a subtle rhythmic pressure, that maintains a remarkably unbroken melodic flow, even carrying through distinct moments of formal articulation, especially in the first movement. The three movements are formally integrated and achieve an emotional coherence that suggests an unstated autobiographical impulse.

The contributions of harmony and texture to the Sonata's character are critical. The distinctive coloration of the harmony is connected to melodic phrases; one passage of five measures has been cited as an example of "harmonic congruence" by Edward T. Cone, by which he means harmonies containing the same pitches as the melody being accompanied. The level of dissonance, owing mostly to suspensions, is surprisingly high considering the overall "sweetness" and generally benign mood; it serves gently but persistently to encourage the flow of events.

Unlike the E-minor Cello Sonata, the piano here never seriously challenges the leading melodic role of the violin, which sings from beginning to end. Far from having a reduced role in the dialogue, however, the second voice has been enriched by an interplay of motivic figuration and metric cross-currents. In this way, the piano plays an equal role in generating form, but with little of the overt struggle found in the earlier duo. In an inscription, Brahms apparently connected this work to lyrical G-major sonatas by Mozart (K. 301) and Beethoven (Op. 96), as well as to a quote from Goethe's *Queen of Heaven:* "Come, rise to higher spheres." The meaning of this quote may become clearer when we compare the sonata to the songs (Brahms's own Op. 59/3–4) upon which it is based.

The use of the metric materials in the first movement has made it the *locus classicus* for Brahms's mature rhythmic technique. His use of hemiola reaches its apex here. The twelve eighth-notes of each 3/2 measure (groups of 4) can be re-divided to imply two different meters, 6/4 (six groups of 2) and 12/8 (four groups of 3). That all three can be suggested simultaneously without any sense of artifice (as in the first page of the movement) speaks to the thoroughness with which this technique has been assimilated into an expressive language.

Large-scale instrumental works based on songs are a feature of the oeuvre of Schubert, whose "Wanderer Fantasy" Liszt embraced as a forerunner of his own explorations in continuous, integrated form. In his First Violin Sonata, Brahms explored methods which offer a distribution of the underlying song material into three related but self-contained movements, going beyond both Schubert and his own earlier efforts in this direction.

These three movements are of traditional design. The first is a "lyric" sonata form in G major (the opening theme reappearing in the tonic at the beginning of the development); the second is an expanded ternary form *(A B A B A)* in E♭ major; and the third, a rondo in G minor based on the *Regenlieder* (Rain Songs), has a subtle design which offers two episodes and a coda based on a recapitulation of the second episode.

The movements are connected on two levels. The first involves subtle and wide-ranging transformations of a group of succinct melodic motives, most of which occur in the opening material of the work: three drawn from the underlying song material occur in the first four measures, and two new ones appear in the answering four-measure phrase. The most conspicuous of these is the "motto rhythm," three D's in a long-short-long pattern that occurs in the most varied rhythmic and formal circumstances throughout the Sonata, and which is set in the beginning of the *Regenlied* to the syllables "Wal-le re-[gen]."

Additional motivic material appears later, the most important being the beginning of the theme of the second movement, a four-note motive of two thirds moving in opposite directions, derived somewhat indirectly from first-movement material. This motive plays an increasingly important role in the third movement: it modifies the song theme in its third measure, which helps to generate a related answering theme (and forms a connection to the "droplet" piano figuration common to song and sonata); it generates the entire "Slavic dance" theme of the first episode, and it provides an answering theme for the second episode.

The second level of integration between movements involves more immediately audible references to material from previous movements. Two occur in the third movement. The first is an extended quotation of the principal theme of the slow movement, in its original key, as an episode of the rondo. The next is the reappearance of this same material in the tonic major; this key has not been heard since the first movement. The ensuing coda uses a form of the motto rhythm that can refer equally to the beginnings of the first or the third movements, and serves, therefore, as a subtle but clear peroration of the whole, an enactment of recollection on a psychological as well as musical level.

The songs (a two-part unit) around which the sonata is built form the beginning of the third movement; programmatically the first two movements might stand for the series of prior experiences which the narrator of the song recalls. Emotionally significant material in the first movement includes transformations of the motto as two equal notes (a spondaic rhythm) which evolve from the repeated-chord accompaniment in the beginning into a plausible representation of a heartbeat when the opening theme returns to round out the second group. A second suggestive motive is a six-note scale figure, used in both ascending and descending directions, which first appears almost immediately, in measure 6. It initiates much of the rhythmic and melodic flow in the movement, and acts in opposition to the hesitancy implied in the first idea. It pervades the end of the exposition, the beginning and middle of the development, and offers a new countermelody to the recapitulation of the second theme. In ascending form, it leads to the climactic high point of the coda.

The conclusion of the second song, *Reminiscence,* and of the Sonata display critical emotive differences: the song ends with a Picardian third in what is still clearly a minor context, while the coda to the Sonata moves fully into major well before the end. In both, the motto rhythm of the song is reiterated by the piano at different pitches. The final line of the song speaks of hot tears on the poet's cheeks, which the two statements of the motto seem to seal as a permanent condition. At the end of the Sonata, the motto is passed back and forth between the instruments in overlapping statements, as if they were calling their farewells to each other across an increasing distance. It is bathed in the tonal transformation of minor to major and the gentle arrival of the plagal cadence, whose benediction echoes the spirit of the conclusion to the *Alto Rhapsody*. This ending displays a sense of reconciliation to the fate against which the song had seemed to protest. It is hard not to hear it as a great, if retrospective, love duet. The melodic material is literally a quote from the opening of Robert Schumann's *Davidsbündlertänze*, where it is marked *Motto von C.W.*

Laurence Wallach

Sonata No. 2 for Cello and Piano in F Major, Opus 99

Composed 1886; published 1887

Movements: 1. Allegro vivace; 2. Adagio affettuoso; 3. Allegro passionato; 4. Allegro molto

The Sonata in F Major for cello and piano was announced in the autumn of 1886, after Brahms's return from one of his summer vacations filled with creative work. "Are you expecting Hausmann?" Brahms inquired offhandedly of his Viennese friend Maria Fellinger, shortly after his return from the beautiful Swiss Alpine town of Hofstetten, on Lake Thun, near Bern. Needing no more prompting, Frau Fellinger soon arranged an informal *soirée* at her home, inviting the virtuoso cellist Robert Hausmann to come from Berlin as guest of honor; and there, on October 29, with Brahms playing the piano, the F-major Sonata received a hearing. The work was tried out again on November 23 at a formal *soirée* in the home of Theodor Billroth, and the following evening it was given its first public performance.

Upon returning to Berlin, Hausmann showed the new work to Elisabet von Herzogenberg, one of Brahms's closest musical confidantes, who wrote most perceptively of it to Brahms:

> So far I have been most thrilled by the first movement. It is so masterly in its compression, so torrent-like in its progress, so terse in the development, while the extension of the first subject on its return comes as the greatest surprise. I don't need to tell you how we enjoyed the soft, melodi-

ous Adagio, particularly the exquisite return to F♯ major, which sounds so beautiful. I should like to hear you play the essentially vigorous Scherzo—indeed, I always hear you snorting and puffing away at it—for no one else will ever play it just to my mind. It must be agitated without being hurried, legato in spite of its unrest and impetus.

Frau Herzogenberg went to the heart of the matter when noting the compression in the first movement, which is built from two tiny motives—the rising fourth and the descending second with which the cello opens the movement—and, as Arnold Schoenberg noted, "Nothing is repeated without promoting development." Schoenberg remarked in 1931:

> Young listeners will probably be unaware that at the time of Brahms's death, this Sonata was still very unpopular and was considered indigestible.... [T]he unusual rhythm within ... 3/4 time, the syncopations which give the impression that the third phrase is in 4/4 ..., and the unusual intervals, the ninths contained in the fifth bar, made it difficult to grasp.

Schoenberg also noted how quickly the theme was developed; even the standard repetition of the opening phrase is an expansion and development of the original phrase, giving the listener little quarter. Yet it is for just this reason that the movement is so exciting, so "torrent-like."

Taken as a whole, the F-major Sonata is an imposing work, not only in its large, four-movement design but also in its technical difficulty. The Brahms biographer Walter Niemann has speculated that it was written especially for Hausmann, with the unique features of his cello in mind. According to contemporary accounts, Hausmann possessed a tone so large and luminous that he could easily rise above the fortissimo of a grand piano, a feat he was repeatedly called upon to accomplish in this sonata.

George Bozarth

SONATA NO. 2 FOR VIOLIN AND PIANO IN A MAJOR, OPUS 100

Composed 1886; published 1887

MOVEMENTS: 1. Allegro amabile; 2. Andante tranquillo. Vivace (alternativo); 3. Allegretto grazioso (quasi Andante)

Brahms's Second Violin Sonata, composed in the summer of 1886 in the Swiss town of Hofstetten on Lake Thun, near Bern, forms part of a group of chamber works (including Opp. 99, 101, and 108) that display a tauter, more condensed style than earlier compositions, yet with no loss of lyricism. Brahms's friend Elisabet von Herzogenberg described the Sonata as being "constructed in the plainest possible way from ideas at once striking and simple, fresh and young in their emotional qualities, ripe and wise in their incredible compactness."

The Sonata has sometimes been referred to as the *Meistersinger* Sonata because the shape of its opening melody (as well as its harmony and voice-leading) resemble Walther's "Prize Song" in Wagner's opera. That similarity may be coincidental, but Brahms himself acknowledged the indebtedness of the first movement's second subject to his own song, *Wie Melodien zieht es mir*, Op. 105/1, which was composed in the same summer. Commentators have detected echoes of at least three other Lieder in this sonata, including *Komm bald*, Op. 97/6, in the same key, and two other songs of Op. 105, *Immer leiser wird mein Schlummer* and *Auf dem Kirchhofe*.

Whatever the plausibility of these specific associations, there is little question that the Sonata as a whole is one of Brahms's most songful and appealing chamber works, as suggested even by his tempo heading for the first movement, Allegro amabile. The movement shows how Brahms could at this phase of his career construct a sonata form that is expansively lyrical yet dynamic. As in several of his mature works from the Fourth Symphony on, the exposition is not repeated, and the development section begins with the main theme on the tonic. Among the noteworthy features is Brahms's ability to rework earlier thematic shapes into new ideas. In the middle of the development section, the closing idea of the exposition is refashioned into a full eight-measure melody. This procedure of lyrical or melodic fulfillment is one that Brahms employs in many of his greatest sonata-form movements.

Another remarkable moment occurs at the end of the development section, which concludes tranquilly and stably on a remote C♯-major chord. As a complete surprise, the recapitulation begins in the home key in the next measure. There has been no traditional harmonic preparation, no "push" toward the return. Rather, it has come in an understated, calm manner fully characteristic of this chamber work.

The middle movement of the Sonata is an ingenious alternation of andante and scherzo elements. Donald Tovey called this movement a "counterpart in pastoral comedy" to the similar conflation in Brahms's F-major String Quintet, Op. 88. The Andante portion, in duple meter and beginning in F major, is almost neo-Baroque in its polyphonic weaving of elegant lines. The Vivace, an energetic folklike dance in D minor and triple meter, presents a thorough contrast. Brahms's tonal mastery is fully in evidence in this movement. The Andante returns not in its original key, but in D major, the parallel (rather than relative) major of the Vivace's key, and only gradually slips back into F major. The last time around, the Andante again returns in D major, but only for a moment. Its second phrase already falls into F major, the key that is sustained through the final, coda-like reappearance of the Vivace.

The Rondo Finale of the sonata is marked by Brahms as Allegretto grazioso (quasi Andante). Such an indication is more typical of Brahms's interior movements and suggests that the tempo—despite the cut-time signature—should not be too fast. Here, as in the first movement and the slower portions of the middle movement, it is gentle lyricism that prevails. The main theme has rightly been called by Tovey "one of the great cantabiles for the fourth [G] string." On wings of song, it carries this great Sonata to its affirmative but understated conclusion.

Walter Frisch

Sonata No. 3 for Violin and Piano in D Minor, Opus 108
Composed 1886–88; published 1889

Movements: 1. Allegro; 2. Adagio; 3. Un poco presto e con sentimento; 4. Presto agitato

Brahms began his third and final Violin Sonata in the summer of 1886 on Lake Thun, Switzerland, contemporaneously with the Second Cello Sonata, Op. 99; the Second Violin Sonata, Op. 100; and the Third Piano Trio, Op. 101. Unlike these other works, though, he appears not to have completed the Sonata at that time. Only two years later, in 1888, did members of the Brahms circle, including the Herzogenbergs and Clara Schumann, see the entire work. It was published in April 1889 with a dedication to Brahms's close friend, the conductor and pianist Hans von Bülow.

The D-minor Sonata partakes of the marvelous economy of expression and means that characterizes the other chamber works of 1886. Unlike Brahms's two other violin sonatas, this one has four movements corresponding to the traditional types. Yet even with this structure, the whole work lasts just over twenty minutes in performance.

The outer movements are darker, stormier counterparts to those of the A-major Sonata. The main theme of the opening Allegro unfolds high in the violin over an agitated, syncopated accompaniment on the piano. The second theme, introduced by the piano in F major, allows in a few more rays of light. Yet even here, lyric expansiveness is curtailed or subverted by such devices as giving a normally weak eighth note a sforzando accent. The most astonishing aspect of this movement is the development section, which is underpinned throughout by an A (or dominant) pedal point sounding for 47 measures. Over this pedal the piano weaves arpeggios and the violin takes up fragments of the first theme. At the end of the development the melodic material seems literally to unravel into garlands of eighth notes, out of which the recapitulation emerges.

The development has left unfinished business, unreleased energy. Soon after the recapitulation begins, a secondary development bursts out, also functioning as an extended transition to the second group. The coda of the movement transposes to the tonic the ominous pedal point of the development section, and the movement ends with a brightening to the major mode.

The Adagio, which takes over the first movement's concluding key of D major, is one of Brahms's most condensed slow movements. It consists of a broad melody that is repeated in varied form, with no intervening or contrasting episode. As Tovey aptly observed, "Such simplicity comes of the concentration of a life's experience; it cannot be imitated by merely writing a tune and refusing to develop it."

The delicate Scherzo, marked "Un poco presto e con sentimento," might be Brahms's briefest instrumental movement; it clocks in at only three minutes in most performances. The movement is also one of Brahms's most original in terms of form, harmony, and phrase design. The overall structure is a kind of *A B A*, within which the harmony wanders widely and imaginatively from its F♯-minor home base, reaching a remote F minor at the end of the middle section. There are moments in this Presto that sound, because of the way in which harmonic progressions refuse to follow Classical precedent, as if they might be from an impressionist work by Ravel or Fauré.

The Finale of the D-minor Sonata is a powerful sonata Rondo in which the pent-up energies of the preceding movements seem to be fully unleashed. It begins in what Malcolm MacDonald has characterized as Brahms's "galloping 6/8 scherzo style." But the rhythmic profiles of the movement's themes vary widely and subtly: the second theme is a hymn-

or chorale-like melody that slows the forward flow, only to give way to a more fluid closing theme. Like the preceding movements in this Sonata, the Finale reinvents Classical forms with deceptive simplicity. The three-key design of the broad exposition is D minor–C major–A minor. Especially distinctive is the remoteness of the second key from the tonic (one would expect F major), and the presence of a minor dominant as the third key, instead of the customary major.

Walter Frisch

Two Sonatas for Clarinet and Piano in F Minor and E♭ Major, Opus 120
Composed 1894; published 1895

MOVEMENTS: I: 1. Allegretto appassionato. Sostenuto ed espressivo;
2. Andante un poco Adagio. 3. Allegretto grazioso; 4. Vivace.
II: 1. Allegro amabile. Tranquillo; 2. Allegro appassionato. Sostenuto;
3. Andante con moto. Allegro. Più tranquillo

The early months of 1894 were particularly melancholy ones for Brahms. In February he lost two of his closest friends, Theodor Billroth and Hans von Bülow, and he was further saddened by the death of another colleague, the great Bach scholar Philipp Spitta, in April. Brahms sensed that the end of his own creative career was at hand. But once again he had occasion to hear Richard Mühlfeld's clarinet playing and was inspired to resume composing. In May, several of Brahms's Viennese friends opened their stately rooms for a festival of chamber music, and Mühlfeld came from Meiningen to take part. The cellist Robert Hausmann was also present, as were the archivist Eusebius Mandyczewski, the critic Eduard Hanslick, the composer Ignaz Brüll, the pianists Anton Door and Julius Epstein, and the singers Josef Gänsbacher and Gustav Walter. A photograph was taken of this group on May 7, Brahms's sixty-first birthday, and the high spirits of the occasion are clearly in evidence—Hausmann stands behind Brahms, poised as if playing the composer like a giant cello! The musical result of this occasion was Opus 120, two Sonatas for Clarinet and Piano, composed that summer at Bad Ischl. Both works were rehearsed in September, and on September 23 they were performed by Mühlfeld and Brahms at a private concert in Berchtesgaden for the duke and duchess of Meiningen. In November, the Sonatas were played several times during a reunion in Frankfurt of Clara Schumann's closest friends, and in early January 1895, they were given their public premiere in Vienna. Once the Sonatas had been published, Brahms presented his autograph manuscripts of them to his "Fräulein Klarinette" with the dedication, "To Richard Mühlfeld, the master of his beautiful instrument, in sincerely grateful remembrance."

As Karl Geiringer has noted, one finds in the Clarinet Sonatas "a wonderful exploitation of the possibilities of the clarinet, particularly in the effective change from the higher to the lower registers, coupled with a certain austerity of tone; a tender melancholy, which seldom breaks out into more energetic or joyous accents; and a splendid perfection of form in all the movements." In the F-minor Sonata the progression of movements is standard—an opening sonata-allegro followed by a slow movement in ternary form with varied reprise, a minuet and trio, and an animated rondo Finale. But, as Geiringer remarked, "What a profusion of individual attributes!" The initial movement grows organically from the two opening melodies of the piano and the clarinet, each of which is immediately developed in alternation, thus in effect masterfully combining sonata, rondo, and variation procedures. Further reworkings and redefinitions of these materials are in store in the development proper, in the retransition to the recapitulation, and in the coda, where, after these many transformations, the themes are now intoned softly, mystically. The movement ends with a Picardy third, and a victory over thematic complexity and minor tonality seems to have been won, though the feeling is perhaps one more of resignation than of conquest. The subsequent movements continue the major mode—a contemplative Andante and Ländler-style Allegretto grazioso in A♭ major, and a rondo Finale in F major—but economic development of thematic materials remains the order of the day. Even the seemingly simple Viennese Ländler is brimming with counterpoint, as its melody reappears in imitation, inversion, and stretto. The sharp ear also notes that the tune itself is a transformation of the first melody of the opening movement, its nature now entirely congenial. With an energetic, somewhat Mendelssohnian Finale, Brahms brings this work to a rousing close.

Brahms often composed pieces in pairs, the second complementing the first in mood and manner. One thinks of the Piano Quartets, Opp. 25 and 26, the two String Quartets, Op.51, even the first two Symphonies, Opp. 68 and 73. Such is the case with the Clarinet Sonatas. Standing in marked contrast to the restless opening gestures of the F-minor Sonata is the gently undulating amabile melody that initiates the E♭-major

Sonata. One is transported to simpler times, to the genial realm of the Biedermeier Schubertiade. To be sure, the "turn" motive at the head of the theme finds immediate and dynamic development, as is Brahms's manner, but impassioned outbursts are rapidly quelled. The theme in the dominant provides a close canon between clarinet and piano, yet the affect is not learned, so deftly is the counterpoint sketched; a second section in this key is all rippling triplets against soaring duple melody. The genial flow of this sonata-form movement is not even interrupted by clear-cut sectional divisions into exposition, development, and recapitulation. This mood piece, so unlike the virile, assertive allegros of most sonatas, ends molto dolce, tranquillo.

Having more than fulfilled the need for lyricism with his opening movement, Brahms proceeds directly to an Allegro appassionato with all the sweep of a Viennese waltz, but cast, like so many numbers in his second, darker set of *Liebeslieder Walzer,* Op. 65, in the minor mode—such is life and love! The other half of the Dual Monarchy is heard from in the central trio, which strikes a noble Hungarian pose reminiscent of the song *Magyarisch,* Op. 46, No. 2, and the early *Variations on a Hungarian Song,* Op. 21, No. 2. Again, the leave-taking is gently done.

The final movement, a set of variations, is based on a motivically tight, classically balanced melody, Andante con moto, that bears a strong resemblance, as Harris Goldsmith has observed, to the theme of Robert Schumann's *Andante and Variations for Two Pianos,* Op. 46, a work that was a favorite of Brahms's and one that he had often performed with Clara Schumann and other pianists in the 1860s and had edited for publication in its early reading with two cellos and horn in 1893. The playful exchange of filigree figures between performers that characterizes Schumann's first variation is the method of Brahms's third variation. And after the rigors of variation, both sets return to a tranquil mood. A final virtuosic flourish, which recalls the metrical hijinks of the young Brahms, closes the work on a merry note.

George Bozarth

6

TRIOS

TRIO NO. 1 FOR PIANO, VIOLIN, AND CELLO IN B MAJOR, OPUS 8
Completed 1854 (revised 1889); published 1854 (1891)

MOVEMENTS: 1. Allegro con moto; 2. Scherzo. Allegro molto; 3. Adagio non troppo; 4. Finale. Allegro molto agitato. Revised Version: 1. Allegro con brio; 2. Scherzo. Allegro molto; 3. Adagio; 4. Allegro

The B-major Piano Trio is two compositions, one in essence a very late critique (1889) of a very early work (1854). When Brahms's publisher and friend Fritz Simrock bought the rights to his first ten published compositions in 1888, he offered Brahms the opportunity to revise them at will. Brahms settled on Op. 8, completely rewriting almost everything except the Scherzo and the opening thematic groups of the remaining three movements. Most listeners know only the mature version; although Brahms himself made no effort to suppress the original and it certainly merits more frequent revival, it is virtually never performed. Musicologists, however, have found the first version fascinating as a rare example of near juvenilia by Brahms, who routinely recomposed and/or destroyed works he found unsatisfactory and also obliterated nearly all sketches, drafts, and other evidence of the compositional process.

In a letter to Clara Schumann after the revision, Brahms accurately referred to the "wild" character of the early version, which above all sprawls: the Adagio, for example, has five loosely assembled sections (in an *A B A' C A"* form). The Piano Trio quotes directly from works by Schubert (the Lied *Am Meer*) in the first interlude of the Adagio and by Schumann (the C-major Fantasy, from a passage that itself quotes Beethoven's *An die ferne Geliebte*) in the final Allegro. It imitates the styles of several composers: Mendelssohn in the Scherzo, Schumann in the second interlude of the Adagio, Bach in part of the second group of the opening movement. That second group itself strings together an assortment of musical topics—an instrumental recitative followed by what sounds unmistakably like a Bachian chromatic fugue subject, both in G♯ minor, and a concluding E-major theme in musette style—all of which are replaced by a fugato in the recapitulation. While much of the Piano Trio is beautiful despite its wildness, the writing for the ensemble is sometimes thin and ineffective, and the work falls flat at certain key moments—for example, directly after the initial group in the first Allegro, in the coda of the Scherzo, and at the end of the second interlude in the Adagio.

Brahms retained most of the fine original Scherzo—Mendelssohnian because of the leggiero articulations and fast passagework in the piano—and its slower, waltz-like Trio, confining his revisions to the coda and details in the scoring elsewhere. In rewriting the rest of the early Piano Trio, he posed himself problems in compositional logic: What might each opening thematic group suggest about the shape of the movement as a whole? For the Adagio, he composed a single interlude to replace the earlier pair. In the Adagio's opening theme, contrapuntal statements by the strings had completed antecedent phrases set for piano in the chordal manner of a hymn, the entrances of the two instrumental bodies gradually coming closer together and then overlapping. Brahms apparently decided that the abstract quality of the writing implied a more subjective middle section, since he composed for it an ardent minor-mode melody, which he gave initially to that most Romantic of instruments, the cello. Like the other movements, the revised Finale (a sonata/rondo hybrid in B minor) is more coherent than the original. The opening group and the subsequent elaborations of it retain the warmth and restlessness of the first version, yet the new second theme sounds oddly prosaic, the only miscalculation in the revised version.

The opening Allegro, a vast improvement over the original, demonstrates most clearly the mastery of the mature Brahms. His recasting confirms at least one correspondence between the early and late styles: the original lyric shape of the first thematic group entails much repetition, and he could accommodate this again thirty-five years later—see, for example, the first movement of the F-major String Quintet, Op. 88—if not in the string quartets of the intervening period. The initial group is essentially songful and "closed" but is also capable of rising to a powerful climax. In the early version, Brahms had followed it with many small, static gestures, finally resorting in the coda to a frantic acceleration to whip up momentum toward closure. In the revised version, he allowed the breadth and other qualities of the first group to determine the form of the movement: although the original version is longer, he made the individual gestures of the later one larger and more passionate, more in keeping with the sweep of the opening theme. Thus, he composed a second thematic group as lyrical as the first and even more dynamic, repeatedly using suspensions, a kind of stressed dissonance that he particularly liked, to arouse almost painful expectations of resolution. And while a number of cadences punctuate the development, it does not become episodic, as in the original. When the first theme takes shape again at the joint between the development and recapitulation, it gains harmonic stability only gradually and it is drastically abridged, in keeping with Brahms's habitual practice in his later years. After the intensity of the rest of the movement, the new coda can afford to luxuriate, as it now does, in the beauties of both themes.

Margaret Notley

TRIO FOR PIANO, VIOLIN, AND HORN IN E♭, OPUS 40
Composed 1865; published 1868

MOVEMENTS: 1. Andante; 2. Scherzo. Allegro; 3. Adagio mesto; 4. Finale. Allegro con brio

The last of the series of chamber works which began with the Sextet in B♭, the Horn Trio stands apart by virtue of its tone color and form. It is unusual enough that its status as genuine chamber music was challenged by its first critic, Selmar Bagge, who assigned it to the category of an occasional piece *(Gelegenheitsstück)*, and expressed doubts about the appropriateness of the instrumentation. More than any other work by Brahms, the form and content of this Trio are determined by its instrumental color. Performers today still share some of those doubts; when played on contemporary instruments, there are severe balance problems which can only be resolved by extra restraint on the part of the horn player. Yet, this most substantial work in the horn player's repertory needs to be considered in the context of the instrument that the composer originally intended.

Although Brahms allowed performances on the valve horn, he designed this piece for the "hand horn." That instrument carried powerful early associations for the composer which are incorporated into this composition. Chief among these is the connection to his parents and childhood; the hand horn was one of the four instruments on which he was instructed by his father, who played it professionally. A crucial role in linking the third and fourth movements is played by a quotation from a folk song that he learned from his mother. The Trio was completed in May 1865, three months after her death (on February 1), and the slow movement in E♭ minor, if not the whole work, shows evidence of being an elegy in her memory. A more traditional, less personal association is indicated by an anecdote: When walking with Albert Dietrich in the Schwarzwald above Baden-Baden, Brahms pointed out a specific spot "on the wooded heights above the fir trees" as the place where he conceived of the Trio's opening theme. The evocation of nature, the woods, and hunting inspire music that looks back to the Serenade in D and forward to several of the *Haydn* Variations. All three of these works have strong connections to the style of Haydn.

Using only one crook for the whole piece (putting the horn in the key of E♭ major) not only limited the range of keys available but required Brahms to work with a kind of precompositional dynamic and timbral configuration built into the choice of notes available to him. The first movement can demonstrate how these considerations contributed to the musical results. The form is unique for an opening movement in Brahms: it is expanded ternary, *ABABA,* lacking a development section with its varied tonal areas. The opening theme is built on a motive of a fifth between open notes followed by a half-step lower-neighbor produced by inserting and withdrawing the hand from the bell of the horn. "Foreign" key areas are restricted; the new notes needed in these key areas are almost all half-stopped, and readily available (the exception is the A♭ above middle C, which is fully stopped and more difficult to play in tune). Such areas have a slightly muted quality that gives them a distinctive character, to the benefit of the musical architecture.

The second movement, a Scherzo, eschews binary form in favor of a compact sonata that evokes a rustic scene, while the Trio is a through-composed Ländler in which the horn assumes the main melody throughout, the only section in the work where this is the case. Here, too, the key of A♭ minor imparts a distinctly haunting color to the horn melody that is well matched to the mood.

With nostalgia and high spirits as the principal moods thus far, the Adagio mesto emerges as the center of gravity; its somber weight increases the intensity of the work. The key, tonic minor, had already been touched in the opening movement; the secondary area, G♭ major, played an important role there too. Thematic and motivic material further recall that movement, but now the timbres and registers reach their darkest moments; this was the movement about which Clara wrote, "[it was] wonderful, but indeed hard to understand on first hearing." Perhaps unsuspecting listeners may truly experience the Trio as an "occasional piece" for two movements, but at this point they have to reconsider their expectations.

The distinguishing formal feature of the Adagio is the use of a fugal exposition and episode as second subject, initiated by the horn, which is elevated to an equal role in the instrumental partnership. Although the overall form is ternary, the emotional weight requires that the reprise be extended by rhetorical interruptions: a slow-tempo quote of the folk song *Dort in den Weiden steht ein Haus* (There in the Willows a House Stands), on horn accompanied by violin alone, alternates with the fugue theme in an ascending sequence, leading to a climactic statement of the opening material. Here the horn unleashes its full power on a previously unheard fortissimo high C, followed by a steep descent of two and a half octaves to low F, one of the most difficult and unstable notes on the hand horn. It is in this movement that the most characteristic colors combine with the most intense emotions.

The concluding Haydnesque sonata form performs the role of an eighteenth-century *Kehraus* (last dance) Finale: send 'em home whistling. If Brahms romantically burdens listeners with private grief in the third movement, he immediately makes up for it in the fourth by irresistibly entertaining them. The horn gets to exercise thoroughly its open, rustic sound quality and temperament, beginning with a full-tempo expansion of the folk tune already foreshadowed, punctuated by "Halloo" signals.

The transitional theme, again in G♭ major, is underpinned by a single, open, pulsating note on the horn, circumventing the instrument's darker color. A similar strategy is used in the most "foreign" area of development, where the horn pulses quietly on a single fractionally stopped pitch (written as B♭) during nine measures of C♯ minor. The retransition loses the violin entirely as the horn "Halloos" through keys, colors, and speeds before finding its companion and the tonic key simultaneously. In a totally uninhibited coda, the piano slips out of key twice, only to be firmly brought back into line by the buoyant tonic arpeggios of its companions. This Finale gives full emphasis to the affirmative mood, balancing both the pensive opening and the elegiac Adagio.

Laurence Wallach

Trio No. 2 for Piano, Violin, and Cello in C Major, Opus 87

Composed 1880–82; published 1883

Movements: 1. Allegro; 2. Thema mit Variationen. Andante con moto;
3. Scherzo. Presto; 4. Finale. Allegro giocoso

What made Brahms so cheerful at Ischl in the June months of 1880 and 1882 may have been the enjoyment of his fully developed compositional powers; this Olympian work speaks to a serene vision of Classical form in which four movements of original design fit together with unobtrusive perfection. It shares not only its key but its character with two favorite works by Schubert, the "Great" C-major Symphony and the Grand Duo, D. 812. Underlying material whose use corresponds to Schoenberg's concept of the *Grundgestalt* pervades the work. Brahms's "basic shape" is an expanding wedge: a single- or two-voiced texture that moves outward (or conversely contracts inward). Within this shape, emphasis is given to the notes C–E–A–F–(G) or their chromatic variants. These general characteristics manifest themselves in endlessly varied forms and temporal dimensions, growing into or out of each other seamlessly through the process of "developing variation."

The opening theme, on strings in octaves, initiates the melodic form of the expanding "wedge," its first note the center around which alternatively higher and lower notes expand toward the dominant. Registral expansion continues, with piano added, to the end of the theme, where the space between outer voices has been enlarged to more than five octaves. In the middle phrase, piano and strings pull in opposite directions, maintaining balance through contrary motion. When the opening theme returns in the strings, variants in both hands of the piano emphasize its motion in opposing directions; in all, three rhythmic versions of the same theme sound simultaneously.

An incisive motive built out of compressed, contracting wedges in both piano and strings animates the transitional material in this movement while the third theme, grazioso, narrows space and sonority gradually, leading to the octave G's in the piano. This moment seems to end the exposition, and another expanding series of wedges begins with a tremolo version of these octaves.

Instead of a recognizable development, however, the first theme returns in the tonic, leading to an unexpected variation in the cello: the theme is metrically expanded so that one measure of the original now occupies two, tempo is speeded up (animato), the harmony moves to the Neapolitan area, the accompaniment races in triplets. The whole experience is enough of a surprise that the listener might not immediately recognize the identity of the theme.

Retransition and recapitulation lead to unison C's and, unexpectedly, beyond; the surprise variant again appears, harmonically unstable and moving away from the tonic. A new consequent to the theme finally reveals the coda; the piano joins the strings for a final tutti statement, and the movement ends. Revealed is an original two-part form combining elements of sonata, rondo, and variation growing out of expansive impulses inherent in its *Grundgestalt*.

The theme of the next movement, in A minor, fulfills an alternative harmony implied by the opening four pitches. It is a "double" theme, the piano playing an equal role with the strings in five variations, the last stretched to form a coda. These all use the "double" relationship to generate varied expansions and contractions between the two sound-groups. The sound-world of Brahms's Double Concerto is foreshadowed in variation 3. Unaccompanied triple-stops initiate close interactions in which expansion within one sound-group is complemented by contraction in the other. The time-scale of these interactions expands all the way to the coda, with its stretched cadence.

The C-minor Scherzo, lighthearted cousin of the third movement of the Piano Quintet, might have been composed by Mendelssohn were it not for the continued workings of the *Grundgestalt,* chromatically modified as a harmonically elusive diminished seventh, C–E♭–F♯–A. The unstable opening is so designed that it grows smoothly out of the A minor of the previous movement.

Further chromatic variation occurs as the violin's effort to outline a tonic triad is thwarted by chromatic neighbors of G, particularly the flattened A which forms the climax of the phrase. The "development" expands from the same pitch A♭, and contains another expanded area, E, the "flatted sixth of the flatted sixth"! Retransition is effected by an apparent "resolution" of the A♭ to G, which continues down one more half-step to F♯, bringing a return of the whole *Grundgestalt*. The reprise has even less to do with stable tonic harmony than the beginning; its rising sequence moves through five ascending whole steps as Brahms flirts with symmetrical (i.e., non-tonal) relationships.

In its final incarnation, with a chromatically raised third note, the *Grundgestalt* receives its most compact statement in the first bar of the Allegro giocoso. The pitch constellation, C–E–F♯–A–G, now includes a stabilizing fifth note. Also included are a countermotive in the piano which moves to the diminished seventh on the third beat, and a repeated-note pattern that transforms the ominous rustling of the Scherzo to a jovial chuckle. Although relaxed and generous in its themes, there is here a concealed economy that controls every detail.

After the quiet introduction, the *Grundgestalt* bursts forth in a double-thematic wedge characteristic of climactic moments elsewhere. New themes result from motivic expansion of the sequential thirds near the start of the work. They can be heard a bit later in the transition, followed shortly by the "new theme" and somewhat after that, the "double" closing theme, in which cello and piano simultaneously state their own variants. The piano's triplets supply further variational material, and the wedge shape plays a spectacular role in contrary piano arpeggios.

Characteristic harmonies here bear a close relationship to the *Grundgestalt*. The harmonic plan revisits its first two notes, C and E, as a structural chord progression appearing four different times in the movement; associated with it is another harmony, a dominant seventh based on B. At two crucial junctures, it is used to lead deceptively back to tonic reprises, preventing them from sounding predictable. This is important, since the main theme is heard six times, only once away from the tonic.

That exceptional (non-tonic) reprise begins the coda as a rhythmic expansion, parallel to the one in the first movement. It leads back to the tonic and a no-holds-barred celebration of the *Grundgestalt* in double-thematic form. All this good cheer in the home key might seem like bluster were it not for the condensed return of identifying harmonic characteristics of the movement and of the whole piece.

Laurence Wallach

TRIO NO. 3 FOR PIANO, VIOLIN, AND CELLO IN C MINOR, OPUS 101

Composed 1886; published 1887

MOVEMENTS: 1. Allegro energico; 2. Presto non assai; 3. Andante grazioso; 4. Allegro molto

Having completed the F-major String Quintet in 1882, it would be another four years before Brahms concentrated again on chamber music. During the summer of 1886, while living in a rented villa in the Swiss resort town of Hofstetten, near Lake Thun in the Bernese Oberland, he completed three major chamber works: the F-major Cello Sonata, Op. 99, the Violin Sonata in A Major, Op. 100, and the C-minor Piano Trio, Op. 101. At this time in the composer's life he appeared less frequently as a performer, preferring to play only his new compositions. The first performance of the Trio took place in Budapest on December 20, 1886, when Brahms was joined by two great virtuosos of the day, violinist Jenö Hubay and cellist David Popper.

For Clara Schumann, the Trio was a "wonderfully gripping" work. She wrote in her diary in June 1887: "What a work it is, inspired throughout in its passion, its power of thought, its gracefulness, its poetry. No previous work of Johannes has so completely carried me away." The C-minor is the shortest of the three piano trios, less than half as long as the B-major, Op. 8, and shorter than the C-major, Op. 87, written four years earlier. Drama and conciseness of expression are paramount, while lyricism, although still apparent, receives less emphasis. Indeed, each movement is seemingly pared down to as few measures as possible.

The first movement is one of Brahms's most relentlessly powerful. Even during the broadly lyrical second subject, there is no relaxation from the ardent, driven quality of the music that is proclaimed at the outset by the declamatory first subject. A dotted-rhythm pattern, first used as a transition theme, becomes the basis for much of the development as well as the extended coda, which contains some of Brahms's grittiest, perhaps angriest, music. This rhythm, first encountered in the *Tragic Overture* and later in the coda of the E♭-major Rhapsody for Piano, Op. 119/4, was never used by Brahms with such sustained force as it is in this trio. At only 234 measures and lacking an exposition repeat (which Brahms had originally included), this is the shortest first movement in all of his chamber music.

The understated and ghostly second movement, also in C minor and a kind of *musique nocturne* not unlike the Intermezzo of the G-minor Piano Quartet, Op. 25, rarely exceeds the dynamic of "piano." As in the Intermezzo, the strings are muted throughout. The sinuous writing of the first section gives way to a more rhythmically based middle section, itself in ternary form but not what could be called a proper trio. Here, in a repeated motive, masterfully scored, pizzicato arpeggios provide the momentum for the piano (at one point marked "sotto voce ma agitato") to complete its short melodic phrases. The movement, as tersely written as the other three, ends in a whisper, as if embarrassed for having drawn attention to itself.

According to Michael Musgrave, the slow movement, in a simple three-part song form, draws on Brahms's "love of the irregular meters of Serbian folk song." Alternating between a measure of 3/4 and two of 2/4, Brahms originally conceived the C-major main theme in 7/4 time. A principal feature is the alternation between piano and strings and the relative absence of the three instruments playing together. With little modulation throughout the three sections (the middle is in the relative minor and alternates bars of 9/8 and 6/8, or three beats and two beats), the movement is one of Brahms's least complicated structures in both form and harmony, but also one of his most charming.

What Tovey called the "grimly energetic" Finale is in 6/8 time and in a highly concise sonata form with a short development. One of the most striking aspects is the unpredictable rhythm, due not only to Brahmsian hemiola effects but also to his penchant in the work for accents on unaccented beats. There are times when the rhythms cast a *trompe l'oreille* effect that make it seem as if the tempo has suddenly changed. This effect is most evident in the meno Allegro sections, where cross-rhythms are the norm. The apparent instability created by these rhythms, as well as the unrelieved dark color of minor keys, gives this movement a restive quality until the broad and triumphant coda in the tonic major is finally reached.

Todd Crow

TRIO FOR PIANO, CLARINET AND CELLO IN A MINOR, OPUS 114

Composed 1891; published 1892

MOVEMENTS: 1. Allegro; 2. Adagio; 3. Andantino grazioso; 4. Allegro

In the early months of 1891, an event took place that provided the impetus for Brahms's final four chamber works. On March 13, the composer departed Vienna for a week-long stay at the court of Meiningen. The aristocratic surroundings of a ducal court might seem a strange place for as bourgeois an artist as Brahms to seek diversion, but the enlightened duke and duchess of Meiningen had long admired Brahms's music and were entirely willing to overlook his lower-class origins and personal eccentricities. Yet it was more than the congenial social atmosphere that attracted Brahms. The court orchestra at Meiningen, organized by the great conductor Hans von Bülow, was one of the finest in Europe—indeed, in 1885, they had been entrusted with the world premiere of Brahms's Fourth Symphony—and from their playing, Brahms may well have expected to gain the inspiration he needed to resume composing after a hiatus of several months. But if it was orchestral writing he had in mind, it was in the realm of chamber music that inspiration came.

Even since the mid-1880s, Brahms had been aware of the artistry of Richard Mühlfeld, Meiningen's principal clarinetist, but on this visit he was particularly impressed by Mühlfeld's playing. One can only speculate on how the tone of "this melancholy singer of the orchestra" reflected Brahms's own frame of mind (we know, for instance, that at this time Brahms was not only contemplating retirement as a composer but was also considering the provisions of his last will and testament). Brahms requested that his "dear nightingale," his "Fräulein Klarinette," as he was wont to call Mühlfeld, perform a private recital for him. The clarinetist played one piece after another from his extensive repertory (including the Mozart Clarinet Quintet and the Weber concertos), and Brahms queried him closely on the nature of his instrument. The seed had been planted, and when Brahms next visited Meiningen, in November of 1891, he brought with him two new works, both composed during his summer vacation at Ischl—the Clarinet Trio in A Minor, Op. 114, and the Clarinet Quintet in B Minor, Op. 115. The Trio was tried out at *soirées* on November 21 and 24 by Mühlfeld, Robert Hausmann, and Brahms; its premiere took place in Berlin on December 12, 1891, with the same performers. Of Mühlfeld's playing, Clara Schumann noted that it was "at once delicate, warm, and unaffected, and at the same time it shows the most perfect technique."

The opening movement of the Trio grows out of the simplest of musical material—a rising arpeggio and the descending scale that follows at the outset of the piece. Organic and contrapuntal development of these ingredients begins immediately and permeates the entire movement, simultaneously unifying and diversifying. The mixing of instrumental registers and colors in the quiet Adagio that follows is particularly subtle. With the Andante grazioso, we are reminded that Brahms composed this Trio while at Bad Ischl and in close contact with his good friend Johann Strauss, Jr—the opening section is one of the most graceful *Wienerwalzer* ever written, a delicate and touching homage to the waltzes of Schubert and the long-lost Biedermeier age, while the Trio section, with its yodeling clarinet, is a Ländler, the Austrian folk dance whence the waltz sprang. With the brief Finale, a rather fluid rondo, we move even closer to folk style, with Eastern European mixtures of 2/4, 6/8, and 9/8 meters deployed in a fiery minor mode.

George Bozarth

7

QUARTETS

QUARTET NO. 1 FOR PIANO, VIOLIN, VIOLA, AND CELLO IN G MINOR, OPUS 25

Composed 1861; published 1863

MOVEMENTS: 1. Allegro; 2. Intermezzo. Allegro, ma non troppo; 3. Andante con moto; 4. Rondo alla Zingarese. Presto

Brahms made his Viennese debut as a performer and composer with his First Piano Quartet in G Minor, Op. 25, a work that looks back to that city's illustrious past, especially to its native son Schubert, as well as forward to its modernist future, in particular to the thematic techniques that Schoenberg would later hail in his famous essay "Brahms the Progressive."

The exact chronology of this work's genesis in unclear. Parts of the G-minor Quartet may well have gestated for years, and even been tried out by Joseph Joachim and Karl Bargheer in 1859, but in the absence of concrete documentary evidence, we are left with Brahms's own date in his catalog, "fall 1861." During the previous summer he had shown movements of the piece to valued musical friends and advisers such as Clara Schumann, Joachim, and later Adolf Schubring. The work is cast in four movements: an expansive opening one, an introspective Intermezzo, an Andante con moto, and a furious Hungarian Finale.

Clara Schumann played in the first public performance on November 16, 1861, in Hamburg, and on the same day one year later, Brahms himself presented the Quartet in Vienna. He had arrived in the city in September and already tried out the work at the home of his new friend Julius Epstein, himself a formidable pianist. Epstein promptly introduced Brahms to Joseph Hellmesberger, whose Hellmesberger Quartet was the premier chamber ensemble in Vienna at the time. After reading through the Quartet at Epstein's, the violinist, not given to flattery, declared, "This is Beethoven's heir!" and informed Brahms that he wanted to present the work at his next subscription concert.

The November 16, 1862, performance with the Hellmesberger Quartet proved a qualified success. Brahms was encouraged to give his own concert two weeks later, at which he played his *Handel* Variations, Op. 24, and the same ensemble premiered the Second Piano Quartet in A Major, Op. 26. Eduard Hanslick reviewed the events and offered an overview of "possibly the most interesting among our contemporary composers." He had doubts, however, about the G-minor Quartet, finding the themes "insignificant . . . dry and prosaic."

Simrock published the Quartet in the late summer of 1863, shortly after its companion piece, the A-major Piano Quartet, Op. 26. Hanslick was not alone in his reservations about the G-minor Quartet. After publication, the number of performances increased, but the critical response was mixed. The first movement received most of the criticism. Clara Schumann registered her initial reaction in a letter to Brahms: "The first part seems to me too little in G minor and too much in D major, and the absence of G minor makes it lack clearness." After premiering the work, she wrote in her diary: "The Quartet only partially satisfies me; there is too little unity in the first movement, and the emotion of the Adagio is too forced, without really carrying me away. But I love the Allegretto in C minor and the last movement."

Joachim voiced similar concerns about the lack of "invention" of the spacious first movement, with its long exposition and prolific principal and subsidiary themes. The opening of even quarter notes is calmly presented in bare octaves. Musicologist Carl Dahlhaus has remarked on the theme's brevity and, echoing Hanslick, on the insignificance of the material, but points to the thematic implications and elaborations that so attracted Schoenberg—the first measure is freely inverted, presented harmonically, and transposed, all within the following seven measures—such "compositional economy," writes Dahlhaus, "the building of music out of minimal capital, was taken to extremes by Brahms." Indeed, although apparently generous in its variety of themes, the work reveals, on closer inspection, that the themes are often related to one another, especially by characteristic intervals and rhythms. After a measure of silence, the first group continues with a brief modulation to the relative major, then returns to the tonic for an elaboration of the opening material. At length, the cello, in a high register, initiates the vast second subject group in D minor, which the piano takes up in octaves. The theme is wonderfully transformed to D major, a brightening that also becomes more expressive. The movement combines austerity—such as the spare beginning and evaporating conclusion—with Brahmsian lushness, especially passages in thirds and sixths that foreshadow folklike elements heard in succeeding movements.

The manuscript shows that for the second movement, Brahms changed the traditional designation of "scherzo" to "intermezzo." This may have been at the suggestion of Clara Schumann, who wrote in July 1861: "I should not call it a scherzo, I can only think of it as an Allegretto, but it is just the piece for me." Brahms's slowing down of the pace in the G-minor Quartet became a characteristic feature in many of his later multi-movement works, including the intermezzos of the the Third Symphony, which is in the same key, and those of Symphonies Nos. 1 and 2. The third movement is marked Andante con moto. Because the tempos of the middle movements are fairly similar, as are their contrasting double theme groups to begin (a Schubertian feature), Brahms sought to create contrast between them in affect, by, for example, opening the second movement with muted strings and providing a march in the middle of the third.

If the Quartet as a whole looks to Vienna's past and future, the rousing Finale, which has proved the most popular movement ever since the first performances, glances sideways to Hungary. It is a breathless Rondo *alla Zingarese* that begins with frantic three-measure phrases in a pervasive homophonic texture. Joachim, who had already written a "Hungarian Concerto" dedicated to Brahms, wrote: "You have outstripped me on my own territory by a considerable track." Not only is the energy of this movement remarkable, but also the texture, sonority, and harmonization, especially in the imitation of the dulcimer.

It is fitting for a work that looks back to Viennese Classicism, and to Brahms's beloved Schubert, that it should so attract the founder of the Second Viennese School. Schoenberg acknowledged his debt to Brahms's technique of "developing variation," but to illustrate his points in his critical essays he focuses on other compositions, mostly chamber works. Perhaps Schoenberg's analysis of the G-minor Quartet is to be found in his orchestration of the piece, which Otto Klemperer premiered in Los Angeles in 1938. In a letter to a local critic, Schoenberg explained his reasons for undertaking the project: "1. I like the piece. 2. It is seldom played.

3. It is always very badly played, because the better the pianist, the louder he plays and you hear nothing from the strings. I wanted once to hear everything, and this I achieved." (Brahms published his own arrangement for piano duet, although he requested not to be identified as the arranger.)

Christopher H. Gibbs

QUARTET NO. 2 FOR PIANO, VIOLIN, VIOLA, AND CELLO IN A MAJOR, OPUS 26
Completed 1861; published 1863

MOVEMENTS: 1. Allegro non troppo; 2. Poco Adagio; 3. Scherzo. Poco Allegro; 4. Finale. Allegro

Well before Brahms made his first trip to Vienna, Viennese musicians had begun to appreciate the beauties of Schubert's great but long-neglected instrumental music. During those same years of reacquaintance with Schubert's instrumental works, chamber music started to assume some of its former importance in the city. Between the death in 1830 of Ignaz Schuppanzigh, whose string quartet had premiered the music of Beethoven and Schubert, and the formation of the Hellmesberger Quartet toward the end of the 1840s, no string quartet had performed publicly in Vienna on a regular basis. The Hellmesberger Quartet gave its first series of concerts in the 1849–50 season, and as early as its second season performed not yet published chamber masterpieces by Schubert. Brahms thus found a congenial atmosphere when he came to Vienna in the fall of 1862 to perform his Piano Quartets in G Minor and A Major, for he himself had focused on the chamber genres in the second half of the 1850s, also a period for him of intense engagement with Schubert's instrumental music.

The A-major Piano Quartet, completed in the fall of 1861, like the other chamber music from the late 1850s and early 1860s, attests to the impact of Schubert upon Brahms. With the F-minor Piano Quintet, Op. 34, the A-major Piano Quartet most clearly demonstrates his reception of Schubert, audible above all in the breadth and lyricism of both pieces, but also in more specific compositional choices made in each movement. Despite the strong Schubertian influence, this is ambitiously original music. Certainly, in at least one area, Schubert did not offer Brahms a model, since he apparently did not compose a single piano quartet. And the A-major Quartet stands out for the richly varied textures that Brahms imagined for the medium: for example, the striking antiphonal effects of the opening, which, with its full chordal writing and subtly archaic harmonic style, hints at the late-sixteenth- and early-seventeenth-century polychoral music that he also came to know well during the 1850s.

Brahms's resourceful use of the instrumental group accounts for the extraordinary expansiveness of this Quartet, the longest of all his chamber works. Beginning with the "polychoral" opening, he created a sound-world of calm beauty in the first movement by placing the piano against the string ensemble and allowing each of the two instrumental bodies its own statement of all of the various themes and their continuations. (The second thematic group is especially extended; toward its end, the anachronistic harmonic style of the opening can briefly be heard again.) In this movement, Brahms reserved the minor mode for the development section, even cadencing prematurely in A minor rather than allowing harmonic tension to build before the return of the first theme. But why undermine the usual effect at the point of recapitulation? He seems to have wanted to emphasize modal contrast over harmonic release. This use of the major-minor opposition on a grand scale again suggests Schubert, as do the three character variations of the first theme that begin the development. In a final passage of antiphonal writing, the coda presents both the original and transformed versions of a fragment from that theme.

The beginning of the Poco Adagio, a lush *Nachtstück* (Night Piece) in E major, places the piano as Romantic protagonist against the string chorus. Both the individuation of the strings and the reconciliation of piano and strings help shape the course of this vast ternary form, which manages to weld a profusion of picturesque details (for example, an ominous recurring figure in the bass, harplike broken chords that appear only in the piano) into a compelling whole. The movement begins with a glorious melody given to the piano, an inexact doubling by the muted strings creating a halo of sound around it; the piano alone plays the impassioned B-minor theme that serves as foil to the opening. In the rest of the central section, the unaccompanied strings play ethereal counterpoint, the piano following with a loose elaboration of the treble strand against the massed strings. From the middle of the movement on, the string voices become more distinct, but the piano and string ensemble also begin to come closer together; in the modified repetition of the opening section, the strings, for the first time unmuted, take the lead—even in the appassionato theme, now in F minor—until the final synthesis in the coda.

The hothouse atmosphere of the second movement lifts in the Scherzo, a sonata form. Both this movement and the Finale use popular-sounding themes in a Schubertian vein—Max Kalbeck called the Finale "an anticipation of Viennese character transmitted through Schubert"— which, as often in Schubert's later works, are then subjected to extensive, intense elaboration. The two themes of the Scherzo's exposition appear first in a bare setting that again separates the piano and strings, but the more complex textures engendered in the development section continue into the recapitulation. Antiphonal exchanges between the strings and piano in the Trio, also a sonata form, overlap in canonic imitation in the first theme and make quiet, hazy plateaus of sound in the second theme, a pastorale, and in the development, which is based on it.

For the final Allegro, Brahms uses a hybrid (sonata-rondo) form that Schubert had favored, and he also spins out the movement to Schubert-ian lengths, justifying the large amount of repeated material by varying the instrumentation. More than elsewhere in the Quartet, the give-and-take between the strings and piano determines the shape of the second thematic group. As in similar moments in movements by Schubert, this group begins with an extended distant chord that is ultimately integrated into E major, the most typical secondary key in A major; the same remote harmony becomes the point of departure for a quasi-development section. In this Finale a number of events, especially the transitions, create an effect of unbounded musical space, seeming to stretch into the beyond. The particular quality of the juxtaposed popular and sublime elements may represent the most profound Schubertian influence of all.

Margaret Notley

Two String Quartets for Two Violins, Viola, and Cello in C Minor and A Minor, Opus 51
Composed 1865–73; published 1873

MOVEMENTS: I: 1. Allegro; 2. Romanze. Poco Adagio; 3. Allegretto molto moderato e comodo. Un poco più animato; 4. Allegro. II: 1. Allegro non troppo; 2. Andante moderato; 3. Quasi Minuetto, moderato. Allegretto vivace; 4. Finale. Allegro non assai

The two String Quartets, Op. 51, in C Minor and A Minor, were dedicated to Brahms's close friend, the physician Theodor Billroth, a talented amateur musician who sponsored a regular series of musical evenings in Vienna. Billroth and Brahms traveled frequently to Italy together, and Brahms took Billroth's opinions on musical matters quite seriously. Ironically, Brahms's respect for Billroth's musical judgment was greater than his respect for the professional critic Eduard Hanslick, the mutual friend of Brahms and Billroth. Hanslick later edited "Who Is Musical?", a posthumous, book-length essay by Billroth published in 1896. The essay, a combination of psychology and aesthetics, intertwines its argument with a highly refined degree of historical reflection. Brahms's dedication of these two quartets to Billroth was not merely a matter of personal sentiment. Like Brahms, Billroth was a committed advocate of Classical compositional traditions, but unlike Brahms, Billroth was virulently opposed to Wagner and particularly appalled by *Die Walküre,* the premiere of which he attended.

The Op. 51 quartets were composed during Brahms's maturity and on the brink of his sustained foray into symphonic form. Their publication represents a pivotal moment in Brahms's sense of his own craft as a composer. He reputedly wrote as many as twenty quartets during his career up to 1873, all of which he subsequently destroyed. That he felt these two works were worthy of publication indicates that in formal structure and resolution they met Brahms's exacting standards for handling the essential procedures of classical composition. They were a vindication of Classicism and therefore a highly appropriate gesture of affection and respect for his anti-Wagnerian friend.

Only three string quartets composed by Brahms survive. Haydn, who can be considered the founder of this form, composed sixty-eight, Mozart twenty-three, and Beethoven sixteen. The extent to which Brahms viewed tradition as a compulsory foundation for composition but at the same time a challenge becomes evident in this comparison of numbers. From the perspective of one analyzing these quartets, it is regrettable that Brahms destroyed all his sketches and preliminary drafts. Brahms, himself a scholar who possessed fragments of Beethoven's sketchbooks in his own collection, knew very well the dangers inherent in providing future generations access to sketchbooks and notebooks. The specter of Beethoven, in fact, hovers explicitly over Brahms's own string quartets, serving as the focal point of orientation just as he did for Brahms with respect to the symphony. As Brahms himself put it, "The three quartets Opus 59 [of Beethoven] represent the highest achievement an individual can realize in terms of creativity and craftsmanship." Beethoven's late quartets, Brahms believed, further extended this achievement.

Brahms's quartets provide an excellent means of understanding his notion of how a piece of music based on Classical procedures should work. Brahms's student Gustav Jenner related his teacher's belief that sonata form must evolve logically out of a theme: "The sonata form must of necessity emerge from an idea." It was this notion that inspired Arnold Schoenberg's later argument regarding the significance of "developing variation" as a key to Brahms's compositional technique. In both quartets, the tightness of structure is audible from beginning to end. Brahms defined the success of the elements of sonata form, however (as in the case of the first movements of these quartets), by the way they finally worked as a whole, not only as movements in themselves but as parts of a multi-movement work. In other words, the process of development as the piece moves forward must result in more than the sum of the individual steps.

Brahms achieves this result in both quartets, and particularly in the C-minor Quartet, by making incremental steps in the development of an opening musical idea that eventually result in a radical transformation—that is, the creation of a new group of thematic ideas. Small transformations therefore flower into dramatic alterations. In the C-minor Quartet, one may hear an integral relationship between the main themes of all four movements. That relationship lends a logical structure not only to the first movement but to the work in its entirety. Furthermore, the choice of C minor as a tonality relates the entire work to tradition, back to Beethoven (particularly Opp. 13, 67, and 111). Yet another Beethovenian model is the Piano Sonata Op. 2/1 in F Minor, which beautifully exemplifies the transformation of the main motif through a transition to the secondary theme. Elements from disparate first movements of Beethoven's early piano sonatas are found united in the structure of Brahms's C-minor Quartet.

The C-minor Quartet can be considered almost cyclical in composition, in part because of the close relationship between the first and second movements. The first movement is in C minor, the second in A♭ major. The third movement alternates between F minor and F major, and the last movement once again is in C minor. The correspondence of the second movement, the *Romanze,* with the beginning of the first movement is based on the three-note leading motive (including further developed variations). The C-major Finale of the first movement (which can be related to the F minor / F major of the third movement) simultaneously allows for the entry of the A♭-major recapitulation from the first movement to be transformed at the beginning of the second movement. A♭ major is, on one hand, the subdominant of C minor, and on the other hand, the parallel key of the subdominant F minor—the key of the third movement. Pursuing this notion of a cyclical structure further, we can also note that the main motive of the third movement, the Allegretto molto moderato e comodo, is developed out of the first movement, though not from the leading motive but rather from the middle section of the main theme.

The last movement of this quartet draws together aspects of a continuous development of material presented in the first three movements as well as a recapitulation of aspects of the entire quartet. Here Brahms employs as a kind of motto, a theme split off from the main motive of the first movement which he modifies in the first two measures. But he utilizes this moment of splitting-off itself as a recurrent impetus by repeating the motto in decisive places throughout the movement. On the whole, the Quartet is a well-chosen and convincing example of the realization of Brahms's notion that a piece of music organized around the traditional sonata form should be nothing less than the unfolding of a single musical idea.

In contrast to the dynamically progressing C-minor Quartet, the A-minor Quartet is characterized by its lyrical intensity. Again Brahms displays his skill in making small aspects of development turn into new ideas. The step-by-step modification of the main theme in rhythm, melody, and harmony becomes the basis for a continuing development. Once more Brahms uses sections of the main material through a splitting-off of the motive. For example, early syncopations in the first and second violins prepare the cello line at measure 20, which constitutes a key transitional moment. The viola accompanies the theme with triplets, which are themselves variations of the main motive in reverse. This procedure underscores Brahms's focus on thematic development from the start and creates a kind of natural and appealing symmetry. The symmetry extends to tonalities as well. The first A-minor movement is followed by a second movement in A major. These tonalities are reproduced in the third movement, which is both in A minor and A major. The last movement is once again in A minor. This organizing principle of symmetry is mirrored in detail throughout the quartet.

The formal structure of the Finale is complex; some have considered it a sonata movement and others a rondo. However, Brahms surely realized that the movement combined both of these formal aspects in very specific and individual ways. This is not only suggested by the continuous structure of the formal elements but also by the fact that the secondary motive runs through all harmonic levels (though the main motive appears three times in A minor and is condensed in the A-major coda)—beginning on the whole in the dominant and continuing C major / F major / A major without ever arriving as an independent formal element within the movement—as we would expect in a rondo. Surprisingly, Brahms introduces here, with the threefold repetition of both the main and secondary motives, a structural series reminiscent of the one he used in the first movement of the C-minor Quartet. In that quartet, the closely interrelated thematic development (which includes the two inner movements) results in a fourth movement at once economical and concise. By comparison, the Finale of the A-minor Quartet is characterized by an emphasis on contrasts, sustained naturally by thematic development and transformation. The two inner movements set an example and influence this process decisively. The second movement can be considered a tripart song form, in which the second section offers a decisive contrast to the first. The third movement is once again motivated by sharp contrast, in this case between minuet-style material in 3/4 time in A minor and a fast, duple-meter scherzo-like dimension in A major. The last movement, however, brings all this to a conclusion. Its hybrid form heightens the elements of contrast among the themes and of all formal strategies presented earlier, which Brahms then explicitly brings to resolution.

In the A-minor Quartet even more than the C-minor, Brahms focuses on how music can utilize radical contrast without sacrificing structural coherence. The tradition of sonata form dictates that main and subordinate themes should be contrasting, and every composer struggles with how to achieve a sense of contrast without compromising the integrity of the whole. Easy, arbitrary opposition can result in formlessness and the absence of audible interrelation. In the A-minor Quartet, Brahms brilliantly avoids this danger. Conversely, too much uniformity raises the equal danger of monotony. Unlike Liszt, Brahms was no friend of monothematic forms, but he demonstrates his mastery in creating effective contrasts using the same shared thematic building blocks. The C-minor Quartet, in turn, is a virtuosic statement on how contrast may emerge through close derivations and resemblances.

The String Quartets of Op. 51 are compelling examples of how self-conscious loyalty to tradition can lead a composer to something truly novel. One of the most frequently discussed features of the musical sensibility of the nineteenth century is its obsession with organic unity. Following the example of Beethoven's Ninth Symphony, composers from Mendelssohn to Mahler sought ways to structure four-movement works into seemingly naturally developed entities. In much symphonic music after Berlioz, composers resorted to the use of repeated thematic material. Another strategy was to redress the balance between first and last movements, giving the final movement a weight that could subsume and summarize earlier events. This obsession with unity in larger musical structures having discrete movements extended also to the quartet form. Without resorting to blatant repetition or expanded final movements—or the increasingly popular alternative of extramusical narrative—Brahms found a way to reconcile the imperatives of Classicism with his own contemporaries' desire to experience through music a sense of aesthetic integration. Brahms, after all, was a composer in the age of Marx and Darwin, an age that specialized in finding universal theories through which radical change, conflict, and difference could ultimately be explained in a comprehensive scheme of truth. Brahms's emphasis on thematic transformation, variation, and musical strategies of reconciliation was particularly suited to the quartet and its strict limitation to four voices. In Op. 51, Classicism and the impulses of musical Romanticism find their own magical reconciliation.

Klaus Kropfinger and Leon Botstein

QUARTET NO. 3 FOR PIANO, VIOLIN, VIOLA, AND CELLO IN C MINOR, OPUS 60
Composed 1855–75; published 1875

MOVEMENTS: 1. Allegro non troppo; 2. Scherzo. Allegro; 3. Andante; 4. Finale. Allegro comodo

The origins of the last of Brahms's three piano quartets, the C-minor, Op. 60, date back to what is often called his *Sturm und Drang* period, a time at least five years before the composition of the Piano Quartets, Opp. 25 and 26. In 1855–56, he wrote a three-movement piano quartet in C♯ minor that included an Andante in E major and a scherzo-like Finale. After several private performances of the quartet, Brahms was dissatisfied, withdrew the work, and ceased further revision. It was not until almost twenty years later that he revisited the score, transposing the original outer movements into a key a half-step lower and writing two new movements.

While the original three movements no longer exist (they were probably destroyed), the composer's own worklist confirms that the first two movements of Op. 60 are from an earlier period and the last two from the winter of 1873–74. Recent research has demonstrated the likelihood that the Scherzo of Op. 60 was originally the Finale of the C♯-minor Quartet; that the first movement remains essentially a revision of its earlier counterpart; and that the E-major Andante, as we know it now, is completely different from that of 1855–56. The premiere of Op. 60 was in Vienna's Musikvereinsaal in November 1875, when Brahms was joined by members of the Hellmesberger Quartet.

In an often quoted remark made in 1868, Brahms instructs his friend Hermann Deiters on the meaning of the opening of the original first movement: "Now imagine a man who is just going to shoot himself, because nothing else remains for him to do." The quotation is a reference to the last chapter of Goethe's *The Sorrows of Young Werther,* in which the hero shoots himself over his unrequited love for a married woman. In the wake of Robert Schumann's death in 1856, the young Brahms attempted to resolve his passionate feelings for Clara Schumann, which by this time had reached a feverish pitch. While it is only speculation whether or not this particular anguish—the emotional torrent surrounding his decision to renounce a formal union with the woman he loved in favor of dedicating his life to his art—is reflected in the Quartet, the consequent first movement of Op. 60 is one of his most powerful and introspective narratives.

For Brahms, as for Beethoven, C minor was a key of driving intensity, restlessness, forcefulness, and drama. At the time he labored with the revision of the Piano Quartet, he had recently completed the String Quartet Op. 51/1, and was working on the First Symphony, Op. 68, both in C minor. In many structural and harmonic details, the first movements of the Piano Quartet and the Symphony are similar. A few of these commonalities include the introductory character of the opening of the Quartet that parallels that of the Symphony; the key of E♭ minor at the end of the exposition/beginning of the development in both works; and the prevalence of motives rather than extended melody (with the significant exception of the Quartet's expansive second theme, which in the exposition is followed by four variations). The wailing and pleading phrases of the Quartet's extensive coda, symphonic in its scoring and a virtual tragedy within a tragedy, lead to a closing that brings back the opening motive of the movement (sometimes referred to, not without reason, as the "Clara" motive, a descending two-note phrase). The unanticipated tranquillity of the final few bars is also reminiscent of the end of the Symphony's first movement.

The second movement, again in C minor and in a driving 6/8 rhythm, is not only characteristic of other Brahms scherzos (notably those from the Piano Quintet, Op.34, and the *Sonatensatz* for Violin and Piano), but is akin to the Symphony's first movement. The formal terseness is such that there is no trio section, but instead a brief and less demonic section that insinuates the tonic major (but never comes to rest in it) and features a melodic outline inflected with Hungarian rhythms. The final bars of the movement are as massive in their orchestrally conceived sound as those in the coda of the first movement.

The slow movement (in E major, the same key as the analogous movement in the Symphony) begins with one of the longest and most luxuriant melodies in all of Brahms, a theme first spun out in the cello, then in a duo for violin and cello. For the first and only time in the Quartet, the emotional temperature subsides so that the general countenance of the movement is calm and reflective.

The last movement is close in spirit to some later works (especially the Finale of the Violin Sonata in G Major, Op. 78) in its songlike grace that hardly camouflages an underlying anxiety and discontent. The sequential and fragmentary nature of the intricate development section gives it an almost dreamlike and meandering quality, while the quasi-religious second theme in chorale style contributes yet another dimension in a collection of seemingly disparate elements. In fact, the movement is an elaborate complex of highly integrated motivic and harmonic components. Whereas the closing of the first movement was the outcome of exhaustion, this movement ends abruptly and irresolutely. Clearly Brahms was not writing for mass acceptance; of all his chamber works, this one undoubtedly caused him more suffering than any other and is thus perhaps the most autobiographical. In 1880, Clara Schumann told Max Kalbeck, "To me he is as much a riddle—I might almost say as much a stranger—as he was twenty-five years ago."

Todd Crow

QUARTET NO. 3 FOR TWO VIOLINS, VIOLA, AND CELLO IN B♭ MAJOR, OPUS 67
Composed 1875; published 1876

MOVEMENTS: 1. Vivace; 2. Andante; 3. Agitato (Allegretto non troppo);
4. Poco Allegretto con Variazioni. Doppio movimento

Striking a tone suggestive of the bucolic summer days spent in Ziegel-hausen near Heidelberg in 1875, during which Brahms composed the String Quartet in B♭, Op. 67, three of the four movements find their roots in the folk idiom so dear to Brahms. The scherzo-like Vivace, a rhythmical romp of shifting accents and meters full of echo effects and dashing fiddle work, opens with a theme that brings to mind both the *Hunt* Quartet of Mozart and the Scherzo of Brahms's early String Sextet, Op. 18; the movement modulates into a second theme steeped in the Bohemian folk style popularized by Dvořák. In place of the usual third-movement scherzo Brahms composed a passionate, agitated Ländler in D minor, described by him as "the most amorous, affectionate thing I have ever written." The culminating Finale, a set of variations with a few surprises, is also based on a folkish theme remarkable for its foreshortened close (seemingly two measures too soon). In this movement, all proceeds normally for three variations; but then the tonality begins to rove, first to B♭ minor, then on to D♭ major and G♭ major (Variations 4–6). The expected return to the home key occurs in Variation 7, now coupled *not* with the Finale's melody, however, but with a recapitulation of the theme of the opening Vivace; additional material from the first movement appears in Variation 8, reinforcing the cyclical nature of the whole quartet. All that is left now is for the Vivace and Finale themes to be interwoven contrapuntally, which takes place, with further developmental feints and flourishes, in the closing measures.

Only in the Andante does Brahms's music dwell wholly in the realm of art music. The soaring melody, spun out over throbbing chords, bears clear kinship to many another Romantic theme, like, for instance, the slow movement of Brahms's favorite Schumann symphony, the Second. "Such an Adagio," Brahms wrote to Clara Schumann, "only a German can compose, for only his deeply serious eye can still look forth full of love amidst great suffering." The autograph of the quartet (in the Pierpont Morgan Library) reveals that Brahms had originally conceived this movement in a more traditional format. After the opening melodic section in F major and a contrasting section in D minor that alternates passages reminiscent of the Baroque French overture with others suggestive of transcendental moments in Beethoven, a varied return of the initial section, once again in F major, was to have rounded out the movement. Written on two large sheets pasted over the original version is a considerably more dramatic reading: the middle section is expanded by six improvisatory-style measures of disorienting chromatic modulation that now lead to a varied reprise of the opening material in the "wrong" key of D major, and it is a full sixteen measures before the "correct" key, F major, is finally approached and achieved, just in time for the final climactic statement of the main theme. A brief coda suggests further complications, but a blissful close is soon at hand.

George Bozarth

8

QUINTETS

QUINTET FOR PIANO, TWO VIOLINS, VIOLA, AND CELLO
IN F MINOR, OPUS 34

Composed 1861–64; published 1865

MOVEMENTS: 1. Allegro non troppo; 2. Andante, un poco Adagio;
3. Scherzo. Allegro; 4. Finale. Poco sostenuto. Allegro non troppo

Even more than the First Piano Quartet in G Minor, the Piano Quintet in F Minor embodies a powerful lyricism enacted within a unified formal space of large dimensions. Given its perfect fit of form and gesture to timbre, it is surprising that the string-piano combination only appeared in the third version of this work. Widely acknowledged as the fruition of Brahms's early maturity, the Quintet succeeds through the balance it strikes between intense individualism of ideas and breadth of organizational plan, which connects the smallest motivic detail to the largest dimensions of formal design. An initiator of this design, the first movement offers a highly charged dialectic. Although resolved within the movement, it continues to provide energy for further confrontation, struggle, and reconciliation in the course of the rest of the work. Crucial to this plan, which bears no resemblance to the Lisztian idea of integrated form, is the use of a small group of energetic motivic particles adaptable enough to fit widely varying musical environments; the most significant of them is the half-step, most often appearing as D♭–C (6–5 of the F-minor scale) but which can be reversed or used as a neighbor figure. Brahms's profound study of Beethoven, his choice of the *Appassionata* as one of the models for this work, and his previous success with variation form prepared him for the challenge.

The potential energy of the opening suggests the breadth of the whole discourse by virtue of its restraint, but it soon bursts out in powerful accents leading to a driving lyricism unique to Brahms, which continuously points to new formal pathways. Large-scale two-part period structure, found throughout the Quintet, is used without any sense of predictability. This is not always the case with Schubert, who provides the formal model here; in Brahms, the second part always redirects the line and harmony of the first. In the long second theme group of the first movement, a variety of phrase materials is involved in a dialogue between determination and hesitation, held tightly together by obsessive triplets. A closing complex, based on the "horn fifths" motive that carries connotations similar to those of Beethoven's *Farewell* Sonata, calms the music down and renders the meter ambiguous; by the transition to the development the now hesitant beat has been thoroughly displaced.

The success of the rest of the movement lies in its ability to maintain the energetic oppositions of the exposition (through key change and variation) and to trace their further implications. Brahms mediates the demands of large-scale Classical form and personal style, brought about through a rapprochement of the influences of Beethoven and Schubert. The explosive energy of Beethovenian motivic materials drives the form: the semitone motive guides harmonic motion at structurally crucial points, particularly at the recapitulation of the second group with its last-moment return to home key. Schubert's formal model offers broadly laid out double periods, loose key relationships, particularly what Tovey calls "purple patches" (apparent digressions into remote harmonic areas), and shifts between major and minor. A characteristic expressive result is a sense of unwillingness to abandon the moment. Even more than Schubert in the best of his late instrumental works, Brahms tightens up the connections between paragraphs and reflects structural relations with motivic detail: the second theme's "purple patch" key, C♯ minor, is generated directly by motivic voice-leading.

Lyricism and the tendency toward continuous evolution lead Brahms to vary where Classical form requires repetition. At the beginning of the recapitulation, emulating the *Appassionata*, Brahms brings back the opening theme in upper strings over a dominant pedal in the cello, but Brahms disguises the moment even more thoroughly than Beethoven with migrating harmonies in the piano. In his later music, Brahms finds concise ways to achieve a varied formal symmetry; here, structural variation complements broad two-part phrase structure to fill out the temporal framework. The result is a symphonic breadth that found its ultimate destination, appropriately, in the symphonies.

In the second movement, the "Slavic" voice (melody in thirds, syncopated accompaniment, scale steps borrowed from the minor) harbors a potential for instability. Such tendencies are effectively restrained for twenty-eight leisurely measures before they finally pull away into the "purple" realm of the flatted sixth, foreshadowed by earlier "borrowed" moments. The middle section, with dramatically sweeping upward octaves and arpeggios, displays Brahms's early tone of romantic extravagance that was on the verge of disappearing from his music; it is the least emotionally restrained lyrical passage in the Quintet, and by the end of the long transition back to the opening material, with its falling echoes, it seems already far in the past.

Beginning with an energized pulsation and an ambiguous ghost of the Andante's key, the Scherzo bursts forth with highly charged energy in a dialogue between the demonic and the grandiose, in which the driving anacruses expand to trumpet calls reminiscent of Beethoven's Fifth.

Included is a double-fugue exposition and episode in E♭ minor followed by a furiously grinding restatement of the second introduction and main theme. The final thirty-five measures maintain this extraordinary turbulence with the help of the half-step motive in its most single-minded appearances, as a cadential appoggiatura that brings the Scherzo to a halt. The Trio, while reasserting lyricism, maintains connections to the first movement and to the Scherzo through the rhythm of the double anacrusis, which is subdued but present for all but eight measures of the middle phrase. The mood is detached, almost Olympian, foreshadowing the corresponding moment in the Piano Trio Op. 87, but with the shadow of the Scherzo running through it.

The final movement, an "amplified binary" rondo, seems the most formally relaxed, following models by Mozart and Schubert, but it bears the burden of the Classical "last movement problem," which becomes particularly onerous where expectations of interrelatedness and formal cohesion have been raised. The dialectic of this Finale involves the confrontation between a chromatically ambiguous slow introduction and a folk-style rondo theme. The discrepancy between the tragic intensity of the introduction and the low-key consolation of a Slavic-colored dance movement is maintained throughout the movement; further tonal and rhythmic disorientation provided by the second (double) theme, which reappears in ingeniously varied guises, is answered by the reprises of the main theme.

In preparation for the first reprise, Brahms offers a halting, stripped-down variation which almost seems cross-indexed to the main theme of the Finale of the Schubert Duo; this prepares for the theme's unaltered restatement, energetic by comparison. The final statement of the theme is prefaced by a transition, tranquillo, that manages to suggest both the harmonic ambiguity of the slow introduction and a yet more schematic version of the rondo theme itself.

With the bass apparently stuck on D♭ (6), Brahms suddenly takes off on a variation of the theme in 6/8, a Presto non troppo in the same key as the second group of the first movement, C♯ minor. (A model might be the Finale of Beethoven's *Serioso* Quartet.) This audacious surprise incorporates various aspects of the first and third movements and cascades toward what seems to be a brilliant cadence. But the usefulness of surprise is not exhausted. Having apparently achieved everything but rhythmic stability (presumably to be supplied by multiple repetitions of the final chord), Brahms unpredictably restarts the rhythmic flow with a motivic 5-♯ 4 convulsion, leading to an extensive coda of one hundred measures. Included is a transformation of the second theme contrapuntally layered over the rondo theme, and, after a final pause, the rhythmic dislocation of the beginning of the Scherzo. The stabilization of this rhythm puts in place the final element, and the movement ends with a sense of concision rather than exhaustion. It is as if these hundred measures serve as coda to the entire Quintet, not just the last movement, as does Beethoven's finale to the *Eroica*. A sympathetic critic, Hermann Deiters, drew the line at the extension of the coda of the last movement. What Deiters viewed as excessive can now be heard as both a brilliant deception and an assertion of self-confidence.   *Laurence Wallach*

Quintet No. 1 for Two Violins, Two Violas, and Cello in F Major, Opus 88
Composed 1882; published 1882

Movements: 1. Allegro non troppo ma con brio; 2. Grave ed appassionato. Allegretto vivace. Presto; 3. Allegro energico

Brahms composed his F-major String Quintet for the Mozartean medium of two violins, two violas, and one cello (rather than the Schubertian two cellos and one viola), apparently beginning and finishing it during the spring of 1882. He based the middle of its three movements on a neo-Baroque sarabande and gavotte that he had written for solo piano and then suppressed in the mid-1850s. The two pre-existing dances would thus seem to be the germ of the Quintet; in any case, the compound movement that emerged from their recomposition and joining is the soul and center to which he made the outer movements defer.

The first Allegro begins with a drone fifth in the cello and second viola. Although this specific pastoral sign, an allusion to rustic bagpipes, quickly disappears, the atmosphere of an idyll is maintained. Themes unfold in a leisurely and lyrical manner, and Brahms has chosen secondary keys (D major and A major) that by convention stand in a "bright" relationship to F major. The development becomes only briefly tangled before reverting to the open textures characteristic of this Allegro. Tension builds, nevertheless, because of the unusually long pedal point on the dominant, over which thematic fragments are recalled, first dreamily but then with growing excitement, culminating in the return of the opening theme, made whole again.

Since he destroyed his own copies of the early sarabande and gavotte, Brahms certainly did not intend for us to know that he based the core movement on them; copies that he had given to friends resurfaced only in the twentieth century. But he also did not obscure Baroque references in the movement. Keeping the telltale accented second beat of the sarabande, the three Grave portions eventually use all of the original dance; the two interludes are respectively in the manner of a quick pastorale and, less exactly, a presto gavotte. Even more to the point, the alternating sections with their contrasting tempos represent the Quintet's slow movement and Scherzo, the former by tradition much weightier and more deeply felt that the latter.

When Brahms reworked his two dances, both originally in A, he left the gavotte-based sections in A major, and transposed those taken from the sarabande to C♯ (minor and major). The dramatic shape of the composite hinges in part on the question of which key will be allowed to end, and thus become "the key of" the movement as a whole. The formalist observation about the eventual triumph of A major, that that key plays an important role in both the first movement and the Finale, explains little. According to that point of view, Brahms could have replaced the slow sections in A major/minor and the scherzandos in C♯ major, as long as he concluded in A major, but that would have made the movement—and the

Quintet—nonsensical. What matters above all is that *the key of the scherzandos should prevail:* his decision to make a compound movement involved more than just making its key fit into a pattern with the outer movements.

Indeed, the alternation of the two movement-types, with the gestures at the boundaries between them, creates an intense plot. The high spirits of the first quick section already seem to mock the solemnity of the opening Grave. This Allegretto vivace retains most of the formal features characteristic of scherzos and other dance-based movements (like the original gavotte), preserving even the traditional repetition of the first strain. But the form does not complete itself; falling into fragments toward an inconclusive end, it yields to the returning Grave. The second Grave and succeeding Presto intensify the affective qualities of the first Grave and Allegretto vivace, C♯ in the process becoming associated with the tragedy and seeming inexorability of the slow-movement sections, A major, with the good cheer of the scherzandos. This time, A major does not give way, instead spilling over into the final return of the Grave, which then proceeds to modulate back to C♯. During the course of the movement, Brahms has strengthened the sense of a drama being played out through codas at the end of each Grave section that seem to reflect on the action. And in the third of these, he exerts his agency. At the end, after audibly deliberating on the two keys, going back and forth between their tonic triad, he (or his musical persona) *chooses* A major, with all of the implications that this key has acquired in the movement: this unusual gesture—quiet yet underscored—is the defining moment in the Quintet.

How does a composer end a multi-movement piece after such a richly plotted center? In Brahms's Quintet, with another Baroque reference and much hilarity: Max Kalbeck wrote that "the spiritually shadowed *Mater Dolorosa* of his Adagio, which bears the scherzo in her womb, must give birth to world-vanquishing humor as Savior" in the Finale. The last movement begins with what sounds like a rambling, rhythmically unfocused fugal subject, which enters four times in alternating tonic and dominant forms: thus, a fugal exposition, the beginning of a Baroque genre that connotes learnedness and elevation. When the Finale does become rhythmically grounded, it also becomes resolutely unfugal, at first both boisterous and homophonic. After the original juxtaposition of fugal and homophonic textures, Brahms certainly does allow in a number of passages in a more elevated style, including a lovely lyrical second theme in A major and a great deal of complex imitative counterpoint.

The complete disappearance of fugal signal and the ultimate triumph of the exuberantly homophonic theme nevertheless effect a reversal of the expectations initially aroused, which makes the movement as a whole sound humorous. But it is high comedy.

Margaret Notley

QUINTET NO. 2 FOR TWO VIOLINS, TWO VIOLAS, AND CELLO IN G MAJOR, OPUS 111
Composed 1890; published 1891

MOVEMENTS: 1. Allegro non troppo ma con brio; 2. Adagio; 3. Un poco Allegretto; 4. Vivace ma non troppo presto

Brahms for a while considered the G-major String Quintet to be his final musical statement, as his biographer Max Kalbeck noted and evidence in the letters confirms. What kind of composition did Brahms decide, however briefly, to make the culmination of his life's work? In the pages Kalbeck devotes to the Quintet, he focused first on its references to the sounds of Vienna:

> No other work of Brahms—excepting perhaps the first set of *Liebeslieder* and the Waltzes Op. 39—more clearly draws attention to the place of origin through the local accents peculiar to it than the G-Major Quintet. It is characteristic of the composer, even more characteristic of his place of residence, in which German sense of humor and Slavic melancholy, Italian vivacity and Hungarian haughtiness have found their compromise [*Ausgleich*].

Like many passages in Kalbeck, this may at first seem blather, but it bears a closer look. On the eve of World War I—the last volume of the Brahms biography, in which this appeared, came out in 1914—Kalbeck chose to write about the Quintet's Viennese character, an amalgam of qualities from at least four different ethnic groups. The excerpt may tell us less about Brahms than about Kalbeck, who was undoubtedly stretching a point for his own political agenda. Yet Hungarian (or gypsy) and Slavic idioms apparently do pervade the last three movements, and Kalbeck's comments highlight the interesting fact that Brahms, whose own German pride easily veered into jingoism, should have allowed so many specifically non-German references into what might have been his last work, completed in 1890 when Austria's nationality problem was already becoming critical. Brahms used similar features objectively, as picturesque folklorisms, in a number of other pieces (for example, the Finale of the G-minor Piano Quartet or the Hungarian Dances). In the later chamber music, however, such references had become part of his own personal language, and the G-major Quintet in particular stands out for its allusiveness.

The Quintet is also remarkable for the beauty of its textures, its sheer sound. The first movement evolves from an incomparably rich opening theme that begins to fragment almost immediately; with the nearly constant shimmering of tremolos, this creates an aural image of something resembling luxuriant, asymmetrical growth. The second thematic group, on the other hand, sounds like a waltz: one of the work's "local accents." The actual development section begins with the transformation of the dance theme—very ordinary elements from it isolated and placed in relief against the tremolos from the opening—followed by vigorous working-out of motives from the first theme, and then by visionary changes rung on those same thematic fragments, which become increasingly remote from their original forms. During this latter process, a new theme merges motives from the opening with a repeated-note figure. This short theme, too, fragments, and its motives undergo further changes that culminate in a long dissonance. As if in quotation marks, a version of the fourth measure from the opening reappears—the recapitulation could in fact have proceeded here, but it would have sounded abrupt. In keeping with the continuously evolving nature of both the first theme and the development section, that theme only gradually takes shape again at the point of recapitulation.

Brahms based the second movement more completely on a type of Viennese popular music: the gypsy café music of the time. Hanslick considered the Adagio to sound Slavic, but it has an array of effects that others believe mark a work as *à l'hongrois* (short subphrases, dotted rhythms, augmented seconds, tremolos that imitate the cimbalom), and it seems to evoke a gypsy style in which a soloist emerges from the band to play an elaborate improvisation. Because of the singular form in which Brahms cast the movement, the Adagio does more than recreate a vernacular style. This form, the topic of much critical discussion, can be described as free variations on an open-ended theme, or, even better, as several views of the theme, for it is not so much varied, in the usual sense, as given different emphases in a series of presentations, irregular in length and progressively developing. Even this does not capture the expressive curve of the movement. The theme sounds in the beginning almost like a march, but when it pauses on a dominant chord, one of the violas breaks free in the first improvisational solo. The drama of the movement centers on the inevitable return of the processional opening after the repeated attempts to alter its course, to take it somewhere else.

The Quintet concludes with two movements that again draw on dance rhythms linked with Brahms's Vienna: a G-minor quasi-Ländler standing in for the scherzo, a waltz in G major as its trio, and a finale with a first thematic group in the manner of a *csárdás*. In the Ländler-like outer dances of the third movement, Brahms has used the so-called gypsy scale (in G minor: G–A–B♭–C♯–D–E♭–F♯–G), interpreting and reinterpreting its characteristic notes, to some extent adapting the typical form of the scherzo to the harmonic tendencies of the scale, but in any case allowing it to imbue the movement with its color. The final Vivace ma non troppo presto has its own harmonic peculiarities, opening in B minor and moving only in the ninth measure toward the expected G major. Throughout the movement, Brahms plays with the relationship between B minor and G major and with the fact that the first group has several detachable components: despite the folkloristic features (including an eventual rowdy *csárdás* in the coda), the construction is in no sense primitivistic. Kalbeck observed that the Quintet is "characteristic of the composer, but even more characteristic of his place of residence." Put more accurately, the materials are typical of late-nineteenth-century Vienna, their transfiguration in the Quintet, of Brahms.   *Margaret Notley*

QUINTET FOR CLARINET, TWO VIOLINS, VIOLA, AND CELLO IN B MINOR, OPUS 115

Composed 1891; published 1892

MOVEMENTS: 1. Allegro; 2. Adagio; 3. Andantino. Presto non assai, ma con sentimento; 4. Con moto. Un poco meno mosso

Brahms resembled Mozart in his cultivation of a wide variety of chamber subgenres and, especially, in his turn to the clarinet as a chamber instrument late in life. Like Mozart, Brahms attributed the inspiration to write for this instrument to the playing of a particular clarinetist—in his case, Richard Mühlfeld. With the Clarinet Trio, Op. 114, the Clarinet Quintet apparently dates from 1891, although letters between Clara Schumann and Brahms from three years before refer to a mysterious, "fierce" *(grausame)* Clarinet Quintet in E Minor; in any case, Brahms chose to present Opp. 114 and 115 as a pair of works that he composed in 1891 under the spell of Mühlfeld's playing. The Clarinet Quintet has the subdued, unearthly beauty of sound that characterizes many of Brahms's later works; it can also lay claim to being the quintessential "autumnal" work of the composer.

Works for string quartet and piano or wind instrument traditionally tended toward concertante style; in this Clarinet Quintet, however, solo-versus-tutti textures, which would present the clarinet as protagonist, appear sparingly, the clarinet usually modulating the sound of the strings in more subtle ways. Beyond that, Brahms minimizes any sense within each movement of vaulting tonal trajectories, as created most famously by Beethoven in his middle period: this is not heroic music. Subsidiary keys tend to sound more like inflections of the main key than strong tonal others that will eventually be subjugated. The key scheme of the Quintet is organized around B minor and its relative major, D, but at a crucial point Brahms undermines the distinction between the two. This eroding of the opposition between major and minor basic to the sign-system of expression in tonal music is one of a number of features in the Quintet that communicate ambivalence and also, ultimately, resignation.

Toward the beginning of the first movement (in B minor), Brahms prominently mixes in D major, the goal of the exposition. The opening only gradually evolves into a theme; for much of its length, this statement seems rhythmically and harmonically ungrounded, as if it would avoid becoming a stable "subject." Each time that the theme reappears there-after, its fluid design allows it to be in some way truncated or telescoped: for example, when the exposition is repeated, the D major of its close connects directly with the D-major moment in the first theme, bypassing the opening measures altogether. A more forceful, fully formed part of the exposition, the transition theme, becomes the center of the development section, where its character undergoes a complete transformation: it is not—or, at least, not only—what it had seemed to be. Brahms's conception of key permits the recapitulation to come almost to a close in G major, which is, nevertheless, only an aspect of the main key; the last-minute regaining of the tonic in a coda emphasizes the tragic finality of the B-minor ending.

The clarinet takes the lead over muted strings in the second movement, dolce and also, in several respects, nearly immobile. Toward the close of the first large section in a tripartite form, the clarinet asserts it-self, disturbing the regularity and repetitiveness heretofore present in the movement, in preparation for an elaborate quasi-improvisation *à l'hongrois* in the middle section. Yet even during most of the impassioned rhapsodizing, the opening motive remains the underlying, obsessive focus of the movement, and the tonic (B major in the outer sections, minor in the middle one) stays basically unchallenged until almost the end. The gypsy soloist does finally break free to wander through remote harmonies, but does not get far before being pulled back to common ground.

While the third movement continues the pattern of incorporating blunted or equivocal gestures, it nevertheless ends up sounding more optimistic than the other movements in the Quintet. Through his mature years as a composer, Brahms created a succession of introspective scherzo-substitutes like this one. Here he not only transformed the character of the scherzo, but also played on the customary three-part form (scherzo-trio-scherzo), again using the permeability between B minor and D major. The movement begins as a D-major Andantino, which cadences twice in B minor only to conclude in D major. A new section, a presto "trio" in B minor, turns out to be a sonata form, in which thematic fragments from the D-major section reappear (and at the original pitch level). Was the D-major Andantino a slow introduction? Not exactly, for its closing phrases return in the coda of the sonata form, which thus ends in D major with a nod toward the traditional three sections. But neither does the movement observe the principles of contrast and containment that help define the genre of scherzo and trio, for it refers to boundaries and differences only to blur them.

Brahms composed the fourth movement as a set of variations on a theme of his own devising, with Bachian counterpoint between the cello and first violin. All five variations maintain the form of the theme, which makes D major the goal of its first strain. While each presents the theme in a new guise, the variations otherwise remain discrete entities: the only overall rhetorical plan would seem to derive from the cumulative effect of the theme's recurring form. The final variation changes the meter from duple to triple, turning the theme into a plaintive waltz. Unlike the others, this variation does not close, leading instead into a coda that recalls harmonically reinterpreted shards from the opening of the first movement. Although a series of illusory cadences on major chords delays closure, an unequivocal B minor, as in the first movement, becomes the tragic *telos* of the Finale and thus the Quintet as a whole.

Margaret Notley

9

SEXTETS

SEXTET NO. 1 FOR TWO VIOLINS, TWO VIOLAS, AND TWO CELLOS IN B♭ MAJOR, OPUS 18

Completed 1860; published 1861

MOVEMENTS: 1. Allegro ma non troppo; 2. Andante, ma moderato;
3. Scherzo. Allegro molto; 4. Rondo. Poco Allegretto e grazioso

According to entries in a personal inventory of his works, Brahms completed the B♭ String Sextet in the summer of 1860. Six years had thus elapsed since he had considered a chamber piece to be ready for publication. In contrast to the B-major Piano Trio of 1854 (Op. 8, original version), the Sextet displays a full mastery of compositional craft, a natural continuation of his accomplishments in the two Serenades (Opp. 11 and 16) from the late 1850s: Max Kalbeck observed correctly that "the Op. 18 Sextet is scarcely thinkable without both Serenades as antecedents." As in the succeeding six chamber compositions, Brahms chose a medium that invited much repetition with varied scoring, and he placed a premium throughout the Sextet on skillful writing for the ensemble, on the rich fullness of sound that had sometimes eluded him in the B-major Piano Trio.

Compared with the three Piano Quartets, movements of all of which probably date back to before the Serenades, and indeed with the early Piano Trio, the Sextet in several respects suggests a scaling-down of his ambitions. He chose a chamber genre for which a piece by Louis Spohr offered the only significant precedent, and he concluded it with a modest Scherzo and Rondo that would not have sounded out of place in early Beethoven. Other influences come through, especially in the first Allegro and the Andante, where a seemingly erratic chord and a foreign style, respectively, give the movements a more dramatic, differentiated shape, but the work as a whole radiates a Classical poise.

While the opening Allegro ma non troppo makes it clear that Brahms had thoroughly assimilated many features of Schubert's late, great instrumental works—their lyricism and harmonic originality, and also the carefully modulated phrase rhythms that hold the large forms together in so convincing a fashion—he did not assay the searching sublimity of Schubert's late style in it: the movement remains for the most part serene and euphonious. The most surprising movement comes at the beginning of the second group, which, as in many of Schubert's sonata forms, consists of two large sections, followed by a closing theme. After the transition has settled on a dominant pedal in the key of F major, an A-major triad, vivid in these surroundings, enters by upward chromatic motion in the first violin and then in the bass—pianissimo, like a sudden vision—only to be rationalized within F major. When the same Schubertian chord enters a second time, it seems more possible that the expanded repetition of the Ländler-like theme could close in A, but the A-major triad is again found to fit within F. The development section presents its distorted, fragmentary version of the exposition, which again leads to the dominant of F. An E-minor triad, the chord that enters thereafter, now by downward motion in the first viola, sounds less irrational and thus less startling than the exposition chord; although it also seems more stable, at least in the first phrase, in the second, it leads toward the retransition and then the recapitulation. The coda concludes with a variation of the closing theme in a waltz rhythm with pizzicatos in all six strings, an effect of charm and textural beauty in keeping with the aesthetic evident throughout most of the Sextet, the exception being the set of variations that constitutes its slow movement.

Brahms based the Andante, in D minor, on a standard Baroque theme called *la folia*, originally a bass line to be improvised upon, but later used in notated sets of variations. Although he changed the meter from triple to duple time and somewhat altered both the harmony and the usual treble line, the derivation of his theme from the archaic source remains audible; moreover, his own set of variations, five in all, begins as a pastiche of Baroque divisions, each of the first three variations subdividing the beat into progressively more parts to create a sense of increasing speed.

The B-major Piano Trio had similarly invoked Baroque topics in the musette-like closing theme and, especially, the unfortunate Bachian fugato of its first movement. Brahms integrated references to the extraneous style much more successfully in the Sextet by making the collision of discourses the point of the movement, by forming the set of variations around the very opposition between latter-day subjectivity and the monumental, impersonal quality of both the Baroque theme and the technique of divisions. Idioms that sound somewhat out of place in Baroque style intrude in the second and third variations. The climax of the movement comes at the end of the third variation; tension is released, and identifiably Baroque features disappear altogether in the *maggiore* fourth and fifth variations. When the theme returns after the final variation, this moment juxtaposes minor with major, Baroque with nineteenth-century discourses; the coda synthesizes the two styles. Brahms himself thought highly enough of this wonderful movement to arrange it separately for piano as a birthday present to Clara Schumann.

Margaret Notley

Sextet No. 2 for Two Violins, Two Violas, and Two Cellos in G Major, Opus 36
Composed 1864–65; published 1866

Movements: 1. Allegro non troppo; 2. Scherzo. Allegro non troppo; 3. Poco Adagio; 4. Poco Allegro

In July 1864, Brahms wrote to his friend Julius Otto Grimm, "I'd like to know how it is in all the houses where one used to go so happily. Also write me of that house and gate . . ." In his oblique fashion, Brahms was referring to the Göttingen home of Agathe von Siebold, a professor's daughter and singer to whom he had been secretly engaged at the beginning of 1859—and then had jilted in the wake of the Leipzig fiasco of the D-minor Piano Concerto. For some reason, in 1864 that old romance had been weighing on Brahms's mind. The report from Grimm was unsparing: "At that house and gate things have sadly changed. . . . Since last year, Agathe has been a governess in Ireland. . . . It got [to be] too much for her in Göttingen; she wanted to find a job for herself and get away from the shadowed pages of her life."

Soon Brahms made a trip to Göttingen to revisit the streets he had walked with Agathe. In September, back at his summer quarters in Baden-Baden, he composed the devastated and exalted songs of Op. 32, the most telling of them, *Nicht mehr zu dir zu gehen* (To go to you no longer): "I would like to stop living, to perish instantly, and yet I would like to live for you, with you, and never die." The same month he composed the first three movements of the G-major String Sextet, completing it the following May.

The result is one of his most magnificent chamber works, more complex, integrated, colorful, and mature than its predecessor, the B♭ Sextet. The first movement is lyrical but with an undercurrent of unrest. The second movement is a scherzo, medium in tempo and in 2/4 rather than the usual 3/4, thus another of the Intermezzos with which Brahms replaced the traditional scherzo in many of his chamber and orchestral works. The leading theme of the second movement comes from a neo-Baroque piano gavotte he had written in the 1850s; in contrast to its gentle elegance, there is a scherzo-like Trio, marked Presto giocoso, in 3/4. The third movement comprises a set of variations, Adagio, based on a sketch Brahms had sent Clara Schumann in 1855. Despite a brightly rhythmic fugal variation in the center, the dominant tone of the third movement could be called wandering, empty, tragic—close to the devastated tone of some of the Op. 32 songs. The Finale, in contrast to the "gypsy" character of the finales in his preceding chamber works, has something like the racing 3/4 vivacity of a scherzo, immediately contrasted with a warm section of *moll-Dur* (mixed minor and major) melody having the gentle lilt of a dance. As Michael Musgrave notes in *The Music of Brahms,* elements throughout the work echo Schubert's string quartets and quintet.

The opening movement shows what Brahms had learned by age thirty-one as a shaper of expressive and inventive sonata forms. It begins with a murmuring half-step ostinato on G–F♯ by the first viola. With interruptions, this figure persists through much of the first theme group. In that figure lies the main technical gambit of the opening section: What harmonies may be superimposed on a given half-step ostinato? At the beginning Brahms builds a striking tonal shift out of two distant keys that can contain the G–F♯ oscillation, G major and E♭ major (the oscillation gives a major-minor inflection to the latter key). The linked rising fifths of the opening melody—G–D, E♭–B♭—define those two keys, which dominate the opening pages; thus a motivic figure produces a larger-scale tonal element. The half-step oscillation goes on and on, stopping only to resume, changing to other pitches, and ushering in new keys.

These devices show the depth of Brahms's craftsmanship, though they hardly imply the elusive but deeply expressive world of the Sextet. But the technical and expressive are inseparable in this work. The oscillation, for example, is nominally an accompanying figure, yet it moves continually from foreground to background, persisting like an obsession that moves in and out of consciousness. As he had done in earlier works, Brahms thematicizes accompaniment figures, integrates the traditional sense of melody and accompaniment, unifies foreground and background; and the linked fifths of the opening unite the local thematic level with the larger harmonic structure. (All these procedures were to have a profound influence on Arnold Schoenberg.)

Perhaps the most arresting thing in the first movement is the overall thematic process, beginning with the rising fifths of the opening melody. From that point scraps of themes succeed one another, seeming to accumulate rather than just pass by. Step by step, each turn of melody building on the last, we move toward something hinted at in a motivic fragment here, a rhythm there. The second theme group arrives with a melody more extended than any so far, and builds yearningly toward a dancing, ecstatic climax that has been gathering since the beginning of the piece. That climax flares in a simple but urgent line with a poignant harmonic suspension underneath.

That is the climax of the exposition, a moment of dazzling emotional power, the more remarkable for the simplicity of means: a line in even quarter notes, as simple and ingenuous as a little waltz. The impact of the climax, its meaning for all the abstractness of meaning in music, is created by an extraordinary marshaling of every musical dimension: a coalescing of thematic elements that seem to produce the climactic melody as inevitably as a flower blooms; the brilliant scoring, the instruments soaring into the high register; the position of the climax within a subtly original sonata-form exposition in which everything points to the end of the second theme group; the rhythmic complexity of the buildup paying off in lilting simplicity, which soon falls into metric shifts combined with breathtakingly fresh harmonies, mounting to a luminous culmination and afterglow that, in context, seems almost sexual.

In fact, there is a secret lying behind that climax, those particular notes: the pitches spell out Agathe von Siebold's name. This procedure of spelling words with notes had for centuries been a means of evoking things symbolically in music. Brahms perhaps learned it more directly from Robert Schumann, who in his *Carnaval* and other works uses letter-cabala to represent places and people. In the first movement's climax, the pitches of Brahms's melody are A-G-A-D-H-E (H being the German name for the note B). The missing letter T is represented by the suspended D that comes in under the melody—so, A-G-A-D-H-E. At the same time, the D forms part of another word, made of the second A of the upper melody, the suspended D, the E of the next melody pitch. The other word is A D E, farewell. *Agathe, farewell.*

"By this work," Brahms told friend Josef Gänsbacher, "I have freed myself of my last love." In it he freed himself of more than love, if indeed he did that. For the listener, the impact of the climax is as abstractly musical as anything critic Eduard Hanslick could have asked for in his doctrine of "absolute music." Knowing the secret (Joachim certainly did, among other friends of Brahms) adds nothing definable to the effect. In contrast to the personal elements and symbolism of earlier Brahms music—such as the opening of the First Piano Concerto, composed in the wake of Robert Schumann's breakdown, and which, after endless agonies, never quite settled into perfect shape—the weight of experience in the G-major Sextet does not strain against the musical dialectic, did not seduce Brahms from his task as composer. Melody, harmony, texture, timbre, and form coalesce to make the climax what it is: *those* notes, *those* rhythms, at *that* moment in the form.

In the G-major Sextet, Brahms freed himself not only from the memory of lost love and gnawing guilt, but from the burden of his life in his art. After this there are few games with pitch-symbols in his music. From this point on, in large degree Brahms disappeared behind his work as behind a mask. This is not to say that his own experience vanished from his music—witness, for example, the *Alto Rhapsody*—but rather, autobiography receded into the background, as private inspiration and impetus.

The G-major Sextet was the first work of Brahms's to be premiered in the United States, in Boston at the Mendelssohn Quintet Club on October 11, 1866. The first European performance came on November 20 of the same year, in Zürich.

Jan Swafford

The music room of Brahms's
home at Karlgasse 4.

Part Three

SOLO
PIANO MUSIC

INTRODUCTION

At the very heart of Brahms's compositional genius is the piano. From his most significant teacher Eduard Marxsen, Brahms received his primary training on that instrument. Although he reputedly did not have a particular taste for practicing, and it is not certain that he ever harbored the ambition to be a piano virtuoso, he continued to play to the end of his life. The piano was firmly rooted as Brahms's central medium of musical expression. For Brahms the piano, both solo and in ensembles, constitutes the principal element in his compositional output, from the Op. 1 Sonata to the late piano works such as the Intermezzos, Op. 117. As a youth, he made his first public appearances playing in the harborside inns of Hamburg. This was admittedly not the noblest use of Marxsen's rigorous classical instruction, but for Brahms it was an indispensable means of bringing much needed funds into the family. It was not until 1853 that Brahms was able to use his talents at the keyboard to make a successful foray into the upper echelons of the profession of music.

Brahms's piano performances—more often than not of his own compositions—constituted the primary component of his public performing life. He also had a career as a conductor, though ultimately it was not a very notable one. It was only during Brahms's lifetime that conducting emerged as a distinct and self-sufficient career. Mendelssohn, of course, had achieved distinction as a conductor, and later Strauss and Mahler were known as composer/conductors, but among Brahms's contemporaries, Hermann Levi, Hans Richter, and Hans von Bülow represented the group of musicians who for the first time became world famous solely on the basis of their conducting.

The primacy of the piano for Brahms fairly reflects the significance of that instrument in nineteenth-century European culture. Although one can speak of important changes in the violin in terms of technique (in modes of bowing, vibrato, and fingering) and materials (the introduction of coiled metal strings, different configurations of bridges, bass-bows, chin rests, shoulder rests, and the positioning of the neck) the violin achieved its basic shape by the early eighteenth century and remained essentially the same instrument throughout the nineteenth century. The same cannot be said for the piano. Between the death of Beethoven and the 1860s (the crucial years of Brahms's early development) the piano was the object of constant technological innovation and fierce commercial competition. Radical modifications in the action and construction of the frame in turn influenced character and tension of the stringing, creating a fundamentally altered sound from the instrument for which Mozart had written. By the mid-1860s the piano had evolved nearly into its modern form. Therefore, the instrument for which Beethoven wrote his last three piano sonatas and the *Diabelli* Variations was also essentially different from that for which Brahms wrote his Intermezzos. The mid-century innovations of American manufacturers, particularly Steinway and Chickering, represented the most important stage in the evolution of the modern piano. During the 1860s and 1870s, the American piano took Europe by storm.

Brahms came of age using an intermediate form of piano construction represented by the Streicher piano, inherited from Schumann, which he had in his home in Vienna. Even though this Streicher would increasingly seem old-fashioned, it and the equally anti-progressive Bösendorfers which Brahms played in public in Vienna were distinctly modern sounding—brighter, more metallic, and richer in tone—than the pianos of the previous generation. It should be noted that Brahms was familiar with and liked the Bechsteins and Steinways he heard in the 1880s. Brahms's good friend Friedrich Ehrbahr was Vienna's second most important piano manufacturer, whose instruments (unlike those of Ludwig Bösendorfer) were distinctly imitative of the Steinway piano, as were the Brechsteins. It was, after all, in Ehrbahr's piano showroom that many later orchestral pieces by Brahms were first heard in their piano reductions.

The driving force behind this extraordinary innovation in the piano was societal. The demand for musical culture among literate, middle-class Europeans exploded during Brahms's lifetime as a consequence of increased affluence and literacy. There was therefore a palpable and economically viable market for a versatile, stable instrument that could offer a satisfying musical experience when played either by itself or with any combination of voices or other instruments, adequate for the home, the salon, and the concert hall. The new piano proved the ideal medium. It could evoke the full range of harmonies of an orchestra, allowing it to reproduce reductively every type and form of music. Furthermore, it did not have to be constantly tuned, and therefore could be owned and used at much wider levels of proficiency from beginner to virtuoso, with tolerable results for all. By the end of the nineteenth century the piano had become a major consumer item, the equivalent of the present day's radio, tape, and CD player, available in all conceivable sizes, shapes, and prices. One telling example of its preeminence in musical culture is Richard Wagner's devotion to it. Wagner wrote no music at all for the piano, though he used it constantly. For Wagner and Brahms alike, and for their contemporaries in Europe and America, the piano was the single most influential factor in the making and playing of music.

Not surprisingly, then, Brahms wrote from the beginning to the end of his career for the instrument as a freestanding, autonomous vehicle, capable of transmitting a full musical experience without assistance from the voice or another instrument. Despite its technical difficulties, Brahms's solo piano music, although now a regular part of the concert stage, was written to the very end of Brahms's career with the expectation that it could be learned and played by amateurs. This in part helps explain why in Brahms's piano music there is a remarkable emphasis on Classical and early Romantic models. Through his piano music, Brahms was intent on displaying to listener and performer alike the possibilities of musical discourse without reference to an extramusical program. The playing and listening to the piano became an act of musical education for the player. Furthermore, as much of his piano music also reveals, like the song but even more so, the solo piano repertory in accordance with Romantic tradition offered the ideal opportunity for a dialogue through music between the musician and one's inner self. In this sense Brahms followed in Schumann's path. For both composers, the piano was a vehicle of self-realization, of improvisation and exploration through music in solitude. And that is part of its continuing appeal for performer and listener today. Brahms's piano music, in its self-conscious imposition of distance between itself and the theatrical, explores the intimate in music.

The most frequent forms in Brahms's piano music are hallmarks of Classical procedure: sonatas and variations. The variations—the *Haydn* Variations for two pianos, Op. 56b, the *Handel* Variations, Op. 24, and the

Paganini Variations, Op. 35—are perhaps the most distinctive and unusual. Formal variations provided Brahms with an ideal vehicle for the ex-
hibition of his unequaled mastery of the traditions of thematic
transformation. In this respect Brahms declined to follow in Schumann's
footsteps, and did not write short works or cycles of works with programmatic and literary meanings. If the association between Brahms and
the ideology of "absolute" music articulated by Eduard Hanslick has any
validity, it can be demonstrated with affirmative results in his piano variations.

A decisive connection between Brahms's piano output and the work of
his mentor Schumann rests in Brahms's clear subordination of virtuosity to the inherent requirements of musical form and content that
emerge from Classical procedures. This is not to suggest that Brahms's
music is not some of the most technically challenging ever written;
though Brahms eschews evident pyrotechnics and the theater of virtuosity, much of his piano music is in its own way pianistic and virtuosic.
His interest in piano technique is indicated by the fact that he wrote exercises for the piano and transcribed major works of music for it. The key
contrast here is with Franz Liszt, who represented for Brahms the darker
side of the piano's popularity in the nineteenth century. The anecdote
which tells of Brahms's visit to Liszt's Weimar residence, where Brahms
fell asleep during Liszt's performance of his B-minor Sonata, is a telling
biographical vignette. There is little in Brahms's piano music that re-
motely resembles Liszt either formally or superficially. Like Schumann,
Brahms had little respect for the cult of piano virtuosity that preoccupied
the European public from the era of Liszt and Thalberg to the several
generations of Liszt pupils and protégés of Brahms's Viennese contemporary and great piano pedagogue Theodor Leschetizky (1830–1915).

If the piano made music accessible to a consumer class more than ever
before, it also produced a class of eager spectators with Philistine tastes.
Against them and the musicians who catered to them, Schumann in the
1830s launched his blistering and unrelenting attacks. Foremost among
the offenders were pianist-composers who wrote music that seemed
flashy and personality-driven. At the other end of the scale were composers who wrote piano music for the amateur public that was vacuous
and made no demands on the player. These were the progenitors of a
genre which became wildly popular during the later part of the century
in Brahms's maturity—salon music for piano alone. This trivial, sentimental, and pathetic music was beloved by amateurs and even more by

music publishers. If Schumann's example left a lasting imprint on Brahms, it can be best discerned in the unrelenting seriousness of his piano music. If in other genres Brahms has been fairly accused of being obsessed and hampered by the weight of the past, in his music for solo piano, although the debt to tradition is no less, there is very little hint of its ever having been a burden. The late Intermezzos make this point most eloquently. Brahms, when writing for the piano, displayed a fearlessness in taking on Schumann's challenge to write piano music for both the amateur and the concert stage which could sustain the daunting standard of the thirty-two sonatas of Beethoven.

10

SONATAS

SONATA NO. 1 IN C MAJOR, OPUS 1
Composed 1852–53; published 1853

MOVEMENTS: 1. Allegro; 2. Andante; 3. Scherzo. Allegro molto e con fuoco; 4. Finale. Allegro con fuoco

Among the works Brahms played for Robert Schumann when Brahms visited the older composer in Düsseldorf on September 30, 1853, was the Piano Sonata in C Major, somewhat disingenuously published in 1853 as Brahms's Op. 1, even though the autograph manuscript identified the work as his fourth sonata. It is not difficult to read between the lines of Schumann's enthusiastic assessment of this work as a "veiled symphony": There is something symphonic about Brahms's treatment of the piano here, for his sonata exacts from the pianist formidable technical demands and from the instrument a variety of hues and textures, as if Brahms were indeed endeavoring to create an orchestral composition at the keyboard. Opus 1 also possesses, as Schumann observed, a profoundly lyrical quality that often brings the sonata close to the realm of the German Lied.

This second point bears stressing, for the first of the four movements of Op. 1 to be composed, in April 1852, was the Andante, based on what Brahms understood to be an old German *Minnelied, Verstohlen geht der Mond auf* (Stealthily rises the moon). Brahms found this song in the anthology *Deutsche Volkslieder,* compiled by Andreas Kretzschmer and Anton Wilhelm von Zuccalmaglio during the late 1830s. We now know that Zuccalmaglio tampered with some of the melodies in this collection, so the authenticity of Brahms's source remains somewhat in question. Be that as it may, Brahms found in this imagined courtly love song inspiration for a romantically effusive set of piano variations in C minor. In the four stanzas of the poem, the unnamed male protagonist implores the rising moon to entrance the beautiful Trude with its magical rays. The form of the Andante parallels the poem. After the presentation of the theme, in a simple chordal style, we hear three variations that treat the melody with progressively more expansive music, suggesting the course of the rising moon and introducing new melodic contours and harmonic digressions. Appended to the last variation is a subdued, tranquil epilogue in which the opening motive of the melody is exchanged, duetlike, between the tenor and soprano registers, to suggest the "two faithful hearts" of the poem.

The sonata was thus inspired by a specific poetic idea, which, happily for the modern listener, Brahms took the trouble to identify in his score. Elsewhere in Op. 1, Brahms also approached the realm of folk song, by devising original thematic material that simulated the quality of folk song. For example, in the first movement, the hauntingly beautiful second thematic group, in the submediant A minor, is folk song–like in character; in particular, one passage in this section, marked by widely spaced chords and a drone bass, exudes an exotic fragrance that some listeners in Brahms's time would no doubt have associated with Scottish folk song. The Finale of Op. 1 actually offers a direct and traceable link to Scotland. In 1853, the year the sonata was finished, Brahms made clear his reliance on folk song to Albert Dietrich, a young composer in Schumann's Düsseldorf circle, and, furthermore, disclosed that the central A-minor episode in the Finale was inspired by Robert Burns's poem "My Heart's in the Highlands." The poem would have been known to Brahms, through Schumann's setting in the song cycle *Myrthen,* Op. 25, as *Mein Herz ist im Hochland.* (As pointed out in the scholarly literature, Burns's poem may easily be underlaid to Brahms's melody.) To be sure, Schumann would have delighted in the hidden words of these songlike passages, the poetry of which, he claimed, would have been readily communicated to the listener.

The other feature of Brahms's score that attracted Schumann's critical gaze, its symphonic character, is boldly manifest at the very outset of the composition: the full, rich chords seem to announce that this piano sonata reaches the utmost limits of the genre and its instrument. The full-bodied opening is often compared to that of another "symphonic" piano sonata, Beethoven's great *Hammerklavier,* though on closer inspection, Brahms's opening clearly derives from the beginning of an earlier Beethoven Sonata, the *Waldstein,* with which it shares its key, C major, and several other analytical details. As tradition dictated, Brahms cast his first movement in the mold of sonata form, though he treated that hallowed form with considerable ingenuity by applying the technique of thematic transformation. Much of the development, for example, is devoted to the second thematic group, which experiences a remarkable series of metamorphoses. One of them is first treated in imitative counterpoint, and then allowed to evolve into a robust, rising theme presented in the bass in octaves, an adaptation that actually brings the theme close to the first phrase of the *Minnelied* in the Andante. In two more transformations, the rising figure appears as a lyrical, expressive theme in the treble and, in the middle register of the piano, as a series of subdued horn calls (a clear symphonic reference). The horn calls then grow in intensity and spill over into the recapitulation, at first harmonically colored to de-emphasize the tonic C major in favor of the subdominant F major, and thus to obfuscate the structural break.

For the third movement of the sonata, a rambunctious Scherzo in E minor, Brahms may have had in mind Beethoven's symphonic scherzos. The head motive of the Scherzo is actually taken over from a cadential figure in the final three measures of the Andante, a thematic link that ties the inner movements together. The contrasting middle section of the Scherzo, a Trio in C major, again shows the lyrical side of Brahms's musical personality and betrays, in certain turns of phrase, the influence of Mendelssohn.

The energetic Finale falls into a somewhat predictable rondo scheme with a refrain and two episodes, according to the plan *A B A C A* plus coda (the second episode, *C,* ushers in the A-minor melody inspired by the Burns text). But utterly unpredictable is the very opening of the movement, which establishes as the refrain a powerful transformation of the opening theme of the first movement. Just as the two inner movements are linked by a common thematic idea, so are the outer movements, though now in a considerably more explicit way: the thematic substance of the refrain is nothing less than a metrical and rhythmic transformation of the sonata's opening measures and the Finale is nothing less than a rehearing and transformation of the first movement. For Brahms at the middle of the nineteenth century, the technique of thematic transformation, usually associated with the music of Berlioz and Liszt, Brahms's compositional antithesis, represented a powerful and viable compositional tool. And, by basing his Op. 1 on a poetic idea, the young Brahms was able to traverse what would later become the great divide in nineteenth-century German music, between the absolute and referential schools of music aesthetics.

R. Larry Todd

Sonata No. 2 in F♯ Minor, Opus 2
Composed 1852; published 1854

MOVEMENTS: 1. Allegro non troppo ma energico. Andante con espressione; 2. Scherzo. Allegro; 3. Trio. Poco più moderato; 4. Finale. Introduzione. Sostenuto. Allegro non troppo e rubato

The F♯-minor Sonata, Op. 2, is the earliest complete sonata (and example of sonata form) by Brahms that survives. It was composed in November 1852 and thus predates all but the second movement of the C-major Sonata, which was published as Op. 1. Even at a young age, Brahms was highly self-critical: at least two other piano sonatas appear to have been written and destroyed by him before Op. 2. When it appeared in February 1854 from the publisher Breitkopf & Härtel, Op. 2 was dedicated "with deepest respect" *(verehrend)* to Clara Schumann, with whose life Brahms had become so profoundly involved since the previous autumn.

The Sonata provides a fascinating window onto the musical personality of the young Brahms, not yet twenty when it was composed. The piano style, especially the frequent, thundering octave passagework in the first movement, is less reminiscent of Beethoven or other obvious "sonata" forbears than of the virtuoso manner of Liszt and other keyboard titans of the 1840s. Also Lisztian in spirit—or, more precisely, early Romantic, since we also find it in Schubert and Berlioz—is the kind of thematic transformation by which Brahms relates the opening figures of all four movements. He was never again to apply this principle as overtly to his large-scale works.

What distinguishes Brahms from most of his contemporaries, however, is that Romantic methods are here put into the service of a continuous and logical process of thematic development that is more characteristic of Beethoven and the Classical composers. In the exposition of the first movement of Op. 2, each segment—first group, transition, second group, codetta—is made to grow almost didactically from the opening motivic gesture. There is no better example than this movement of Brahms's fabled mingling of Romantic and Classical practice.

The second movement is cast as a theme and three variations. It is one of the first examples we have from Brahms's pen of a form he was to cultivate throughout his career. Although the source of the theme is not identified by Brahms in the score, he admitted to Albert Dietrich that the melody could be fitted to the words of an old German *Minnelied, Mir ist leide* (It is painful to me), a characteristic example of medieval poetry which tells of admiration from afar for a noble lady. Recently, George Bozarth has suggested that the variations can be seen to follow quite closely the sense and structure of the poem. It is tempting to speculate that although the movement predates Brahms's first encounter with Clara Schumann, it might have come to represent their relationship. In the second movement, as in the first, Brahms takes up a Classical structure, but modifies it with Romantic procedures. The second variation, for example, expands—really explodes—the second part of the theme into a massive climax in D major.

The third movement of the Sonata acts as almost a further variation of the Andante theme, which is transformed note for note into a mercurial Scherzo in B minor. The Trio section returns to D major, the key of the climax in the previous movement, and reinterprets the Scherzo's 6/8 meter in a more lilting, lyrical mood.

The imposing slow introduction to the Finale, marked Sostenuto, restores gravity to the same basic thematic material. In the Allegro that ensues, the theme now takes on the feel of a dramatic ballad that unfolds over a steadily flowing accompaniment. The fast part of the Finale is a full-fledged sonata form, replete with athletic and difficult piano writing and a wide range of expression. In the flamboyant coda, the thematic head motif is given a last apotheosis in the remote key of C major, after which Brahms indicates Molto sostenuto and cuts the tempo in half, almost to that of the introduction. A final improvisatory flourish of trills, chromatic runs, and scales brings the piece to a powerful close in the key of F♯ major.

As a whole, the F♯-minor Sonata shows Brahms giving full reign to his Romantic instincts while at the same time manifesting his affinity for the more Classical unity and sobriety that were to become such an important part of his musical personality. The dazzling thematic transformations and keyboard pyrotechnics are always rationalized structurally.

Walter Frisch

SONATA NO. 3 IN F MINOR, OPUS 5
Composed 1853; published 1854

MOVEMENTS: 1. Allegro maestoso; 2. Andante. Andante espressivo;
3. Scherzo. Allegro energico; 4. Intermezzo. Andante molto (*Rückblick*);
5. Finale. Allegro moderato ma rubato

In the tempestuous Sonata in F♯ Minor, Op. 2, Brahms came unusually close to the pianism of Liszt. Compared with this predecessor, the F-minor Sonata displays an increase in the control with which Brahms balances Kreislerian wildness with complex motivic variation, songfulness, and large-scale proportion. It is clear that Brahms's ambition to integrate large forms needed to discover the longer-range implications of large, even flamboyant gestures whose effects were so immediate. In the service of this goal, a nexus of Brahmsian traits is already firmly in place, especially a fertile sense of thematic and motivic variation, a related interest in variations of rhythm and pulse at the service of structure, and a fondness for rich keyboard sonority.

Present also are Brahmsian melodic fingerprints, such as the theme built from a chain of descending thirds at the beginning of the slow movement, or a basic Brahmsian ascending motivic outline, *sol-do-re-mi* (add *fa* between the last two and you have the Andante molto of the fourth movement), and its retrograde *mi-re-do-sol* (plainly used in the second and subsequent episodes of the Finale). Absent, however, are the sense of concentrated statement, the complex interplay between texture and voice-leading, the finely controlled use of harmonic ambiguity, the sonority that seems to spring organically from the fundamental idea of the individual work. A degree of diffuseness and conventionality allows listeners to hear Brahms's connections to his predecessors of Schumann's generation.

It has been observed that all the moments of this Sonata in the submediant (D♭ major), in whatever movement they occur, correspond to each other, and may even be viewed as variants of the same *Urmelodie*. That fact, taken together with the chronology of the Sonata's creation, leads to an interesting glimpse of Brahms's compositional process in his most successful early attempt at large-scale form. Two of the inner movements, Andante and Intermezzo (*Rückblick:* backward glance), were already in existence when Brahms arrived for his month-long stay at the Schumanns' in October 1853. There he completed the Scherzo and the two large-scale outer movements (save for some pre-publication revisions).

The simplest version of the D♭ theme is the closing episode of the second movement, marked Andante molto. It is adumbrated by the middle section in the same key. It can also be found in the Trio of the Scherzo, where it forms a lyrical contrast to the energetic rhythms of that movement's outer sections. This last seems to be the version most directly alluded to in the *Rückblick,* where the tonal context is ambiguous but relates to the key of the movement, B♭ minor (relative of D♭ major). Thus, when Brahms came to tackle the more challenging sonata form of the first movement and sonata-rondo of the last, he had a well-established network of thematic and motivic materials upon which to expand.

Brahms apparently worked backward into the first movement. Although the powerful opening hurls out a pithy but expansive motive that reaches beyond itself registrally, harmonically, and rhythmically, it is in fact a derivative of the static lyric material whose clearest statement (in the aforementioned key of D♭) occurs only toward the center of the movement, as are corresponding variants in other movements. This theme seems to have been the ontological starting point for the movement and the initial gesture is derived from it. That the first movement appears as a trajectory built on the energy of its opening motive speaks to Brahms's ideals and growing powers of construction. The lyrical moment in question does not behave as a climax or culmination, as it would for such composers as Sibelius or Ives. Their use of fragments which coalesce into themes offered a significant formal innovation. Here, the process generates a Brahmsian episode at a lower energy level surrounded by more vigorously directed material such as will be found later in the symphonies.

Another characteristic structural moment is an inventive retransition which is actually a disguised version of the main theme, presented in the tonic key. When the "official" recapitulation arrives, we realize that we have already heard it and recognize another fingerprint of the composer: being in the moment and simultaneously experiencing the moment as already past. Such "backward and forward" references, however, can also seem like formal weaknesses. The grandiose sense of summing up found in the closing measures of both outer movements seems inflated or at least a self-conscious attempt to punctuate a significant discourse rather than the inevitable goal of a continuous thematic and harmonic process.

Evaluations of this work vary widely. Backed by statistics, it can be viewed as one of the most successful piano sonatas of its century. This status is in a sense insured by Brahms's decision never to write another.

Its long-range strategy of structural unity through the addition of a fifth movement is clearly effective; the *Rückblick* brings piano writing to the brink of the orchestra, with timpani rolls and suggestions of brasses in its evocation of a *Marcia funèbre,* as well as an impressionist moment on an unresolved dominant ninth that suggests the woodwinds of Debussy's *Prélude à l'après-midi d'un faune.* Similarly effective is the quotation of three lines of poetry at the head of the Andante, suggesting a song-not-quite-without-words in clear *Volkston* (folkmanner). The ballade-like structure of this melody carries through the episodes and generates the throbbing and overt Romanticism of the Andante molto mentioned above as the *Urmelodie* of the whole sonata. The irresistible Scherzo builds on the generic strengths Brahms already exhibited in his free-standing Scherzo, Op. 4, as well as the *F-A-E* Sonata movement.

There is a sense of the whole, a breadth of view that validates the process of thematic and tonal interconnectedness among all movements. Not only the innovation of an interlude, but also the bold stroke of ending the Andante firmly in a key other than that of its opening, speak to Brahms's willingness to rethink multi-movement form. Also impressive is the control over rhythmic flow found in the Finale, whose second and third episodes parallel those of the slow movement in the key and status as variants of the *Urmelodie.* This movement begins, like the first, with a motive that cuts itself short, requiring response. Brahms's voice is unmistakable in the gruff, low tessitura, which calls forth an antiphonal response from a higher choir, one which matches rhythmic with harmonic displacement in ways that will be fruitful for the development of the first theme. This opening dialectic is both characteristic and promising. The second theme, however, reverts to the conventional, despite the *F-A-E* motive upon which it is built. The subsequent episode in D♭ aspires to an obsessive Beethovenian pulse. It displays harmonic ingenuity over a fixed pedal but ultimately feels stretched out and static.

Following the reprise, the second D♭ section reveals the *mi-re-do-sol* motive in the style of a fraternal or communal song which will be used with great rhythmic flexibility and which combines contrapuntally not only with other thematic materials but even with itself at a variety of speeds. The use of varied rhythmic materials in this movement constitutes its most successful formal feature, including varied groupings and tempos to suggest the kind of unfettered motivic discourse that animates Brahms's later large-scale forms. The way in which Brahms doubles the tempo and moves into the parallel major demonstrates not only his affinity for scherzando writing and playful counterpoint but also his command of shifting tempo in relation to motivic variation. This discovery will be put to significant use in finales (for example, the Piano Quintet in F Minor, Op. 34) and other movements in extended Classical forms (for example, the second movement of the Piano Trio No. 2 in C Major, Op. 87).

Laurence Wallach

11

VARIATIONS

VARIATIONS ON A THEME BY ROBERT SCHUMANN
IN F♯ MINOR, OPUS 9
Composed 1854; published 1854

In June 1853, Clara Schumann began work on a birthday present for her husband, a piano composition titled *Variations on a Theme by Robert Schumann*, Op. 20. For her theme she borrowed a wistful twenty-four-measure sketch in F♯ minor, the second of five *Albumblätter* Robert had incorporated into his collection of piano miniatures published the previous year as *Bunte Blätter*. Clara's work included ten variations, in the final one of which she wove a phrase from her own *Romanze* published in 1839 (in the *Quatre pièces caractéristiques*, Op. 5). This bit of self-quotation, a kind of musical signature, continued a process Robert had begun in 1833, when he found in Clara's *Romanze* the inspiration for his fanciful variation set, *Ten Impromptus on a Theme of Clara Wieck*, Op. 5. At that time, Robert was twenty-three, and Clara fourteen. By 1853, after thirteen years of marriage, Clara was the mother of six children, and Robert, struggling in his capacity as the municipal music director of Düsseldorf, was beginning to show clear signs of mental deterioration; this culminated in crisis in February 1854, when he attempted suicide by plunging into the Rhine River.

In May, after Robert was admitted as an inmate at an asylum near Bonn, Clara gave birth to their seventh child. Throughout this difficult time, she was not permitted to visit Robert, and her principal source of emotional support was the young Brahms, who began to bring her, as she recovered from childbirth, individual piano variations on Robert's *Albumblatt*. The result of this recuperation was Brahms's own set of *Varia-*

tions on a Theme by Robert Schumann, published in 1854 as his Op. 9, an extraordinary work that impresses as a kind of musical journal of the artistic relationship between the Schumanns and Brahms.

The variation set comprises Schumann's theme and sixteen variations, which divide into two halves of eight variations each. In the first half, Brahms retains the tonic key of F♯ minor, thereby imposing a somewhat arbitrary tonal coherence. But the treatment of the theme in the first eight variations is anything but arbitrary. In the first variation, the theme is inverted to the bass, and in the second, the theme is rhythmically reshaped by means of a syncopated figure and metrically altered (from 2/4 to 9/8), so that it is more or less fully disguised. In the third, Brahms indulges in a play of register, continually crossing the hands, so that the theme appears now in the treble and now in the bass; in addition, he begins to introduce harmonies foreign to the orbit of F♯ minor, giving the theme an additional disguise. The fourth variation, marked Poco più moto, reestablishes a melodic line in the soprano, but a line that, again, seems well removed from the original theme. In the fifth and sixth variations, a capricious scherzo punctuated by staccato octaves and a turbulent Allegro, we lose more or less all traces of the original theme. In the seventh, a subdued Andante, individual pitches from the theme are frozen and sustained through a shifting series of expressive sonorities. Only in the eighth variation does Brahms reintroduce the theme, intact, in the soprano, but now a new compositional technique is deployed in the bass. What initially appears as nothing more than an undulating tremolo accompaniment turns out, on closer inspection, to be a canonic imitation of the theme an octave below.

Brahms's contrapuntal gambit probably owes its inspiration to Clara, who had included a canonic variation in her set. But the turn to artful counterpoint at the midpoint of Brahms's composition, subtly introduced as it is, adumbrates a more prominent development in the second half of the work, in which contrapuntal techniques emerge in full prominence. Thus, in the tenth variation, the bass line of the theme is set against its mirror inversion. In the fourteenth variation, Brahms employs canon at the second above, and in the fifteenth, at the sixth below. Including the eighth variation, Brahms thus devotes four variations, or one-fourth, of his composition to contrapuntal manipulations. The conspicuous use of these learned techniques is, in itself, an act of homage to Schumann, who, during the 1840s, had studied counterpoint together with Clara, and had examined that most intellectual branch of musical composition in such works as the Six Fugues on BACH for Organ, Op. 60, and the canonic Studies for the Pedal Piano, Op. 56, both from 1845.

Two other features of the second half of Brahms's Op. 9 also call for special comment. First, Brahms now moves away from the tonic key of F# minor, prolonged through the first eight variations, in order to explore the subdominant B minor (No. 9), submediant D major (No. 10), Neapolitan G major (No. 11), and G♭ major (No. 15), before concluding (as did Clara in her variation set) in F# major (No. 16). These tonal excursions are accompanied by a remarkable series of thematic allusions to other works by Schumann. Thus in No. 9, Brahms invokes the B-minor *Albumblatt* from Schumann's *Bunte Blätter,* Op. 99, and in No. 10 not only alludes to the slow movement of Schumann's String Quartet Op. 41/1 but quotes the theme of his Impromptus, Op. 5 (a theme, as mentioned earlier, that Robert, in turn, had borrowed from Clara's *Romanze*). The fourteenth variation seemingly alludes to the nocturne-like piece "Chopin" from Schumann's piano cycle *Carnaval,* Op. 9. And finally, in No. 16, Brahms extracts the bass line of Schumann's theme, accompanying it with sparse chords in the treble, a distinctive texture that brings to mind the conclusion of Schumann's Impromptus, Op. 5. In sum, Brahms's variation set evolves as a process of thematic invention and discovery to become a work imbued with Schumann's characteristic love of quotation, allusion, and carnivalesque masks.

R. Larry Todd

11 Variations on an Original Theme in D; 13 Variations on a Hungarian Song in D, Opus 21
Composed 1857, 1856; published 1861

The year 1856 saw Brahms undertaking a "correspondence course" in counterpoint with his friend Joseph Joachim in which the two criticized each other's compositions. When Joachim sent him some variations on an Irish folk song, Brahms—who had already written variation movements in the piano sonatas Opp. 1 and 2, and one independent set on a theme by Robert Schumann, Op. 9—was moved to make general remarks critical of both Joachim and himself:

> From time to time I reflect on variation form and find that it should be kept stricter, purer. The Ancients were very strict about retaining the bass of the

theme, their actual theme. With Beethoven the melody, harmony, and rhythm are so beautifully varied. I sometimes find, however, that the Moderns (both of us!) more often (I don't know the right expression) worry the theme. We anxiously retain the entire melody, but don't manipulate it freely. We don't really create anything new out of it; on the contrary, we only burden it. The melody thus becomes scarcely recognizable.

Later that year, Brahms turned again to writing variations, in a pair of works that reveal a new tendency evident in his compositions: exploring different ways of varying a theme that arise from the nature of the theme itself. The two Op. 21 variation sets have rarely been regarded as a pair because Brahms's friend and biographer Max Kalbeck asserted that the *Hungarian Song* Variations (No. 2) were written before Op. 9, possibly as early as 1853, shortly after his trip with the Hungarian violinist Eduard Reményi. (Brahms wrote down the theme twice in that year.) There has also been a widespread perception that No. 1 repudiates rather than complements No. 2 in that it is "stricter and purer," while Brahms was later critical of No. 2 (in a letter of 1869 to the critic Adolf Schubring). But there is no evidence of No. 2 before 1856, and Brahms's own catalog merely lists No. 1 as "beginning of 1857" and No. 2 as "earlier?" Moreover, Brahms's interest in things Hungarian was rekindled in early 1856, when Clara returned from a concert tour there. The most significant common features of the two sets appear in no other independent set by Brahms: minor-mode variations limited to a single large group, a linking of most of the major variations by melody or speed of figuration, and a "finale" that includes a reworking of the first variation. The greater sophistication of No. 1 reflects not a development away from No. 2, but a response to its more sophisticated theme, Brahms's first to be composed especially for variations. Moreover, each set appears to draw on one of the two Beethoven sets that Brahms had performed earlier in 1856: No. 2 recalls the C-minor Variations, WoO 80, with its eight-measure theme and group of opposite mode variations where the theme melody goes into the bass, while No. 1 employs the constant-harmony techniques with only occasional melodic references that characterize Beethoven's E♭-major *Eroica* set for piano, Op. 35.

The theme in the Hungarian set, with its alternating measures of triple meter and common time, its syncopations and stamping energy, is a mere eight measures long, and is immediately "contradicted" by an initial large grouping of variations in the minor (Vars. 1–6). These flamboyant *minores* cohere as pairs and small groups based on rhythm while keeping the theme's melody recognizable and placing it either in the bass (as in Vars. 1 and 3), the treble (Vars. 4 and 6), or divided between them (Vars. 2 and 5). The long series of variations in major that follow (7–13) connects Variations 8–11 by a pervasive tonic pedal and Variations 9–13 by an increase in both dynamics and rhythmic speed. Variation 9, a later poetic insertion, is pivotal in altering the metrical pattern of the theme and introducing a new melodic pattern that returns in the bass of Variations 10 and 11. As a climax to the long chain of variations increasing in their speed of figuration, the Allegro Finale is a rondo whose refrain, a variation of the theme, gave Brahms a good bit of trouble. In a letter to Joachim, he wrote: "Particularly in the Finale a nasty youth is simply raging, and I'd very much like to fashion a more respectable fellow, not raising a racket as sometimes [happened] in the sonatas." He also mentions that Clara did not care for the appearance of B♭ minor in the Finale, in a section recalling the explosive impact of Variation 1. Possibly the criticisms from his friends prompted Brahms to revise the Finale, whose autograph manuscript looks different from the other pages. Such revisions might have overlapped with the composition of Op. 21/1, and accounted for the aforementioned question mark in Brahms's catalog ("earlier?").

In contrast to the Hungarian song, the much longer theme of Op. 21/1 is poetic and contemplative, with an extended tonic pedal for the first six and last five measures. Nearly all of the major variations form pairs (Vars. 1 and 2, 3 and 4, 5 and 6) in which the second intensifies some aspect of the first, while the minor group (Vars. 8–10) provides the last element before the Finale (the major-minor arrangement opposite to that of Op. 21, No. 2). The Finale is a kind of expanded variation-as-coda whose continuing trill and increasing figuration recall the last variation of Beethoven's E-major Piano Sonata, Op. 109. In figuration and affect, this set looks back to the Schumann set, Op. 9 (the canonic Var. 5, the espressivo agitato of Var. 10) and also forward to Brahms's *Handel* Variations, Op. 24 (the syncopated Var. 3, the martial, dotted Var. 8). At the same time it seems to mark the emergence of Brahms's own voice in variations, beholden neither to a characteristic theme (a national dance or song, for example) nor a beloved mentor. The theme is neither "worried" nor "burdened," but often simply taken as an outline to be filled in, whether in structure, harmony, or melodic contour.

Elaine Sisman

25 VARIATIONS AND FUGUE ON A THEME BY HANDEL IN B♭, OPUS 24
Composed 1861; published 1862

Wagner said that Brahms's *Handel* Variations showed "what could still be done with the old forms," a grudging but genuine acknowledgment of the work's power, reported by Max Kalbeck. Brahms himself called it his *Lieblingswerk* (favorite piece), and Clara Schumann, for whom it was written as a birthday present, described it as uniting art and inspiration. Indeed, by choosing a theme from Handel's *Suite de Pièces pour le Clavecin* (second volume, 1733, an aria already given five variations by Handel), Brahms signaled his intention to explore the heritage of the form. But generalized Baroque elements—including the canonic Variations 6 and 16, the "music box" of the Couperin era (Var. 22), the Siciliana (Var. 19)— are by no means Brahms's only models here. One could also point to myriad other specific appropriations of rhythmic and textural ideas from the great variation sets of the past, notably Bach's *Goldberg* and Beethoven's *Diabelli* Variations, as well as contemporary styles. The very first variation, for example, stands in the same relation to the theme as the first of the *Goldberg* Variations: a rhythmically active recasting of the constructive segments of the aria, even using the same sixteenths-and-eighth pattern in the right hand (dactyl) against an eighth-and-sixteenths pattern in the left (anapest). The "galloping" anapest figurations of Brahms's Variations 7 and 8 recall the fifteenth of the *Diabelli* set, perhaps mediated by the identical rhythms in the third of Schubert's *Death and the Maiden* quartet variations (a work which already resonated powerfully in the tolling conclusion to the variations in the String Sextet Op. 18 and its piano arrangement). The sparkling *sciolto* Variation 14, with its ascending-octave bass line and trilled right-hand attack, evokes the Allegro Var. No. 16 of the *Diabelli;* the playfully imitative Variation 3, that of Beethoven's Nos. 11 and 19; the Romantic chromaticisms of Variations 2 and 20 perhaps extend those of Beethoven's Nos. 3 and 12. More general topical references to contemporary styles include étude (Vars. 2, 4, 21, 24), introspective character-piece (Vars. 5, 12), triumphal march (Var. 25), and Hungarian rhapsody (Var. 13), now with the gravity of an overture, perhaps to introduce the second "half" of the variations much as the *Goldberg* Variations have an explicit *ouverture* at their midpoint in Variation 16.

The strictness of the piece is often noted, yet the term does not seem adequate to describe such richly expressive variations. Once again, Brahms's own words on variation help to identify his approach. Writing to the critic Adolf Schubring in February 1869, Brahms made trenchant comments that placed himself within a historical lineage:

[I]n a theme for [a set of] variations, it is almost only the bass that *actually* has any meaning for me. But this is sacred to me, it is the firm foundation on which I then build my stories. . . . If I vary only the melody, then I cannot easily be more than clever or graceful, or, indeed, [if] full of feeling, deepen a pretty thought. On the given bass, I invent something actually new, I discover new melodies in it, I create. . . .

He told his composition pupil Gustav Jenner that "the bass is more important than the melody," not because it remains exactly the same, but because a variation of the bass can modify the entire character of the melody more strongly than can a variation of that melody only. By the bass, he clearly did not mean just the bass *line*, but rather a broader *basis*, including the harmonic structure, the melodic contour, and the underlying motives: a kind of distilled essence. In fact, identifying the bass as the most important element of the theme enabled him to project radical recastings of the theme's elements against a relatively stable background, the "firm ground" on which he "builds his stories."

One of the most rewarding aspects of the piece from the performer's point of view is Brahms's consistent attention to inner lines (Vars. 2, 11, 12) and to strongly profiled thematic elements in the left hand (Vars. 12, 17, shared by left and right in 18), usually in the more lyrical variations. These enable the pianist to vary the performance of the repeats by a change of emphasis, bringing out now the upper, now the inner line, and thus to expose some of the intricate motivic connections between theme and variations. The theme itself, only eight measures long but with repeats, was memorably described by Max Kalbeck as "chiseled from marble." Its clearly defined motives—three ascending steps (m. 1), lower-neighbor figure (left hand, mm. 1, 2), three repeated notes (upper notes of left hand, m. 1), contrary motion (m. 5)—give rise to numerous intricate variants. Moreover, each variation takes up a new rhythmic motive (or longer pattern) in a new texture. In Variation 2, for example, in the context of a three-against-two étude, the neighbor figure is elaborated in triplets against a contrary-motion bass, while the newly chromatic linear motion gives rise to new harmonic goals and the first minor inflections in the piece. The harmonic language continues, on a somewhat smaller scale, the substitutional harmonies Brahms associated with his *Schumann Variations*, Opp. 9 and 23. The melody of the second phrase moves up to the third degree while remaining in the tonic; in Variations 5, 6, 7, 9, 11, 13, 14, 19, and 20, the key follows suit, moving up a third to the mediant: D minor in major-mode variations, D♭ major in minor-mode variations, the sole exception being in Variation 9, D major in major mode. Variation 9 also writes out the repeat of the second half in order to elevate its first phrase to F♯ major, a magical moment in which the solemn progression of octaves in contrary motion is lit from within.

The fugue not only caps the apparently untoppable final variation; it also recrosses the motivic and harmonic territory of the set. The fugue subject, a distillation of thematic motifs with the contour of the theme melody, is heard in inversion (creating contrary motion) and augmentation, as well as in the tonic minor, D♭ and G♭/F♯ majors, and in the thirds and sixths of so many of the variations. In structure, the fugue also revisits the paired variations like 7 and 8, 11 and 12, 23 and 24, each of which increases in intensity, as well as the chain of decreasing intensity and greater lyricism in 14 to 18, because the buildup in thickness and dynamics occurs during paired subject areas, while the quieter lyrical passages function as episodes. Finally, the tolling right-hand octaves, recalling the chimes at the end of the fancy-dress ball in Schumann's *Papillons,* form a brilliant conclusion over the entire range of the piano.

Elaine Sisman

STUDIES FOR PIANO: 28 VARIATIONS ON A THEME BY PAGANINI IN A MINOR, OPUS 35
Composed 1862–63; published 1866

Brahms designated these pieces primarily as "studies" and secondarily as "variations," even if they are now more typically listed by their subtitle than by their main title. If this designation provides a credible explanation for the peculiar fact that he published them as two independent books of fourteen "studies" each, the explanation is partial at best, for he clearly intended them as much for public performance as for private practice, as indicated by the substantial coda he provided for each book.

Brahms's pianistic studies with the virtuoso Carl Tausig during the early 1860s, in some ways analogous to his earlier studies in composition with Joseph Joachim, were the most immediate inspiration for Op. 35.

On a more practical level, these variations helped Brahms to bridge the gap between the studio and the concert hall; he referred to the works as his "finger exercises" and used them precisely in that way, yet performed them in public as a prideful demonstration of his sometimes disputed credentials as a virtuoso pianist. More broadly, Brahms's choice of theme indicates a network of compositional influences. Paganini's artistic virtuosity, preserved above all in his *Twenty-four Caprices,* had already inspired pianists of the previous generation to both emulation and imitation, as they attempted in their individual ways to place virtuosity in the service of art, in many cases using Paganini as a direct model. Thus, Chopin's *Etudes,* Liszt's *Grandes Etudes de Paganini* and *Etudes d'exécution transcendante d'a près Paganini,* and Schumann's *Studien nach Capricen von Paganini* (Op. 3), *Etudes de concert d'après des Caprices de Paganini* (Op. 10), and *Etudes symphoniques* virtually define the genre to which Brahms was contributing. More specifically, Brahms carefully situated his two sets among those of Paganini, Liszt, and Schumann. Thus, he chose the theme of Paganini's Caprice No. 24, which also presents technical studies in the form of variations, equally appropriate for practice or performance. Moreover, Brahms chose a caprice that Schumann had not arranged, but that Liszt had used to conclude his set, so that Brahms's Op. 35 augments Schumann's two sets of *Paganini* Studies while effectively displacing Liszt's less ambitious adaptation of the Twenty-fourth Caprice; this indication of his affiliation with Schumann and against Liszt finds possible echoes both in Brahms's publication of two parallel sets and in his title, which, like Schumann's in Op. 3, uses the less common designation of "Studien" rather than "études." And, finally, the structural parallel between Paganini's Twenty-fourth Caprice and Schumann's *Etudes symphoniques,* alternatively titled *Etudes en forme de variations,* provided Brahms with the kind of nested model he liked to use as a compositional starting point, at the same time allying him once again with Schumann.

In concert, Brahms's Op. 35 presents the performer with problems logistical as well as technical, for each set offers a complete, self-sufficient treatment of the theme. Clara Schumann objected to the arrangement in two books, urging cuts and a rearrangement into one set. Presumably, she would have excised (or, perhaps, exorcised) the more difficult "witch" variations she could not master, although her inability to perform them may have been a moot point after her failure to please either Brahms or her audiences with his *Handel* Variations. Brahms's preferred solution, as offered to Moriz Rosenthal, was to perform the first set and continue with the second if the audience hadn't had enough; thus, the second book might serve as an encore for the first. Yet this is less than satisfactory, and gives the impression of a somewhat tedious retelling of a story already concluded, not only starting over with the same "Once upon a time" but, for most audiences, deviating only slightly from the first telling, with differences more technical than aesthetic. One has to think that Brahms's "solution" was offered partly in jest, for who would be expected to prepare the entire second book—scarcely shorter nor less difficult than the first—purely on the disingenuous speculation that an encore might be requested after the first book? In any case, Brahms did give his blessing to integrated performances of the two sets; one such arrangement (performed by Heinrich Barth in 1880) incorporated three variations from the second set within a truncated version of the first, comprising a total of twelve variations.

Despite their shared parentage, however, the two sets have distinct personalities. The shape of book 1 is determined partly by an ostinato element that first appears in Variations 2 through 4, resurfacing in the later major-mode variations (11 and 12). In the second book, a number of elements introduced in the first book emerge with greater force. Thus, the violinistic tone of the theme itself, effectively canceled by overt pianism early in the first book (notwithstanding the arpeggiations of Variation 3), is pointedly recalled in book 2: in Variation 6, when Paganini's infamous left-hand pizzicato is suggested by the left-hand grace notes added to an otherwise unaccompanied right hand; in Variation 8, when Brahms specifies that the staccato should be rendered *quasi pizz.;* and in the forceful unison gestures that dominate Variations 9 and 10 and much of the coda. A typical Brahmsian play with cross-rhythms, incidentally indulged in the first book, is intensified in the second, with the three-against-two textures of Variations 1, 2, and 5, and the coda; the alternating 6/8 and 3/4 configuration of Variation 12; an occasional five-against-two texture in Variation 14; and, most extraordinarily, the nine-against-four texture heard throughout Variation 7.

There is some indication as well that Brahms did consider the larger span—that is, embracing both books within one gesture—even if he does not manage to temper significantly the deadening effect of a story twice-told. Thus, we might note the intensifications in the second book of devices introduced in the first, and the spacing of more relaxed variations across the two books. A more subtle indication is his deployment of another typical Brahmsian device—a kind of mirror-image counterpoint, with one hand simultaneously reflecting the other—which occurs mainly in the early stages of the first book and in the later stages of the second, thus helping to define a larger shape for the whole.

Raymond Knapp

12

MISCELLANEOUS WORKS FOR PIANO

SCHERZO IN E♭ MINOR, OPUS 4
Composed 1851; published 1854

The Scherzo Op. 4, composed in August 1851, is the earliest surviving work by Brahms to which a firm date of origin can be attached. Just over eighteen years old, Brahms was a young pianist-composer who had still not ventured far beyond his native Hamburg and a fairly restrictive musical training. The Scherzo thus offers a fascinating glimpse into a musical mind very much in the formative stages of development.

Any composer sitting down to write an independent scherzo for piano at mid-century would almost certainly have had Chopin as a model. It is thus odd that the pianist William Mason reported (many years later) that in 1853 Brahms denied having been familiar with Chopin's music when he wrote Op. 4. To be sure, Brahms's teacher Eduard Marxsen is known to have kept the young pianist on a strict diet of Bach and the Classical masters. But it is unlikely that Brahms could have escaped exposure to Chopin, to whose Scherzos (especially No. 2 in B♭ minor and No. 4 in C♯ minor) Brahms is clearly indebted in genre, musical style, and even details of phrase structure. (Later in life Brahms became a proud admirer, and editor, of Chopin's music.)

Brahms's Scherzo, which last about nine minutes in performance, is (like those of Chopin) built sectionally. A scherzo proper alternates with two large, independent trios. The Scherzo itself is a free and imaginative adaptation of sonata form. After a repeated exposition that modulates to the minor dominant (an unusual choice of key), the "development" is dominated by a bold new theme in the tonic, which some commentators have interpreted as a reference to Heinrich Marschner's opera *Hans Heiling* (1832).

The first Trio, in the key of the parallel major, E♭, is a study in contrast between descending octave passages and quirky melodic phrases that are harmonically and rhythmically open-ended. The second Trio, marked Molto expressivo, dips to a more remote, third-related tonality, B major, confirmation of which is, however, kept skillfully at bay by a broad, Chopinesque melody in C♯ minor over a flowing arpeggiated accompaniment.

Even in this early work we can see an interest in thematic coherence and development that suggests how thoroughly Brahms had studied—and valued—his Haydn, Mozart, and Beethoven. He attempts to impart continuity across Op. 4 by motivically linking the different segments. Thus, for example, the descending scale that forms the main theme of Trio I derives from a similar figure near the opening of the Scherzo and reappears in still another form as a melody over the rolling accompaniment in Trio II.

Whatever it may owe to Chopin and other composers, the piano idiom of Op. 4 is also very characteristic of what we will come to associate with the mature Brahms. The thick chordal style, often with doubled thirds and sixths in the right hand, is an especially Brahmsian fingerprint. Also the contrapuntal texture, especially in portions of the Scherzo itself, shows that even in 1851 Brahms had an interest in the genuinely polyphonic capabilities of the keyboard. These pianistic elements are joined to, or complemented by, a rhythmic-metric language of great force and originality. It is clear from the Scherzo that by 1850 Brahms had pretty much turned his back on the more superficial, salon-style pianism and piano works of many of his contemporaries. He was already set on a course that would bring Romantic and Classical elements into a unique synthesis.

Walter Frisch

4 BALLADES, OPUS 10
Composed 1854; published 1856

1. Andante
2. Andante

3. Intermezzo. Allegro
4. Andante con moto

The designation of "ballade," when applied to a piece for solo piano, seemed to mean different things to different composers in the nineteenth century. The most celebrated examples of the type remain those by Chopin, who was the first to use the title for non-texted music. Although Chopin's ballades established a fairly consistent generic profile—in which an episodic treatment of songlike material seems to trace an unspecified narrative while avoiding predictable formal outlines—they have inspired much speculation regarding his intentions. And, despite their popularity and presumed influence in spawning a sizable repertory of piano ballades, other composers apparently felt little obligation to use them as models, even in a very general sense. As a result, the piano ballade became a diverse genre marked by a freedom of approach surpassed only by other "wild-card" genres such as the fantasia, capriccio, and rhapsody. Although the title "ballade" implies at least some connection to the type of narrative poem or song that bears the same name, this connection is typically manifest mainly in terms of its evocative material and tone, and resists codification.

While Brahms's Op. 10 Ballades seem to have no obvious model, they—like many ballades written after mid-century—are more in keeping with Mendelssohn's lyrical *Songs without Words* than with Chopin's dramatic conception of the type. But the Brahms set also stands apart from more general trends, for it seems to be the first instance of a genuine Ballade *cycle*, with four individual pieces intended to be performed together. If this much seems clear from various musical connections among the four, and from Brahms's designation of the third piece as Intermezzo, which was only later used by him as a title for independent pieces, there remain many points of confusion.

Are all four pieces ballades? After all, none is individually labeled as such, and the third is distinguished from the rest as an Intermezzo. Might we not be better off understanding only the first piece as a genuine ballade? While Herder's translation of *Edward* was the basis for the opening piece, none of the others has a specified poetic source. If we are to understand the set as a cycle, do the individual pieces function as part of a larger narrative, as in many song cycles? Or are they related only as musical statements, as seems more likely? And, if the latter, what are we to make of the fact that the cycle ends in a key quite distant from that of the opening, despite the close relationship between the keys of the successive pieces? The lack of traditional harmonic closure seems odd unless we imagine some kind of narrative progression across the individual pieces.

These and related questions may perhaps be put aside, if not to rest, with the reminder that the designation of "ballade" and "intermezzo" are emblems of a Romantic vagueness that was particularly attractive to Brahms during the mid-1850s, just after meeting Robert and Clara Schumann, along with others of their circle, such as Joseph Joachim and Julius Otto Grimm, to whom the Ballades are dedicated. Particularly revealing in this regard is Brahms's prominent use of the *F.A.F.* musical motto, which, according to Max Kalbeck, he adopted during this period. Standing for "Frei aber Froh" (free but happy), in response to Joachim's motto "Frei aber Einsam" (free but lonely), Brahms's motto purportedly stems from Schumann's practice of using musical ciphers to imbue musical motifs with private significance. Thus, Brahms's second piece begins with a version of the motto (F♯–A–F♯), immediately repeated), which serves as the basis for much of the figuration in the final two pieces in the cycle. To be sure, this indication of a possible personal significance does not actually explain much to us, beyond reinforcing an air of secrecy and the kind of hidden meanings that are probably not meant to be deciphered.

What does seem clear, however, is that Brahms wanted the four pieces, when performed together, to project an open-ended musical continuity—suitably ballade-like—based on a linear progression of keys and a recycling of motives and textures from the earlier pieces in the later ones. Thus, for example, he uses a special kind of counterpoint throughout the cycle, in which one hand plays an inverted version of the other, and he manages a kind of leap-frog harmonic continuity through the succession of keys within and across the four pieces.

Even if the words of Herder's translation fit only imperfectly beneath the opening sections of the first Ballade, *Edward,* the probing questions and evasive responses of the original poem, concerning the blood dripping from Edward's knife, are vividly reproduced. In particular, Brahms seems to suggest Edward's duplicity by switching the upper and lower melodic lines for his second response to his mother's questions. It has been suggested that Brahms here reworked an intended vocal setting as a non-programmatic solo piece, or, alternatively, recast the poetic ballade in programmatic terms. Neither explanation is completely satisfying, however. If the intensification of the dialogue in the middle section may be taken programmatically, the correspondence here to a vocal model is tenuous at best. And the concluding, abbreviated return to the opening, however satisfying in musical terms, cannot be convincingly interpreted as programmatic, for instead of Edward's admission that he has killed his father according to his mother's wishes, we are left with her opening question, seemingly unanswered.

Extending the archlike structure of the opening Ballade, Brahms in the second Ballade (Andante) provides a five-part structure (roughly *A B C B A*), placing the minor-mode digressions of the second and fourth sections, which recall the confrontational dialogues of *Edward*, between more soothing sections, which also recall *Edward*, in motive and texture if not in mood.

The third piece, the Intermezzo, is the shortest of the four, and presents itself almost as a scherzo within a traditional four-movement cycle, especially as it follows the relatively slow and digressive second piece. Its lyrical central "trio" recalls both Edward's initial "answers" in the opening Ballade and the off-beat accompaniment figures of the second piece.

The final piece works many subtle effects. At the outset, the opening melody in 3/4 sounds against an accompaniment that echoes the 6/8 scherzo rhythms of the Intermezzo, taking part in a recurring play with two-against-three rhythmic textures begun in *Edward*. In the middle section, the slow-moving melody is placed within the accompaniment instead of above or below it: the indication here is to play "with intimate sentiment but without marking the melody too strongly." Perhaps the most subtly nuanced effect is harmonic, set up with the opening slide into the major mode from the minor; the payoff in this case is reserved for the end, when an extended return to the music of the middle section, in the tonic minor, slides inevitably back into the major with a final return of the opening.

Raymond Knapp

8 Piano Pieces, Opus 76
Composed 1878; published 1879

1. Capriccio. Un poco agitato
2. Capriccio. Allegretto non troppo
3. Intermezzo. Grazioso
4. Intermezzo. Allegretto grazioso
5. Capriccio. Agitato, ma non troppo presto
6. Intermezzo. Andante con moto

7. Intermezzo. Moderato semplice
8. Capricco. Grazioso ed un poco vivace

With the publication of Op. 76 in 1879, Brahms introduced his first instrumental masterpieces in miniature. Here he eschews the extroverted virtuosic style of his previous sonatas or variations and, in the suite-like organization of the work, avoids the multi-movement, large structural statements of his chamber pieces. In the process, he discovers a more intimate, subtly nuanced palette of colors while relinquishing none of his characteristic control over motivic development, complexity of thought, tonal relationships, and their consequences. These brief masterworks are distinguished by a sense of balance in which every aspect of compositional technique is amply in evidence, but it is the ebb and flow of feeling that dominates the surface of the composition: the cadential, modulatory, and motivic elements work in the service of a romantic imagination finding expression. Although performing the pieces requires an accomplished pianist, there is never a moment when a display of virtuosity overshadows the development of the composition or disrupts the mood of the work. In this regard, these works have more in common with Schubert's *Moments musicaux* and Schumann's short works than they do with Chopin, whose Preludes are more self-consciously original and owe their pianistic flamboyance more to ornamentation (at its highest level) than they do to motivic development.

These eight pieces are divided evenly between capriccios and intermezzos, whose contrasting moods of activity and repose are underpinned more by a loose scheme of keys than by formal procedures. Taken as a whole, the capriccios assume the role of greater structural weight, at the beginning of the set (Nos. 1 and 2), in the middle (No. 5), and at the end (No. 8), while the intermezzos provide moments for relaxation and introversion. The first two capriccios flow together from the churning emotions of the first in F♯ minor into the playfulness of the second in B minor. The dominant-tonic relationship of these keys on the sharp side of the circle of fifths is then balanced in mood and harmony by the following two intermezzos, both of which explore the flat side: A♭ (No. 3) and B♭ (No. 4). Number 5 is the stormy center of gravity, like a concentrated knot of intensity in C♯ minor that is gradually smoothed out through the next two intermezzos in A major (No. 6) and A minor (No. 7). The process is then completed by the last capriccio, which settles into the purer realm of C major. Such an anomalous succession of keys would be quite unusual in a sonata-style framework; certainly Brahms was stimulated by the freedom of composing within a less formal structure that allowed him to make such a proposition and carry it through to its resolution.

The gradual and intuitive grounding of large-scale form through a sequence of movements reflects the nature of the works within their own forms. In each piece, a pervasive ambiguity of rhythm and local harmonic color takes place within a greater, simpler harmonic structure. The triadic harmony gradually becomes more clearly delineated through root movement in the bass—most pieces end with long dominant-tonic pedals in the bass. They all share the feeling at the end that as the harmonic framework becomes more stable and the original ambiguity disappears, the hidden potentials of the motives continue to reveal themselves. The result is strikingly different from that of the short piano works of Beethoven, such as the sets of Bagatelles (which undoubtedly served as an inspiration for Brahms). In Beethoven, the drive toward more concentration takes place primarily in his larger works, in which small motives become the source of entire movements. Conversely, in his smaller works, the ideas themselves tend to be more long-breathed. Brahms, however, unifies the two styles through regular (and irregular) Romantic, songlike phrases within which his motives are subject to continuous, concentrated variation and development.

Although the capriccios tend toward more formal sophistication and surface activity, in both genres Brahms's technique of "developing variation" is equally noticeable. This technique, which he refined throughout his career, reached a new level of subtlety during the years he wrote these compositions. As in the first movement of his Second Symphony, Op. 73, the material is audibly spun out from the opening motives through sequences, transposition, invertible counterpoint, inversion, augmentation, etc. In such a large sonata-form movement as the Symphony, Brahms must fashion several highly contrasting themes and characters in order to create large, dramatic periods, but in these short works, the smallest nuances of texture create slight shadings of a single feeling.

One aspect of the developing variation that is amply in evidence is a procedure that could be called the motivic drive to opacity: a motive or interval (an inner voice, for example) that at first goes unnoticed and is therefore transparent, gradually assumes a more prominent role and becomes more opaque. Thus in No. 1, from the very first measure, the agitated, restless mood of the piece is established by shifting accents in a descending three-note motif that is transposed up an octave within the first half of each measure. The second phrase introduces a melodic four-note motive into the foreground and drives the piece through sequential modulations, as the three-note descent unifies the two sections by slipping into the accompaniment. The octave as an interval of transposition is almost imperceptible, but by the time of the return to the key of F♯, the octave has been integrated into the three-note motive itself to form a delicate filigree in the right hand above the repeat of the restless opening material. As this filigree condenses, the octave plays a more prominent role, until oscillating octaves have been distilled out of the texture and are all that remain in the spent quintuplets of the written-out ritard. Simultaneously, the complex relationship of minor seconds, both chromatic and diatonic (particularly of the flat-sixth degree), become more starkly audible, culminating in the final octave appoggiaturas (D–C♯) before the closing chords.

This tendency toward opacity is not necessarily the audible end of a goal-directed form. In the more modest pieces, such as No. 7, there is no finale-like summation; rather, a passionate theme is framed by a more placid, elegiac processional. In the first section, a repeated chromatic neighbor and a syncopation appear separately and without immediate consequences, but these fleeting ideas are combined at the very beginning of the contrasting section to create the more plaintive, agitated mood that is the driving force of the central melody. The potential of the ideas is revealed in the middle of the frame, and at the end they are themselves recalled in their original context.

Even in such a carefree, dancelike piece as No. 2, not one element is introduced that does not somehow play a role in the outcome. All of the intervals of the sixteenth-note melody become the subject of variation. Brahms mines the character of the legato inner voice to create the central melody. It is this inner voice, embedded in the texture toward the end of the piece, that eventually seizes control and leads the work chromatically downward as it relaxes into its conclusion.

While the second melody in No. 4 is spun out of the first chiefly through inversion, its undulating accompaniment is kept firmly if subtly in place by inner pedals. This technique allows the bass part the freedom to imitate the melodic voice until it gradually assumes the role of pedal point toward the end of each phrase. During this time, an E♭ is quietly insistent as the inner pedal of the first phrase and its restatement, until in the final measures it springs to life as full-fledged harmony in a sudden E♭-minor arpeggio.

In Nos. 3, 5, 6, and 8, Brahms exhibits a unique, rhythmic flexibility exceeding that of any composer before Debussy. In the turbulent, rhythmic complex of No. 5, the theme itself consists of characteristic Brahmsian cross-rhythms; a chromatic inner voice of steady eighth notes mediates between the firm duple octaves of the bass and the increasingly intense melodic triplets of the top voice. This effect is varied and intensified through a rhythmic transformation when the meter switches obsessively back and forth between 2/4 and 6/8, and through enjambment over the bar-line as, in the coda, Brahms pulls together the very basis of all of the motives into a rhythmic fusillade condensed into five eighth-note patterns that simultaneously expand and contract to six eighths and, finally, an insistent nine eighths before the final cadence.

Brahms's rhythmic explorations lead not only to formal inventiveness but also to the great mystical lyricism of his work. In No. 3, the high tessitura and regular rhythm in the left hand generate a certain serenity that is contradicted by the breathlessness of the constant syncopations in the right hand. When these syncopations finally come to rest on a downbeat chord, they are followed by the surprising introduction of triplets, which, while already a new rhythmic element, are also felt more as groups of four and five (because of their melodic shape and occasional grace notes) than as a regular pattern of three. In No. 6, the hands switch their relationship between triplets and duplets in each phrase of the piece and the syncopations of the left hand become more stable in the second section, which forms the basis for the coda. In the final piece, No. 8, the virtuosity of the pianist comes into the foreground and the range of the keyboard is wider than it is in the previous pieces. Although this capriccio represents the resolution of the previous explorations into a mood of joy and uplift, the rhythmic complexity, matched by the harmonic variety, make this resolution no straightforward matter. Brahms characteristically avoids the C-major triad itself until near the end of the work, and the weak-beat accents throw the weight of the harmony constantly into the next measure. Unlike in his large sonata forms, all of the conflicts, stormy and reticent, of the previous movements are resolved within themselves, leaving this last piece the latitude to be the least resolved, the least harmonically grounded, and the most joyous in its freedom.

As uniquely structured and intuitive as the forms of these pieces may seem, the experiments begun here are a point of departure that Brahms continued to explore in his later sets of short piano works. Even more important, these discoveries in a freer context were incorporated into his sonata structures. In the Third Symphony, for example, a Romance (i.e., intermezzo) becomes worthy of a symphonic context (i.e., the third movement). Brahms became universally hailed as a master of form because the discoveries he made in pieces such as these miniatures infused his larger works with a formal integration and originality that never superseded the possibility for intimacy, introspection, and finely crafted nuance.

Mark Mandarano

2 RHAPSODIES, OPUS 79
Composed 1879; published 1880
I. Agitato; II. Molto passionato, ma non troppo allegro

The year 1879 found Brahms in the middle of his most productive period, and in a hiatus between orchestral efforts—the previous summer's Violin Concerto and the next summer's two Overtures, and with the Second Piano Concerto in progress. In the summer of 1879, Brahms produced the gently lyrical First Violin Sonata and followed up the eight piano miniatures of Op. 76—in some degree probably earlier work—with the Two Rhapsodies of Op. 79. Together, these two summers' keyboard pieces are the only purely piano works Brahms had composed since the Sixteen Waltzes of 1865 (if we accept that the *St. Antoni* Variations for two pianos are a stop en route to an orchestral work), and the last before the late piano works of 1892–93. In short, having impressed the Schumanns early on with his piano sonatas, and being admittedly more comfortable composing for the piano than for any other medium, Brahms paradoxically gave up sonatas entirely, resorting to collections of Romantic-style miniatures, and spent the heart of his career barely composing solo piano music at all.

The biographical question, then, has always been why Brahms produced this small burst of piano miniatures in the later 1870s, and more particularly: Why the tumultuous, impassioned, High Romantic tone of the Op. 79 Rhapsodies, so much in contrast to the comparatively impersonal tone of the other music of this period?

To the degree that the question can be answered, the clue lies in the dedication of the Rhapsodies to Elisabet von Herzogenberg, a musical amateur then living in Leipzig with her composer husband, Heinrich. As a teenager, Elisabet had briefly been a pupil of Brahms shortly after he arrived in Vienna. Despite her extraordinary talent as a pianist and potential composer, and a charm of person and personality that were already becoming legendary, Brahms confessed to Julius Epstein that he was afraid of his feelings for her. Then, in 1874, Brahms renewed his acquaintance with Elisabet and befriended her husband; the two together formed the nucleus of a Brahms faction in generally unfriendly Leipzig.

In all of this, Brahms was repeating an old pattern: fleeing from his feelings for a woman, but entering a friendship with the family once she was safely married and admiring the lady from a distance. With Elisabet, however, the connection was far more than that; she had an extraordinary command of music and considerable critical powers. In the 1870s, she became one of the small circle of friends from whom Brahms asked for comment on new works (the others included Clara Schumann and Joseph Joachim). By the period of the Rhapsodies, Brahms depended more on Elisabet than on Clara, and followed her advice more consistently than he generally did with any adviser in his maturity—to the degree of revising and suppressing songs exactly as Elisabet suggested. Perhaps only Joachim's contributions to the Violin Concerto and earlier to the First Piano Concerto rival the impact this female friend had on the music of the old bachelor and misogynist Brahms.

In short, Elisabet von Herzogenberg was one of the most important of Brahms's platonic muses, and hence, perhaps, the tone of the Rhapsodies that he dedicated to her. Both are intense in gesture, with some of the most advanced and restless harmonies Brahms ever wrote: long stretches that refuse to cadence, to rest, even to define the key clearly. Rhapsody No. 1 in B Minor, laid out in *ABA*/coda form, is notable for its swirling rhythms expressing searching harmonies. For contrast, the middle section, though thematically derived from the opening material, is a stretch of placid and lyrical B major. If the main theme of the B-minor Rhapsody is gasping and fiery, the sonata-form G Minor is more compact and flowing, but the tonal implications of its surging opening are remarkably elusive—what Arnold Schoenberg admiringly named "roving harmony." That idea gives way to a second subject highly unusual for Brahms, a pounding, ominous bass line under a repeated triplet figure that grows from soft to loud like a mounting obsession; the idea recurs even more relentlessly in the development section.

Opus Nos. 76 and 79 are well on the way to Brahms's late piano works, which might be called scientific essays in compositional craft in the guise of little salon pieces. How and to what degree the Rhapsodies reflect his tumultuous feelings for Elisabet von Herzogenberg can only be specula-

tion. Certainly, though, they reinforce the impression that under the relentlessly guarded surface of old-bachelor Brahms raged passions that he
only occasionally, and in telling circumstances, allowed to trouble the
usually magisterial surface of his mature music.

Jan Swafford

7 FANTASIAS, OPUS 116
Composed 1892; published 1892

1. Capriccio. Presto energico
2. Intermezzo. Andante
3. Capriccio. Allegro passionato
4. Intermezzo. Adagio
5. Intermezzo. Andante con grazia ed intimissimo sentimento
6. Intermezzo. Andantino teneramente
7. Capriccio. Allegro agitato

Friedrich Schlegel wrote: "A fragment should be like a little work of art,
complete in itself and separated from the rest of the universe like a hedge-
hog." The seven short pieces that constitute Op. 116 bear the general
designation *Phantasien,* in spite of the fact that none of the separate works
are so named; they are either Capriccios or Intermezzos. Number 4, the
central piece, originally bore the title *Notturno.* That Brahms was not
happy with these titles is indicated by his request for help in finding alternate ones from friends. What he meant to signify by *Phantasien* remains provocative but obscure: it may point to a seriousness, a "purely
music" intention in Hanslick's sense, of fantasy as the "true aesthetic
moment of music." At the same time, it hearkens back to the world of
E.T.A. Hoffmann and of Robert Schumann, whose works Brahms was
editing at this time. Qualities of the eccentric, bizarre, and humorous,
noted in Op. 116, are linked to the realms of Hoffmann's *Kreisler* and
Schumann's *Kreisleriana,* the only work of that composer to bear the specific designation *Phantasien;* several interesting parallels exist between the
two sets.

Phantasien is distinguished from the remaining late sets by its network
of interconnections. Brahms's own statement to Simrock, who proposed
to publish the set in two volumes, is ambiguous; he wrote that "the first
two and the last three should be published together." Since the two published volumes contained the first three and the last four, Simrock seems

to have either ignored or misinterpreted Brahms's wish. Jonathan Dunsby takes Brahms's statement as calling for one volume of five pieces, to which two, Nos. 4 and 5, were later added. Although the unusual interdependence of individual pieces in Op. 116 had been noticed (based on motivic correspondences or an overall tonal plan), the specific details of connection and plan were first fully spelled out by Dunsby as complementary elements of a "multi-piece."

The extensive evidence of motivic connections and tonal architecture is convincing, but leaves open the questions of Brahms's original intent and of the aesthetic status of the result. His own comment, when such motivic connections were pointed out, was that he was unaware of them and viewed them as an indication of limited imagination. Despite this typical disclaimer, Op. 116 as a cycle displays a wide variety of formal strategies, a concentrated refinement of keyboard style, an exploration of rhythmic displacement and ambiguity, further blurring of the distinctions between melody and harmony, and a mingling of voices from the composer's past and present, all held in balance by architectonic forces that retain an air of mystery, an atmosphere of the fragmentary and aphoristic.

Freed from the "symphonic imperative" by his "retirement" from composition, Brahms revisited issues of structure while renewing his commitment to the aesthetics of Romanticism. In the privacy of a "confidential relationship" with his "beloved keyboard," as Edwin Evans says, the composer explored the more radical implications of his mature musical language. Metric ambiguities are pushed to new lengths in the final Capriccio (a total of 60 measures including repeats). Passages of fluid meter occur in every piece, but particularly in No. 2, whose middle section is built out of phrases of five-, ten-, and fifteen-measure lengths, marked off by multi-layered note groupings defined in various ways by left-hand patterns, by shapes of figures or melodic phrases (not the same grouping) in the right hand, and by harmonic motion. The relationships of these non-coinciding elements is firmly controlled by Brahms's unfailing sense of variation and tonal direction. As listeners, we wander blindly in this strange terrain, but are benevolently guided by one who lives there.

The three Capriccios evoke Schumann's and earlier Brahms's *Sturm und Drang* manner. While there is no question about the originality of tone and method in No. 1, both No. 3 and No. 7 seem to evoke the clichéd turbulence of the 1820s and 1830s, especially in the latter's use of bare diminished-seventh chords and literal sequences. Seen from the perspective of the "multi-piece," however, such moments offer a framework for the gnomic or fragmentary qualities of the Intermezzos, particularly Nos. 4 and 5. Such characteristics reflect a mood of musical recollection, rather than regression. While the echoes of Brahms's Op. 10 Ballades have been detected in the last three pieces, parallels may also be found between the G-minor Capriccio (No. 3) and No. 7 of *Kreisleriana:* both are in the subdominant area of the principal key of the set, both are built on writhing arpeggiated seventh-chords (especially diminished or half diminished), and both incorporate a marked contrast between turbulence, even violence, and lyrical serenity. In Schumann's case, this last comes in a peaceful coda, while Brahms more conventionally builds songful contrast into the middle of a ternary form, shaping it in swelling phrases (particularly in minor harmonies) that connect to the outer sections. Of all earlier groupings of *Charakterstücke* (not including sets of variations or sectional pieces like the "Arabesque"), the most integrated are *Kreisleriana* and *Carnaval,* which we can view as forerunners of Op. 116.

It is in the Intermezzos, however, that Brahms pushes his harmonic and textural explorations to new lengths. Although the range of modulations may be reduced, voice-leading assumes a new motivic significance. In No. 2 in A minor, the harmony (left hand) includes a chromatic preface to the arriving tonic chord. Two measures later, the identical pattern, with new melody, suggests a harmonic transition, while in the next measure, the very same notes represent a reversal of ornamental and stable tones.

Motivic voice-leading is also responsible for the instability of Intermezzo No. 4, which hovers between E major and C♯ minor, settling at cadences only on the dominants of both, until the very end. This is the least stable "final" cadence and individual tonal structure of the seven. It serves as a fragmentary piece in the center of the set, located between symmetrically arrayed pairs of pieces which share formal types: Nos. 1 and 7 are the most rounded and elaborate, Nos. 2 and 6 are ternary with varied reprises, and Nos. 3 and 5 are simpler ternary forms. Though more harmonically grounded than No. 4, No. 5 uses fragmentation to produce both subtle humor and strong dissonance, generated through ingenious symmetrical action of the hands on the keyboard.

The Intermezzos are all quite delicately scored, and even the interior Capriccio shows surprising textural economy. The final Capriccio asserts its significance in its central section by developing a complex middle-voice melodic (later chordal) texture with surrounding material in contrary motion, and then by linking this to the return of the tonic through a flying cadenza that has elements of Baroque organ music and even Baroque violin style. Its adaptation of bariolage to the piano is spectacular, preparing for the condensed, breathtaking climax of the concluding reprise.

Laurence Wallach

3 INTERMEZZOS, OPUS 117
Composed 1892; published 1892

1. Andante moderato
2. Andante non troppo e con molto espressione
3. Andante con moto

Brahms referred privately to these three Intermezzos as "cradlesongs of my sorrows," and gave the following inscription to the first in the set:

> Schlaf sanft mein Kind, schlaf sanft und schön!
> Mich dauert's sehr, dich weinen sehn.
> (Schottish. Auf Herders *Volksliedern*)

> Sleep softly, my child, sleep softly and well!
> It grieves me much to see you weep.
> (Scottish. From Herder's *Folk Songs*)

As is typical for Brahms, he leaves unstated considerably more than he tells us. Taken by itself, the inscription suggests a simple lullaby, yet it points to much more disturbing subject matter, for the source poem details the bitter sorrow of romantic betrayal and abandonment by the child's father. If we feel encouraged by this to dig still deeper—and Brahms's private reference offers further incentive—we may choose to believe, as many have argued, that the other two Intermezzos have a similar origin and expressive intent, that they too have a poetic basis, and may also be construed as lamenting lullabies. Taken to its extreme, this line of inquiry has led George Bozarth to conclude, following Max Kalbeck, that the first two Intermezzos are settings of stanzas 1–3 and 4–7 of "Schlaf sanft mein Kind," respectively, while the third continues with the next poem in Herder's collection, "O weh! O weh!, hinab ins Thal!" (Oh woe! Oh woe!, deep in the valley). And the claim is eminently plausible, especially when we consider, as Bozarth points out, that Brahms actually copied out both poems in a notebook.

But discovering a poetic basis for the Intermezzos does not help us much with fundamental problems of genre and performance. In other sets of piano pieces by Brahms, in particular the Op. 10 Ballades and the Op. 116 Fantasias, internal musical features have been seen to argue persuasively that the set should be performed as a group, but such claims are seldom made with regard to Op. 117. Even if he was more specific in his title than in others of the late sets (thus, these are not merely *Klavierstücke*), his enumerating them as "*Three* Intermezzos" seems to indicate, as with Op. 79, a collection of individual pieces rather than a genuine cycle. Moreover, the genre of intermezzo, however loosely Brahms might have conceived it, would appear to indicate that they should be performed in between other pieces. Although the suggested poetic basis indicates that the second Intermezzo might reasonably follow the first in performance, especially given the close relationship between their respective keys (E♭ major and B♭ minor), the argument is considerably less persuasive when extended to the third Intermezzo (in C♯ minor). And if, ultimately, the issue of performance must be resolved through a careful consideration of the effect produced by three successive Andante pieces—the latter two, moreover, in the minor mode—most have felt that the intensification of effect does not compensate adequately for the lack in variety.

Yet, the many parallels between the Op. 117 Intermezzos and the Op. 10 Ballades should give us pause. As in Op. 10, Brahms begins Op. 117 with the hint of a poetic source; in both cases, a mother confronts her child with the absence of the father. To be sure, the latter parallel may reasonably seem somewhat forced—after all, there are differences between sleeping babies and bloody knives, even if both are in this case tokens of paternal absence. But the shared basis in Scottish folk poetry, as collected by Johann Gottfried von Herder, and the strategy of heading only the first piece with a poetic source, even if the remaining pieces seem to have a similar inspiration, might encourage us to notice also that Op. 117, no less than Op. 10, offers subtle musical links among the individual pieces, involving motive, texture, and harmony.

The apparent harmonic disjunctures, for example, recall Op. 10 in their open-ended, leap-frog harmonic continuity even if the connection between the first two Intermezzos (in E♭ major and B♭ major) is enforced only after the fact by the retention of a disturbing E♭ in the bass at the beginning of the second Intermezzo. Texturally, all three Intermezzos bury their melodies within figurational textures; the third Intermezzo acts to some extent as a summation of this strategy, frequently placing the melody in an inner voice beneath repeated tonics, as in the opening of the first Intermezzo and, in the middle section, recalling the figurational interweaving of melody and accompaniment that dominates the second Intermezzo. Even more striking are the motivic links among the three Intermezzos, with their obsessive retracings of a melodic minor third; again, this is underscored in the final Intermezzo, especially with its pointed recollections, at the outset, of the stark octaves and rhythmic motif that lead away from the opening "stanza" in the first Intermezzo. Frequently, the deployment of motivic and textural recollections also points to subtle harmonic connections among the Intermezzos. Thus, the transitional passage from the first Intermezzo, to be recalled in the third, approaches D♭ minor (enharmonically, C♯ minor) before settling back into E♭, whereas the figurational leaps in the A-major section of the final Intermezzo, initially to F, from C♯ (enharmonically D♭), and the melodic insistence on D♯ in the outer sections (enharmonically E♭), reinforce subtle harmonic links between the otherwise distant tonalities of A major and B♭ minor in the first case, and C♯ minor and E♭ major in the latter.

Whether performed separately or together, all three Intermezzos offer moments of profound disquiet. In the first Intermezzo, the placid tranquillity of the opening stanza dissolves completely even as its melody continues, and even before the minor-mode middle section, marked pianissimo sempre ma [somehow] molto espressivo. The restless, unstable theme of the second Intermezzo emerges occasionally in the major with more stability, yet an unhappy oscillation between B♭ major and D♭ major near the end leaves this alternative hanging. In the final Intermezzo, it is the major-mode central section, offered tentatively between the more securely declaimed minor-mode sections, that is most disturbing, particularly in its tendency to send unexpected notes floating into the upper register, and to leave them there, unresolved.

Raymond Knapp

6 Piano Pieces, Opus 118

Composed 1892; published 1893

1. Intermezzo. Allegro non assai, ma molto appassionato
2. Intermezzo. Andante teneramente
3. Ballade. Allegro energico
4. Intermezzo. Allegretto un poco agitato
5. Romanze. Andante
6. Intermezzo. Andante, largo e mesto

In 1892 and 1893, as he was turning sixty and had but half a decade remaining in his life, Brahms published four collections of shorter piano pieces: Opp. 116, 117, 118, and 119. These collections, containing twenty pieces in all, rank among the most impressive and individual accomplishments of his final years. The music reveals all of the hallmarks of Brahms's mature style: it is introverted and subdued, darkly muted and deeply serious, and it offers few compensations for the casual listener in the form of easy, expressive effect or outward display. All twenty pieces are lyrical in character, turned inward as if addressed primarily to the composer himself, or at best to a select handful of listeners. In external form, they are entirely unremarkable, cast without exception in straightforward *A B A* forms; they employ a harmonic language that is, when viewed casually, conservative, considering the time of composition; and they remain relatively uniform in rhythm and texture. The comfortable pleasures afforded by superficial rhetoric are abjured. The life of this music resides not on the surface but underneath, partially hidden in its inner, deeper structure. It speaks a language of pronounced technical and expressive concentration, yet one that is also deeply personal, as if transmitted on a one-to-one line of communication.

Opus 118, the third of these collections, contains six pieces, four titled Intermezzo and the remaining two—the third and the fifth—Ballade and Romanze. (These titles may hint at the music's character but they tell us little else.) One recognizes at once that what is heard is not intended for casual communication: seemingly essential information is withheld as the music unfolds, requiring that we struggle to grasp the underlying process. The very first piece, for example, an Intermezzo in A minor, fails to provide a clear definition of its key until it is essentially over, its initial tonic cadence being followed by only a brief, confirming coda. The opening phrase begins forthrightly enough, in F major, but then the music quickly turns toward C major as perhaps a more likely tonal goal. Yet the question of whether C major is tonic or merely the dominant of the originally suggested F remains unanswered; and the exact repeat of the phrase does nothing to settle the matter. By the time a second, longer, and contrasting phrase reaches its conclusion, moreover, it is evident that neither C nor F can prevail: the music has finally found its way to A minor—which is converted to A major during the coda. Stability is hard won, and it remains tentative at best, the tonal ambiguities set out in the initial gestures never being fully resolved.

The difficulty of music to locate its true path, either structurally (as in the search for key) or expressively (as in the search for a proper "tone," always seemingly an issue for Brahms), lies at the heart of the composer's late style and has much to do with those qualities of reticence and regret, of melancholy and longing, so commonly associated with it. One feels that here Brahms is striving for a level of expressive immediacy that is simply no longer readily available to him but has become attainable only through great effort and conscious calculation.

One experiences this feeling with special poignancy in the almost mordantly somber E♭-minor Intermezzo that closes Op. 118. The simple, extremely repetitive unaccompanied figure in the upper register with which the piece begins, encompassing only three different pitches (the first three of the tonic scale), frames a melodic line suspended in uncertainty, unsure of its whereabouts or intentions. This line soon spawns an arpeggiated diminished-seventh accompaniment that appears to evolve directly out of it (a typically Brahmsian feature) but that manages only to intensify the uncertainty. This diminished seventh, in principle capable of resolving in any number of ways (Brahms offers little to restrict the possible meanings), seems determined to avoid them all, arpeggiating forlornly up and down through the lower reaches of the keyboard as if lost in rumination. When it finally does move to a tonic triad, it does so irregularly, and rather than relaxing, moves restlessly beyond it. The articulation of the home key is thus relegated to a passing moment and then immediately abandoned, as if in apology. As in the first Intermezzo, tonic definition is undermined, yet the effect is utterly different, since here there is little doubt about what key we are in. But the tonality asserts itself so indirectly, through shadowy surrogates rather than emphatic representatives, that the result is equally compromised and conflicted.

In this music, Brahms appears to have reached the realization that traditional musical language can remain viable only by reflecting upon its state of disintegration. Traditional functions continue to assert themselves but they demand extraordinary effort and artifice to do so. Consider the fourth Intermezzo, where a quasi-canonic, inversional imitative pattern appears between the lower voices of the two hands in the outer sections (replaced in the middle one by a strict, non-inversional canon at the octave), propelling the music forward as if by some external force. The combination of learned contrapuntal technique and lyrical intimacy projects faithfully—and movingly—that twilight moment in Western music's evolution where the traditional language of post-Renaissance composition is reaching the end of its long blossoming.

Similarly telling are the arcane melodic connections that link the contrasting middle sections of all of these pieces to their outer ones, so that they appear to emerge from their surroundings as if by some mysterious alchemy. Brahms's message seems clear: music can continue to exist only by reflecting upon the very difficulty of its continuing existence.

Robert P. Morgan

4 PIANO PIECES, OPUS 119
Composed 1892; published 1893

1. Intermezzo. Adagio
2. Intermezzo. Andantino un poco agitato
3. Intermezzo. Grazioso e giocoso
4. Rhapsodie. Allegro risoluto

> Johannes Brahms, who is by far the most gifted, if not the only worthy living representative of German Classical music, has, perhaps owing to advancing age, confined himself recently to minor efforts; but even for these gratitude should be displayed while they continue to take the form of such small but exquisite gems for pianoforte solo as the series just published as Opp. 118 and 119.

An English critic, writing in *The Musical Times* on February 1, 1894, greeted the publication of Brahms's final piano works as further extending the tradition of German instrumental music. But in the twentieth century, the composer Arnold Schoenberg would see in these enigmatic miniatures not so much links to the German musical past as signs of Brahms's forward-looking, modernist tendencies in his closing years. For some hundred years, these works have continued to hold a special allure for musical scholars: if the pieces look back, with a certain nostalgia, on Brahms's position as the musical heir of Beethoven, Schubert,

Mendelssohn, and Schumann, they also look forward, in their thematic restraint and formal concision, to the experiments of Schoenberg and his disciples.

Like the Six Piano Pieces, Op. 118, the Four Piano Pieces, Op. 119, were composed during the summer of 1893. Brahms sent them to Clara Schumann before releasing them to the music firm of Simrock, to be issued in November of that year. In earlier collections of piano pieces, including Opp. 76 (1879) and 116 (1892), Brahms had experimented with alternating arrangements of two contrasting types of miniatures, the capriccio and intermezzo. If the capriccio was characterized by a fanciful, extroverted manner, the intermezzo explored the intimate, lyrical, and introverted side of musical expression. The juxtaposition of these two types recalled for Brahms Schumann's habit, in his great piano cycles of the 1830s, of reflecting the dual sides of his musical personality (Florestan and Eusebius) in sharply delineated types of pieces. Now in Op. 119, at the end of his career, Brahms dispensed entirely with the Capriccio, replacing it with a Rhapsody, by far the most ambitious and technically challenging piece of the set. The Rhapsody appears as the fourth and final composition of the opus, and is preceded by three Intermezzos, a contrasting group that serves as a counterweight.

Taken as a whole, the four compositions reveal a clear tonal ordering. The first two, in B minor and E minor, are related by a fifth. The third, in C major, lies a major third below the second, and a minor third below the Rhapsody, in E♭ major. The first two pieces are in sharp keys; the third is in the "neutral" key of C major; and the Rhapsody stands by itself as the only one of the four in a flat key. Finally, the first two pieces are in minor keys, while the last two are in major keys. Accompanying these arrangements of sharp and flat, of minor and major tonalities, is a progression of mood from the most intimate and dreamlike (the Adagio of No. 1) to the most energetic and robust (the Allegro risoluto of the Rhapsody). Numbers 2 and 3 depict emotional states that lie between these two extremes. Thus, No. 2 is marked Andantino un poco agitato and Andantino grazioso, while No. 3 has the heading Grazioso e giocoso.

In terms of their formal design, the first two pieces fall roughly into ternary *ABA* structures, with a contrasting middle section. In No. 3, Brahms dispenses with the contrasting section, while in No. 4, he builds a much more complex structure, based on three different thematic ideas arranged according to the symmetrical scheme *ABCBA*(Coda).

Brahms scholars have often commented on the thematic and motivic concentration in Op. 119. Thus, No. 1 is built upon a descending chain of melodic thirds, a simple melodic pattern that Brahms had explored in a variety of earlier works, including the slow movement of the Piano Sonata in F minor, Op. 5, and the first movement of the Fourth Symphony, Op. 98, and would revisit in the third of the *Vier ernste Gesänge*, Op. 121 *(O Tod, O Tod, wie bist du)*. In No. 2, Brahms derived all of his material from an opening head motive that reduces to six pitches; while in No. 3, a compact motif of just four pitches was sufficient to inspire the composer. But notwithstanding this remarkable economy of means, the listener is also impressed, paradoxically enough, by the melodic richness of the opus. Through a process of thematic variation and metamorphosis, Brahms was able to transform the basic building blocks of his pieces into highly imaginative edifices of sound. In No. 2, for instance, the opening motive in E minor reappears, in the "contrasting" middle section, as a lyrical waltz theme in E major that initially borrows the pitch structure of the original motive and then blossoms into a self-contained miniature. To accomplish this transformation (from Andantino un poco agitato to Andantino grazioso), Brahms subjects the opening material to a series of compact variations, in which the punctuated sixteenth-note pattern of the opening measures is rhythmically adjusted to syncopated triplets and then even eighth notes. In effect, the agitated opening is gradually transformed, along with the essential motivic material, into a gracious, songlike utterance.

Undoubtedly the most adventurous of the four pieces is No. 1, in which Brahms explores a highly dissonant harmonic language. Here the basic melodic material, a sequence of descending thirds, is amassed vertically to produce a series of shifting seventh and ninth chords, dissonant structures that vitiate any sense of firm grounding in the tonic key, B minor, which, through the course of the piece, is implied rather than directly stated. Only in the closing measures is a cadence on B minor attained, but only through a complete sequence of thirds, B–G–E–C#–A#–F#–D–B, that is allowed to discover its roots in the tonic triad. Schoenberg's concepts of "hovering tonality" and "developing variation," and Anton Webern's concept of "constant variation" arguably may trace their origin to this late miniature abstraction of Brahms.

R. Larry Todd

13

PIANO FOUR HANDS

VARIATIONS ON A THEME BY ROBERT SCHUMANN IN E♭, OPUS 23

Composed 1861; published 1863

After the Op. 21 variations of 1856–57, Brahms next turned to piano variations in 1861 with a pair of large-scale works, the *Handel* Variations, Op. 24, in September and the four-hand *Schumann* Variations, Op. 23, in November. (It is unclear why the opus numbers are not chronological, especially in light of the publication of Op. 24 in 1862 and Op. 23 in 1863.) These were the last works he completed in Hamburg before moving to Vienna the following year. His interest in the variation form may have reemerged after he made a piano arrangement of the D-minor slow movement of the String Sextet Op. 18 as a gift for Clara Schumann. Possibly his old association of variations with the Schumann circle, vivid in Op. 9, may have revived as well, prompting the choice of theme in Op. 23 and the dedication of the autograph of Op. 24 to "a dear friend," on the occasion of Clara's birthday. As in the earlier pair of Op. 21 variations, the nature of the theme forecasts important features of the variations, such as the conclusions of funeral march (Op. 23) and fugue (Op. 24). Paired works enabled him to deal with, even reconcile, the older and newer models of variation form that he both admired and struggled against. (Although Op. 21 is the first actual pair, the *Schumann* Variations Op. 9, may be thought of as encapsulating an "internal pair" because of Brahms's split persona in the work, identifying some variations with "Brahms" and others with "Kreisler," much as Schumann had labeled his *Davidsbündlertänze* with Eusebius and Florestan.) Variation themes exert both a constructive and an emotional force, and the "aura" of Schumann's so-called last thought—the theme he wrote and started to vary shortly before throwing himself into the Rhine in 1854—wafts over the piece. Brahms chose it for its personal meanings, its "melancholy sound of farewell," and he admitted that the variations were not far removed from that idea.

The *Schumann* and *Handel* Variations have one strikingly similar variation, and the difference in their treatment suggests the differences in Brahms's approach to those themes. The sixth variation of the *Handel* and the fourth of the *Schumann* sets are each two-part imitative *minores* with both hands in octaves, appearing relatively early in each cycle. Several features point to Op. 24, Var. 6 as a variation on a Baroque theme: despite its expressive distance from the theme (prepared somewhat by the preceding variation in minor), it is entirely canonic, and resembles the theme melody. Opus 23, Var. 4 is only intermittently canonic, and is more consciously "mysterious" in such evocative details as a hollow-fifth cadence, repeated notes or tremolo in the lowest registers of the piano during the second reprise, and syncopated sigh-motifs to replace the canon. It is also the only variation in that set without any overt melodic resemblance to the theme whatever, even its upbeat. Based instead on the descending fifth of the theme's cadential measure, it seems to function as a mood piece rather than as part of a variation group. Brahms's choice of theme thus suggests which set of historical references and models—the stricter or freer interpretations of melody, bass, harmony, and structure that he later characterized as "creating something new on a given bass" (see Op. 24)—should operate within a single variation set.

One of the most interesting pieces of Brahms reception is the lengthy review and explication of this work published by critic Adolf Schubring in 1868 in the *Allgemeine musikalische Zeitung* as part of his extensive series on "The Schumann School." Schubring offers a ringing endorsement of the necessity of "thematic work" as the essence of the "logical" art of music, and seeks first to describe the motivic kernels of the theme (the three opening notes of the melody (G–F–E♭); the first three notes of the bass, (E♭–E♭–E♭); the last two notes of the melody, (B♭–E♭), and their constructive elaboration in the variations). Then, however, he turns to the "spiritual content" of the work, which he finds as necessary to understand as the form. Here is the outline and conflation of Schubring's two descriptive modes:

Var. 1: E♭. Complete melody of the theme (with suspensions and chord resolutions), motive 3 in the bass. Tender melancholy.

Var. 2: E♭. Double diminution of the inverted first motive and fourfold diminution in the upper voice of the second motive. Pain, first mild, then harsh and harsher, finally throbbing and hammering.

Var. 3: E♭. Upper voice fashioned from the first motive, in the bass the inversion of the third motive in fourfold diminution. "O sweet, bitter pain, why are you so dear to me!"

Var. 4: E♭ minor. The diminished third motive, treated canonically. Dirge, in which in the second part muted drums join the two lamenting voices.

Var. 5: B major. Five voices treated in strict double counterpoint; the main melody is at first in the two middle voices, the two upper voices imitate the bass canonically, voice exchange at the repeat. "Who has ever heard me lament? My heart is breaking with sadness."

Var. 6: E♭. Double counterpoint, freely treated; the upper voice has the entire first motive but in varied rhythm, the lower voice varies the first motive, with diminutions and additions. As the text of the main motive: "On, take courage, quiet your lamenting."

Var. 7: E♭. Three voices, in undulating contrary motion, bring first only two notes of the main motive; then later the three descending notes of the main motive. A melody of indescribable grace emerges in the second half, while the second player has a dominant pedal, the undulating motive of the variation, and the third motive. "Tears still tremble in your lashes, and see, you are already smiling again."

Var. 8: G minor. Motive 1 in both voices; the bass has the third motive and imitates the main motive of the variation in the second half; double counterpoint. Rhapsody of sadness.

Var. 9: C minor. First part in strictest double counterpoint; upper and lower voices use a combination of all three motives. Determined pulling oneself together, mixed with outbreaks of quivering pain.

Var. 10: Funeral march. Middle voice has motive 2, then motive 1, then motive 1 inverted and in diminutions; free double counterpoint; coda with the original theme. "Ah, they have buried a good man, (coda) but to *me* he was more! *Requiescat in pace et lux perpetua luceat ei!*"

Schumann's theme was not published until Brahms brought it out in 1893, and the variations that Schumann wrote on it did not appear until 1939. Thus, the circumstances of their composition were not known outside the Schumann family circle. Brahms's reasons for choosing this private theme and writing a piece by turns lighthearted, wistful, and elegiac, are not known; it was published with a dedication to Julie Schumann, who was sixteen when it was composed and eighteen when it was published. Certainly the genre of four-hand piano music was designed for intimate gatherings rather than the concert hall, and the dedication to Clara's daughter rather than Clara herself perhaps recognized the consoling power of domestic performance.

Elaine Sisman

16 WALTZES, OPUS 39
Composed 1865; published 1866

In 1864, the Viennese publisher C. A. Spina released the posthumous first edition of Franz Schubert's Twelve Ländler for Piano, D. 790. This beautiful collection, Schubert's finest, had been edited, anonymously, by Brahms, working from an autograph in his own private library. A few months later, in January 1865, evidently stimulated by the experience, Brahms composed his own collection of Waltzes for Four-Hand Piano, Op. 39. To his friend Eduard Hanslick, dedicatee of the cycle when it appeared in August 1866, Brahms described the music as "two books of innocent waltzes in Schubertian form." But this lineage would have been clear enough even without the acknowledgment, for, like his predecessor's dances, Brahms's waltzes stand worlds apart from those composed in the tradition of Lanner and the Strauss family—the former more or less intimate sets of pieces for use as *Hausmusik,* the latter orchestral, decidedly public affairs, meant for ballroom dancing.

In structure, too, Brahms's set diverges from the standard practice of the 1850s and 1860s. In the hands of Johann Strauss, Jr., the Viennese waltz cycle had come to consist of a fairly small number of dances, linked where necessary with transitional material and framed with an introduction and coda. By contrast, Brahms's waltzes follow the normal Schubertian plan, whereby the cycle is made up of a lengthier series of brief pieces lacking the separate introduction, transitions, and coda.

Not all latter-day Schubertians were as true to the master's practice. For example, Liszt's *Soirées de Vienne,* nine arrangements of groups of Schubert dances published in 1851, are showpieces for piano in the manner of the arranger's original works of the time. By the same token, in three arrangements of Schubert dances dating from the 1860s, Johann Herbeck followed a distinctly modern formula, setting the numbers for orchestra and supplying slow introductions and transitions of his own. In other words, Brahms's original cycle recalls the collections of Schubert more faithfully than do the arrangements of either Liszt or Herbeck.

The Op. 39 Waltzes even open with a dance bearing numerous resemblances to a Schubertian predecessor, the *Atzenbrugger Deutsche,* Op. 18, No. 2. This similarity should come as no surprise, for being untried in the world of dance music and, by 1865, scarcely having veins surging with *wiener* blood, Brahms quite naturally looked for guidance to Schubert, native son of the imperial city, master of her dances, and a composer from whom he had already learned a great deal about "serious" forms, especially the sonata.

The "Schubertian form" of Brahms's remark to Hanslick thus squares with the facts. The description of his waltzes as "innocent," however, could only have been made tongue in cheek, since the pieces in Op. 39 display many of the refined features taken for granted in the composer's larger works. Normally such pieces would be straightforward affairs. Dance music, after all, is tied to repeated rhythmic (and often melodic) patterns. One need only recall Strauss's *Blue Danube* Waltz, the beginning of which comprises six nearly literal statements of the principal motive. (This work provided Arnold Schoenberg, in "Brahms the Progressive," with his example of musical "baby talk.") In contrast stands Brahms, who seized every opportunity to employ his characteristic developing variation, practicing what Schoenberg was later to preach in his dictum that "a stricter style of composition . . . demands that nothing be repeated without promoting the development of the music."

The third dance of Op. 39, in which Brahms derives nearly all his sixteen-bar melody from a single rhythmic motive, is a case in point. The opening four measures present several related versions of this cell, each involving a descending fourth or fifth followed by a repeated note and then an ascending interval. The next three measures yield a second generation, a modified melodic configuration now fleshing out the familiar rhythm. Only in the eighth measure is the cell absent from the melody. But here, coinciding with the cadence ending the first half of the dance, the motive is developed further in the left-hand part. The normal state of affairs is immediately restored, however, when the melody takes up the new, "left-hand" version at the outset of the second half, leading it into a further set of motivic variants before arriving at the final cadence. Other dances evolve along similar lines. In the last dance—which comes on the heels of the cycle's most overtly "popular" number, a charming Ländler nowadays heard all too often in distressing Muzak arrangements—we find Brahms indulging his taste for contrapuntal artifice: here the variation is worked out in invertible counterpoint.

David Brodbeck

14

ORGAN

11 CHORALE PRELUDES, OPUS 122
Composed 1896; published 1902

1. Mein Jesu, der du mich
2. Herzliebster Jesu
3. O Welt, ich muss dich lassen
4. Herzlich tut mich erfreuen
5. Schmücke dich, o liebe Seele
6. O wie selig seid ihr doch
7. O Gott, du frommer Gott
8. Es ist ein' Ros' entsprungen
9. Herzlich tut mich verlangen
10. Herzlich tut mich verlangen
11. O Welt, ich muss dich lassen

As is well known, Brahms was profoundly interested in the history of music. The chorale-prelude form is most commonly and properly associated with Johann Sebastian Bach. The other nineteenth-century composer for whom the chorale prelude was an important form was of course Felix Mendelssohn, who was in part responsible for the Bach revival of the early nineteenth century. Mendelssohn not only wrote organ works of his own modeled after Bach but also published a version of fifteen Bach chorale preludes for organ in 1846. The important Peters edition of the Bach organ works was published in Leipzig in the 1840s.

Though Brahms did not write extensively for the organ, (except as part of the instrumental ensemble in choral music) that instrument had for him close personal associations with key people and moments in his life. Robert Schumann was an enthusiastic proponent of the Bach revival and it is likely that Brahms's first introduction to Bach's organ works happened in the context of his friendship with the Schumanns. When he engaged in counterpoint studies with Joseph Joachim in 1856, he wrote many of his exercises for the organ. Of those early works, only four have survived. Brahms published two of them himself (the Fugue in A♭ Minor and the Chorale Prelude and Fugue on *O Trauerigkeit*) and two others (Prelude and Fugue in G Minor and Prelude and Fugue in A Minor, dedicated to Clara Schumann) were discovered years after his death. It is therefore not entirely surprising that in 1896, Brahms returned to the organ as his final vehicle of musical expression in a long and venerable career. Upon hearing the news of Clara Schumann's death in May, Brahms rushed frantically to Frankfurt and then to Bonn for her funeral service; in his haste, he caught the fever that led to the discovery of his own fatal liver cancer. As Brahms's pocket calendar indicates, seven of the chorale preludes of Op. 122 were written shortly after Clara's death when Brahms was at Bad Ischl. The final four preludes were completed between the 15 and 30 of June 1896, also at Bad Ischl. Though Brahms played these works for friends in the summer of 1896, he did not send them to his publisher; Op. 122 was published posthumously in 1902.

Though completed near the end of Brahms's life, the preludes appear to be based on material he worked on at several points in his life before 1896. Numbers 5 and 6 possess a close similarity to one of the earlier chorale preludes that Brahms wrote in 1856. As Michael Musgrave has noted, the final chorale prelude bears a distinct resemblance to the opening of the final movement of *Ein deutsches Requiem*. In the set of the eleven, two chorales are used twice, one *O Welt, ich muss dich lassen* in No. 3 and No. 11, and the other, *Herzlich tut mich verlangen,* in Nos. 9 and 10. Copies of these chorale melodies were made by Brahms sometime between 1854 and 1856; they therefore arguably recall the period of his life in which Joachim and the Schumanns figured prominently. As his final work, then, Brahms returned to the organ after a forty-year interim and created a composition that embraces some of the earlier phases of his life, as well as earlier eras of music history.

Perhaps because of this intersection of music history with a profoundly personal history, the chorale preludes have a lyrical and compelling spirituality about them. Though the model and example of Bach are consistently audible, they are distinctly Brahmsian. They mirror Brahms's remarkable modesty about his own musical accomplishments, displaying his sense that his own achievement was not one of isolated originality but of a respectful extension of a musical and religious tradition, introduced to him by his earliest, and most extraordinary friends.

Leon Botstein

Brahms drinking afternoon coffee at the home of Johann Strauss in Bad Ischl, 1894.

Part Four

SOLO
LIEDER

INTRODUCTION

The solo song, the Lied, can be considered with little doubt a truly distinctive dimension and revealing emblem of nineteenth-century music. Haydn, Mozart, and Beethoven wrote secular songs, but from a post-Brahmsian perspective the break between the Classical and the Romantic is most striking in the Lied, particularly given the transformation of the form evident in the music of Franz Schubert. Music historians have been accustomed to stress continuities between the Classical era and nineteenth-century Romanticism. This sense of continuity has been underscored by the early-twentieth-century critical tradition regarding Brahms initiated by Arnold Schoenberg. Schoenberg credited Brahms with appropriating and transforming Classical procedures so that they became integral and pathbreaking dimensions of late Romantic music. The most frequently cited historical dimensions of Brahms's work emphasize his debt to the Classical and Baroque eras.

This argument of continuity is convincing, but there is also another aspect to be considered. Schubert became so important a figure to subsequent generations of composers precisely because he went beyond Beethoven and certainly Mozart and Haydn. That achievement—the originality of Schubert—was located squarely in his massive output of Lieder; his contribution to the form was a defining part of the ideology of nineteenth-century musical Romanticism. For Schubert's successors, particularly Mendelssohn, Schumann, and Brahms, the song form was an indispensable medium in the same way the opera was pivotal to composers in the age of Mozart. In fact, for Haydn and Mozart the opera aria was their primary secular vocal medium. Lieder appealed to the sensibility of an emerging, literate, introspective audience in the early nineteenth century that turned to music as a unique and welcome form of subjective expression. Insofar as Romanticism in both literature and music can be understood as facilitating the exploration of subjectivity, the Lied offered the ideal vehicle in its combination of two favored modes of expression—poetry and music. As poetry broke away from its eighteenth-century conception (in theory if not in practice) as a basically social activity functioning to describe the finite forms of a communally experienced world—society, politics, morality—it became redefined as a self-conscious presentation of language, as a figurative expression of interiority, designed to facilitate personalized sentiment, intimacy, and differentiated readings. In this context, music (already perceived as directly addressing the emotions), if used in combination with the poetic, exponentially enlarged the possibilities. Brahms, using both banal and exquisite poetry, followed the lead of the early Romantic practitioners and theorists. He proved his mastery at not only illustrating apparent linguistic meaning but in suggesting multivalent, subjective responses to meaning, including contradiction, irony, and hidden allusion. Following Schubert, Brahms realized the Romantic's dream by opening a wide variety of subjective readings in performance and hearing.

The Lied also appealed to composers, professional and amateur performers, and listeners as a result of the obvious fact that more than one person is required to realize the form. The Lied form was designed primarily for domestic surroundings and for the more intimate group socializing that became commonplace in the nineteenth century. The circumstance of two individuals working together with text and music to generate an artistic communication concerning profoundly personal and intimate matters of emotion regarding crucial moments in life, particularly those surrounding love and death, is reminiscent of a sublimated sexual experience, a fact not lost on critics or novelists of Brahms's generation, such as the Swiss writer Gottfried Keller. The song form, unlike the solo piano work, is an instrument of intimacy but not solitude. It differs from the violin or cello sonata or the four-hand piano genre because it is a duet with words and a program. The song was for the nineteenth century a vehicle of intimate communication as well as an "abstract" musical event whose realization more often paralleled the issues raised by the poetic content: desire, loss, fulfillment, remembrance.

In Brahms's remarkable corpus of Lieder, the full range of the Romantic tradition of songwriting may be found. He used all of the available models, from strophic to through-composed. Brahms's output stands out, however, from that of Schubert and Schumann in the number of songs which utilize folk poetry and texts. By the 1850s, the national cultural sensibility which was first visible in the second decade of the nineteenth century and derived from an alliance between the Romantic movement and post-Enlightenment cultural politics had come into full bloom. After the first edition of *Des Knaben Wunderhorn* in 1805, Brahms and his generation became engaged in the preservation and extension of a particular construct of an authentic, premodern folk heritage. This was not particularly a preoccupation of Schubert's, who was not German but Viennese and who died well before the tidal wave of modern nationalist sentiment.

Ultimately, however, it is the unique combination of profundity and accessibility integral to Brahms's musical personality which definitively characterizes his Lieder. Whether in the *Vier ernste Gesänge*, Op. 121, or his settings of the poetry of Count Adolf Friedrich von Schack, in which the melancholy and self-reflective resignation regarding many matters of life, especially those surrounding intimacy and attachment, are given expression, Brahms has succeeded in reaching many generations of listeners. Perhaps a partial explanation for his particular accomplishment distinct from that of his illustrious predecessors, Schubert and Schumann, is the fact that, of these three great song composers, only Brahms reached middle and old age with the clarity of his mind intact. The later songs of Brahms are unique because of the confluence of emotion and music that bring to the listener a range of wisdom and pathos unlike anything to be found in either Schubert or Schumann.

NOTE: In order to preserve Brahms's use of the words *Gesänge* and *Lieder*, both of which are normally rendered in English as "songs," the original German terms have been retained in the headings that follow, as has the conjunction *und* in "Lieder und Gesänge."

15

SOLO LIEDER

6 GESÄNGE, FOR TENOR OR SOPRANO, OPUS 3
Composed 1851; published 1854

1. Liebestreu [Reinick]
2. Liebe und Frühling I (Wie sich Rebenranken schwingen) [Fallersleben]
3. Liebe und Frühling II (Ich muß hinaus) [Fallersleben]
4. Lied aus dem Gedicht "Ivan" [Bodenstedt]
5. In der Fremde [Eichendorff]
6. Lied (Lindes Rauschen in den Wipfeln) [Eichendorff]

The earliest songs of Brahms are a group of eighteen works composed between June 1851 and July 1853. They were eventually published as Opp. 3, 6, and 7. Brahms wrote a number of songs prior to that time, but they are lost. The six songs of Op. 3 were not the first to be written; much of Opp. 6 and 7 were written earlier. Opus 3 is dedicated to Bettina von Arnim, whom the twenty-year-old Brahms met in 1853 through his new friend Joseph Joachim. Bettina von Arnim was a well-known figure in the German Romantic circles. As a child she knew Goethe and Beethoven. She was the wife of Achim von Arnim and the sister of Clemens Brentano, the two Romantic writers responsible for the folk-text collection *Des Knaben Wunderhorn*, which had so great an influence on German Romantic music, and particularly on the work of Brahms and Gustav Mahler. Robert Schumann was especially fond of Bettina and dedicated his set of songs Op. 133 (1853) to her. Joachim was close to Bettina's daughter, Gisela, who married Hermann Grimm, the son of the famous expert on language and folklore, Wilhelm Grimm. For the young Brahms, Bettina was possessed of a certain aura. She represented a direct connection to the greatest figures of German culture, and, as Karl Geiringer has noted,

Brahms's dedication of his first published songs to her constitutes a declaration of allegiance to the ideals of Romanticism.

The songs of Op. 3 reveal not only the striking talent but an uncanny refinement uncharacteristic of a young composer. Brahms thought well enough of these songs to reissue them in 1888 with some revision. The first song, the E♭-minor *Liebestreu* (True Love), to a text by the poet Robert Reinick, has generally been regarded as a seminal masterpiece. This was the work that Brahms performed for Joachim at their first meeting. The song, marked sehr langsam, relates an exchange between mother and daughter, in which the mother encourages the daughter to forget an unrequited love and to dispense with sorrow. But the young daughter insists on her fidelity to her love. The entire song is constructed as an elaboration of the intervals presented in the opening theme. This song has a particularly intimate quality, and clearly foreshadows the subtle design and compact emotion of the finest songs of the mature Brahms. The composer himself was perhaps aware of its preeminence in the set, for he chose it as the first number, though it was not first to be composed in the period from 1851 to 1853. Brahms was perspicacious enough to realize the emotional power and weight this first song would lend to all of Op. 3.

The next two songs, settings of texts by Hoffmann von Fallersleben, are both entitled *Liebe und Frühling* (Love and Spring). Both are in B♭ major; Op.3/2 is marked moderato ma non troppo and Op. 3/3 is marked vivace con fuoco. The second stanza of Op. 3/2 contains a direct reference to the aria "Batti, batti," sung by Zerlina in Mozart's *Don Giovanni*. (Brahms later said that the song had been inspired by his passion for a young woman who performed that role.) The song has often been singled out for its use of counterpoint. In Op. 3/3, Brahms displays a certain adventurousness of harmonic exploration. As in *Liebestreu*, the two *Liebe und Frühling* songs offer deft and virtuosic demonstration of music as evocative of the texts, particularly the overt contrasts and connections between emotion and experience. Opus 3/4, to a text by Friedrich Martin von Bodenstedt, is again in E♭ minor with the marking mit feurigen Schwung (in a passionate manner). The final two songs are settings of texts by Joseph von Eichendorff. *In der Fremde* (Among Strangers), Op. 3/5, composed in November 1852, is marked poco agitato and is in F♯ minor. Op. 3/6, simply entitled *Lied*, is marked poco allegretto and is in A major. The two Eichendorff songs are perhaps more illustrative than evocative of the text. Opus 3/5 is often compared with the opening song of Schumann's Op. 39, the *Liederkreis*, not only because both songs are in the same key but because for his version Brahms used Schumann's alteration of Eichendorff's text.

Many of the Op. 3 songs were originally intended for domestic use and publicly performed only much later. These songs date from 1853, the most pivotal year of Brahms's life, in which he traveled on the legendary concert tour with the violinist Eduard Reményi. This was the moment when Brahms for the first time met the leading musicians of the age. Opus 3 was recommended for publication by Schumann and forms one of the reasons behind Schumann's famous encomium of Brahms in the 1854 article entitled "New Paths," an act of generosity which would ironically haunt Brahms for the rest of his career.

Many composers have in their juvenilia works of an ambitious scope which reflect a grandiosity and fearlessness we frequently associate with youth. It is quite revealing of Brahms's character that his early forays into composition focus on the miniature form, and in the case of Op. 3, on highly structured texts with relatively unambiguous meanings. The virtuosity of the young Brahms as a composer therefore was revealed not in scale but in the intricacy and command of through-composition, variation, counterpoint, harmonic contrast, and the interplay of voice and accompaniment. These skills are put to the service of texts in the spirit of the Romantic ambition to fuse music and language so that neither text nor music would be subordinate to the other. Opus 3 reflects the advice that Brahms gave to his only student of composition, Gustav Jenner: when setting a poetic text to music, a composer should know the text intimately, particularly in terms of its structural and metrical characteristics. Brahms urged that any composer wishing to set a text should read and re-read a poem out loud in order to find the proper breaks in the poetic declamation. That technique permitted Brahms not only to set a text but to use music to augment and supplement the communicative power of language.   *Leon Botstein*

6 GESÄNGE, FOR SOPRANO OR TENOR, OPUS 6
Composed 1852–53; published 1853

1. Spanisches Lied [anon.; trans. Heyse]
2. Der Frühling [Rousseau]
3. Nachwirkung [Meissner])
4. Juchhe! [Reinick]
5. Wie die Wolke nach der Sonne [Fallersleben]
6. Nachtigallen schwingen lustig [Fallersleben]

Six more songs from the years 1851–53 became Op. 6; despite their later opus number, however, most were composed somewhat earlier than Op. 3, primarily in April 1852. Opp. 6/5 and 6/6, like Op. 3/2–3, are set to texts by Hoffmann von Fallersleben and date from July 1853. Opus 6 is dedicated to the two pianist sisters Luise and Minna Japha, whom Brahms had first met while in Hamburg. It was Luise who in 1850 persuaded Brahms to send a parcel of his works to Robert Schumann; Schumann returned the package unopened. Three years later, when Luise was studying piano with Schumann, she and Brahms renewed their friendship within Schumann's circle.

The first number of Op. 6, entitled *Spanisches Lied,* is set to a text translated into German by novelist and poet Paul von Heyse (the son of Felix Mendelssohn's tutor in Classical languages). This text was also set many years later by Hugo Wolf. Brahms's song is marked Allegretto and is in A minor. Opus 6/2 is in E major, entitled *Der Frühling* (Springtime), and is marked con moto. The text is by Johann Baptiste Rousseau. This song is a cheerful affair: many observers have noted that Brahms omitted the third stanza of the poem which suggests the underside of the experience of joy during springtime. The coherence of the mood of the song was apparently crucial to Brahms, and therefore, he chose not to complicate the song's spirit with more than a quiet, gentle conclusion. This happy work possesses an almost Hungarian aspect. Opus 6/3 is called *Nachwirkung* (Aftereffect). Marked poco agitato, it is built on the idea of contrast and is in A♭ major. Here Brahms makes very effective use of the 9/8 rhythm. The first four songs of this set—including Op. 6/4, titled *Juchhe!* (Hooray!), to a text by Robert Reinick, in E♭ major and marked con moto—all make inventive use of the inherent tension between triple and duple rhythm within 6/4 and 9/8 meters. *Juchhe!,* in strophic form with three stanzas, has sometimes been seen as a tribute to Mendelssohn.

The last two songs of Op. 6 are in B♭ major and A♭ major respectively, one marked poco andante and the other marked allegro non troppo, and both set to texts by Fallersleben. These final numbers are directly concerned with the illustration of nature: each contains musical illustrations of birdsong. In No. 5, Brahms again utilizes a strophic form and reserves the third stanza for the description of an eagle ascending and descending in the sun. Number 6 harks back in its rhythmic structure to the triple-duple meter interplay of the first songs. It is a remarkably beautiful song and with No. 5 constitutes an attractive closing group to the set of six. Number 6 closes in a melancholy manner characteristic of the later Brahms: quietly, with an appropriate musical setting of the image of a flower that refuses to bloom. As a whole, the cycle points to Brahms's lifelong attachment to nature and his view that nature highlights the predicament of the modern individual as bittersweet and painful. The instability of emotion and the inevitable sorrow in human relationships are at once mitigated and also deepened by the sense of life, joy, and renewal which is inspired by the solitary encounter with nature.

Leon Botstein

6 GESÄNGE, OPUS 7
Composed 1851–53; Published 1854

1. Treue Liebe [Ferrand]
2. Parole [Eichendorff]
3. Anklänge [Eichendorff]
4. Volkslied (Die Schwälble ziehet fort) [trad. Scherer]
5. Die Trauernde [trad. Scherer]
6. Heimkehr[Uhland]

The six songs of Op. 7, like Brahms's two earlier sets of Lieder, date from before April 1853, and therefore before Brahms's departure from Hamburg and his encounter with Schumann. Though they can only be admired as juvenilia which contain certain indications of the composer's as yet not fully developed powers, they have held special interest for scholars because of a number of biographical intersections. For one thing, the set is dedicated to Albert Dietrich, the forgotten third member of the famous F.A.E. (*frei aber einsam;* free but alone) group which collectively composed the violin sonata based on those initials. Dietrich, who outlived Brahms by more than a decade (he died in 1908) was a fine composer of Lieder in his own right, though little remains in the repertory. His ambitions in vocal music were perhaps even greater than those of Brahms, as his efforts and limited success in opera suggest, but his place in music history remains secured almost exclusively by his relationship to Brahms.

An even more significant biographical aspect of this set, however, is the fact that it contains Brahms's earliest song—or at least the first song he saved—*Heimkehr* (Homecoming), set to a text by Ludwig Uhland. *Heimkehr,* marked allegro agitato, is written in B minor but ends strongly in the major. Placed last in the cycle, the song has often been compared to Op. 3/1, *Liebestreu,* in order to demonstrate Brahms's early affinity to the song form. *Liebestreu,* composed two years later, can be seen as a version of *Heimkehr* which avoids the earlier song's melodramatic artifice and resolves its disproportionate style. It was perhaps with self-conscious scrutiny that Brahms chose to open the three sets he published in this period, Opp. 3, 6, and 7, with the later, more successful effort, and conclude them with his first attempt.

Though all of the songs of Op. 7 are settings of texts from various sources, including poems of Ferrand and Eichendorff and folk songs from Scherer's 1851 collection *Deutsche Volkslieder,* they bear a marked similarity in subject matter. All of them deal with aspects of loneliness, despair, and the daunting prospect of the fulfillment of the promise of love. The protagonists are young women who have been left alone, whose anxieties about being abandoned are alleviated by either the anticipation or reality of their lovers' reappearance. The apparent coherence of the subject matter has led some observers to suggest that Op. 7 may have been a kind of draft or experiment for a possible operatic subject (which might also explain the oddly theatrical style of No. 6, for example). All these songs reflect something of an illustrative musical sensibility. In the first number, *Treue Liebe,* marked andante con espressione and in F♯ minor, echoes of water are heard in the piano. Horn calls signal the context of the hunt in No. 2, *Parole* (Watchword) in E minor, which shares a marking of andante moderato with No. 3, *Anklänge* (Sympathies) in A minor. Both of these Eichendorff settings constitute the apex of the opus in view of the way Brahms's enormous psychological empathy is mirrored in his brilliant use of harmony. The two folk-song settings, *Volkslied* (Folk Song) and *Die Trauernde* (The Grieving Girl), show Brahms's attempt to imitate a somewhat old-fashioned folk sound, but here again there is a distinctly melancholy character to his manipulation of the conventions of folk simplicity. *Die Trauernde* also provides some further biographical insight, because years after it was written, it became the basis of some variations composed by Heinrich von Herzogenberg, aspiring composer and husband of Brahms's close friend Elisabet. Though Brahms was certainly appreciative of the tribute, his professional assessment of Herzogenberg's variations remained tactfully enigmatic.

Leon Botstein

8 LIEDER AND ROMANCES, OPUS 14
Composed 1858; published 1861

1. Vor dem Fenster [trad. Simrock]
2. Vom verwundeten Knaben [trad. Herder]
3. Murrays Ermordung [Percy; trans. Herder]
4. Ein Sonett (Ach könnt ich, könnte vergessen sie) [attrib. Count
   Thibault; trans. Herder]
5. Trennung [trad. Zuccalmaglio]
6. Gang zur Liebsten [trad. Zuccalmaglio]
7. Ständchen (Gut Nacht, gut Nacht) [trad. Zuccalmaglio]
8. Sehnsucht [trad. Zuccalmaglio]

The eight songs of Op. 14 have generally been regarded as the inception of a new period in the evolution of the composer's skill in Lieder, as
the first indication in Brahms's music of a dimension of an aesthetic and
cultural point of view that would remain with him throughout his life.
Opus 14 also points to an historical development in nineteenth-century
German thought and taste which Brahms embraced enthusiastically and
which deeply influenced his choice of subject matter in his subsequent
Lieder. For a number of historical reasons, including the impact of the
Napoleonic invasions, early-nineteenth-century German reaction against
the influence of the French Enlightenment, nascent industrialization on
the European continent before 1848, and the evolution of literary Romanticism, German intellectuals and artists at mid-century developed an
affection for an artificial but highly alluring construction of a folk past.
German art became dominated by images based on contemporary reen-
actments of an idealized and simple rural past that was perceived to be
at the root of the best in the modern German national character. The
most eloquent philosophical and ideological expression of this Romantic recreation of German folk culture occurs in the writings of Johann
Gottfried von Herder, whose conception of history candidly relied on
the idea of a distinctive evolution of national character, language, and
race. In German music, the obsession with this construction of folk identity, like most extremes, produced some ironic consequences. The revival
of interest in folk roots throughout Europe was a symptom of an odd discomfort with the notion that the German accomplishment in music as
an art form had outgrown its folk origins and become a universal language of art. This concept became so pronounced that by the early twen-

tieth century observers would claim that of all European countries, Germany had alienated itself, or rather progressed away most radically the most, from an authentic folk past.

Brahms is rightly viewed as a cosmopolitan figure, but his patriotic inclinations indicate that he was also not entirely out of step with his times. Though he also used folk inspirations for some of the earlier Op. 7 songs, the Op. 14 numbers demonstrate a more intense and complex relation to folk sources from many cultures. Opus 14 shares the same acute interest that produced the *Volkskinderlieder* and *Deutsche Volkslieder* composed that same year. Though the original sources for Op. 14 seem eclectic, they share elements that provide evidence for Brahms's intention possibly to form a cycle out of these Lieder. For instance, No. 3, named *Murrays Ermordung* (Murray's Murder), in *A B A* Liedform, marked con moto and in E minor, is based on a well-known Scottish ballad, "The Bonny Earl o'- Moray," and No. 4, marked langsam in A♭ major, is a lyrical, introspective song based a sonnet by the thirteenth-century troubadour Thibault IV, Count of Champagne. But both of the texts that Brahms uses are adaptations by Herder that complement the German origins of the rest of the sources. Opus 14/1, *Vor dem Fenster* (Before the Window), marked andante in G minor, employs a dialogic format as a lover sings to his sweetheart through the window at night while everyone else sleeps. Opus 14/2, again taken from Herder, is titled *Vom verwundeten Knaben* (The Wounded Boy) and is marked andantino in A minor. It is a mournful ballad describing the endless character of grief. Opus 14/5, *Trennung* (Parting), is marked sehr schnell and is in F major; it concerns a young girl's sorrow at watching her lover dash off on his horse. Opus 14/6, marked andante con espressione in E minor, is a strophic setting of the internal striving of a lover longing for the excitement of the secret tryst as he attempts to express his emotion in writing. This song's particular power derives partly from Brahms's experiments with the vocal range, and the piano as responsive to the voice, so as to express the thwarted longing. Opus 14/7, *Ständchen* (Serenade) in F minor is a setting of a text in which a male voice sings his beloved to sleep and wishes her a peaceful and comforting night with dreams of him. The piano's quietly insistent repetitions evoke calm imagery of moonlight and the night. Opus 14/8, *Sehnsucht* (Desire), marked andante and in E minor, is through-composed. It is Tyrolean in origin and is a sentimental setting of a woman whose lover is at sea. All of these songs share the personal subject matter and evocative moods as-

sociated with the conventional lives and concerns of idealized country
folk, the perceived cultural basis of national characteristics, particularly
among German-speaking peoples.

Leon Botstein

5 Poems, Opus 19
Composed 1858; published 1862

1. Der Kuß [Hölty]   4. Der Schmied [Uhland]
2. Scheiden und Meiden [Uhland])   5. An eine Äolsharfe [Mörike]
3. In der Ferne [Uhland])

Brahms's use of folk sources during this period of his composition
continued with the *Gedichte* of Op. 19. There was one notable exception.
Of these five songs, all written between September 1858 and May 1859,
the last, Op. 19/5, in A minor and moving to A major, is a setting of a
poem by Eduard Mörike, *An eine Äolsharfe* (To an Aeolian Harp). The
poem, occasioned by the death of Mörike's brother, uses the Romantic
convention of the harp to suggest the relationship between nature and
music. Brahms mixes recitative with song powerfully in this setting of a
text which employs metaphors of nature for the expression of internal
emotion. Though it uses all of the musical conventions associated with
the harp's sound, it is nevertheless marked by tremendous harmonic variety and an expressive, imaginative realization of the vocal line.

The Mörike setting stands out among the other numbers, which consistently retain the aura of the folk-song subject matter and sound effect
that pervade so much of Brahms's music during these years. One of the
finest examples of Brahms's penchant for onomatopoeia occurs in the
other well-known song of this group, No. 4 *Der Schmied* (The Blacksmith)
in B♭ major. Brahms distinguishes the sound of the different hammer
strokes of the blacksmith and his apprentice through the piano accompaniment, as part of his wonderful parallel between the dark and intense
character of the artisan's craft and the power of love. Brahms gives a special musical emphasis to the closing lines, which describe the flames
emerging from the blacksmith's forge, evocative of his passion.

Opus 19/2, called *Scheiden und Meiden* (Separation and Avoidance),
which Brahms marks "not too slow but with powerful expression" (in D
minor), and No. 3, *In der Ferne* (In the Distance), marked for the same
tempo and beginning in D minor but ending in D major, share the same

textual source as *Der Schmied*, the poetry of Ludwig Uhland. Both of these songs, however, are meant as complements to one another; they certainly share a sensibility and thematic material, and comprise what Clara Schumann identified as one of Brahms's best attempts to approximate the popular folk-song idiom. Opus 19 opens with a song based on a poem by Ludwig Hölty, *Der Kuß* (The Kiss), marked poco adagio and in B♭ major. Brahms makes very clever use of phrase structure to illustrate the internal trajectory of a lover's first stolen kiss. Both the music and the poem evoke the disquieting power of "innocent" kissing to engender desire when there is no prospect of fulfillment.

Leon Botstein

9 LIEDER UND GESÄNGE, OPUS 32
Composed 1864; published 1864

1. Wie rafft' ich mich auf in der Nacht [Platen]
2. Nicht mehr zu dir zu gehen [Daumer]
3. Ich schleich umher [Platen]
4. Der Strom, der neben mir verrauschte [Platen]
5. Wehe, so willst du mich wieder [Platen]
6. Du sprichst, daß ich mich täuschte [Platen]
7. Bitteres zu sagen denkst du [Hafiz; trans. Daumer]
8. So stehn wir, ich und meine Weide [Hafiz; trans. Daumer]
9. Wie bist du, meine Königin [Hafiz; trans. Daumer]

According to an entry in Brahms's own index of his works, the *Lieder und Gesänge*, Op. 32, were composed in September 1864 in Baden-Baden. Conforming to his usual practice of setting clusters of texts from the same poetic collection or by the same poet, Brahms turned here to verses by August von Platen (Nos. 1 and 3–6) and the fourteenth-century Persian poet Mohammad Shams od-Din Hafiz in translations by Georg Friedrich Daumer (Nos. 7–9). The second song, *Nicht mehr zu dir zu gehen* (To go to you no more), is based on a traditional text, also as transmitted by Daumer. While Kalbeck claimed that some of the songs were drafted before September 1864 (by his account the ever popular ninth song, *Wie bist du, meine Königin,* was originally a half-step higher, in E major), it is probably safe to assume that the majority took definitive shape during the composer's stay in Baden-Baden.

This scenario would place the *Lieder und Gesänge* in close proximity to two other projects that occupied Brahms at various points throughout the 1860s: his setting of the fifteen *Magelone Romanzen*, Op. 33, and the cantata *Rinaldo*, Op. 50. The Op. 32 Lieder display important links to both of these works. In Kalbeck's opinion, the languishing hero of *Rinaldo* is "once again ensnared by his old travails" in Op. 32. The publication history of the *Lieder und Gesänge* is in turn bound up with that of the *Magelone Romanzen*. In early October 1864, Brahms submitted the first six of the *Romanzen* (Nos. 7, 8, 12, and 13 may also have existed in some form by that time) and the whole of the Op. 32 set to Breitkopf & Härtel, which rejected them, in part because of the technical demands of Brahms's piano parts. Both sets were issued by the Swiss publisher Rieter-Biedermann in the following year: the *Lieder und Gesänge* in January or February and the six *Magelone Romanzen* in September.

For many commentators, Op. 32 represents a watershed in Brahms's development as a song composer. Here, the expansive, almost operatic designs of some of the earlier *Magelone Romanzen* (for example, Nos. 3 and 6) give way to simple strophic patterns (Op. 32, Nos. 3 and 5)—that is, to Lieder in the narrow sense of the term—or to modified strophic and *ABA* forms in the remaining *Gesänge*, all of which are enriched by subtle variation procedures. Moreover, the extroverted tone of the *Magelone Romanzen* recedes in favor of a decidedly inward tone.

These traits are well exemplified in the melancholy *Nicht mehr zu dir zu gehen*. Notable for its flexibly wrought vocal line, this song puts into practice the advice Brahms gave to his pupil Gustav Jenner some years later: the aspiring song composer, Brahms maintained, "should carry the poem in [his] head for a long time . . . paying especially close attention to the declamation." Brahms's concern with the rhetorical dimensions of the text emerge in the pregnant pauses and irregular phrase-lengths that impart a recitational quality to *Nicht mehr zu dir zu gehen*. At the same time, the syntactic freedom of the vocal line is grounded by the piano part, which provides motivic continuity through its development of a brief sigh figure and of the pattern first announced in the left hand in measures 1–3. Functioning at once like a ground bass and a migrating *cantus firmus* (even the voice shares in its presentation), this pattern is a close relative of the descending tetrachord associated since the seventeenth century with vocal laments. Its use in this song projects the text as a plaint for a forlorn lover whose thoughts are poised midway between life and death.

To what extent, however, do this song and its neighbors form part of a unified cycle as opposed to a random collection? Although Brahms did not call the Op. 32 songs—or any of his other sets, for that matter—a cycle, it is evident from their tonal and harmonic disposition that he attempted to fashion more than a mere succession of discrete pieces. The overall tonal plan features movement from the minor keys of the first six songs to the major keys of the last three, while most adjacent songs either share the same key or, more often, articulate a relationship by a third or a fifth. The attenuated or inconclusive final cadences of several songs (for example, Nos. 2, 4, 8) serve as agents of continuity in that they heighten our expectations of more to come. The closing C-major chord of No. 6 can be heard as a dominant (given the emphasis on B♭-minor harmonies in the preceding measures), and thus dovetails neatly with the F-major tonic of No. 7. Motivic links among the songs are comparatively few, but noteworthy all the same. The languid descending gesture from the piano postlude of No. 2, for instance, is absorbed into the accompanimental figuration at the beginning of No. 3.

Of course, issues of cyclic unity cannot be divorced from textual considerations, especially considering Brahms's complaint, made late in life, that most singers grouped his songs quite arbitrarily in performance, thinking only of what suited their voices and not realizing the trouble he had taken "to assemble his songs like a bouquet." In the *Lieder und Gesänge,* this concern emerges in Brahms's disposition of the texts to suggest an affective trajectory, an inner narrative of emotional states. His arrangement of the poems traces a course from the brooding melancholy of the opening "wandering" song *(Wie rafft' ich mich auf in der Nacht)* to the rapturous lyricism of *Wie bist du, meine Königin.*

This psychological journey unfolds in three stages, the first of them delineated in Nos. 1–4. (Brahms himself insisted that if the songs were to be issued in several volumes, the opening four settings should be kept as a group; Rieter-Biedermann complied.) All four of these texts can be read as laments over a lost or unapproachable beloved or as portrayals of loneliness and alienation. Just as significant, however, is their expression of a temporal dilemma. What seems most to distress the "lyric ego" of the poems is the inexorable slipping away of time: "O weh, hast du die Tage verbracht" (Alas, how you have squandered your days) we hear in No. 1, and "jener Mensch, der ich gewesen . . . wo ist er nun?" (that man I used to be . . . where is he now?) in No. 4. Moreover, the texts abound in images of time's passage, such as the rushing millstream of Nos. 1 and 4 and the withered trees and yellowing leaves of No. 3. Brahms was highly sensitive to this imagery and to the larger poetic theme in which it was implicated. If the steady triplet motion in No. 1 is a musical code for the millstream, the song's marchlike rhythms point even more emphatically to the relentless flow of time. In No. 3, the images of organic decay—emblems of the transience of all living things—find a musical equivalent in a melody imbued with the quality of a dimly remembered, doleful folk tune.

Numbers 5 and 6 mark the second stage of the inner journey of the speaker, who at first makes a valiant attempt to escape from the fetters of sensual love but later resigns himself to having lost his beloved. This new phase is articulated musically by the wrenching diminished-seventh chord at the beginning of No. 5 (the same harmony is echoed quietly in the subsequent song), and then by Brahms's recourse to quasi-orchestral textures, propulsive triplets, and piercing fanfares in the piano part of the song.

The final chapter of the affective narrative comes in Nos. 7–9. Now the beloved is viewed as an object of adoration in spite of her "bitter utterances" (No. 7) and "angry replies" (No. 8). In the last song (No. 9), the speaker delights in the bliss of physical union, as roses and zephyrs displace the images of withering trees and harsh winds from earlier poems (Nos. 3 and 5). The music portrays this shift not only tonally (by turning to major keys) and melodically (through heightened lyricism), but texturally as well. Indeed, all three songs feature understated duet textures, either within the right hand of the piano part or in the interaction between piano and voice. Already employed to good effect in the plaintive No. 6, the two-part writing suggests that the previously forlorn speaker is carrying on an inner dialogue with his beloved.

This is not to say that the Op. 32 songs represent a direct translation of poetry into music. As Brahms put it, a musically realizable poem should contain a gap or "weak spot" that a composer "enters" in order to cast the meaning of the poem in a new light. The composer found such a gap in the final poem of the set, "Wie bist due, meine Königin." Ostensibly a celebration of ecstatic union, this text provided Brahms with the impetus to call the happy ending of the set into question through his remarkable use of harmonic color. In the third strophe of the poem, the beloved appears as one who remains "wondrous" *(wonnevoll)* even in a desolate wilderness, while in the fourth strophe the sensuous embrace of the lovers is described as a blend of pleasure and pain. Brahms already accents the painful side of the equation in his setting of the third strophe with a striking excursion into the minor Neapolitan region (E minor). As with so many of his harmonic strategies, this one derives from Schubert, probably from the conclusion of the second movement of the String Quintet D. 956. In *Wie bist du, meine Königin,* Brahms exploits the minor Neapolitan harmony for a distinctly poetic purpose: to unmask the poem's image of perfect bliss as an illusion. In addition, the Neapolitan's appearance here indicates that the tortured sentiments uttered earlier in the *Lieder und Gesänge* have not been expunged: the harmony strongly colors the settings of precisely those lines from the first and fourth poems where the lyric ego voices profound despair over the ephemeral nature of existence. To put it in terms of Brahms's own aesthetic, the composer filled the gaps in his poetic texts with musical memories of an anguished past. The beloved, as portrayed in Brahms's song, is not quite as wondrous as the figure in Hafiz's (or Daumer's) poem.

John Daverio

Romances from L. Tieck's Magelone, Opus 33

Composed 1861–68; published 1865–69

1. Keinen hat es noch gereut
2. Traun! Bogen und Pfeil sind gut
3. Sind es Schmerzen, sind es Freuden
4. Liebe kam aus fernen Landen
5. So willst du des Armen
6. Wie soll ich die Freude
7. War es dir
8. Wir müssen uns trennen
9. Ruhe, Süssliebchen
10. Verzweiflung (So tönet denn)
11. Wie schnell verschwindet
12. Muß es eine Trennung geben
13. Sulima (Geliebter, wo zaudert)
14. Wie froh und frisch
15. Treue Liebe dauert lange

In the absence of any opera by Brahms, his choice of narratives for other genres assumes unusual interest as an indicator of his taste and affinity for specific dramatic themes. A particular attraction to medieval legend is evident in most of the sources Brahms apparently contemplated for operas he never wrote, as well as for realized works such as his cantata, *Rinaldo,* Op. 50, and the *Romanzen aus L. Tieck's Magelone,* Op. 33.

The *Magelone Romanzen* are neither as self-contained musically as Beethoven's *An die ferne Geliebte* (1816) or Schumann's *Dichterliebe* (1840), nor as coherent in their narrative as Schubert's *Die schöne Müllerin* (1823), yet all three earlier works were clearly relevant to the inception of what is usually regarded as Brahms's lone essay into song cycle. In April 1861,

Brahms accompanied the eminent baritone Julius Stockhausen (1826–1906) in complete performances of the Beethoven, Schubert, and Schumann cycles in Hamburg, and he began composing the first four of the fifteen *Magelone Romanzen* just a few months later.

Central to the question about the status of Op. 33 as a song cycle is the relationship between the poems Brahms set and the story on which they comment. Whatever the possible musical interdependence of the fifteen songs, any narrative connection depends on knowing the accompanying novella by Ludwig Tieck (1773–1853), in which eighteen poems are interspersed in the brief chapters.

Tieck's *Wundersame Liebesgeschichte der schönen Magelone und des Grafen Peter aus der Provence* (The Wondrous Love Story of the Beautiful Magelone and Count Peter of Provence) first appeared in the second volume of a collection of *Volksmärchen* (Fairy Tales) that Tieck published in 1797 under the pseudonym Peter Leberecht. (Brahms apparently used the second edition, drawn from *Phantasus, eine Sammlung von Märchen, Erzählungen, Schauspielen und Novellen* [vol. I; 1812].) Tieck, a prominent writer, critic, and translator, who helped edit A.W. Schlegel's celebrated translation of Shakespeare, was also intensely attracted to medieval themes. In the story of Count Peter and Magelone, he ingeniously cast a Romantic tone, at once more sentimental and exotic yet less religious, on a distant, twelfth-century tale of chivalric love.

The poems Brahms set accompany a story that is not readily apparent when detached from the novella. Such poetic interpolations, like those in Goethe's *Wilhelm Meister,* had prompted earlier Lied collections (for example, Schubert's Op. 62 [D. 877] and Schumann's Op. 98a). Abstracted from the prose narrative, the poetry is merely suggestive of affect. Indeed, had Brahms simply called this collection *Fifteen Songs,* those ignorant of the background of the poems might have sensed a similar emotional progression of love, separation, and reunion as that found in the *Nine Lieder und Gesänge,* Op. 32, which cleverly assemble unrelated poems by August von Platen and Georg Friedrich Daumer.

Many of Brahms's contemporaries, however, would have known the basic legend of the love of "Count Peter of the Silver Keys" for the fair princess from Naples, even if not in Tieck's telling of it. Young Brahms himself probably first encountered G.O. Marbach's simpler folk version of the familiar tale in 1847 while teaching piano to Lieschen Giesemann. That idyllic time left its mark—the fourteen-year-old Brahms could finally quit his despised job as pianist in the taverns of the Hamburg harbor and savor the beautiful nature of Winsen an der Lühe. (Musicologist Thomas Boyer even discerns an autobiographical identification of Brahms with the hero of the *Romanzen*.)

As the story begins, a wandering minstrel suggests that Peter, son of the count of Provence, travel to learn about the world. Peter sets off with three rings from his mother. Hearing of the beautiful Princess Magelone, daughter of the king of Naples, Peter arrives there with armor and horse emblazoned with two silver keys, amazes all with his jousting, and woos the princess with the assistance of her maid Gertraud. Peter gives Magelone the three rings, accompanied by love songs he has written in her praise. Although betrothed by her parents to another, Magelone agrees to flee with Peter and they set out on a coastal course back to France. After singing her a lullaby, Peter chases a raven that has swooped down and snatched a red silk bag containing the three rings. In his pursuit, Peter gets separated from Magelone, becomes lost at sea, and is eventually captured by Moorish pirates. He is taken to the sultan of Babylon, whose beautiful daughter Sulima is attracted to him. Thinking Magelone dead, Peter agrees to sail away with Sulima, but a vision of his beloved inspires him to escape, and they are ultimately reunited.

Some of the poems Brahms set (he omitted the first one and penultimate two from Tieck's novella) are lyrical meditations on the evolving narrative, while others are "songs" within the story itself, beginning with the minstrel's worldly advice and concluding with a spring song of love (a unison duet). In addition, there are the love songs that attend the giving of rings (Nos. 4, 5, 7) and the lullaby (No. 9). Peter is the "persona" for most of the songs, although No. 11 is for Magelone (for which Brahms narrows the vocal range while expanding the chromatic inflection of the melodic line), and No. 13, a simple jaunty tune, belongs to the exotic Sulima. Brahms includes a fair amount of word-painting and atmospheric accompaniments, and the moods extend from somewhat folklike songs of wandering to elaborate operatic-style arias.

Formally, Brahms cast most of the fifteen songs in rondo-like structures (such as the first two and last two), two- and three-part forms, varied strophic settings, and entirely through-composed (No. 6). Whereas Schubert wrote eight of the twenty songs in *Die schöne Müllerin* strophically, Brahms sets only No. 13 in that way, and even there divides the six stanzas into two larger sections comprising a repeated *A A B* structure and takes some liberties at the end.

While in recital and on recordings today, Op. 33 is usually heard in its

entirely, lasting nearly an hour, its genesis and initial performances en-
dorse no such unity. Brahms wrote the first six songs during 1861–62 and
they were published in two volumes as Op. 33 in 1865 with no indication
of further installments to come. Apparently Brahms was satisfied that
these six were self-sufficient. The remaining songs evolved over the next
six years, only to appear in three more volumes in December 1869. All of
the known first performances, moreover, presented the songs individually. If this seems to vitiate further the coherence of the cycle, it should
be remembered that Schubert's *Die schöne Müllerin* and *Winterreise* were
likewise originally published in installments and that they too were not
performed as cycles in public until Stockhausen took up their cause in
the mid-1850s, first in concert with Clara Schumann, and later with
Brahms. (That Brahms dedicated his *Magelone Romanzen* to the great
singer thus assumes added significance.)

The year after the complete publication of Op. 33, Brahms wrote to
critic Adolf Schubring that one need not hear all fifteen *Romanzen* performed together, nor "pay any attention to the narrative at all." Brahms
states that "it was only a touch of German thoroughness" that led him
to compose "through to the last number." Another contemporaneous
report contends that Brahms "was, in general, opposed to the performance of all the songs as a cycle."

Brahms commented on this issue many times over the next twenty-five
years, and took flatly contradictory positions. His instructions to publishers are the most significant statements because they determined how
the songs would be available to performers and public. Brahms wrote in
1875 to the Swiss publisher Rieter-Biedermann that the songs have "absolutely nothing to do with the *Phantasus* and the *Liebesgeschichte vom Peter*.
Really, I have just set the words to music and no one should be concerned
over the landscape . . . or anything else." When Otto Schlotke provided a
running narrative of the plot placed between the songs, Brahms complained, "But it has nothing to do with my songs, just as little as the
whole *Rittergeschichte*. Don't let it be printed!" Yet Max Friedländer, an authority on German Lied and former student of Stockhausen, reported
that Brahms told him after a performance in 1886 that he would like to
see a new edition introducing the poems and conveying the mood that
inspired their composition.

If Brahms's own statements can thus be cited to support both separation and unity, and even though their creation spanned some eight years,
there are internal musical justifications to respect the coherence of the

cycle. The songs project a logical tonal scheme in the succession of keys, beginning and ending in E♭ and usually proceeding by fifth and third. Some songs seem to lead to, or effortlessly follow from, a neighboring one, and commentators have even noticed a recurring motivic connection between an arpeggiated E♭–B♭–G that begins the vocal line in the first song and reappears in others (e.g., Nos. 2,3,5,10,15).

The *Magelone Romanzen* have held an ambiguous place in critical esteem. While they do not achieve the level of the great, inspiring cycles, their relative obscurity has caused them to be underrated. Only the haunting lullaby has prospered independently from the other songs. The standard designation "song cycle" may in fact be misleading. Brahms called the pieces "Romances," yet they differ considerably from his two other Romance collections, Opp. 14 and 84, which emanate more of a folk style and include strophic structures. Indeed, the *Magelone Romanzen* are surprisingly far removed from Brahms's favored folk style and often project a structural and textural complexity more associated with his keyboard and instrumental music. The recurring charges that many of the songs are too operatic, that the vocal style can be too difficult, elaborate, and long, and that they indulge inappropriate word repetition, betray a reified view of the Lied and of the *Liedercyklus*. Even given Brahms's own contradictory, perhaps ambivalent, position on their independence or unity, the fifteen songs nevertheless evolve from and evoke the medieval themes that so attracted him. Brahms's revealing query, "Aren't the *Magelone Romanzen*, after all, a kind of theater?", invites us to view the *Magelone Romanzen* in operatic terms as a series of reflective arias enjoyable without descriptive recitative, as lyrical intermezzos that can be separated from a timeless tale.

Christopher H. Gibbs

4 GESÄNGE, OPUS 43
Composed 1857–64; published 1868

1. Von ewiger Liebe [Fallersleben]
2. Die Mainacht [Hölty]
3. Ich schell mein Horn ins Jammertal [trad. Uhland]
4. Das Lied vom Herrn von Falkenstein [trad. Uhland]

These four songs, published in 1868, form one of the more heterogeneous of Brahms's Lieder collections, and he had not always intended to group them together. On March 11, 1868, Brahms and the baritone Julius Stockhausen had included the songs *Von ewiger Liebe* (Of Everlasting Love) and *Die Mainacht* (May Night) at a concert they gave in Zürich. The Swiss publisher Jakob Rieter-Biedermann was present, and he expressed a strong desire to issue the two settings, both of which have since established themselves as among the most famous of the composer's Lieder. Brahms had, however, already undertaken to let his principal publisher, Fritz Simrock, have some songs around the same time. "If I take two out of the middle," he told Rieter-Beidermann, "I can put in order a collection of Lieder only poorly." In the end, companionship won out over questions of musical orderliness. On July 5, Brahms explained the sacrifice he was making on behalf of his Swiss friend: "I am in the middle of putting together a small pile of songs, and since I am happy to give you the two you wanted, I shall no doubt throw the poets into complete confusion." Had Brahms not allowed Rieter-Biedermann to have *Von ewiger Liebe* and *Die Mainacht,* he might well have grouped the former together with the other settings of folk poetry included in his Lieder sets Opp. 47–49, which he offered to Simrock, and the latter with either the two further Hölty songs of Op. 46 or the single setting of the same poet *An ein Veilchen* (To a Violet), found in Op. 49. Since the nightingale figures prominently in *Die Mainacht,* Brahms may well have originally intended the song as a natural companion piece to *An die Nachtigall* (To the Nightingale), Op. 46/4.

Von ewiger Liebe sets a folk poem originally transmitted in the Saxon dialect known as Wendish, in a translation by Leopold Haupt and Heinrich Hoffmann von Fallersleben. The text is one that may have given Brahms pause for thought. Six years earlier, in 1858, during the period when he was conducting a women's choir in Hamburg, Brahms had written a bridal chorus with soprano solo, to words by Uhland. One of its melodic ideas—a phrase setting the words "Das Haus benedei' ich und preis' es laut, das empfangen hat eine liebliche Braut" (I bless and praise loudly the house that has received a beloved bride)—reappears in strikingly similar form in *Von ewiger Liebe,* where it expresses the young girl's affirmation, "Eisen und Stahl, man schmiedet sie um, unsere Liebe, wer wandelt sie um?" (Iron and steel may be forged anew, but who could change our love anew?) At the time Brahms composed his bridal chorus, he was deeply attached to Agathe von Siebold. Their relationship was painfully broken off after less than a year. Perhaps it is no coincidence that around the same time he composed *Von ewiger Liebe,* Brahms immortalized

Agathe by encrypting her name in the opening movement of his G-major Sextet, Op. 36.

The narrative of *Von ewiger Liebe* is of great simplicity. A young man is seeing his beloved home. As they walk along a dark country lane, he is anxious lest she should be caused pain by what others think of their relationship. She responds with an expression of faith in the constancy of their love. The opening section sets the scene, with the darkness of the landscape mirroring the intensity of the young couple's emotions. Short-breathed phrases repeated almost obsessively deep in the bass of the piano, with the accompaniment subtly doubling or anticipating the vocal line, a refusal to allow even a glimmer of major-mode consolation—these features enable the music's intensity to grow even before the man begins to speak. When eventually he does, the animation of the piano part increases, with a sudden surge of triplets anticipating the 6/8 rhythm of the song's final section. Horn calls accompany his words, with driving triplets suggesting the wind and rain that he fears will form a backdrop to their parting. With his bitterness, the music's pace increases, the horn calls become more insistent, and a remarkable atmosphere of intensity and anger is created. Not for nothing did even Hugo Wolf, normally no Brahms lover, admire this song.

Gradually, the song subsides toward its final section. Here, in the major, the woman quietly proffers her assurance of love. The steadfastness of her feelings is echoed in the static quality of the music, which unfolds to unchanging harmony, with a single repeated note chiming through the piano part. Their love, she says, is stronger than iron and steel; and when the same music returns a few measures later, Brahms lends it added emphasis through a subtly enriched sonority. The chiming note, moreover, is now syncopated—hinting, perhaps, at the forger's hammer transforming the pliant metal into new shapes. A final triumphant affirmation of the eternity of love, and this remarkable song is over.

The British musician Sir George Henschel found himself on one occasion en route from Coblenz to Wiesbaden, in the company of Brahms. The two discussed art in general, and creativity in particular. According to Henschel, Brahms took as his example of the latter the opening of the second song in Op. 43, *Die Mainacht,* composed in 1866:

"There is no real creating," [Brahms] said, "without hard work. That which you would call invention, that is to say, a thought, an idea, is simply an inspiration from above, for which I am not responsible, which is no merit of mine. Yea, it is a present, a gift, which I ought even to despise until I have made it my own by right of hard work. And there need be no hurry about that, either. It is as with the seed-corn; it germinates unconsciously and in spite of ourselves. When I, for instance, have found the first phrase of a song, say [here Brahms sang the opening of "Die Mainacht"], I might shut the book there and then, go for a walk, do some other work, and perhaps not think of it again for months. Nothing, however, is lost. If afterward I approach the subject again, it is sure to have taken shape; I can now begin really to work at it. But there are composers who sit at the piano with a poem before them, putting music to it from A to Z until it is done. They write themselves into a state of enthusiasm which makes them see something finished, something important, in every bar."

The quietly understated beginning of *Die Mainacht* is, indeed, an inspiration of great naturalness. Hölty's poem contrasts the loneliness of man with the tranquillity and harmony of nature; and Brahms finds the perfect musical metaphor—a floating melody of profound calm, which nevertheless carries with it a distant undercurrent of restlessness. The song begins as though in midstream, and it is notable that not once until the very end is the chord of the home key sounded in root position. Elsewhere, Brahms prefers the second inversion of the chord, a more dissonant and less final form. It is the failure of the music ever to reach a resolution that conveys so perfectly the image of someone who will never again see the object of his love, wandering disconsolately through the peacefulness of a moonlit night.

Die Mainacht was also set by Schubert, with a curiously Mahlerian melody that serves all four verses of Hölty's poem. Brahms, however, omits the second verse, so that his song can unfold as a simple ternary design. It may well be that in any case, the composer felt uncomfortable with the sentimentality of the missing stanza, in which Hölty praises the nightingale's wedded bliss. Brahms's middle section introduces the cooing doves, their inseparableness suggested by a piano accompaniment in smoothly repeated thirds. But with a passionate outburst, the man turns away from the harmony of the scene, seeking "darker shadows." The final section returns to the melody of the beginning; but now it rises to a new high point, as the tears flow at the pain of lost love.

The third of the Op. 43 songs, *Ich schell mein Horn ins Jammertal* (I Blow My Horn in the Valley of Tears), is a straightforward arrangement of the first of the five Op. 41 songs for male chorus, and Brahms told Rieter-

Biedermann that this "must absolutely be pointed out to the public." The four-part choral writing of the original is, in fact, transferred whole-sale to the keyboard, while the singer doubles the piano's top line throughout. Brahms makes no attempt to render the accompaniment id-iomatically pianistic—indeed, he is careful to retain the music's archaic modal flavor, with root-position chords used throughout. The song itself is one of the many manifestations of the composer's affection for early music. Its source is the earliest of all printed German song collections, the *Liederbuch* published around 1512 by Arnt von Aich. The evocative title, "I sound my horn in woe," owes its origin to Duke Ulrich of Württem-berg, who may well have written the song himself. The duke, a renowned hunter, was betrothed as a child to Sabina of Bavaria, a niece of Emperor Maximilian. Their wedding took place in 1511; but the marriage was loveless, and the duke laments the loss of the woman who had always been the object of his affections, Countess Elisabeth of Brandenburg. The countess is likened to the noble animal who escapes the hunter's clutches: he has to content himself with a common hare.

Also of sixteenth-century origin is the text of the last Op. 43 song, *Das Lied vom Herrn von Falkenstein*. It appeared in the first volume of Johann Gottfried von Herder's influential *Volkslieder* of 1778–79 and from there found its way into the collection of folk poetry *Des Knaben Wunderhorn*. Brahms appears to have used this later source for his text, though he may well have taken the opening two verses from Ludwig Uhland's *Alte hoch- und niederdeutsche Volkslieder*, published in 1844.

Brahms sets the ballad in curious fashion, for much of its length mak-ing no distinction between the two strongly opposed protagonists—the stern and unyielding Falkenstein and the woman in white he meets as he rides across his domain. Nor does the composer allow the narrative to de-velop: this is essentially a strophic setting, with the verses separated by a six-measure transition whose "sighing" phrases suggest the notion of pleading. Contrast is offered by a more tender middle section, in which the woman thinks of her lover festering in Falkenstein's jail. The rugged beginning, with the voice and piano in unison and the first verse unhar-monized throughout, is clearly a portrait of the baronial lord. The young woman greets him quietly and submissively, to the same music. As she speaks of honor, she becomes more assertive, and Brahms at last provides a harmonization of the stanza's final three measures. Only with the fourth stanza is the complete motif harmonized—and here the vocal line assumes a different cast, with the woman's determination mirrored in drumlike repeated fourths. Following the more gentle middle section (its urgency nevertheless indicated in Brahms's marking of *drängend*), this is the form which her declamation will henceforth take. Falkenstein, rather than face the shame that would be involved in fighting a woman, agrees to release her lover on condition that they leave the borders of his realm—a condition she indignantly rejects.

Misha Donat

4 GESÄNGE, OPUS 46
Composed 1864–68; published 1868

1. Die Kränze [Daumer]
2. Magyarisch [Daumer])
3. Die Schale der Vergessenheit [Hölty]
4. An die Nachtigall [Hölty]

The groupings of Opp. 46–49 constitute a collection of works all completed around the summer of 1868, though many of them have origins in earlier versions. Significantly, in Brahms's opus catalogue Op. 46 follows directly on *Ein deutsches Requiem*, Op. 45, and Op. 50 is *Rinaldo*. These twenty-one songs are therefore preceded by a seminal work of both musical and biographical significance and followed by Brahms's only attempt into the field of musical drama. The mid-1860s represent a difficult time in Brahms's life. In 1865 his mother died and the following year his father remarried. The *Requiem*, performed in part in December 1867 in Vienna, did not meet with immediate approval. Earlier that same year, any residual hope of returning to Hamburg to a suitable professional post had been dashed. Although Brahms had conducted the Singakademie for one year in Vienna, he had not yet come to feel entirely at home in that city.

The instability of Brahms's life at this point may explain why this period is dominated by the resurrection of older compositions and why this opus in particular is filled with songs of introspection and pensiveness. Opus 46 consists of two pairs of songs. The first pair is a set of translations by Daumer. *Die Kränze* (Wreaths) is marked ziemlich langsam and is in D♭ major. In this jewel of a song, the rhythmic patterns of the music mirror those of the text. Few of Brahms's songs so effectively evoke the overwhelming sense of pain and sadness. Number 2 is a Hungarian song entitled *Magyarisch*, an andante in A major. Again Brahms follows the evocation of the text closely with matching harmonic colors. In *Magyarisch* Brahms returns to a folk idiom, though the song is not quite as Hungarian as the title suggests. Its place in this setting, however, is justified by the text, which carries forward the theme of internal suffering, grief, and pain.

The second pair is settings of poems by Ludwig Hölty. *Die Schale der Vergessenheit* (The Cup of Forgetfulness), marked lebhaft (but not too quickly) is in E major and was written in 1864. Opus 46/4 *An die Nachtigall* (To the Nightingale) is marked ziemlich langsam and uses a text which Schubert also set to music in 1815 (D.196). Philipp Spitta described this number as possessing a "feverish, burning pain." According to Hermann Deiters, Brahms did not care much for this song; its publication was a result of Julius Stockhausen's advocacy. The work has been noted for its avoidance of a clearly rooted harmonic character and its display of passion. The song, like many others in Brahms's oeuvre, employs the objects of nature as the medium through which the protagonist expresses a struggle with love.

Leon Botstein

5 LIEDER, OPUS 47
Composed 1860–68; published 1868

1. Botschaft [Hafiz; trans. Daumer]
2. Liebesglut [Hafiz; trans. Daumer]
3. Sonntag [trad. Uhland])
4. O liebliche Wangen [Flemming])
5. Die Liebende schreibt [Goethe]

Like many of the songs of the late 1850s, the five songs of Op. 47 reflect Brahms's deep attachment to Agathe von Siebold, and communicate a wide range of emotional responses to love; this is especially true of the closing number of Op. 47, *Die Liebende schreibt* (A Woman in Love Writes). It is a setting in E♭ major of a sonnet by Goethe, and suggests Brahms's full awareness of compositional precedence. The same text was set by Mendelssohn, published posthumously as part of his Op. 86, and, appropriately, became one of his most popular songs. Schubert also put this text to music in 1819 (D.673) though the song was not published until 1832. In a letter to Brahms in 1869, Philipp Spitta praised the composer for structuring the music closely along the lines of the poem and compared Brahms's setting favorably to Mendelssohn's version. He felt that by adhering to the structure of the poem, Brahms effectively evokes the sense of loneliness and fear which the love-sick protagonist expresses.

The first two songs of Op. 47, entitled Botschaft (Message), and *Liebesglut* (The Passion of Love), are both settings of translations by Daumer of the fourteenth-century Persian poet Hafiz. *Botschaft* is marked grazioso in D♭ major and quickly became one of Brahms's most popular songs. Many observers remark on Brahms's deft use of the tension between duple and triple meter and the effectiveness of the codetta of the song. *Liebesglut* is marked appassionata, beginning in F minor and concluding in F major. It is characterized not only by rhythmic ingenuity but by a dialogue between major and minor and shifting tonalities. Number 3, *Sonntag* (Sunday), in F major and marked nicht zu langsam, is set to one of Uhland's many poems written in a folk idiom, a sensibility which Brahms appropriated effectively to create another of his most popular songs. There is an affecting simplicity to the work, deriving partly from its strophic and quite predictable phrase structure. The accompaniment suggests the innocent and naïve setting. Number 4, *O liebliche Wangen* (O Lovely Cheeks), with a text by Paul Flemming, is marked lebhaft and is in D major. This passionate song is fast-paced and the juxtaposition of major and minor at the end of every strophe underscores the aspect of intense and unfulfilled desire.

Leon Botstein

7 LIEDER, OPUS 48
Composed 1855–68; published 1868

1. Der Gang zum Liebchen [anon. trans. Wenzig]
2. Der Überläufer [Des Knaben Wunderhorn]
3. Liebesklage des Mädchens [Des Knaben Wunderhorn]
4. Gold überwiegt die Liebe [anon. trans. Wenzig]
5. Trost in Tränen [Goethe]
6. Vergangen ist mir Glück und Heil [trad. Mittler]
7. Herbstgefühl [Schack]

Though most of Brahms's song sets are not cycles in a strict sense, it has often been pointed out that they tend to share a sensibility and self-reference that suggest a sense of cohesion and interconnectedness among the individual numbers. The kind of flexibility afforded by this mere suggestion of relation (as opposed to the more formal narrative unity of a cycle) is quite conducive to the complex portrayals of volatile human emotion that are the major subjects of Brahms's songs, for it provides space for a perpetual reevaluation of each song's perspective. Can anything, Brahms asks, be said conclusively about the nature of love? This skeptical element perhaps explains a particular pattern that may often be discerned, in which the final song is placed as a dramatic contrasting comment on the prior numbers. Opus 48 is no exception in this regard; this set of seven songs culminates in a closing song which challenges the sensibility of the "cycle."

In this case, the first six songs all possess a relationship to the folk idiom. Opus 48, Nos. 1 and 4, are translations from the Czech by Joseph Wenzig. Number 1 is reminiscent of the slow waltz; Brahms wrote this in 1868 and used it to create a folk mood which allowed him to include two songs of an earlier provenance: Nos. 2 and 3, both of which were written before 1860. Number 2, *Der Überläufer* (The Deserter), marked andante con moto in F♯ minor, and No. 3, *Liebesklage des Mädchens* (The Maiden's Love Lament), marked etwas langsam in B major, are based on texts from *Des Knaben Wunderhorn*, the collection edited by Achim von Arnim and Clemens Brentano. In both songs, the protagonist expresses despair at being betrayed in love, No. 2 from the perspective of a man, No. 3 of a woman. Opus 48, Nos. 4 (in E minor) and 5, share a strophic form to express their laments on the nature of love. Number 5, *Trost in Tränen* (Comfort in Tears), employs a dialogue form mirroring the two voices of the poem. It is a setting of a poem by Goethe, in which Goethe himself borrowed the opening line from a folk song. It is marked andante and begins in E major, closing in E minor. Number 6, entitled *Vergangen ist mir Glück und Heil* (Happiness and Well-being Have Been Lost to Me), is a Doric-mode setting of an old German chorale. Of the set, this song has attracted the greatest interest of scholars because it demonstrates Brahms's interest in archaic song forms. In terms of the thematic subject matter, however, Brahms places this self-conscious song in the penultimate place as if to set up the wholly modern character of the final song.

All of these songs share the melancholy, unifying subject of grief, but they in no way prepare for the final number of the opus, the intensity and beauty of which serve as a clarifying comment on the relative nature of grief. It is not an accident that the two songs preceding No. 7 suggest the possibility of consolation. This thought is far from the text (by Schack) and music of *Herbstgefühl* (Sense of Autumn), No. 7, which is marked

ziemlich langsam and is in F# minor. When Brahms sent this song, which
Spitta described as "powerful in its dark moods," to Clara Schumann as
a present, she wrote back saying that she could never play through the
piece without bursting into tears. The text of the song may remind one
of the dark, somber mood of Simon's aria at the end of Haydn's *The Seasons,* in which winter rather than autumn functions as a metaphor for the
recognition of mortality and the pointlessness of life. But while Haydn's
vehicle is the voice of an old man who would be prone to such reflection,
Brahms's song dramatizes the pessimism of a man nearing middle age,
still young and strong enough to feel desire, but verging on the realization that the moment of promise has passed. Since the song's appearance,
observers have noted a direct reference to Schubert, whose song *Der Dop-
pelgänger* was on Brahms's mind as he was composing this work. The terrifying sadness of the musical setting is unrelieved, as is signified by the
dying out of the song in the depths of the bass register of the piano.

Leon Botstein

5 Lieder, Opus 49
Composed 1868; published 1868

1. Am Sonntag Morgen [anon; trans. Heyse]
2. An ein Veilchen [Hölty]
3. Sehnsucht [anon. trans. Wenzig]
4. Wiegenlied [trad. Scherer])
5. Abenddämmerung [Schack]

In Op. 49 Brahms creates a parallel grouping to Op. 48, with the final
song again expressive of disconsolation and set to a text by Friedrich von
Schack (1815–1894). *Abenddämmerung* (Evening Twilight) is marked
ruhig and is in E major. Once again Clara Schumann perceptively commented that the intense sadness of this song seemed inappropriate to
someone of Brahms's relative youth. Brahms utilizes a rondo form in
which the music of the opening stanza returns twice. Many observers
have commented on the remarkable subtlety, complexity, and striking
quality of the piano accompaniment. Philipp Spitta identified a
Beethoven-like mysticism in the song. Max Friedländer found the dissonances "reassuring" and most recently, Lucien Stark has argued that the
song is permeated with nostalgia. Brahms was clearly taken by the melancholy resignation of Schack's poetry. Schack—a patron of the arts, a col-

lector, and a poet, literary historian, and translator—was, like Brahms, oppressed by the sense of "lateness" of the contemporary world. Schack lived primarily in Munich, and was a prolific writer who became the leading expert in the history of the Spanish theater. His translations of the classics of Spanish and Portuguese literature became standard in the German-speaking world, and his poetry was extremely well received. Schack was ennobled in 1876. One of his primary interests was the question of the relationship between East and West; he published a philosophy of history entitled *Evenings of the Orient*. His three-volume autobiography, *Half a Century,* is an important document of late-nineteenth-century politics and culture. An especially interesting point of connection between Schack and Brahms is Schack's intense interest in contemporary painting. Schack assembled collections of Schwind, Feuerbach, Böcklin, and their contemporaries, which are now part of the state collections in Munich and housed in the famous Schack Gallery. If one wanted to gain a sense quickly of Brahms's aesthetic tastes in contemporary painting, the holdings in the Schack collection would mirror them precisely.

Immediately preceding this great closing song is a work which truly made Brahms a household name. Number 4 is the famous *Wiegenlied* (Lullaby), marked zart bewegt (delicately moving) and in E♭ major. It was composed in 1868 to celebrate the birth of the second child of Arthur Faber, a wealthy industrialist, and Bertha Faber, one of Brahms's oldest acquaintances whom he had known in Hamburg. Bertha (a native Viennese who had spent considerable time in Hamburg), first suggested to Brahms that he come to Vienna. The song was first performed by Luisa Dustmann-Meyer and Clara Schumann in Vienna, where Arthur and Bertha Faber then lived, in December 1869. The first stanza is from *Des Knaben Wunderhorn,* and the second was written by Georg Scherer. Here Brahms's imitation of a folk-song style was more successful than he would have wished. The song in many bowdlerizations and arrangements became world famous.

Number 1, *Am Sonntag* (On Sunday Morning), marked andante espressivo and in E minor, is a translation by Paul von Heyse from a popular song from Tuscany. Number 2, *An ein Veilchen* (To a Violet), is also a German version by Ludwig Hölty of an Italian poem by Giovanni Battista Zappi. Once again in this pairing of songs, Brahms employs a favorite method of juxtaposing male and female in dialogic opposition. In No. 1, a woman describes her attempt to come to terms with her lover's infidelity. In No. 2, the male lover wishes for his lover to see the tears he sheds because his fidelity is not reciprocated. No. 2 is marked andante and is in E major. No. 3, entitled *Sehnsucht* (Desire) in A♭ major, is another Wenzig translation of a Czech text from Bohemia. The first three songs are all through-composed, making the final two more striking since the famous *Lullaby,* No. 4, is strophic in structure. In putting the group of five songs together, it should be noted that as in Op. 48, the final song is substantially longer than the others. Furthermore, just as Op. 48/7 picks up some of the opening rhythmic character of No. 6, Op. 49/5 picks up the hint of the waltz from No. 4, as well as the rhythmic displacements over the bar-line. In organizing the songs from this period into collections, Brahms had a particular dramatic and emotional strategy in mind. One might say that in Opp. 47–49, and particularly Opp. 48 and 49, there is the hint of a nascent philosophy of history. Contemporary texts, or at least as in the case of Op. 47 a more modern text (Goethe), are juxtaposed to more archaic poetry and folklike sentiments. The contemporary and the modern emerge as the bearer of the profoundly sad, the melancholic, and the pessimistic. They offer a bittersweet recognition of the elusive character of happiness, the loss of innocence, overwhelming presence of death, and the pain of desire.

Leon Botstein

8 Lieder und Gesänge of G. F. Daumer, Opus 57
Composed ?1871; published 1871

1. Von waldbekränzter Höhe
2. Wenn du nur zuweilen lächelst
3. Es träumte mir, ich sei dir teuer
4. Ach, wende diesen Blick
5. In meiner Nächte Sehnen
6. Strahlt zuweilen auch ein mildes Licht
7. Die Schnur, die Perl an Perle
8. Unbewegte laue Luft

The eight songs of Op. 57 were published in December 1871 by Jakob Rieter-Biedermann. Although the exact date of composition is not known, they may have been written as early as the summer of 1868. All the texts are credited to Georg Friedrich Daumer (1800–1875), although three are translations by him. The texts of Nos. 1, 4, 5, 6, and 8, published in Daumer's *Frauenbilder und Huldigungen,* originated with Daumer. No. 2, published in Daumer's *Hafis: eine Sammlung persischer Gedichte,* is a translation of a Persian poem by Mohammad Shams od-Dīn Hafiz. No. 3 from *Polydora: ein weltpoetisches Liederbuch,* is a translation of a Spanish poem. No. 7, from the same collection, is translated from Sanskrit.

Although drawn from a number of volumes, the poems share the same theme of unrequited love, and all are characterized by an undisguised eroticism. For instance, the text of the middle section of No. 5 reads: "Ah, that man who has looked upon your face, to whom your spirit has entrusted that sweet ardor which blazes in it, for whom your kisses have burned, who has ever lost all his senses for joy upon your bosom." This explicitness drew a great deal of attention, with many of Brahms's friends chastising him for choosing such texts. The eighth song, with its description of swelling hot desires and heaving breasts, provoked the most criticism; Elisabet von Herzogenberg claimed to have defended the song despite its having upset her self-described prudish sensibilities. Similarly, Doris Groth, wife of the poet Klaus Groth, repeatedly praised the music of Op. 57, noting its sensitivity and intense effect on the listener, but she complained that the texts were not so beautiful. The critic Hermann Deiters must have had similar thoughts, stating that the songs were not suitable for common folk (*Allgemeine musikalische Zeitung,* 1875). According to Klaus Groth, Brahms imagined that Daumer the man would somehow embody the themes of his poems. But Max Kalbeck relates that, when the poet and the composer met in Würzburg in 1872, Brahms found Daumer to be an old man who claimed that he had always loved only one woman—his wife, who, Brahms noted, was as withered as the poet himself.

Beyond the eroticism, each song is intensely moving, and Brahms portrays the agony of the male protagonist with great sympathy. Nineteenth-century critics uniformly acclaimed these works, and, in her volumes on contemporary music, La Mara (Marie Lipsius, 1837–1927) described their infinite beauty and richness, and approvingly quoted Hermann Kretzschmar's remark that one puts aside the first four songs "as if one had heard a great tragic opera." When performed together, these four songs feel overwhelming, in part because of the wide array of emotions that are experienced in such a short time. From the fervid declaration of love in the first song, with its buoyant melodic line, to the relatively controlled emotion and resigned patience of the second, we experience the jarring pain in the realization that the woman never returns the protagonist's love. In the fourth song, the outer sections portray the anguish of love, while the more serene, chorale-like opening of the middle section represents a time when the character's soul will be at rest and his passion subsided.

The last four pieces are turbulent settings, characterized by numerous operatic gestures. The eighth, *Unbewegte laue Luft*, begins with the piano suggesting the tepid stillness of nature by the sustained E–F♮–E neighbor motion in the bass. Both the low register of this passage and the predominance of long notes contrast with the high registers and moving accompaniments of the other works of Op. 57. They also contrast with the next passage, in which a splashing fountain is represented by an eighth-note figure ornamented with a trill. As the text turns away from the external scene to the man's stormy passion, the tempo quickens, the dynamic level increases, and more active piano figuration appears. In the first section, the melody falls into tiny segments separated by rests; in the second, the melody is more expansive and the phrases are often longer than four measures. As the man entreats the woman to be with him, the dynamics soften and the piano's tempestuous sixteenths give way to more relaxed triplets. The neighbor motion of the prelude returns and facilitates a modulation to the pastoral key of F major, as the man sweetly invites his paramour to "float this way with your ethereal feet." The song ends with a return to the previous fervid mood, and the high melodic line and loud dynamics emphasize the ecstasy implied by the text.

In *Brahms Songs*, Eric Sams suggests that these pieces represent Brahms's own affection for Clara Schumann, and he believes that Brahms used Robert Schumann's melodic code for Clara throughout Nos. 4–7. This motive is frequently associated with pieces in B major: Sams notes that it appears at the beginning of the B-major seventh song and is then developed for the beautiful and notoriously graphic melodic curve at "deiner schönen Brust" (your beautiful bosom). (The tenderness of this image is created by the softly yearning appoggiaturas and by the harmonies, which wander from the tonic to the remote key of B♭ major.) This recurring motive lends to the unity of the cycle in much the same way as the erotic images serve as unifying threads in the texts. Similarly, sixteenth-note figurations and fast tempos are consistently employed throughout the cycle during the most passionate moments, where they convey the excitement of the protagonist.

Although the songs might have been meant for Clara Schumann, many of them demonstrate the influence of her husband's style of song writing. Robert Schumann's style is particularly evidenced by the manner in which the short melodic segments float over the piano in Nos. 2 and 3. In the case of No. 3, the short segments realistically depict the painful hesitancy of the protagonist's admission that he only dreamed that the woman loved him. By entering in the middle of each 6/8 measure, these segments create the metrical ambiguity that helps to evoke the vagueness of the dream. This haziness is also created by the large-scale harmonic structure, in which a tonic, root-position chord is prominent only on the last word. Even here, however, a minor seventh is added to the chord, and further dissonances adorn the tonic until the final chord of the postlude. Such withholding of the tonic, even though it is strongly implied by the dominant-seventh harmonies, is also evident in many of Robert Schumann's compositions.

Despite the gentleness of No. 3, it also contains the most heart-wrenching moment in the entire cycle. On the first admission that the protagonist is just dreaming, the melody climbs to the high minor sixth (g♮″), the dynamics reach *forte,* and then, as the melody descends, the tempo slows, the dynamics die away, and the phrase breaks off on a glaring, unresolved German sixth chord. After a moment of total silence, the piano reenters in a subdued way, like someone trying to catch a breath after a nasty shock. It begins with low, triplet eighths, and then, in the next measure, resumes the sixteenth-note motion that had characterized the rest of the song. Most of the chromatic notes of the sixth chord that bring such reality to this harrowing moment have been anticipated in the second measure of the prelude. Here a diminished seventh appears over a dominant pedal, and it recurs in the interlude and postlude. In its last appearance it quietly gives way to dominant harmonies, just as the protagonist's agony will be tempered by time. Similarly poignant moments occur in many of the songs—the lingering appoggiatura at the end of No. 7 (as the character dreams of the woman's breasts), and the melancholy melisma that gently falls over a sustained chord at the end of No. 6 (portraying the man's reluctant acknowledgment that the woman's glances show no trace of love), are but two further examples.

Kretzschmar seized on the idea that these works told a story of unrequited, fervid love, and he commended Brahms's brilliant depiction of the man's torment and inflammable emotions. And as late as 1911, La Mara wondered why such pearls were not heard more regularly in concert halls.

Heather Platt

8 Lieder und Gesänge, Opus 58
Composed 1869; Published 1871

1. Blinde Kuh [anon. trans. Kopisch]   5. Schwermut [Candidus]
2. Während des Regens [Kopisch]   6. In der Gasse [Hebbel]
3. Die Spröde [anon. trans. Kopisch]   7. Vorüber [Hebbel]
4. O komme, holde Sommernacht [Grohe] 8. Serenade [Schack]

Op. 58 was published with Op. 57 in 1871 by Jakob Rieter-Biedermann. Although the exact date of composition of each of the songs is not known, most of them were probably composed between 1869 and 1871. In October 1871, Brahms offered these works to the publisher, saying that he and the conductor Hermann Levi had worked on putting them together. Opus 58 includes Brahms's only solo Lied settings of poems by August Kopisch (1799–1853), Melchior Grohe (1829–1906), and Friedrich Hebbel (1813–1863). Max Kalbeck was quite critical of the texts of Op. 58, and in particular suggested that those by Hebbel were dull imitations of Heine. He lambasted not only their general style but even their grammar.

Unlike most of Brahms's Lieder, there are a variety of manuscript sources for the songs of Opp. 57 and 58. There are sketches for two measures of *Unbewegte laue Luft* (Still, Warm Air) Op. 57/8, an early draft of *Vorüber* (Over), and a practically completed version of *Während des Regens* (During the Rain). There are also autograph manuscripts of Op. 57/1, 2, 5–8, and Op. 58/1, 3, 5–7, as well as of the end of Op. 58/8. In his dissertation, *The Lieder of Johannes Brahms, 1868–1871: Studies in the Chronology and Compositional Process,* George Bozarth demonstrates how Brahms reconsidered some of these works. In some cases, he altered the metrical placement of the words, so that they were more accurately declaimed or so that their emphasis was clearer. In other cases, he changed the piano part so that it better aided the general flow and provided firmer support for the melody, particularly at climactic moments. Such changes illustrate the great concern that Brahms had for expressing the meaning and emotions of the texts, as well as for adequately representing their syntactical structure.

The first three songs of Op. 58 are all settings of works by the Silesian-born painter and poet August Kopisch, who was known for his translations of Silesian and Italian poetry into German, as well as for his original works, which show the influence of folk poetry. All three poems employed by Brahms were published in the poet's 1836 *Gedichte. Während des*

Regens (the second setting) is the most humorous, depicting a couple caught in a rain shower. The man hopes the rain will not stop, because as long as it continues they will kiss and embrace. Brahms coyly portrays this desire with unusual elongations on the words "Tropfen" (drop), "Regen" (rain), and "mehr" (more). However, he saves the longest extension for the word "entlassen" (allowed), when the character confesses that he will be permitted to stay only while the rain continues. Some of these extensions are facilitated by changing the meter from 6/4 to 9/4, an alteration that was praised by Hermann Deiters in his 1875 review in the *Allgemeine musikalische Zeitung*. Brahms offers a fairly literal interpretation of the rain with a staccato accompaniment. Whereas Brahms often associates staccato raindrops with descending lines and melancholy moods, here the piano has predominantly ascending figuration, and, with the lively tempo and major mode, it depicts the pleasure of the situation afforded by the rain. Deiters also remarked upon the tone-painting in Op. 58, and in particular on the impatient accompaniment of *Blinde Kuh* (Blind Man's Bluff), the first of the Kopisch settings, in which the idea of a game of hide-and-seek, a metaphor for a man searching out his sweetheart, is conveyed by the two-part imitative counterpoint that runs in unceasing sixteenth-notes throughout the song.

Die Spröde (The Hard-Hearted Girl) also captured the attention of the nineteenth-century critics, with Deiters remarking on its changes in meter, and Hermann Kretzschmar (followed by Max Friedländer) noting the roguish turn in the upper part of the piano's third measure. Kretzschmar thought that this figure belied the otherwise sorrowful setting. Brahms perhaps felt similarly, and, after the song had been published, he changed the original minor-key ending to major. He also had Hermann Levi ask the poet Paul von Heyse to improve on Kopisch's translation. As a result, Heyse rewrote the last lines of each stanza, and these alterations were included in the subsequent editions of Brahms's song.

On the whole, Deiters was most impressed with *O komme, holde Sommernacht* (O Come, Sweet Summer Night) admiring its beauty of expression and pleasant sound, and suggesting that the main rhythmic pattern was closely related to that of the words. The key of this piece, F$\sharp$ major, was not frequently used by Brahms, who seems to have followed Schumann's model in reserving it for particularly ebullient love songs. Schumann's *Frühlingsnacht* (Op. 39/12) demonstrates this key association, and Brahms's song, with its dotted motive and its middle section's repeated-note melody, recalls this earlier work. Both songs are in a fast tempo, and while the piano figurations are different, both call on triplet patterns. Moreover, both songs end with an exalted statement that the girl will be won over. In the Schumann song the nightingales sing, "She is yours!" The Brahms setting, however, is a little less discreet, ending with, "It is then that my sweetheart will surely become mine, the wicked girl!"

After this exuberant fourth song, the following four songs are of a much more pessimistic mood. In particular, Deiters commented on *Schwermut* (Melancholy) noting its doleful rhythmic patterns and expressive harmonies. La Mara was also moved by this song, and she praised the opening low, E♭-minor chords for their anticipation of the protagonist's deathly complaints. As he weeps in agony, the words "vor Schmerz!" (from pain) are set to a stark falling fifth. The unusual dynamic markings also emphasize these words; a brief crescendo leads to *forte* on "vor," but it is immediately followed by a return to *piano* on "Schmerz." As the character lays down his head, thinking only of death, the harmonies suggest the unrelated keys of B minor and then G minor. Although both of the subsequent Hebbel settings are quite melancholy, neither is so intense nor characterized by such despairing music as *Schwermut*.

An early version of *Serenade* already existed in 1867, when Brahms sent a copy of it, along with *Herbstgefühl* (Op. 48/7) and *Abenddämmerung* (Op. 49/5), to Clara Schumann for her birthday. All of these songs are settings of poems by Count Adolf Friedrich von Schack (1815–1894), an art historian and poet. Their despondent mood is thought to reflect Brahms's own depression at a time when he had realized that Hamburg would no longer be his home, but he had yet to establish permanent residence in Vienna. After seeing these works, Clara Schumann wrote on February 26, 1867, reassuring him that he had many reasons to be in higher spirits, including his close friends and his wealth of talent. She concluded, "I hope that you do not often surrender yourself to such a bitter mood."

Of the three Schack settings, *Serenade* is the most relaxed, though even here the character is in a subdued mood, doubtful that he will be able to hold his sweetheart even for one hour. Despite the melancholy text, the song has a charming melodic line. This is typical of Op. 58 as a whole, in which, as Deiters remarked, the melodies have a folklike character but still retain the artistry expected of a Lied. According to George Bozarth, the earlier version of this piece is simpler and even closer in style to a folk song. (Brahms made the revisions to this piece sometime between 1867, when he sent Clara a copy, and 1871, when the work was published, but the exact time is unknown.)

Heather Platt

8 LIEDER UND GESÄNGE, OPUS 59
Composed ?1871–73; published 1873

1. Dämmerung senkte sich von oben [Goethe]
2. Auf dem See [C. Simrock]
3. Regenlied [Groth]
4. Nachklang [Groth]
5. Agnes [Mörike]
6. Eine gute, gute Nacht [Daumer]
7. Mein wundes Herz [Groth]
8. Dein blaues Auge [Groth]

With the exception of the first piece, whose date of composition is not known, the Op. 59 songs were written the year they were published, 1873. Brahms sent them to the publisher Jakob Rieter-Biedermann as two sets, claiming that they were the result of some house cleaning, and describing them as "some extremely lovely, recommendable, agreeable, here and there difficult, moral, God-fearing, briefly first-class songs." Although he required that the publisher keep the order that he had designated, he himself had at one time put together a mini-cycle of the four Groth settings with the two songs known as the *Regenlieder*—*Regenlied* (Rain Song) and *Nachklang* (Reminiscence)—being placed first and last. In letters of 1873 and 1874, both the poet, Klaus, and his wife Doris, who were close friends of the composer, repeatedly thanked Brahms for these settings. During this time they performed these songs, along with others by Brahms including ones from Opp. 33, 57, and 58, as well as Doris's favorite, *Von ewiger Liebe* (Op. 43/1). Doris's letters are filled with unbridled adulation for Brahms's compositions, though she confessed that she and her husband had some difficulties performing them. In some cases, they were assisted by more talented visitors, and on one occasion, Julius Stockhausen, another friend of Brahms and one of the most esteemed Lieder recitalists of the day, sang the *Regenlieder* for them. Stockhausen also performed these two works at the home of Clara Schumann, to whom Brahms had sent them as a birthday present.

The text of *Regenlied* was published in Groth's *Hundert Blätter, Par-*

alipomena zum Quickborn (1854) and the poet inscribed the text of *Nach-klang* in Brahms's copy of this publication. Although performed sepa-rately even during Brahms's lifetime, and despite the fact that Brahms had already completed another setting of *Nachklang* (WoO 23), these two 1873 settings form a discrete pair within Op. 59. Both poems are per-vaded by the image of falling raindrops, and in both, the protagonist is in a pensive mood, dreaming of past, happier times. These songs are un-doubtedly the most successful and best known of those in Op. 59, and in his 1875 *Allgemeine musikalische Zeitung* review of this opus, Hermann Deiters enthusiastically applauded the melancholy melody that perme-ates both songs, as well as the beautiful modulations.

Much of the music of *Nachklang* is derived from *Regenlied*. The recur-ring main theme of both songs (which Brahms used again in the last movement of the G-major Violin Sonata, Op. 78) is characterized by a re-peated note pattern that in the prelude of *Regenlied* is played staccato. While offering a literal interpretation of the raindrops, this theme, along with the constantly falling melodic phrases, conveys an aura of nostalgia. This wistfulness is already suggested by the prelude to *Regenlied*, where the theme begins with bare octaves, and is then repeated in the bass. Both songs are in F♯ minor, and in both the reflective mood is suggested by the slowly declaimed text, the generally high range of the piano and voice, and the harmonic structure. The prelude of *Regenlied* begins on the dominant and reaches a very brief tonic chord as the voice enters. Throughout most of this song, however, the tonic is absent. This type of de-emphasis of the tonic, a not uncommon characteristic for a nineteenth-century composition, was often employed by Brahms, and in his songs he frequently uses the resulting wandering harmonies to create a dream world in which time seems to be suspended.

Regenlied is the more expansive of the two songs and includes a lengthy central section that begins firmly in D major. This section's new chordal texture, 3/2 meter, and its melodic line are suggestive of a chorale, and this association conveys a confident belief in the soul and Creation—a type of steadfastness and childish wonderment that is quite different from the outer sections of the song. After this section the music of the opening is recalled, and it is followed by a ten-measure postlude in which the tonic is resounded in the bass, as if to make up for its absence throughout the rest of the song.

Nachklang starts with the voice's restatement of the opening melody of *Regenlied*. Without the preceding work's prelude, this song does not clearly state the tonic chord until its last word. When sung alone, then, it seems to meander, ever searching for the tonic. When sung with *Regenlied,* this effect is somewhat lessened, as the first song provides the tonal framework for the second. In *Nachklang,* raindrops are compared to flowing tears. Although one might assume that the tears are for a lost love, in the context of the diptych they can also be inferred as being for the lost innocence of childhood. The brevity of *Nachklang* and its employment of the *Regenlied* theme suggest that it is a type of epilogue to the first song.

The other two poems by Groth that are used in Op. 59, *Mein wundes Herz* (My Wounded Heart) and *Dein blaues Auge* (Your Blue Eyes), are also from *Hundert Blätter, Paralipomena zum Quickborn.* Although these works are placed in a parallel position to the *Regenlieder,* as the last two songs of a volume of four they do not form a pair in the same manner and are not textually or musically related. *Mein wundes Herz* is characterized by a complicated, contrapuntal accompaniment in which the opening notes of the melody are woven throughout the piano, appearing in diminution, inversion, and stretto, and finally, in the last measures, in which the loved one is proclaimed to be the protagonist's guiding star, in augmentation. This contrapuntal working out, however, does not hamper the exuberant vocal line.

After the *Regenlieder, Dämmerung senkte sich von oben* (Twilight Descends from Above) has received the greatest critical acclaim of the Op. 59 songs. The text, written by Goethe when he was seventy-nine, juxtaposes images of dark and light, metaphorically representing death and life. Brahms became acquainted with this poem through a setting by his friend Hermann Levi, who then claimed that Brahms used part of his melody; he cited these measures in a letter of January 17, 1899, to Julius Stockhausen. Although Levi and Brahms had at one time been quite close, they grew apart as Levi became more aligned with Wagner and his followers. In this letter Levi criticized Brahms's declamation, finding, like other Wagnerians, that Brahms often placed too much emphasis on unimportant words (as, for example, the melodic ornament on "sich" toward the beginning of this setting). He fiercely claimed that such blunders were intolerable.

Brahms uses every means available to him to conjure up Goethe's nature world. In the first section of the text the darkness of twilight is transformed by the light of the evening star. Correspondingly, the prelude (which anticipates the melody) begins in a low register and is followed by a gradually rising tessitura and increasingly quicker surface rhythms. The harmonic structure also serves as a metaphor for this change, moving from the opening G minor toward E♭ major. Stanza two repeats the first stanza's melody, but encases it in a sixteenth-note countermelody. This Baroque-style invention-texture, combined with the minor key and the low range, conveys the mysteriousness of night in which nothing is seen clearly. The last two stanzas turn to major and their melodies reach out more freely, as the moon's rays suggest optimism. The gently throbbing accompaniment trails the voice, evoking the trembling evening light and the shadows that it casts.

The following song, *Auf dem See* (On the Lake), is an excellent foil to the darkness of *Dämmerung senkte sich von oben*. Its nature images are all lightness, beginning with the blue of the sky and waves. The pedals of the opening phrases suggest this pastoral atmosphere, and the rocking motion of the piano soothes the stormy heart of the protagonist. The contentment of this setting is encapsulated by the sunny E-major key, the predominantly diatonic harmonies, and the chorale-like melody that concludes the outer sections.

The other two songs, *Agnes* and *Eine gute, gute Nacht* (A Good, Good Night), are of a lightweight character, and their harmonic and melodic structures are not quite as complicated as those of some of the other pieces in Op. 59. Like the first song, *Agnes* is in G minor, but unlike all of the other songs, this one is clearly sung from a female's point of view. Each stanza of music is based on the first, with the melody staying fairly constant while the accompaniment changes. The piano alters not only the figuration but also the harmony, and its exquisite, passing chromaticisms in the last stanza bring a certain sympathy to the portrayal of the weeping girl, whose broken heart had up until this time been treated somewhat blithely. With its repeated notes and echo segments, this piece has somewhat of a folklike quality, suggesting the simple-mindedness of Agnes, and this contrasts with the more sophisticated and pathetic setting of this text by Hugo Wolf.

As in Agnes (which alternates 3/4 and 2/4 measures), much of the interest of *Eine gute, gute Nacht* lies in the rhythmic structure. After the prelude, which anticipates the main melody, the piano and voice seem to move independently with the upper line of the piano having a different rhythmic structure and often moving in contrary motion to the voice. This is particularly noticeable at the beginning of the second stanza on the lines, "You shouldn't have fed my soul's flame so cruelly." The true joy of the song, however, is the melody's falling leaps, its pretty appoggiaturas, and its generally sprightly mood.

Heather Platt

9 LIEDER UND GESÄNGE, OPUS 63
Composed 1874; published 1874

1. Frühlingstrost [Schenkendorf]
2. Erinnerung [Schenkendorf]
3. An ein Bild [Schenkendorf]
4. An die Tauben [Schenkendorf]
5. Junge Lieder I (Meine Liebe ist grün) [F. Schumann]
6. Junge Lieder II (Wenn um den Holunder) [F. Schumann]
7. Heimweh I (Wie traulich war das Fleckchen) [Groth]
8. Heimweh II (O wüsst ich doch den Weg zurück) [Groth]
9. Heimweh III (Ich sah als Knabe Blumen blüh'n) [Groth]

For both textual and tonal reasons, the nine songs of Op. 63 appear to form a cycle. Although the texts of the *Lieder und Gesänge* are by three different poets, Brahms clearly designed the sequence of songs to present a narrative in which the hero mourns the loss of his youth and first love. The four Schenkendorf settings *(Frühlingstrost, Erinnerung, An ein Bild, and An die Tauben)* and the three Groth settings *(Wie traulich war das Fleckchen, O wüsst ich doch den Weg zurück,* and *Ich sah als Knabe Blumen blühn),* which Brahms himself designated as "Homesickness," present a melancholy view of departed youth and ephemeral love. These flanking groups of songs enclose two idylls, settings of unpublished poems by Robert Schumann's son Felix, the "Junge Lieder" *(Meine Liebe ist grün* and *Wenn um den Holunder).*

In the opening song, *Frühlingstrost* (Spring Consolation), the spring breezes describe their role in easing the path of love. The poem embodies a complicated change of speaking voice from the lover to the spring breezes themselves. The lover describes the breezes addressing him, trying to console him, "the sorrowful one." In the second stanza, the "airs" *(Lüfte)* seek out the woman, telling her to awaken and search for her lover in the fields. The breezes profess undying devotion, assuring the beloved that they will protect her from the sadness she must feel at the man's departure. In *Erinnerung* (Remembrance), the protagonist returns to places where he once walked with his beloved and recalls how her "wondrously beautiful eyes" filled the entire world with "eternal happiness" and "sweet light." Now, seeing these once familiar sights again reminds him of her, but they make him feel only longing "filled with pain and desire and lack of love." In *An ein Bild* (To a Portrait), the hero sees a picture of the woman he once loved. Like a person who stares into the depths of the sea, ignoring all of the gleaming treasures, or who gazes into the firmament, remaining oblivious to all of the stars but one, the protagonist ignores everything but this picture. Mesmerized by it, he feels that it alone possesses the power to ignite all of his longing, courage, and desire. In the fourth song, *An die Tauben* (To the Doves), the hero in anguish calls upon the doves to carry an urgent message to his distant beloved. Wracked by "eternal torment," he gives them a letter, which says, "Beloved, either come quickly, or seek me in the land of the dead."

The two settings of the Felix Schumann poems represent a retrospective hiatus—an untroubled idyll picturing youthful love fulfilled—within the cycle's larger, tragic narrative. In *Meine Liebe ist grün* ("My Love Is Green"), the protagonist rejoices in his beloved who is "green like the lilac bushes and as beautiful as the sun." His soul, winged like the nightingale and intoxicated with love, celebrates their love in song. In *Wenn um den Holunder* (Around the Elderberry Bush), we discover the youthful lover cuddling his beloved on a mossy bank. Night falls, the village clock chimes, the larks sing their evening prayer, and souls "melt" into one another through "the holy, God-given power of love." The only hint of sorrow is at the parting; at last the protagonist releases his beloved from his embrace, blessing her by kissing her upon the eyes.

With the concluding three Groth settings, however, the mood reverts to the tragic present of the Schenkendorf poems. In the first of the "Heimweh" (Homesickness) songs, the protagonist revisits his birthplace and recalls how, in his childhood, everything about it was magical: the trees and flowers were filled with dreams, and everything sang and glowed. In the song's final stanza, the hero bitterly regrets ever having left his homeland; only in his native woods and fields could he ever hope to still his feelings of longing and yearning. In the second "Homesickness" song, we now encounter our protagonist standing in despair on the edge of the ocean, the infinite, desolate waste of sea and sky mirroring his own internal state. If only he could find the path back to childhood! Why did he ever seek happiness elsewhere, leaving his homeland and his mother? How he misses the peace of being a child in his mother's arms and basking in maternal love. If only he could return to his childhood, untroubled by striving, struggle, and the passage of time. As in the first "Heimweh" song, the concluding stanza is fraught with melancholy: there *is* no path to a second childhood; all that remains is the fruitless search for happiness represented by the empty beach. In the final "Home-sickness" setting, the speaker again returns to his childhood and recalls the sunshine, the light, and the fragrances he "drank in thirstily" in his youth. Now, he searches in vain for a wreath of flowers he wove as a child; but, like the glow of his youth, it has disappeared forever.

Imogen Fellinger has proposed that Brahms's title for this cycle, *Lieder und Gesänge,* is significant because it points to a mixture of formal types; according to Fellinger, the composer carefully distinguished between *Lieder*—that is, strophic and varied strophic songs—and *Gesänge,* or elevated and artificial songs. According to this definition, the strophic or strophic binary songs 5, 6, 7, and 9 are *Lieder,* while songs 1, 2, and 4 in rondo form and songs 3 and 8 in "chiasmus" or "cross" form *(A B B A)* are *Gesänge.* The form of the songs may be clarified as follows:

No. 1, five-part rondo: A_1, B, A_2, C, A_3
No. 2, five-part rondo: A_1, B, A_2, B_2, A_3
No. 3, "chiasmus" form: A_1, A_2, B_1, B_2, A_3
No. 4, five-part rondo: A_1, B, A_2, C, A_3
No. 5, strophic: A_1, A
No. 6, strophic: A_1, A_2
No. 7, strophic binary: A_1, B_1, A_2, B_2, A_3, B_3
No. 8, "chiasmus": A_1, B_1, B_2, A_2
No. 9, strophic binary: A_1, B_1, A_2, B_2

The fact that the first and last songs are both in A major reinforces the hypothesis that these nine songs constitute a cycle (a further unifying feature is that all of them are in the major mode). The second of the "Heimweh" Lieder, *"O wüsst ich doch den Weg zurück,"* is arguably the most famous of the entire cycle. A striking feature of this song is the sudden modulation to F major, the Neapolitan ($\flat$II) of E major. This "wandering" modulation into F major, a key at once so "distant" from and yet close to the E-major tonic, clearly represents the protagonist's "loosing his way" in life—that is, loosening the connection with the "home" (tonic key) of his childhood. The "darkness" of this modulation from the "bright" four-sharp side (E major) to the "subdued" one-flat side (F major) is intensified in the final stanza when F major is converted into F minor; here, the simultaneous reduction of the texture to "bare" or "empty" octaves depicts the vast "emptiness" of the "barren strand" *(öder Strand)*. One might say that, with its melancholy portrayal of the irrevocable loss of youthful innocence and maternal love, and the inevitable decay into entropy and ultimately death, this passage encapsulates the very essence of the entire Op. 63 cycle. The power and eloquence of this song was immediately apparent to early observers, including Billroth, who wrote to Brahms: "The [Groth] poems are magnificent and you have set them to beautiful music with skill and imagination. As far as my own idea of songs goes, I should say that the second, *'O wüsst ich doch den Weg zurück,'* is the best."

Timothy L. Jackson

9 GESÄNGE, OPUS 69
Composed 1877; published 1877

1. Klage I (Ach, mir fehlt) [anon., trans. Wenzig]
2. Klage II (O Felsen, lieber Felsen) [anon., trans. Wenzig]
3. Abschied [anon., trans. Wenzig]
4. Des Liebsten Schwur [anon., trans. Wenzig]
5. Tambourliedchen [Candidus]
6. Vom Strande [trad., trans. Eichendorff]
7. Über die See [Lemcke]
8. Salome [Keller]
9. Mädchenfluch [trad., trans. Kapper]

The songs of Opp. 69–72 were published as a group by Simrock in 1877. Some of these works had been written at an earlier time, but all those of Op. 69 date from the year they were published. Although contrasting in mood, theme, and style, many of the texts of these four collections were written by a small group of poets. Each opus includes at least one text by Karl Candidus (1817–1872) and one by Carl Lemcke (1831–1913). In all, the four collections contain two songs with texts by Gottfried Keller (1819–1890) and two by Goethe (1749–1812). Additionally there are four texts by Joseph Wenzig (1807–1876), all of which appear in Op. 69.

Brahms sent the songs of Opp. 69–72 to Clara Schumann on April 24, 1877. He claimed that Simrock was urgently waiting for them but that first he wanted her advice. Clearly he believed that Clara would not be completely pleased with his work, since he cautioned her to read the texts more than once and hoped that she would not think them too crude. (The letter also includes some discussion of financial matters, but Brahms claimed that he was too embarrassed to admit to the price Simrock was paying for these pieces.) It would seem, however, that Brahms did not subsequently alter any of the works, and perhaps he asked for Clara's comments as a way of appeasing her or to prepare her for works that she might not like. In any case, Simrock had by this time already seen many of these pieces, and in a letter to Brahms of March 29, 1877, he relates how he and one of Brahms's other friends, Theodor Billroth, had enjoyed playing them. On May 2, Clara responded as Brahms had requested. After proclaiming the songs as glorious, she listed each one with a sentence or two of commentary. As Brahms predicted, she was not entirely happy with the music, and many of the texts were not to her taste. In particular, from Op. 69 she was not so pleased with *Klage I* (Lament) and *Tambourliedchen* (Little Drum Song) and she recommended that he not publish *Über die See* (Over the Sea) and *Salome*.

Frau Schumann was not the only one who disliked *Salome*. It was also harshly criticized by Hugo Wolf. Wolf, too, set this Keller text, and in a letter of August 20, 1890 to his friend Melanie Köchert, he rants about Brahms's song-writing style and this work in particular: "What a master of the bagpipes and accordion Brahms is! 'You can't top this!' No one writes more authentic foot stompers than he, and yet, despite all the stompers, 'let's be merry' ditties and doodles, no one can be as melancholy as he ... and so in this familiar, noble, popular vein it yodels away to the end." These allusions to folk music mock the folk heritage of Brahms's Lieder. Brahms, following Schubert, considered folk music as a model for Lieder, and it influenced his declamation, rhythmic patterns, and form. Wolf, however, disapproved of all these elements of Brahms's compositional style, and he was so enraged by Brahms's setting of this Keller text that he even wrote out several measures illustrating for Köchert the older composer's alleged errors.

The folk style that Wolf so disparaged is evident in a number of other settings in Op. 69, and Clara Schumann drew attention to this aspect of *Klage II*. In part these folklike characteristics are due to Brahms's choice of texts, with the first four being translations of folk poetry by Wenzig, and the last being a translation of a Serbian folk song by Siegfried Kapper (1821–1879). Both Wenzig and Kapper were Czech, and both were known for their translations of folk poetry. (Brahms also drew on Kapper's translations for some of the texts of Opp. 85 and 95.) In all of the Op. 69 settings, the resemblance to folk music is witnessed in the easy flowing melodies, with that of *Klage II* being characterized by graceful ornaments on the last eighth of many measures.

Most of the Op. 69 pieces tell of the woes and joys of a young girl, though in *Tambourliedchen,* the girl disguises herself as a drummer boy. Brahms himself described this group to Simrock as *Mädchenlieder,* and recommended that they be advertised as such (letters to Simrock of April 18 and 21, 1877). Billroth recognized this theme and approached these songs with a great deal of excitement. In an October 1877 letter to Hanslick, Billroth described how his daughters were singing them, and he imagined exactly the type of girl who would best represent each song:

> No. 4, an eighteen-year-old girl, blonde, finding the sensual note un-
> consciously through the necessity of nature . . . No.8, a rather original
> sixteen-year-old, black-eyed little girl, full of fun, full of spirits, very quick,
> with natural grace, and singing out with an overwhelming joviality. No.9 . . .
> is a tremendously sensuous and passionate song; it must be sung with all
> that feeling, the *czárdás* getting wilder and wilder. When that girl, after that
> song, meets her Jova, she embraces him as if she would crack all his ribs!

Perhaps in imitation of the folk music of central Europe, this last piece, *Mädchenfluch* (Maiden's Oath), alternates triple-meter sections, characterized by dotted rhythms and rolled chords in the piano, with wilder duple-meter sections, featuring excitedly moving sixteenth-note piano figures. The folk character is also suggested by the raised (Lydian) fourth, which is prominent in the melody of the faster, duple sections. Clara Schumann praised the swing of this setting, but she thought the text ugly. After the introductory remarks of the narrator and the mother, the girl curses her sweetheart, but with each curse she also reveals her desire to have him, and the whole piece ends triumphantly with her calling out, "Bring him to my house!"

The spirited mood of *Mädchenfluch* is similar to that of *Tambourlied-chen,* and both songs are also in A major. Perhaps these similarities suggested the placement of these songs within the Op. 69 cycle. This collection was published in two volumes comprising Nos. 1–5 and 6–9, respectively, with *Tambourliedchen* as the last song of the first volume and *Mädchenfluch* as the last of the second. While this last song drew the imagination of Billroth, *Tambourliedchen* also seems to have had a number of admirers, and it was even performed at one of the Vienna Wagner Society's concerts. This group was known for its criticism of Brahms, and its concerts were primarily intended to promote the work of Wagner and his followers.

The brightness of these A-major songs contrasts with the more resigned moods of *Vom Strande* (On the Beach) and *Über die See*. Both of these songs are set in minor keys and depict a maiden whose sweetheart has abandoned her and is now oceans away. Whereas *Über die See* is a simple, melancholy, strophic song, *Vom Strande* is more varied. Its main stanzas are characterized by a moving folklike melody, not so different in style to that of the other songs of Op. 69, but the refrain is more dramatic. It has a slower moving melody, an unsettling, syncopated bass motion, and it begins on an F-major chord that only gradually progresses to the tonic, A minor. Throughout the song a variety of sixteenth-note figurations depict the waves falling on the shore, where the girl stands calling out to her man. The final cadence of this refrain is somewhat inconclusive, with the melody rising to a scale-degree 5 (rather than falling to the tonic), and the supporting harmonies moving directly from an augmented-sixth chord to the tonic, rather than through a dominant chord. This unsettling cadence, with its high, forlorn melody and bass's descending arpeggio, suggests that the girl's calls will not receive a response.

Heather Platt

4 GESÄNGE, OPUS 70
Composed 1875–77; published 1877

1. Im Garten am Seegestade [Lemcke]
2. Lerchengesang [Candidus]
3. Serenade (Liebliches Kind) [Goethe]
4. Abendregen [Keller]

When Brahms sent the Opp. 69–72 songs to Clara Schumann for her review prior to their publication, he mentioned that in particular he would be grateful for her criticisms of Op. 70. Of these four songs, Frau Schumann most praised the first, *Im Garten am Seegestade* (In the Garden on the Seashore). Its accompaniment also impressed critic Theodor Helm (see his review in the *Musikalisches Wochenblatt*, February 1878), who claimed that it was highly original.

Frau Schumann also seemed pleased with the second song, *Lerchenge-*

sang (Lark's Song) though she did not much care for the melody. The Herzogenbergs, who first viewed these songs with Clara, also had some reservations about this piece, and Heinrich criticized the sparseness of the accompaniment. These first two songs, composed in February and March 1877, have somewhat similar texts: after painting outdoor scenes, which feature the songs of birds, they talk of memories and lost love. Their ethereal moods seem to have provoked Brahms to draw on Robert Schumann's song-writing style, and in particular, his style of independent piano parts. The choice of B major for *Lerchengesang*, as well as the gentle, high arpeggios of the piano (which include one of the highest notes employed in Brahms's accompaniments—f♯″), and the sighing appoggiaturas are reminiscent of the dreamy B-major songs of Op. 57, which also show the influence of the older composer. Somewhat unusual for Brahms, however, are the entire measures in which the piano is silent while the voice sings. Each of the two main sections begins with the voice's melodic segment followed by the piano's touching appoggiaturas. This exchange is like a dialogue between the protagonist and the faraway voices of the past, which gently haunt him. The vast distance in register of the two melodies and the loneliness of the unaccompanied voice create a nostalgic aura, suggesting that the protagonist is out of touch with his current surroundings and that he will never be able to reclaim his past love.

The text of *Serenade* is from Goethe's opera *Claudine von Villa Bella*, though it had already been used as an independent song text by Christoph Gottlieb Neefe (1748–1798), Johann Friedrich Reichardt (1752–1814), Franz Schubert, and Max Bruch (1838–1920). Neefe was a teacher of Beethoven, and Brahms owned a copy of his *Serenaden*, which included this setting. In Goethe's original text, this song is performed, with a zither accompaniment, by the hero, Rugantino. He addresses two of the other characters, Claudine and Lucinde, asking each in turn why delicate souls always torment themselves. Throughout his setting, Brahms employs light two-part writing with the two hands of the piano or the voice and piano exchanging short motives, perhaps alluding to the inner questioning and seeking of the protagonist. Clara Schumann was particularly critical of the text repetitions that Brahms employed during the song's final phrase. Numerous writers in both the nineteenth and twentieth centuries have criticized this type of repetition, with some claiming that Brahms inserted repetitions more for the sake of musical expansion than for textual clarity. In this instance, they might have a case, because the threefold statement of "liebliches" does seem over-wrought for this otherwise tender song. Moreover, the voice's concluding gesture does not do justice to the rest of the melodic line and no doubt contributed to Clara's description of this last phrase as "stiff."

Of the four songs in Op. 70, *Abendregen* (Evening Rain) was composed first, in 1875. Whereas the other three are relatively brief portrayals of eternal longing, this song comprises four stanzas and is almost double the length of the others. The Keller text tells of a weary traveler who be-lieves that his actions have been misinterpreted but that he will be re-deemed after death. It opens with the traveler trudging gloomily through the rain, but it closes with the image of a brilliant "rainbow of honor" en-circling his head. Clara Schumann described this text as bombastic and uninspiring. In a letter of April 10, 1877, Billroth, who had discussed the song with the singers Julius Stockhausen and Amalie Joachim, also raised objections to the text, suggesting that it was more cerebral than poetic. He recognized, however, that this type of text had an appeal to Brahms and he concluded that the composer's music gave a "solemn blessing over the poetry." According to Max Kalbeck, the text had personal im-plications for the composer, symbolizing his feelings concerning his dis-agreement with Wagner and Peter Cornelius. In 1864, Cornelius had given Brahms a holograph copy of Wagner's *Tannhäuser.* The next year, however, Wagner demanded that the score be returned to him, claiming that it had only been loaned to Brahms. Brahms obliged, but felt that he had been misrepresented because he believed the score had been a gift.

Brahms's setting of the text is uneven. The most convincing aspect of the text-music fusion is the tonal metaphor for the change in the per-ception of the traveler. The opening section, concentrating on his dismal life, is in A, while the second section, depicting the high esteem accorded to him after his death, is in C major, a key often used to represent purity. The transition to this key is characterized by a slowly rising series of arpeggios, thought by most commentators to represent the rainbow. The second, slower, and more noble section aptly depicts the raised stature of the traveler, and the part describing his closest friends is set to a partic-ularly moving, chromatic passage. In contrast, the detached accompani-ment (representing the rain) and the repeated-note melody of the first section seem too relaxed for the initial dispirited mood of the text. Fur-thermore, the first full measure of the melody is marred by a rest placed between the syllables of "schimmernd," a type of declamation problem that has aroused the ire of many of Brahms's critics.

Heather Platt

5 GESÄNGE, OPUS 71
Composed 1877; published 1877

1. Es liebt sich so lieblich im Lenze! [Heine]
2. An den Mond [Simrock]
3. Geheimnis [Candidus]
4. Willst du, daß ich geh? [Lemcke]
5. Minnelied [Hölty]

The five songs of Op. 71 were all written in 1877 and, like those of Op. 70, they are of somewhat uneven character and quality. The text of the first is from Heine's *Romanzen*, in which it is titled "Frühling." Initially, Brahms also used this title, but he changed his mind, writing the new title, *Es liebt sich so lieblich im Lenze!* (Love Is So Lovely in Springtime!), into the printer's fair copy. These words recur, with the same music, as the second line of the first and second stanzas, and the final line of the last. The scene portrays a charming shepherdess weaving dainty wreaths, an action that, as in *Der Kranz* (Op. 84/2), Brahms suggests by a contrapuntal accompaniment. The first two stanzas are set to almost identical music, paralleling the closeness of their texts, which describe the river and then the shepherdess and her wreaths. The piano's figuration changes for the next stanza's description of a horseman. Although its animated, triplet staccato motion seems a little forced, as does the modulation to F♯ major, Brahms may have chosen these devices to depict the rider's boldness. The music of the first stanza is then repeated for the last, with alternations to portray the girl's longing and to allow for a new G-major section, representing the forlorn cries of a nightingale.

In *An den Mond* (To the Moon) the protagonist's melancholy is immediately suggested by the minor key and low accompaniment, as well as by the melody's neighbor-note motif (B–A♯–B). This motive, with its uneasy rhythm and dissonances, provides much of the tension throughout the song. First heard in the prelude, it is taken by the melody, and then expanded and embellished across three measures at "der Empfindung Seufzer" (the sigh of feeling). The darkness of this setting is momentarily relieved by a modulation to D major when the protagonist tells the moon that only a look from his sweetheart will heal his heartache. As he claims that only hope keeps him alive, the piece ends with a surprisingly high level of chromaticism. The postlude fades out with variations of the initial chromatic neighbor motive, the lingering dissonances hinting that the man's hope will not be enough to sustain him.

Clara Schumann thought the end of *An den Mond* beautiful, and she was also enchanted by the next song, *Geheimnis* (Secret). This second song was perhaps the best received of those in Op. 71, and Theodor Billroth, in his October 1877 letter to Hanslick, described it as "the most exquisite scent of lilies in the moonlight!" The Viennese critic for the *Musikalisches Wochenblatt,* Theodor Helm, was not quite so impressed, however. Writing in a review of February 15, 1878, he claimed that the song was too much like Schumann's *Der Nussbaum* (Op. 25/3). The quiet scene of a spring evening, in which only a gentle breeze provides motion, is depicted through soft dynamics, pedal points, and the slowly unfolding melody, which is marked *sotto voce*. The figuration of the left hand of the piano generates most of the motivic and chromatic interest of the work. It molds the phrases together, producing the seamless, floating sensation that gives this work its transcendent quality. This effortless, forward motion is also created by the harmonic structure in which a completely unaltered tonic chord is not stated until the end. Over the piano's graceful arpeggios, with their poignant dissonances, the voice has phrases of uneven length. These techniques conjure up a dreamlike atmosphere, which is reminiscent of *Es träumte mir* (Op. 57/3), as well as the B-major songs of Op. 70.

Throughout this piece, the inner voice often repeats a wistful descending tetrachord (G–D), which is characterized by the flattened seventh and sixth scale degrees The only section where this disappears completely is at the end of the first stanza, when Brahms repeats the protagonist's question to the trees: "Why are you standing together like that?" This more assertive section modulates to the dominant, and ends with the only *forte* in the piece. The tetrachord returns for the last stanza, which introduces another elegiac falling figure in the piano. As the speaker finally reveals that the real topic of the poem and of the whispering trees is the couple's love, the tempo slows, the chromaticism increases, and the accompaniment thickens. Stressing this topic further, the words "unserer Liebe" (our love) are spread across seven measures

and the descending tetrachord is repeated in augmentation, over a dominant pedal, and then in its original configuration over a tonic pedal.

Willst du, daß ich geh? (Do You Want Me to Go?) is from a completely different world. The bawdy text, in which a man attempts to persuade a
woman to let him stay the night, appalled both Elisabet von Herzogenberg and Clara Schumann. Theodor Billroth was more appreciative, suggesting (in a letter to Brahms of April 10, 1877) that "a good tenor (but
who?) will drive the women mad" with this song. The man's question
"Willst du, daß ich geh?" forms the refrain, and it is set to chromatically
rising melodic segments over a syncopated accompaniment with uneasy,
repeating bass notes. This melody is also the basis for the first phrase of
each stanza. The first two stanzas are set to the same music. They begin
with a piano prelude that establishes the wild, stormy scene by fast, syncopated rhythms and loud dynamics. In contrast, the roar of the waves
at the beginning of the third stanza is suggested by the piano's contrary-
motion figures, which flow smoothly and softly. In this stanza, the man
asks the woman to keep him safe from the wicked fairy, and the mysteriousness of this creature is alluded to by a subdued chromatic passage.
In the final stanza the man paints a picture of a more pleasant night en-
cased in the woman's warm arms. The stormy introductory measures are
omitted, the tempo slows a fraction, and the key changes to the optimistic tonic major. Once more, the ascending refrain is sounded, but
now it slows and pauses. Suddenly the lively tempo returns, and a loud,
lyrical version of the question is sounded. Whereas the other refrains are
marked tranquillo, dolce, *piano,* and the man seems to approach the
woman with some degree of care, now he is jubilant. Aside from the
melodic changes, the chromatic harmonies, which before had abruptly
broken off on a dissonance, are replaced by an assured move from the
dominant to the tonic, and full chords replace the bare octaves. All these
changes imply that the man received the answer he wished. Simrock (in
a letter to Brahms of March 29, 1877) revealed his pleasure with this outcome, and the song as a whole.

The Hölty text of *Minnelied* (Love Song) had previously been set by
Schubert, Mendelssohn, Moritz Hauptmann, and Louis Ehlert. The ethereal mood of Brahms's piece takes us back to the world of *Geheimnis,*
though here there is an aura of melancholy as the protagonist contemplates what his life would be if his beloved left him. As in the third song,
Brahms relies on pedal points to create the gentle, dreamlike atmosphere.

In the central section, the bleakness of life without his beloved is depicted by a lower, relatively stagnant melodic line, and by a constantly reoccurring soulful diminished seventh. Many of Brahms's contemporaries praised this work's charming lyricism, and Billroth described it as "a transfiguration of the ecstasy of first love." During the late 1870s and early 1880s it was included in numerous recitals, and according to Helm, it was popularized in Vienna by Gustav Walter. Carl Kipke, however, in a review in the November 1877 *Musikalisches Wochenblatt*, chastises the singer Frau Amalie Joachim (a friend of Brahms) for not altering the text so that it would concern a woman's heartbreak rather than a man's. He claimed that it was nonsense for a woman to sing the original text.

Heather Platt

5 Gesänge, Opus 72
Composed 1876–77; published 1877

1. Alte Liebe [Candidus]
2. Sommerfäden [Candidus]
3. O kühler Wald [Brentano]

4. Verzagen [Lemcke]
5. Unüberwindlich [Goethe]

Although published in 1877 and sent at this time with the others from Opp. 69–71 for Clara Schumann's critique, some of these songs were composed earlier. This is the case with *Alte Liebe, Sommerfäden,* and *Unüberwindlich,* which were written in 1876. In her letter of May 2, 1877, Frau Schumann revealed that the first and last songs were already old friends. Indeed, the last song was so well known that the singer Julius Stockhausen used one of its lines, "Hab' ich geschworen tausendmal" (I've sworn a thousand times), to toast Brahms at the party celebrating the Leipzig premiere of the composer's First Symphony. (This 1877 event is recounted by Florence May in *The Life of Brahms.*) Whereas Clara Schumann found some of the songs of Opp. 69–71 to be less than pleasing, she seemed to like all five of Op. 72 and even proclaimed *O kühler Wald* to be "wonderful!"

The first two songs of Op. 72 are set to texts by Karl Candidus. *Alte Liebe* (Old Love) is reminiscent of Schumann, specifically his *Sehnsucht nach der Waldegegend* (Op. 35/5). In both, the nostalgic texts are set in G minor with a meter of 6/4. Brahms's setting includes numerous expressive details; for instance, the low register of the first stanza's accompaniment and the G♭ (♭I) on the word "fernem" (far) suggest the distant country of the swallow; by contrast the modulation to C major conveys the optimism of the words "neues Glück" (new good fortune). The second stanza ends with an E♭-major chord followed by an E♭-minor chord that functions as a transition to the less harmonically stable middle section. Beginning with a dissonant chord (a diminished seventh) and an unexpectedly high melody, this section's constantly changing keys and louder dynamics portray the excitement and frustration of the dream of a lost love. Although the section ends with a cadence in C major, the C chord is altered to form the same dissonant chord that had begun the section. In this way the entire dream is framed by the same chromatic chord.

In the text of *Sommerfäden* (Summer Threads) gossamer threads, hopelessly caught on shrubbery, are compared to the frailty of love. The text's wistfulness is beautifully depicted by the harmonies, rhythms, and textures of Brahms's setting. The piano's two-part counterpoint winds its way around the vocal line like the flying threads, whose weightlessness is further conveyed by the avoidance of a firm tonic chord. The melody seems to occupy a completely different world, perhaps the real world of the protagonist. Initially the piano emphasizes the dominant, while the melody favors notes belonging to the tonic triad. Its more varied rhythms also contrast with the piano's eighths, which continue with such incessancy—not even pausing at cadences—that they seem to be encircling the character uncontrollably. Similarly, the voice and piano begin phrases at different times, and the only time that they move together is in the last line, where the right hand doubles the voice and a more chordal accompaniment is introduced.

The text of *O kühler Wald* (O Cool Forest) is by Clemens Brentano (1778–1842), who, in collaboration with Achim von Arnim (1781–1831), published the well-known collection of folk poetry *Des Knaben Wunderhorn*. This poem, like that of *Alte Liebe*, tells of the songs of a former love reverberating painfully in the heart. The song begins with repeated thick, low chords, suggesting the cool forest, and the melodic line falls into short segments with rests marking the commas in the text (a technique of text setting that Brahms impressed upon his student Gustav Jenner). One immediately senses the protagonist's despair, and this is further stressed at the end of the stanza, where a sustained dominant-seventh chord gives way to silence, rather than resolving to the tonic. The second stanza begins with another startling harmonic and rhythmic gesture.

The protagonist explains that the loved one is buried deep in his heart, and the words "Im Herzen tief" are set to unexpectedly long notes in the flat submediant (F♭ major). The subsequent phrase is a recomposition of the first phrase of stanza 1, and this repetition nicely draws attention to the similarities between the corresponding lines of text. The song comes to a close with the protagonist tenderly remembering his lost love. His wistfulness is suggested by the borrowings from the minor mode and by the melody's final ascending gesture. Like many of the piano pieces by Schumann and Chopin, the final cadence of this song recalls the piano's opening, perhaps implying the continued yearning of the protagonist.

Clara Schumann praised the swing and passion of *Verzagen* (Despair) and she accompanied Amalie Joachim in its first documented public performance on October 31, 1877, in Berlin. Perhaps the virtuosic piano part had particular appeal for Clara, whose own Lieder often included demanding writing for the pianist. The thirty-second-note arpeggiations and neighbor motives that permeate this song are somewhat unusual for Brahms, who tended to favor larger subdivisions of the beat for his accompaniments. Although the idea of using arpeggios to represent the roaring sea might be somewhat trite, Brahms convincingly portrays the intense emotion of the scene through disruptive syncopations and glaring dissonances. The right hand has a melody of much longer notes, and its separateness from the lower, moving figuration suggests the numbness and isolation of the speaker.

The opus ends with Goethe's drinking song, *Unüberwindlich* (Insuperable), which compares women with wine. In contrast to the previous songs, this one begins loudly in a Vivace tempo. Its main motivic idea is from Domenico Scarlatti's Sonata in D (L. 214). Uncharacteristically, Brahms, with some encouragement from his friend George Henschel, bracketed this motive's first appearance in the prelude, and he wrote Scarlatti's name beneath it. This idea spores the initial melodic phrases, and, played staccato as if in imitation of a harpsichord, it sets up the light, detached accompaniment that permeates the song. During the second stanza, part of this motive is also used to represent the popping sound of a wine cork. This humorous gesture is one of the numerous examples of exaggerated word-painting, typical of a good *opera buffa* aria, that characterize this song. Another instance occurs at the end of the first phrase of stanza 1, when octaves and longer notes as well as a move toward C♯ minor convey the fake solemnity of the oath never to trust the bottle. Similar overwrought gestures, including a canon between the voice and bass, and sustained notes doubled in octaves, accompany the man's claim that he has sworn a thousand times not to trust a false woman. The end of the song includes further recollections of the Scarlatti motif, and the melodic line, with its leaps and drawn-out rhythms, suggests a big, operatic conclusion.

Heather Platt

5 ROMANCES AND LIEDER, FOR ONE OR TWO VOICES, OPUS 84
Composed 1877–81; published 1882

1. Sommerabend [Schmidt]
2. Der Kranz [Schmidt]
3. In den Beeren [Schmidt]
4. Vergebliches Ständchen [Zuccalmaglio]
5. Spannung [Zuccalmaglio]

Although first published by Simrock in 1882, Op. 84 was written in two phases. The first three songs, settings of poems by Hans Schmidt, date from the summer of 1881, while the remaining two date from the summers of 1877–79. Brahms took the texts for these last two from the collection *Deutsche Volkslieder mit ihren Original Weisen* (1838–40), and he probably believed that they belonged to authentic folk songs. This collection was published by Anton Wilhelm Florentin von Zuccalmaglio (1803–1869) and Andreas Kretzschmer (1775–1839), and it has become clear that Zuccalmaglio altered many of the original songs and texts and wrote some of the others himself, claiming that they too were folk songs. It is likely that the texts of *Vergebliches Ständchen* (Futile Serenade) and *Spannung* (Tension), as well as those of *Dort in Weiden*, Op. 97/4, and *Klage*, Op. 105/3, were written by Zuccalmaglio. All five settings of Op. 84 are dialogues: the Schmidt settings are dialogues between a mother and daughter, while the Zuccalmaglio texts are dialogues between sweethearts. These types of texts were common in German poetry, and the scene at the window in *Vergebliches Ständchen*, in which an ardent suitor begs to be let inside, was particularly popular.

The title of the opus states that these songs could be performed by one or two voices, implying that two voices could be used for the respective protagonists in each song. The fifth song includes an *ad libitum* second part during its closing phrases, and its first documented performance was as a duet with Ida Huber-Petzold and Adolf Weber in Basel on January 23, 1883. This mode of performance is rarely taken seriously, however, and when one of Brahms's friends, the Viennese critic Gustav Dömpke, suggested that an obbligato second part could be added to *Vergebliches Ständchen,* Max Kalbeck facetiously replied that the song could as well be staged as *"Letztes Fensterln,* ein lyrisch-symphonisch-malerisch-orchestisch-mimoplastisches Gesamtkunstwerk!" (*Johannes Brahms,* III, 337, note 2).

Irrespective of the number of singers, the two characters in these dialogues are often given distinctive music, with the mothers and daughters of the first three songs being particularly clearly delineated. In each piece the two characters are allocated different keys, and in *Sommerabend* (Summer Evening) and *Der Kranz* (The Garland) the mother has a somewhat lower range. Throughout the entire opus, the folklike texts and topics inspired Brahms to write graciously flowing melodic lines—which were praised by many of his friends—and light, supportive accompaniments. Aside from differentiating the characters, most of the songs convey a dramatic, though humorous, progression. *Der Kranz,* for example, begins in G minor, as both women ponder the wreath a boy has given the daughter. The final section, however, changes to the tonic major and introduces a louder, more rhapsodic, and confident accompaniment as the girl confesses that although the wreath has thorns, she thinks about the boy all the time. The couple in *Spannung* (Discord) sing exactly the same music until the end, when the girl decides to stay with the young man despite his reported unfaithfulness. While retaining the same overall melodic character, this section has a more lively tempo, a thicker accompaniment, and modulates to the tonic major. It is at the end of this stanza, where both characters promise to be faithful, that Brahms introduces the *ad libitum* second part. It might have seemed more obvious to begin by using different music for the boy's overtures and the girl's rebuffs, but one has the feeling that the two characters are not really at odds. Despite all her accusations, the girl really does want this young man, and feigns disinterest instead of overtly flirting with him.

Of the five, *Vergebliches Ständchen* is perhaps the most convincing scene, and it quickly became the most popular of this collection. It was frequently performed by numerous singers (including such important male performers as Gustav Walter) and it was extensively discussed by Brahms's friends and foes. Eduard Hanslick, the noted Viennese music critic and close friend of Brahms, greatly admired this song; when he congratulated Brahms on it, the composer, who undoubtedly realized that this song's simplicity and folklike melody would please the critic more than some of his somber pieces, responded somewhat cryptically that he himself was extremely pleased with it and that he knew that nothing truly excellent could escape Hanslick.

Not everyone, however, was so pleased. Hugo Wolf in particular was quite critical of the song's declamation, and in a review of January 10, 1886, he grouped this song with *Der Kranz* and *Feldeinsamkeit* (Op. 86/2) and labeled all three as "gravedigger Lieder." Max Kalbeck, one of Brahms's fiercest supporters, defended the song, calling the criticisms shortsighted and foolish, and he claimed that the declamation was intended to enhance the comic effect.

Vergebliches Ständchen is in strophic-variation form, and the first two stanzas (which introduce the boy and girl) are practically identical. Both begin with the rising arpeggio motif that permeates the song and which is manipulated to lead dramatically into the girl's rejections of the boy in the fourth stanza. The third stanza changes to minor and introduces new eighth-note figuration in octaves, depicting the suitor standing in the freezing cold, shut out from the house and the girl he desires. As the young man begs to be let in, the piano introduces a figure that expands on the opening triadic motive and accents the second beat of every measure. This syncopated figure creates tension and anticipation, which is further increased in the final phrase of the stanza as the piano imitates the voice's rising motives. During the brief interlude leading into the final stanza, the tempo and dynamics increase and the arpeggio motif is stated three times in quick succession, climaxing on an accented chord with a ″—the piece's highest note—in the upper part. This new pitch marks the beginning of the final stanza, in which the girl inverts the boy's greeting of "good evening" and wishes him "good night." The postlude reuses this stanza's interlude (itself a variation of the initial prelude) and quickly regains the loud dynamic level and the climactic a ″. Now this note is marked with a *sforzando* and harmonized with a dissonant chord that resolves to the final authentic cadence. This phrase is the only time that the opening ascending gestures lead to a conclusive authentic cadence, and this conveys the finality of the girl's negative response. Almost all commentators have drawn attention to this conclusion, describing the girl as forcefully slamming the window on her suitor.

Kalbeck suggested that singers of the caliber of Amalie Joachim or Alice Barbi, both friends of the composer, were needed to interpret the delicate humor of this song, which once heard will never be forgotten. Hanslick praised Spies's rendition, noting that she sensitively portrayed the characters without destroying the lighthearted drama. Despite his admiration for Spies, Brahms was said to prefer the performance of Frau Joachim. He also told Friedländer that he wanted performers to make the young maiden sound quite haughty.

Heather Platt

6 LIEDER, OPUS 85
Composed 1877–82; published 1882

1. Sommerabend [Heine]
2. Mondenschein [Heine]
3. Mädchenlied [trad., trans. Kapper]
4. Ade! [trad., trans. Kapper]
5. Frühlingslied [Geibel]
6. In Waldeseinsamkeit [Lemcke]

Published in 1882 with Opp. 84 and 86, most of the songs of Op. 85 were composed in 1878. The Heine poems of the first two songs were originally placed together in the cycle *Die Heimkehr* in the poet's *Buch der Lieder,* and Brahms's settings preserve this pairing, augmenting the verbal connections with musical ties. The remaining four songs of the opus are not so clearly related, though both Kapper settings have a folklike spirit, and the last song, *In Waldeseinsamkeit,* returns to the wistful mood of the first two.

The moon is a central figure in both of the Heine poems, and in both poems its light soothes the troubled protagonist. These songs, marked *langsam,* are in B♭ major, and they share numerous melodic and harmonic ideas. In the second stanza of *Mondenschein* (Moonlight), Brahms quotes the main phrases of *Sommerabend.* In the first song this music is associated with the refreshing golden glow of the moon at dusk, and in the second, it accompanies the description of the moonlight dispelling the horror of the night. In letters of 1878, Brahms and Otto Dessoff, conductor of the Vienna Philharmonic, discussed this recurring music and the associated symbolism. Despite Brahms's explanations, Dessoff remained unconvinced of the effectiveness of the repeated music, because, as he explained, the image of the moon is not precisely the same in both poems. In addition to this quotation, there are a number of other motivic connections between the songs. At the end of the second stanza of the first song, Brahms introduces a sighing appoggiatura figure, which is played over low, sustained chords, suggesting the mysteriousness of the still of the evening. These figures take on greater importance in the second, more melancholy song and they are recalled and transposed on the words "müde Glieder" (weary limbs). A series of related descending appoggiaturas is also used in the final measures of the melody, where they gently flow downward, like the character's tears.

Whereas the first song is full of only pleasant images of dusk, *Mondenschein* begins with an immediate shift to a darker and scarier scene. Brahms underscores this change by beginning without a piano introduction and with an immediate shift to the tonic minor, followed by a cadence on G♭. Similarly the graceful arpeggios of *Sommerabend* are replaced by stark octaves. This darkness, however, is quickly banished by the comfort of the moonlight, accompanied by a return to the main melody of *Sommerabend*. Although this restatement includes a return to the major mode, G♭ briefly reappears in the song's closing phrases, as the protagonist again refers to his torments. This time, however, this chord leads to C♭ major and then back to the tonic. As the protagonist's anguish subsides, relaxing, triplet arpeggios recall the rhythms and lightness of the figuration associated with the enchanting fairy at the end of *Sommerabend*. The final cadence of this song is a restatement of the cadence that had opened *Sommerabend*, though, as is to be expected, this time the tonic chord is sustained for the full measure. Although B♭-major (tonic) root-position chords are relatively rare in this second song, the tonic is never in doubt, and performing the songs as a pair reinforces this idea. Furthermore, the second song's turn to minor is anticipated in the first song, with the piano's final phrases including D♭ (the minor third). This type of pairing of songs by tonal means is somewhat similar to the techniques used to link the F♯ pieces in Op. 59, *Regenlied* and *Nachklang*.

The next two works, *Mädchenlied* (Maiden's Song) and "Ade!" (Adieu!), are settings of poems translated by Siegfried Kapper. The first, a favorite of Clara Schumann, was written in 1878, while the second had an unusually long genesis, having been first sketched in 1877 but not completed until early 1882. *Mädchenlied* is a simple strophic setting with each of the four measures of the main phrase having the same rhythmic pattern and even the same generally descending contour. The most distinctive feature of this slight A-minor piece is its 5/4 meter, which is extended to 6/4 to allow for a typically Brahmsian slower repetition of the last line. Similarly *Ade!* is distinguished by the unusual rhythms in the piano part, which seem too complex for the simple, folklike text.

In *Mädchenlied*, we are told that the young girl is singing of her absent sweetheart. Her continued longing is represented by a melody that fades away on scale degree 3 (instead of the tonic) and by the absence of a clear, concluding authentic cadence. The vocal line of *Ade!* also ends somewhat inconclusively on scale degree 5: as the sweethearts continue to call "farewell" to each other, even though they are so far apart that they cannot see or hear each other, the song fades out and, unusually for Brahms, ends with an eighth note.

The last two songs return to the high standard of the opening two, again contrasting an optimistic number, *Frühlingslied* (Spring Song), with a more melancholy one, *In Waldeseinsamkeit* (In the Loneliness of the Forest). The first begins with a lively, rolling accompaniment. One might expect the voice to open with an octave leap culminating on a strong tonic chord, but instead it leaps a seventh, forming an appoggiatora over a diminished seventh. In this way the music creates the mysteriousness of the fragrances described in the text. This measure anticipates much of the chromatic activity throughout the song, and its E♭ and the B♭ recur in the second stanza, where a subdued, chromatic passage depicts the dreamy protagonist wandering through the fields. The third stanza is marked *animato* and is louder, with a more active accompaniment, portraying the protagonist confidently wishing that his heart will blossom one more time. As if to emphasize his optimism, the piano postlude ends with a crescendo and a chromatic ascent to the tonic. Dessoff praised this song, but he told Brahms that the next one, *In Waldeseinsamkeit*, was among his most beautiful Lieder.

Although in the major mode, *In Waldeseinsamkeit* is not as optimistic and it is set to a much slower tempo. Moreover, throughout the song the tonic minor is often referred to, and the minor third and sixth are featured shortly after the beginning. The minor sixth (G♮) is first introduced by the piano and it then becomes the high point of a beautifully wistful melisma on the word "Sehnen" (yearning). These chromatic pitches anticipate the move to D major/minor in the next stanza. This section describes the protagonist's anguish, and his unsettled mood is also suggested by the dissonances in the piano part, louder dynamics, and more agitated rhythms. In the final stanza, at the sound of the distant nightingale's melancholic song, ascending thirds in the voice are mournfully echoed by the piano. The high g♮ of "Sehnen" is returned for the last line, which ends in a plagal cadence with the voice moving in the upper register from scale degree 3 to 5. For Brahms, these gestures are normally associated with continual yearning, often unrequited love, and we shall see them again in *Es schauen die Blumen* (Op. 96/3). The pathos of this song drew the acclaim of Brahms's contemporaries. Clara Schumann, in a letter to Brahms of July 9, 1878, praised this enchanting ending, and Elisabet von Herzogenberg remarked, in a letter of July 24, 1882, that it was "born of deep personal experience. The man who can listen to it dry-eyed is surely past saving!"

Heather Platt

6 Lieder, for Low Voice, Opus 86
Composed ?1877–79; published 1882

1. Therese [Keller]
2. Feldeinsamkeit [Allmers]
3. Nachtwandler [Kalbeck]

4. Über die Heide [Storm]
5. Versunken [F. Schumann]
6. Todessehnen [Schenkendorf]

As with the Op. 85 songs, most of the songs of Op. 86 were composed in 1878. *Nachtwandler* (Nightwalker), however, was composed in 1877, *Feldeinsamkeit* (The Loneliness of the Fields) in 1879, and the date of the composition of *Über die Heide* (On the Heath) is not known. Op. 86 includes Brahms's only solo Lied settings of poems by Hermann Allmers (1821–1902), Theodor Storm (1817–1888), and Max Kalbeck. Of these writers, only Storm's poetry is still well known, and Allmers acknowledged that his poem "Feldeinsamkeit" was made famous primarily through Brahms's setting.

Therese is a setting of a poem by Gottfried Keller, a poet who knew the music of Brahms and had heard this particular composition. In 1884, Keller decided to revise the poem for its publication in his complete works. Max Friedländer, the acquaintance of the composer and the author of *Brahms Lieder*, reports that he cautioned the poet against these changes, in part because the original text was so well known through Brahms's setting. Keller, however, went ahead, though some time later he told Friedländer that indeed there had been some confusion between the two versions. The various editions also led to one of Hugo Wolf's tantrums against Brahms. In a letter to his dear friend Melanie Köchert, Wolf chastised Brahms for not using the later edition of the Keller poem, which Wolf had used for his own setting. This, of course, was quite ludicrous, as Brahms's setting predates the collected edition of the poet's works that Wolf describes. Moreover, Brahms had great respect for this poet, and in an 1878 letter, he asked Otto Dessoff to consult with Keller about the poem's title, which did not appeal to him. Although it is not clear whether Dessoff discussed this matter with the poet, Brahms kept the title of *Therese*. Ironically, in the later edition of this work, Keller himself suppressed this title, as well as the other female names that he had used for the poems collectively known as *Alte Weisen*.

Brahms wrote this song in May 1878 but he reconsidered the melodic line in 1882. In its original form the opening is characterized by repeated notes. Brahms altered this, however, introducing a more jagged line, characterized by two leaps of an octave, and he sent this new version to his copyist, Robert Keller. He also sent it to the Herzogenbergs, who quickly responded that they much preferred the original version. Two days after their letter, Brahms again wrote to Keller telling him to disregard the changes and to keep the original melody. In this letter of April 28, 1882, Brahms reveals that he was still a little displeased with the final song.

Feldeinsamkeit is one of Brahms's most popular Lieder; it was widely performed during the 1880s and 1890s, and soon after the publication of Op. 86, Simrock released it as a single issue. It has not, however, been accepted uncritically. Brahms arranged for Karl Reinthaler to sing his setting to the author of the original poem, Hermann Allmers, who was not impressed: he claimed that the melody was too artificial and did not capture the dreamy atmosphere he intended. By contrast, he preferred the folklike setting of Gerhard Focken. Nevertheless, encouraged by the poet's friends, Brahms sent Allmers the autograph manuscript of this song for his seventieth birthday. The poem itself did not escape the critics either, with Richard Specht and Klaus Groth questioning the line "gestorben bin," which Groth said should have been "gestorben wär." Groth even suggested to Allmers that he change the text. Gustav Jenner, who became a student of Brahms through the intercession of Groth, recalled that Brahms discussed this song with him and was quite distressed at Groth's actions.

The song is in modified strophic form with the inner phrases of the first strophe being modified to fit the second stanza of text. In this stanza the music moves from the tonic (F major) toward D♭ major, reflecting the character's dream of dying and being able to join the peacefully drifting clouds in the blue sky. Elisabet von Herzogenberg praised this particular passage, obviously hearing the soulfulness of the setting much more clearly than Allmers (letter to Brahms of July 24, 1882). The work also includes numerous instances of explicit word-painting, and their profound effect was praised by Richard Specht. For example, the elegantly rising quarter-note chords of the opening resemble the blades of grass described in the text; an ascending arpeggio represents the word "hohen," and the repeated tonic pedal suggests the stillness of the scene. In the second half of the song Brahms illustrates the notorious "gestorben bin" with bare octaves between the piano and voice—a texture that he frequently employed to depict death.

While Brahms is known for his selection of melancholy and deathly poems, the text of *Nachtwandler* paints an unusually frightening scene, and even Elisabet von Herzogenberg confessed that it took a while for her to appreciate the real beauty of the work. The poem warns against waking sleepers, because in sleep they can overcome ordinarily insurmountable obstacles and avoid all anxiety and longing. Brahms sets this to a chilling lullaby whose 3/4 meter is often organized so as to imply 6/4. In the first measure of the prelude the ominous mood is already established by the oscillating major and minor triads. The song ends portentously with the warning "Woe to the lips that would call out to him!" Brahms slows the tempo at the beginning of these lines and the melody rises and falls like the shape of a lip. As the dynamic level continues to fall, the voice ends on a dissonant chord and the subsequent piano postlude recalls the mood of the prelude.

In *Über die Heide*, the protagonist tramps through the dreary autumn countryside thinking of spring and lost love. The poem comprises four two-line stanzas, and Brahms uses the same music for the first two and a slightly modified version for the last. The third stanza has a new melody and, through word repetitions, is stretched to eight measures instead of the usual four. This is the bleakest stanza, in which the protagonist, encircled by ghostly mists, sees only black vegetation and an empty sky. Brahms's music conveys this agony and frustration through its louder dynamics and richer texture, and although C minor and F minor are alluded to, neither key is established. The repetitions of the four-note octave motive in the deep bass register (which suggests the awkward gait of the character) and of the main four-measure phrase aptly depict the desolate scene. The concluding cadence expands the unsettling chromatic cadence that ends both the first and second stanzas. In each instance, the piano repeats the voice's last segment, suggesting the muffled echo of the man's footsteps. At the final cadence, this motive (itself derived from the bass's octave figure) is repeated an additional time to softer dynamics. This provides a greater sense of finality than the other cadences, whose gripping dissonances evoke the man's bitterness and heartache.

Versunken (Drowned) is a setting of a poem by Felix Schumann, the youngest son of Clara and Robert, who was named for Felix Mendelssohn and was Brahms's godson. The other text by Felix that Brahms set was "Junge Lieder I" (also referred to as *Meine Liebe ist grün*, Op. 63/5), and both settings were intended to delight Felix as well as to comfort Clara, who for many years agonized over her son's deteriorating health. While *Meine Liebe ist grün* is one of Brahms's best-known songs, *Versunken* is not entirely convincing, and Elisabet von Herzogenberg suggested that the melody resembles "forked lightning." Clara Schumann, however, said she liked the work, and in particular the middle section (letter to Brahms of July 9, 1878). She did, however, have criticisms of some of the other Op. 86 pieces, and she suggested a few small changes in the harmony of the next song, *Todessehnen* (Death Wish), though overall she admired this piece as well.

With their expansive settings, *Versunken* and *Todessehnen* turn away from the intense, compressed mode of expression in *Über die Heide*. The text, of *Todessehnen*, by Max von Schenkendorf (1783–1817), comprises five stanzas and traces the protagonist's gradually changing mood from the expression of his grief and heavy burdens to his request for God to release him from life so that he can be one with the spirits. Brahms's setting follows exactly this transition, moving from the F♯-minor, quadruple opening section, with its rigid dotted rhythms and deep accompaniment, to a relaxed, lyrical third stanza that eases into F♯ major for the final two stanzas. This last section, conveying the longed-for spiritual union, is in a triple meter, with a higher register and a hymnlike melody, accompanied by relaxed, ascending arpeggios. Otto Dessoff praised the opening and closing of this song, but he chastised Brahms for the passage using parallel fifths. In response, Brahms cited an analogous passage in the last movement of Mozart's B♭-major String Quartet, K. 458.

Heather Platt

2 Gesänge, for Alto, Viola, and Piano, Opus 91
Composed 1863–64 and 1884; published 1884

1. Gestillte Sehnsucht [Rückert]
2. Geistliches Wiegenlied [Geibel]

Although these two songs, set to texts by Friedrich Rückert (1788–1866) and Emanuel Geibel (1815–1884), are the only solo Lieder by Brahms in which the voices are joined by two instruments instead of just the piano, ensemble Lieder were not entirely unknown in the nineteenth century. For example, Richard D. Green's recently published *Anthology of Goethe Songs* includes two such works: Arnold Mendelssohn's *Am Flusse* calls for voice, lute, and piano (?1904), and Moritz Hauptmann's *Der Fischer* for voice, violin, and piano (1843). Similar ensemble songs were also written by Louis Spohr. In this instance, however, Brahms was not so much experimenting with a genre as writing for specific friends: the singer Amalie Joachim and her husband, the violinist Joseph. Although it is not known whether the couple ever performed these pieces in public together, Amalie did perform them in Vienna on January 7, 1886, with Joseph Hellmesberger playing the viola.

Comprised of 97 and 157 measures respectively, these songs are a return to the expansive, slowly unfolding style of the *Magelone Romanzen*, Op. 33. Both begin with unusually long instrumental preludes, which establish the mood and melodic material of the main part of the songs. The viola and voice, whose similar timbres are fully exploited, are then in constant dialogue, moving imitatively, in contrary motion, or with the viola embellishing the voice's melody, as though improvising all around it. The piano plays a more supportive role and is confined to the lower register, only occasionally playing over the viola's countermelodies.

Gestillte Sehnsucht (Stilled Desire) was the second piece to be written, and Brahms completed it in 1884. At this time, the Joachims had separated, and Brahms thought that the composition and its publication with the earlier lullaby might in some way help to mend the rift. The Rückert text paints a gentle evening scene in which the whisperings of birds and winds seem to offer relief to the heart-heavy protagonist. Although this disquieted spirit is only specifically introduced in the second stanza of the text, it is already suggested in the song's prelude. The viola often plays poignant appoggiaturas or other dissonances against the piano, and the dissonances anticipate the second stanza's move to the tonic minor.

This central stanza is contrasted with the outer ones, emphasizing more the continual longing of the protagonist. The gracious melodic line of the first stanza is replaced by a syllabic line, and in contrast to the rapturous descending phrases of the outer stanzas, the first three phrases begin with ascents, perhaps suggesting the protagonist's anxious questioning as he wonders when his troubles will cease. This stanza reaches an unsettling climax: as the viola and piano parts become more agitated, the voice moves in contrary motion to the bass, and a series of diminished sevenths harmonize the ascent to the melodic peak on e″. This climax occurs as the character describes his yearnings as being so intense that they make his breast heave, and it is further underscored by a crescendo to *forte*—the only place, other than in the prelude, in which this marking is used.

As the protagonist contemplates a more peaceful time, the music returns to the relaxed, lyrical strains and major mode of the opening stanza. These outer stanzas end with the viola echoing the last phrase of the melody, though with slightly altered rhythms and harmonies. In both places Brahms introduces the diminished seventh that appeared in the prelude. This chord includes the B♭ of the tonic minor (the key of the troubled inner section), and Brahms repeats this note in each measure of the postlude, first in the piano and then in the viola. Finally it is treated as an appoggiatura over the tonic and resolves in the penultimate measure. With these repetitions, the minor sixth lingers like the protagonist's yearnings, which (as the title of the song implies and the last line of the text confirms) only subside with death.

Whereas *Gestillte Sehnsucht* was composed for the troubled Joachims, Brahms presented an early version of *Geistliches Wiegenlied* (Sacred Lullaby) to the couple at the time of their marriage in 1863. The composer was dissatisfied with this version and recalled it, but then returned it when the couple's first child was born in 1864. The current version was well known to Brahms's circle as early as 1878; in a letter to Brahms of April 18, 1882, Theodor Billroth requested a copy, describing the song as "so poetic and singular in remembrance." He made a similar comment about *Gestillte Sehnsucht* in a letter of August 6, 1884, and guessed that Brahms would publish it with the earlier lullaby. The viola begins *Gestillte Sehnsucht* by quoting the old hymn *Josef, lieber Josef mein*, which it repeats during the song. This melody establishes the gentle rocking motion and the 6/8 meter, both of which are typical lullaby gestures and had been used by Brahms for Peter's lullaby in the *Magelone* songs, *Ruhe, Süßliebchen* (Op. 33/9). The hymn tune was already known in the sixteenth century, when Walther published a harmonization of it, and it was employed by other nineteenth-century composers including Liszt and Heinrich von Herzogenberg. Herzogenberg, like his wife, was a great admirer of Brahms, and he valued Brahms's opinions of his own compositions. His setting of the hymn is included in his oratorio *Die Geburt Christi* (1894), where it is used for a soprano and bass duet with cello obbligato.

The text of the hymn fits perfectly with that of Geibel, a poet whom Brahms believed was not well enough appreciated. Geibel based this work on a Spanish poem by Lope Felix de Vega Carpio (1562-1635). Both the poem and the hymn are told from the point of view of Mary, who asks for help to sing the baby Jesus to sleep. In the hymn she asks Joseph; in the poem she implores the angels to silence the rustlings of the treetops and cold winds. This text was also set by Hugo Wolf (it is the fourth of his *Spanisches Liederbuch*), and despite the differences in their songwriting styles, both composers give similar interpretations. For example, both use crescendos and chromaticism to represent the noise of the wind. As the text anticipates Christ's suffering, Wolf's setting becomes more chromatic and Brahms's modulates to the tonic minor and changes meter to 3/4. After a restatement of the first section, Brahms concludes with the viola's repetition of the hymn tune.

Heather Platt

5 LIEDER, FOR LOW VOICE AND PIANO, OPUS 94
Composed 1883-84; published 1884

1. Mit vierzig Jahren [Rückert]
2. Steig auf, geliebter Schatten [Halm]
3. Mein Herz ist schwer [Geibel]
4. Sapphische Ode [Schmidt]
5. Kein Haus, keine Heimat [Halm]

In a letter of August 6, 1884, Brahms's friend Theodor Billroth described the songs of Op. 94 with their texts of lost youth and death as a type of winter's journey, and he noted that not everyone would be sympathetic to their somber, reflective mood. In particular he described the poems by Halm as being characterized by an unusual "melancholy bitterness" (a feature of many of this poet's *Trauerlieder*). He claimed that these pieces belong in the same category as Brahms's *Abendregen* (Op. 70/4) and that despite their seriousness, as old age approached, he found them more refreshing than sweet love songs. These pieces were probably written with Julius Stockhausen's voice in mind, and when Stockhausen first sang *Mit vierzig Jahren* (with Brahms at the piano) he burst into tears during the final stanza (see Kalbeck, *Johannes Brahms*, III: 522). Billroth anticipated that this song was intended for this singer and claimed that only Stockhausen "could give it the piety that such nobly conceived and nobly composed thoughts deserve."

There can hardly be a measure of *Mit vierzig Jahren* (With Forty Years) which does not demonstrate the richness of the word-music fusion that is the hallmark of the nineteenth-century Lied. The song abounds with examples of word-painting and finely nuanced harmonies, all of which are coordinated to bring the character and his emotional turmoil to life. The fast ascent of the initial phrase represents the passing of the first forty years of life, while the subsequent softer, lower, longer notes, and a slight pause on "schau'n zurück" (look back) poignantly evoke the man's turn to the past. As he recalls the stillness of childhood and then the noisiness of youth, a sustained phrase is contrasted with a lilting melody and a detached accompaniment.

The dramatic crux of the song occurs at the end of the second stanza. A halting melody with a strident diminished Fifth (doubled in octaves at the piano) captures the protagonist's anguished anticipation of death. At forty, however, life is not over, and the B♭ of the diminished Fifth is repeated and enharmonically reinterpreted to A♯ (the leading tone). This harmonic reinterpretation, which leads from the deathly key of D minor and back to the tonic (B minor), aptly symbolizes the man's realization that indeed life is not yet over. These measures move directly into the last stanza, in much the same way as the man's life continues without break. Brahms avoids a strong authentic cadence until the very final measures of the piece, withholding it until the man's death is described. This final cadence, which uses the major version of the tonic triad, is led into by longer melodic notes and relaxed arpeggios in the piano. Like many other texts set by Brahms, Rückert's poem describes death as a release (a safe arrival in port), and, as Brahms's friends realized, this sentiment is exquisitely reflected in the calmness and ease of the song's concluding phrases.

The Halm text of *Steig auf, geliebter Schatten* (Rise, Beloved Shadow) portrays a grieving survivor creating a vision of his deceased loved one, knowing that she would have encouraged him to go on with his life. It is in a key rarely used in Brahms's songs, E♭ minor, and, as the protagonist realizes that he should not give in to his sorrow, it softly modulates through G♭ major, D major, G minor, to B♭ major. This lyrical inner stanza includes some particularly touching word-painting. For example, life and death are contrasted by high and low melodies, gentle arpeggiations versus sustained chords, and G♭-major harmonies versus a chromatic melody and bass. Encasing this section are two musically similar stanzas beseeching directly the deceased. The main idea of these outer stanzas is a series of descending thirds—a motive that Brahms used repeatedly in his later songs (especially those of Op. 121) to represent death. The melody and bass alternate these motives, much in the way the protagonist is eerily shadowed by his beloved.

In *Mein Herz ist schwer* (My Heart Is Heavy) the wind encircles the protagonist, chilling the night and bringing whisperings of past times, of a castle and a maiden. This archaic image and the endless chasing seem to have prompted Brahms's piano figuration: in even quarters, the hands move in contrary motion, one eighth-note apart. Above this contrapuntal texture the vocal line begins with unusually short segments. Halfway through the first stanza, the piano breaks off and then reenters with nine-part chords punctuating the lines "Treetops whisper far and wide." While these tall chords graphically represent the trees, the abrupt change in texture along with the disruptive harmonic progression are reminders of the protagonist's heavy heart and sleepless night. In the second stanza chromatic harmonies further underscore this anguish. One of its modulatory passages begins on the word "Herzeleid" (heartache) and leads to a very unstable A major on the word "Jungfrau" (young maiden)—the true cause of the pain. This louder, animated central section ends when the man asks where his joy-filled youth has gone, and just as there is no answer to such a question, the tempo slows, and the piano breaks off on an unresolved augmented triad. After a pause the soft opening strains of music are recapped as the last line of text repeats the first line. The final cadence, however, is somewhat unconventional. The expected dominant seventh is altered to include a diminished fifth (D–A♭) and the leading tone is not raised. The resulting dissonance instantly communicates the hopelessness of the protagonist, while the soft dynamics, the piano's low range, and the melody's slow descent convey his resignation.

As if to provide relief from the despondency of the preceding songs, *Sapphische Ode* is in D major. Nevertheless, speaking of tears and a lost love, it is not undiluted happiness. Schmidt's poem compares the loved one's countenance to roses, and the tears falling on her cheeks to the dew on the roses. The two stanzas are set to almost identical music, and throughout, the low, gently throbbing accompaniment and the repeated

D pedal evoke the stillness of the nighttime scene, while the borrowings from the minor mode allude to the protagonist's tender heart. This wistfulness is also hinted at during the postlude, when an inner line of the piano descends through a chromatic tetrachord, a symbol usually associated with death. The name of the song is a reference to the structure of the poem: a Sapphic strophe comprises four lines, the first three having five feet, the last only two.

Constituting only twenty measures, *Kein Haus, keine Heimat* (No House, No Home) is possibly Brahms's most austerely dramatic song. The text is drawn from Halm's narrative *In der Südsee,* where it is sung by the black hero who commits suicide in order to save his former mistress, a fickle young girl. The piano begins with resounding bare octaves and continues with syncopated, low chords punctuating the character's ponderous questions of his existence. On first hearing, the opening melody may seem too simple, but its initial rising third and then its leap of a fifth produce the sound of the man's agonizing moan of "Kein Haus" (no house) and "kein Weib" (no wife). Throughout this phrase, the melody's structure and rhythm mirror the word repetitions and punctuation of Halm's text. Set in D minor, the harmonies rarely move from the tonic, dominant, and subdominant chords, and there is no modulation or unusual chromaticism. Only the last stanza provides any surprise, ending with an equivocal plagal cadence and ascending melodic line, rather than with the expected repetition of the first stanza's authentic cadence and descent to the tonic. Most commentators overlook this work, convinced by its brevity and sparseness that it contains nothing remarkable. Nevertheless, it is exactly these startling qualities that make this piece so intense, rendering a moving and convincing portrayal of the man's despair.

Heather Platt

7 Lieder, Opus 95
Composed 1883–84; published 1884

1. Das Mädchen [trad., trans. Kapper]
2. Bei dir sind meine Gedanken [Halm]
3. Beim Abschied [Halm]
4. Der Jäger [Halm]
5. Vorschneller Schwur [trad., trans. Kapper]
6. Mädchenlied [trad., trans. Heyse]
7. Schön war, das ich dir weihte [trans. Daumer]

Opus Nos. 94 and 95 were published together in 1884. In contrast to the somber, low sound of the Op. 94 songs, which all seem to be told from the point of view of a dispirited male, the songs of Op. 95 are mostly concerned with the lives and loves of young women. They have a predominantly folklike, high-spirited mood and are less chromatic than those of Op. 94. Despite this unifying thread, the texts are from eclectic sources. The first and fifth songs have texts from Siegfried Kapper's *Gesänge der Serben;* the text of the sixth is a translation by Paul von Heyse of an Italian poem; while that of the seventh is a translation from the original Turkish and it was published in Daumer's *Polydora.* The texts of the other three songs, which appear consecutively, are all by Friedrich Halm.

Both of the Kapper songs, *Das Mädchen* (The Maiden) and *Vorschneller Schwur* (Rash Oath) comprise two sections moving from tonic minor to major. This change is accompanied by a change in tempo, with the second tempo marking also indicating a new, more gracious mood. (The second section of *Das Mädchen* is marked animato grazioso, while that of *Vorschneller Schwur* is animato ma grazioso.) Both songs begin with a narrator who introduces a young maiden daydreaming about her future. The changes in the music represent the two possible scenarios that each girl imagines. The girl in *Das Mädchen* contrasts the horrid possibility of an old man as a lover with the more pleasing image of a young lover. *Vorschneller Schwur* traces the maturation process of a similar young girl. In this song, however, the narrator speaks for the entire first stanza, describing how the girl has taken an oath not to pick flowers, drink wine, or kiss boys. Brahms then provides a transitional passage in which the tonic minor and major triads are respectively used to contrast yesterday (when the vow was taken) to today (when the girl reconsiders her hastiness). The soft dynamics, slowing tempo, and syncopated bass notes provide an aura of expectation as the piano gradually unfolds the major triad and leads into the brighter, more confident second stanza. In this stanza, the girl realizes that life would be much better, and she would be happier, if she did drink wine, pick roses, and (most important) kiss her sweetheart. The entire song is based on a single eight-measure phrase which begins by arpeggiating the tonic triad. In almost every instance this triad begins in the upper register but falls into the lower register for its last note (a´). Only when the girl decides to kiss her sweetheart is the triad fully stated in the upper register, and this decision, with the newly attained a´´, is accompanied by a swelling in dynamics and a further increase in the tempo. The final phrases retain this more confident mood, with the last word of the song being ornamented by a jubilant melisma that soars back to the high a″.

Although the voices of the narrator and the maiden in *Das Mädchen* are not so clearly differentiated, Brahms does use many of the same techniques as in *Vorschneller Schwur* to contrast the girl's vision of an old lover with that of a young lover. The first section has a syllabic melody characterized by dotted rhythms, whereas the second has a lyrical, flowing melody and a lighter accompaniment. As in *Vorschneller Schwur*, there is an expectant transition between the two sections; the mode changes to major, the melody begins in a halting manner, the tempo slows, and the piano arpeggiates an augmented-sixth chord. For a brief moment, one ponders whether the girl will be happier, but this question is quickly answered by the commencement of the joyful, lyrical section, which immediately picks up the tempo.

Bei dir sind meine Gedanken (My Thoughts Are with You) and *Der Jäger* (The Hunter), the first and third of the Halm settings, continue the folklike lyricism of the Kapper settings. *Der Jäger*, with its arpeggios, syncopated accompaniment, and key of F major, provides a good introduction to *Vorschneller Schwur*, which begins in D minor and has a melody similarly dominated by arpeggio figures. The second of the Halm settings, *Beim Abschied* (At Parting) is the only text of Op. 95 that is definitely spoken by a male protagonist. Although set in the normally sunny key of D major, the song is permeated with subtle rhythmic and harmonic tensions. When it was first published, the piano accompaniment only changed meter from 3/8 to 2/4 for the last two lines of text, but then Brahms decided to have the piano begin the duple meter as soon as the voice enters (in 3/8). The simultaneous use of these contrasting meters gives the song its breathlessness, and this agitation is further suggested by the fast tempo and the piano's harmonies. Throughout the song, the right hand of the piano gradually moves to and from the note a′. This movement often involves chromaticism and dissonances, some of which allude to the tonic minor. The protagonist is in a depressed mood that he simply cannot shrug off, and these recurring chromaticisms suggest the problems that constantly besiege him. Although he is surrounded by people, none of them comfort him, and the only person who really matters is not there. That this one woman is so important to him is signified by the high, long notes on the word "Eine," as well as by the slowing tempo and minor chords that underscore the words describing her absence.

The title of the sixth song, *Mädchenlied*, suggests a continuation of the innocent world of the Kapper songs. In this instance, however, there is no happy ending. The poem (from which Brahms took only the last two stanzas) tells of a fifteen-year-old girl, thinking of her sweetheart as she washes her clothes. She dreams that on Judgment Day she will be admitted to Paradise but that, to her dismay, her sweetheart will not be there. Despite the simple-mindedness of the girl, the melody is unexpectedly angular, and the restless harmonies contrast with the predominantly diatonic portrayals of the other Op. 95 maidens.

Schön war, das ich dir weihte (Fair Was My Present to You) is the only song of Op. 95 that ends in a minor key. The surprisingly simple prelude, a one-measure syncopated, repeated note, takes us into the joyless world of the protagonist whose love (and gifts) were not returned in kind. Richard Specht, a Viennese music critic and friend of Brahms, stated that this song, with its remarkably calm melodic line, expresses "immeasurable sorrow." The melody begins with brief, halting segments which, being perfectly wedded to the punctuation and flow of the text, suggest that the distressed speaker cannot complete a full sentence without breaking down. The gifts were given with love, and the word "Herze" is set to a dissonant $g\flat''$ that breaks off without resolving. As the character cries for kinder treatment, the music modulates to a plaintive $D\flat$ major and the word "empfangen" (receive) is stretched over a complete measure, with an arching melisma—the only such ornament in the song. This graceful figure reaches a high $g\flat'''$, a note one octave higher than the $g\flat''$ on "Herze."

Heather Platt

4 Lieder, Opus 96
Composed 1884; published 1886

1. Der Tod, das ist die kühle Nacht [Heine]
2. Wir wandelten [trans. Daumer]
3. Es schauen die Blumen [Heine]
4. Meerfahrt [Heine]

This collection comprises settings of three Heine poems and one translation of a Hungarian poem by Georg Daumer (which appeared in his *Polydora*). Brahms's notebook, comprising his handwritten copies of poems, reveals that he had intended to make a cycle of four Heine settings. He did set another Heine poem, "Wie der Mond sich leuchtend dränget," but it was much criticized by Elisabet von Herzogenberg, who clearly stated that it did not meet the standard of the other Heine works (letter to Brahms of May 1885). Brahms must have agreed with her, because he did not release this composition at all. Though composed in 1884, the final group of four songs was published, with Op. 97, in 1886. Each of the Op. 96 pieces demonstrates a masterly fusion of text and music, and all were eagerly applauded by Brahms's contemporaries, including his most loyal friends Theodor Billroth and Clara Schumann.

The first song, *Der Tod, das ist die kühle Nacht* (Death Is Like the Cool of Night) is characterized by numerous graphic touches, and its word-tone synthesis has been praised by many writers, including some of Brahms's twentieth-century critics, like Jack Stein. Whereas the first section compares death to a cool night and life to day, the second describes the unrequited love, represented by a nightingale's song that permeates the protagonist's dreams. The complexity and sensitivity of this setting are obvious from the very first two-measure segment in which the halting, repeated-note melody, descending accompaniment, and the diminished-seventh harmonies (which cloud the C-major tonality) represent death. Life, by contrast, is then symbolized by a sweeter melodic line, an eighth-note accompaniment, and an uncluttered authentic cadence. The unsettling atmosphere of the text's first line is also captured by the piano's syncopations and by the manner in which the voice and piano do not cadence together. In contrast the melody and piano of the second segment do not use as many syncopations and they do end together. The idea of dissonances to represent darkness is continued in the second phrase when the top line of the piano ascends chromatically from c´ to g´, moving the key center toward G minor. This brooding opening gives way to a delicate dream scene in which the piano's range expands and its high, gently rolling chords depict the branches above the speaker's bed. The bittersweetness of the nightingale's song is so effectively portrayed by the sighing appoggiaturas in the melody and the dissonances and high repeated notes of the piano that Richard Specht claimed that "none had ever sung more ardently and yearningly." The melody ends in the upper octave with the last segment softly echoing the preceding one, conveying the longing of the repeated words "sogar im Traum" (even in my dreams). These sad thoughts of love reverberate in the muffled syncopation and dissonances of the postlude.

Elisabet von Herzogenberg praised the beauty and passion of *Wir wan-*

delten (We Wandered), emphasizing the flattering melodic line and the expressiveness of the harmonies. Daumer's poem sets a hushed scene in which the protagonist recalls silently wandering with his beloved, as both were afraid to speak their true feelings. This quietness is suggested by Brahms's choice of the mellow key of D♭ major, and by the predominantly high range of the piano. As the couple walk hand in hand, the piano works in two-part counterpoint, with the lower part imitating the top part in inversion and at a distance of two beats. Throughout the first and last sections the piano has repeated A♭˝s, which represent the sweet-sounding chimes of the lovers' thoughts. At the beginning of the middle section, A♭ is enharmonically reinterpreted to G♯, facilitating the modulation to E major. In the last line, the wonderment of the protagonist is aptly depicted by the flowing melodic line, descending from and returning to the high register, with many of the notes being ornamented by sighing eighths. The postlude echoes the last few notes of the melody as though at a distance, suggesting a cinematic fade as the couple walk on by.

The Heine texts of the remaining two songs end with characteristically biting, ironic twists. In *Es schauen die Blumen* (All the Flowers Gaze) the opening three couplets speak of flowers, streams, the sea, and songs, all of which appear to glow like the protagonist's sweetheart. In the last couplet, however, this character reveals that he is bathing in tears and mournful songs. Brahms follows Heine's change in mood and cuts these last lines off from the preceding ones. After momentarily stopping the piano, he introduces word repetitions extending this couplet to form its own eleven-measure section. Although the melody begins in the same manner as that of the other couplets, it descends and for the first time ends on a low F♯´. This descent, like the new, hesitant syncopations of the bass, evoke the protagonist's sadder mood. The following phrase returns to the initial higher register, but its longer notes similarly suggest his wistfulness. As has often been noted, the ending is remarkably similar to that of *In Waldeseinsamkeit* (Op. 85/6), with a plagal cadence and a melodic line that ascends from scale degree 3 to 5. In both songs, this type of inconclusive cadence suggests the endless longing of the protagonist. In a letter to Brahms of May 14, 1886, Clara Schumann, picking up on this feeling, wrote of *Es schauen die Blumen:* "Oh, how . . . [it] moves one with its cry of despair at the end!"

Whereas Heine's cruel irony could almost be missed with the light, scherzo-like feeling of *Es schauen die Blumen* (a characteristic that some commentators attribute to the influence of Schumann), it cannot be missed in Brahms's brooding setting of *Meerfahrt* (Sea Voyage). Clara Schumann also praised this song, particularly its harmonies. From the initial measures of the prelude, with its low register, undulating motion, minor mode, and harsh appoggiaturas, this piece sounds more like a burlesque barcarole than the mystical waltz tunes described in the text. Snug in a small boat, a couple floats through the evening and is charmed by the music of the isle of the spirits. Despite this alluring sound, they drift sadly by, onto the wider sea. The opening appoggiaturas with their startling dissonances, which Brahms emphasizes by marking *forte*, represent the inconsolable sorrow of the pair. At the description of the strains of the waltz music floating across the water, the accompaniment changes to a vamp-style figuration and the harmonies move toward a cheerful E major. The couple, however, is not to experience the pleasures of this dance, and the new key is not firmly established. Instead, the dance seems to spin out of control, touching briefly on A♭ major, and then repeated, crashing appoggiaturas prepare for Heine's tormented conclusion. The voice breaks off on a high f″ (a striking dissonance against the bass's G♯), and the piano gradually leads into a slower phrase in which the voice reenters and declaims, "wir aber schwammen vorüber" (but we floated past). The opening phrases and tempo then return, with the original appoggiaturas now appearing in the voice as well as the piano. Gradually, as the boat floats away, the melody falls, the dynamics die away to *pianissimo*, and the piano ends on a bare low octave. In her letters to Brahms of May and June, 1885, Elisabet von Herzogenberg repeatedly returned to this song; she was moved by the despairing appoggiaturas and anguished harmonies and haunted by the sadness of the ending. She concluded her letter of May 21–22, in which she discussed most of the songs of Opp. 96 and 97, by requesting that the composer send her an autograph manuscript of this piece for Christmas.

Heather Platt

6 LIEDER, OPUS 97

Composed ?1885; Published 1886

1. Nachtigall [Reinhold]
2. Auf dem Schiffe [Reinhold]
3. Entführung [Alexis]
4. Dort in den Weiden [Zuccalmaglio]

5. Komm bald [Groth]
6. Trennung [trad., trans. Zuccalmaglio]

The six songs of Op. 97 were written around 1885 and then published with those of Op. 96 in 1886. Both collections were released by Simrock and both volumes included drawings by Max Klinger. Klinger's visual interpretations of Brahms's compositions, published in a collection called *Brahms Phantasie,* were much admired by the composer, and he paid tribute to the artist by dedicating the songs of Op. 121 to him. Whereas Op. 96 is a fairly unified cycle, having songs of similar breadth and intensity, Op. 97 is more diverse, including the folk-song setting *Trennung* and the dramatic ballad *Entführung.*

The author of the text of *Nachtigall* (Nightingale) and of *Auf dem Schiffe* (On the Boat) was Christian Reinhold Köstlin (1813–1856), a lecturer in law at the Tübigen University who wrote under the name of Christian Reinhold. His wife, Josephine Lang (1815–1880), had studied music with Mendelssohn, and was a composer of numerous Lieder. Their daughter, Maria Fellinger (d. 1927), was a member of Brahms's circle of friends and was responsible for many of the photographs of the composer that have been widely published. Brahms also used poems by Reinhold in *Auf dem See,* Op. 106/2, and *Ein Wanderer,* Op. 106/5, and he performed these works, along with *Nachtigall* and the first three of Op. 96, at a *soiree* at the home of singer Gustav Walter in February 1885. Brahms invited Maria Fellinger to this gathering, and other guests included Hanslick, Billroth, Kalbeck, and Dömpke. Billroth later opined to Hanslick that though he adored these songs, the performance was not what he would have preferred.

Although the music of *Nachtigall* had originally been used for another text (that of *Ein Wanderer,* Op. 106/5), this first song was much praised by Brahms's friends. Elisabet von Herzogenberg was charmed by it, particularly by the opening, with its grace notes, pretty dotted rhythms, and restless syncopations. In a letter to Brahms of May 21 and 22, 1885, she said it "has the bittersweet of the real nightingale's song; they seem to revel in augmented and diminished intervals, passionate little creatures that they are!" These dissonant intervals are given unusual prominence in the melodic line, and they create much of the harmonic instability of the first section of the song. They also captured the attention of Clara Schumann, who wrote in a letter of May 14, 1886, "How magically the notes of the nightingale strike one's heart strings." The nightingale is but a reminder of a true love, and this connection is explained in the second section, which begins with a less ornate melodic line. This passage draws to a high, loud climax, as the singer freely declaims that the loved one has long since been lost. Time is temporarily suspended, and after a moment's silence, the nightingale's song is repeated like a haunting voice from the past.

Entführung (Abduction) is a return to the chivalric, medieval world of the *Magelone Romanzen* (Op. 33). This is the only Brahms setting of a text by Georg Wilhelm Häring (1798–1871), who wrote under the name Willibald Alexis. Alexis was a novelist in the tradition of Sir Walter Scott, and this ballad tells of an amorous knight who had lain in a bog for six nights before carrying off his Lady Judith on the seventh. Brahms's setting captures the couple's wild ride, with the fast tempo and driving triplet rhythms representing the galloping horse. The melody's triadic motions and the diatonic harmonies, along with the rhythmic patterns, are gestures that Brahms, and Schumann before him, associated with medieval times. The setting is in a simple strophic form, with only the last phrase substantially varied to convey the image of the knight triumphantly proclaiming that on this, the seventh night, he would sleep.

Entführung separates two songs that draw on a folk-song style, *Auf dem Schiffe* and *Dort in den Weiden* (Beneath the Willows). Brahms specifically requested Elisabet von Herzogenberg's opinion of this song, and her letter of June 3, 1885 includes numerous criticisms of it. In particular she asserted that the melody was unvocal and too slavishly dependent on the piano part. The poem, like those of Op. 84, was probably written by Zuccalmaglio. In contrast, the text of the sixth song, *Trennung* (Separation), is considered to be from an authentic Swabian folk song. Brahms's setting is much superior to that of *Dort in den Weiden,* and while the accompaniment is still closely linked to the melodic line, its constant eighths add variety. Brahms gave an autograph copy of this song to Maria Fellinger, who, although born in Swabia, confessed to Brahms that she did not know any folk songs from there.

Between these two folklike pieces is a setting of Klaus Groth's *Komm bald* (Come Soon). Groth gave Brahms this poem for his fifty-second birthday, and both poet and composer sent their respective contributions to Hermine Spies, the contralto with whom both were somewhat infatuated. Brahms and Groth often mentioned Spies in their letters, and Groth described this effort as a "joke of two admirers." Max Kalbeck claimed that Spies's success in Vienna was due to Brahms and he chided the composer for his fawning behavior, saying that Spies "could boast of an impresario such as none of her sisters in Apollo had ever had" (*Johannes Brahms,* IV:37). Richard Specht also disapproved of Brahms's attentiveness to this singer, whose flagging musicality the composer eventually acknowledged.

The protagonist of the coyly titled *Komm bald* roams from day to day wishing his sweetheart were with him. As he dreams, the melody expands on its original strains, and the harmonies search out new keys, flirting with—but never firmly establishing—C and F major. The piano's prelude then returns, and the first stanza of music is altered to accommodate repetitions of the last line of text, "wärst du dabei" (wish you were here). Within these repetitions the word "du" is singled out for special emphasis, being set to longer, higher notes than the surrounding words and being underscored by the piano's gentle appoggiaturas. This treatment, combined with the melody's short segments and the turn to the subdominant, gives the closing phrases a plaintive air.

Heather Platt

5 Lieder for Low Voice and Piano, Opus 105
Composed 1886–88; published 1888

1. Wie Melodien zieht es mir [Groth]
2. Immer leiser wird mein Schlummer [Lingg]
3. Klage [Zuccalmaglio]
4. Auf dem Kirchhofe [Liliencron]
5. Verrat [Lemcke]

The songs of Op. 105 constitute one of the most diversified groupings of Brahms's Lieder, ranging from the simple, folklike style of *Klage* (Lament) to the intensely dramatic *Immer leiser wird mein Schlummer* (Ever Fainter Grows My Slumber) and *Auf dem Kirchhofe* (In the Churchyard). Moreover, the cycle cannot be sung by a single person; *Immer leiser wird mein Schlummer* requires a female performer, and *Verrat* a male. The first two songs were written for Hermine Spies, who sang them to Brahms shortly after they were composed in 1886. *Verrat* (Betrayal) was written in the same year while the remaining two songs were written in 1887–88. Initially, *Klage* and *Auf dem Kirchhofe* were to be published with Op. 106/3–4, and Op. 107/5, and all of these pieces are grouped together in a manuscript that was owned by the publisher Simrock. Brahms, how-

ever, rejected this grouping and instead decided to publish simultaneously three collections of songs. This decision and the ordering of the individual pieces within Opp. 105–107 seem to have preoccupied Brahms
and Simrock during June and July of 1888.

The first two songs of Op. 105 are among the best known of Brahms's
Lieder, and the composer also used their melodies in two of his instrumental pieces. The opening measures of the first are similar to the theme
of the first movement of the A-major Violin Sonata, Op. 100, which was
also composed in the summer of 1886. The melody of the second was
originally used (with a different harmonization and key) as the cello
melody of the Andante of the Second Piano Concerto, Op. 83 (1882).

Wie Melodien zieht es mir (It Runs, like Melodies) is a setting of a poem
by Klaus Groth. As Elisabet von Herzogenberg noted, the text is unusually abstract and it contrasts with the dramatic narratives or emotional
scenes that Brahms typically employed. Its opening stanza invites a musical interpretation, for it describes melodies, which cannot be adequately
defined by words, wafting through the mind like a fragrance. Brahms
bases the other two stanzas of music on that of the first, and as his student Gustav Jenner noted, this is one instance where he alters the music
at the end of the stanzas. These changes are coordinated with the text,
which only suggests the unease of the protagonist during the second
half of the second and third stanzas. There are numerous subtle shadings
in these passages; for example, the short phrase and accompanying cadence in F♯ minor at the end of the second stanza captures the idea of the
melodies suddenly vanishing. Similarly the third stanza introduces further dissonances and more remote keys, as we are told that, despite its
weaknesses, verse does have the power to produce tears.

Immer leiser wird mein Schlummer tells of a girl's valiant fight to remain
alive long enough to see her sweetheart one last time. Throughout the
song, her battle is depicted by the juxtaposition of ascending and descending melodic lines. The final phrase of the first stanza haltingly ascends to d♯″ but then plummets an octave: the girl weeps bitterly as she
has envisioned that her sweetheart has got as far as her door, but no one
is there to let him in. Similarly, the second stanza arpeggiates upward,
but this time it climaxes on a loud f♮″, which is reached at the same moment as the key changes from C♯ minor to D♭ major. Finally, the girl
finds enough strength to cry out for her beloved to come, but this saps
the very life from her, and the melody plunges a tenth and the piano cadences in the lower register. The harmonic progression leading up to

this final cadence has attracted a great deal of comment. It is based on three parallel 6/4 chords that are so unorthodox that Elisabet von Herzogenberg begged Brahms to change them. Nevertheless, both Max Kalbeck and Max Friedländer took her to task and noted the heartwrenching impact of the passage.

The effectiveness of this song has been praised by numerous musicians, and Billroth (a friend of the poet Hermann Lingg) found it so moving that he could not play through it without crying, as he relates in a letter to Brahms of August 18, 1886. Hanslick, in a letter to Billroth, revealed that he could not really appreciate the song (a sentiment that did not surprise the surgeon, who passed the critic's comments on to Brahms). In the press (and later in his book *Musikalisches und Literarisches* of 1889), however, Hanslick was more positive, claiming that he had never before believed that music could portray such profound sadness.

Almost all of the motivic and harmonic material of this song is developed from the initial four beats, including the uneasy syncopated rhythmic patterns of both parts of the accompaniment. This disquiet is established immediately by the first beat. The song begins without a piano prelude and with the bass entering an eighth after the voice and upper parts of the piano. The harmonic structure of these initial beats could be interpreted as an appoggiatura (a figure that pervades the piece) resolving to a dominant seventh, or as a second inversion of the tonic chord, which arpeggiates down to the root at the end of the first measure. This harmonic ambiguity is associated with a metric ambiguity, for one could as well hear the beginning of the piece in 3/2, as in the notated duple meter. Indeed, the nineteenth-century historian and music theorist Hugo Riemann (1849–1919) demonstrated this by rebarring the opening phrases of each stanza. Together, these harmonies, syncopated rhythms, and the metrical ambiguity render a highly affective portrayal of the girl's anxieties and hopelessness.

Of the three remaining songs, only *Auf dem Kirchhofe* reaches the same level of inspiration as the first two. This piece sets a poem by the dramatist and novelist Detlev von Liliencron (1844–1909), whose poetry was influenced by two other poets Brahms also set, August von Platen and Joseph von Eichendorff. Liliencron wrote this particular poem in 1879 on the death of his mother, and he was greatly honored, indeed overwhelmed, by Brahms's setting. Upon being sent a copy of this song by Klaus Groth, he claimed that it was the "highest distinction" and that it gave him "immeasurable joy."

Clara Schumann, in a letter to Brahms of November 4, 1888, praised the first three songs of this opus but described this one as "too dreadfully sad." This powerful work begins with a recitative-like section that contrasts with the lyricism of the first songs of Op. 105, recalling instead the pathos of earlier works such as *An eine Aeolsharfe,* Op. 19/5. Like so many of Brahms's later works, the intensity of this setting is due in part to its compactness and to the angry dissonances of the first section. The second section quotes the Passion chorale *O Haupt voll Blut und Wunden,* and it is clearly set off from the preceding stormy section: the swiftly rising arpeggios alternating with crashing chords are replaced by calmer, chorale-like figuration; the strong dynamics are reduced to *pianissimo*; the key changes from C minor to C major; and the chromatic harmonies of the first section are for the most part put aside. All of these gestures reinforce the idea of the final lines of the poem, that death is a release—an idea that is also in the text of the original chorale.

Immer leiser wird mein Schlummer and *Auf dem Kirchhofe* are separated by a simple folklike setting, *Klage,* which is in strophic form. It comprises three phrases that, unusually for Brahms, are not separated by even the briefest of piano interludes, and the piano part itself, while not slavishly sticking to the largely triadic melody, is quite undemanding.

With its story of unfaithfulness and murder, *Verrat* comes as a shock. Elisabet von Herzogenberg was particularly annoyed by the text, claiming in a letter to Brahms of October 28, 1888, that he should not have set such an unattractive, cheap poem with such a skulking male protagonist. The setting is a return to the dramatic ballad style of Schubert's *Erlkönig,* where a number of characters are presented in a scene. Brahms represents each character by contrasting sections of music. The woman has a lyrical, high melody and a gentle accompaniment, while the evil man has a lower melody, characterized by dry dotted rhythms. When this character pretends to address and threaten the person who has stolen the woman's affections, the harmonies move from B minor to the dark and unrelated key of E♭ minor. As he sarcastically exclaims, "I will bless your wooing!", the harmonies move back toward B and a lyrical, high melody underplays the glee with which he approaches his revenge. This violent act is committed with a repeated *fortissimo* diminished seventh. After a pause the initial stanza of music returns and the villain quietly tells how, in the light of day, the woman will find a dead man on the moor.

Heather Platt

5 Lieder, Opus 106

Composed 1885–88; published 1888

1. Ständchen (Der Mond steht über dem Berge) [Kugler]
2. Auf dem See [Reinhold]
3. Es hing der Reif [Groth]
4. Meine Lieder [Frey]
5. Ein Wanderer [Reinhold]

Most of the songs of Op. 106 were written around the time they were published in 1888, but *Auf dem See* (On the Lake) and *Ein Wanderer* (A Wanderer) were composed earlier, in 1885. These works received mixed reviews from Brahms's friends. Elisabet von Herzogenberg noted their prettiness, but by and large she seemed more impressed with those of Op. 105. Hanslick, however, felt almost exactly the opposite. Whereas he had trouble appreciating such serious songs as *Immer leiser wird mein Schlummer,* and *Auf dem Kirchhofe,* (Op. 105/2, 4), he was quite fond of flowing, folklike numbers like *Auf dem See.* This song has none of the difficult harmonies of some of Brahms's other late Lieder; the melody has a lilting 6/8 rhythm and much of the accompaniment (which Hanslick praised) is characterized by gentle sixteenth-note patterns. In general, Hanslick preferred settings like this one and the Op. 103 *Zigeunerlieder,* rather than Brahms's more somber and dramatic Lieder. His tastes were well known to Brahms and his friends; in a letter to Brahms of July 2, 1876, Billroth wrote that for the most part Hanslick had little sympathy for the " 'out-of-your-soul' sounding music."

The text of the *Ständchen* (Serenade) is by Franz Kugler (1808–1858), and Brahms took it from his *Skizzenbuch* (1830), which included the poet's own illustrations and music. (His compositions include a setting of *Frauenliebe und -leben,* which predates Schumann's setting of the same Adelbert von Chamisso texts.) Aside from being a composer and poet, Kugler was an art historian and biographer of Frederick the Great. *Ständchen* is, however, his only poem to be set by Brahms as a solo song.

Max Kalbeck praised the confident and cheerful tone of the melody of *Ständchen.* The staccato accompaniment is suggestive of a strumming guitar, typical of an evening serenade, or perhaps more literally, the zither referred to in the second stanza. This stanza ends with a description of singing and playing on the flute, fiddle, and zither, and, like his treatment of numerous other references to music making, Brahms expands upon this picture, introducing word repetitions, new accompaniment figurations, and a chromatic detour through E♭ major to B major.

Elisabet von Herzogenberg criticized the repeated rhythmic patterns of *Es hing der Reif* (The Frost Hangs), a type of criticism that often greeted Brahms, though usually it came from his foes like Hugo Wolf. However, Brahms's copyist, Robert Keller, in a letter to the composer of September 24, 1888, numbered it among his favorites. The text by Klaus Groth compares the spring's warmth with blissful passion, but the winter's frost with a woman's rebuff. As the voice enters, the bass of the piano begins a chromatically descending tetrachord that takes some seven measures to complete. This line suggests the hoarfrost in the trees, and it anticipates the cold greeting of the woman. The underlying tension is also suggested by the continual syncopations in the piano part (in which each motive begins on the second half of the second beat—an unusual length for an anacrusis), and by the harmonic structure in which the tonic triad (A minor) is often deemphasized. The subject of rejection occurs frequently in Brahms's Lieder, but it is only in his late works that the penetrating pain is portrayed with such economy and intensity, relying more on subtle harmonic nuances than on expansive melodic lines and complex accompaniments.

Meine Lieder (My Songs) is undoubtedly the highlight of this opus, with its well-shaped melodic line, reminiscent in style of *Wie Melodien zieht es mir* (Op. 105/1), and graceful accompaniment. It is the only one of Brahms's solo Lieder with a text by Adolf Frey (1855–1920), a Swiss poet and professor of literary history. Like *Wie Melodien zieht es mir,* the text refers to the power of song, and in particular to the dark sounds of the protagonist's own songs. The eighths of the piano provide an excellent foil to the vocal line, and during the first section, they sweep gently downward, like the wings of the melody described in the poem. With the sorrowful image of cypresses, however, these figures give way to soft, sustained chords. Although the style of the opening melody returns, the piano does not return to its original figures until the postlude, which repeats and extends the prelude.

With the dispirited protagonist of *Ein Wanderer,* we enter the world of Schubert's *Die Winterreise.* Traveling the road of sorrows, the wanderer of this Reinhold poem is every bit as inconsolable as the man in *Kein Haus, keine Heimat* (Op. 94/5). As in this earlier work, ascending melodies, in this case steeply rising arpeggios, symbolize the protagonist's questioning. The styles of the accompaniments, however, are quite different. Whereas the earlier song had a remarkably simple accompaniment, the piano part of *Ein Wanderer* is contrapuntal, and, in particular, its initial contrary motion graphically depicts the diverging roads described in the first line of the text. A sparser accompaniment, by comparison, is used at the end of the second stanza, where the man imagines that no one would understand if he confessed where he really dwelt. His frustration and disillusionment are stressed as this phrase ends loudly on a sustained dominant seventh, with the voice breaking off on the leading tone (e″). Despite this telling gesture, the song seems overwrought and less dramatically convincing than *Kein Haus, keine Heimat.*

Heather Platt

5 Lieder, Opus 107
Composed 1886–88; published 1888

1. An die Stolze [Flemming]   4. Maienkätzchen [Liliencron]
2. Salamander [Lemcke]   5. Mädchenlied [Heyse]
3. Das Mädchen spricht [Gruppe]

An intriguing aspect of Brahms's lifelong devotion to Lieder composition is his ongoing experimentation with methods of combining his favored strophic form with detailed reflection of the dramatic implications of the text.

The five songs of Op. 107, all presumed to have been composed during the year or so preceding their publication in October 1888, reveal that Brahms, whose vast corpus of art songs yet lacked only the *Vier ernste Gesänge*, was still concerned with the problem of adapting strophic form to expressive purpose. In the first and third songs, *An die Stolze* (To the Haughty Woman) and *Das Mädchen spricht* (The Maiden Speaks), the structure of the poetic stanza dictates that of the strophe, which is repeated virtually unchanged; in the second and fourth, *Salamander* and *Maienkätzchen* (Catkins), the strophe is modified upon repetition; *Mädchenlied* (Maiden's Song) derives the material for its contrasting concluding section from development of the basic strophe.

Brahms chose to set only the first two verses of *An die Stolze* by Paul Flemming (1609–1640), probably because of the parallel construction they share. In each eight-line stanza, the first four lines detail a complaint of the poet against the haughty woman of the title; the fifth line uses three increasingly intense verbs to express his own feelings; and the last three lines, which resume the accusatory tone of the opening, are addressed to the lady herself. Brahms's setting depicts the basic conflict by contrasting a sighingly dissonant vocal line in gradually rising quarter notes with a wide-ranging, flowing countermelody in the piano, suggesting the long-suffering steadfastness of the poet's love despite the fickleness of its object; the harmonies of the more inward fifth line hint at the remote key of the lowered mediant and culminate in a painful, prolonged minor-ninth dissonance; the closing phrases return to the tonic key and increase in length and dissonance, soon abandoning the flowing accompaniment in favor of assertive chords with afterbeats.

In the fanciful *Das Mädchen spricht* by Otto Friedrich Gruppe (1804–1876), a new bride questions the female swallow outside her window. The first three lines of each five-line verse constitute a relatively mundane query: "Was it with your old husband that you built your nest? What do the two of you twitter about in the morning?" But her nuptial happiness intrudes irresistibly: "Or have you only recently pledged yourself to him? Are you newly married too?" Brahms sets the opening lines to short, sprightly vocal phrases in the tonic key while playful rhythms in the accompaniment evoke the swallow's darting movements. But suddenly the piano introduces in *forte* the key of the lowered mediant (♭III), a frequent Brahmsian metaphor for the realm of the imagination; more sustained vocal phrases and a long, gradual slowing and softening imbue the second question with increasing thoughtfulness, which is broken only at the very end of the strophe by the return of the "real-world" tonic key.

In his would-be comic poem *Salamander*, Carl Lemcke (1831–1913) compares a salamander, who "just begins to feel good" when thrown into a fire by a malicious girl, to himself, who "gets a good feeling from fiery love." Brahms sets the first verse with folkloric simplicity in the minor mode; a repetition of the last line of text results in a total of five two-measure phrases. As a musical equivalent to the verbal analogy, Brahms devises a second strophe that is an enlarged major-key variant of the first. It is stretched from ten measures to twelve by the insertion of a measure of piano interlude after its first phrase and an expansion of the last line's repetition. Both of the closing phrases derive from the development of a tiny chromatic motif that showed up in the accompaniment to introduce the reference to fire in the first strophe. The inserted interlude deliciously postpones the first joke, the salamander's unexpected reaction; the elongation at the end emphasizes the later, principal drollery.

The text for *Maienkätzchen* is a poem by Detlev von Liliencron (1844–1909), originally titled *Tiefe Sehnsucht* (Deep Longing). In the first of its three-line stanzas, the poet hails the early spring appearance of catkins, some of which he inserts into his hatband; in the second, he remembers that there once was a time when he did the same to a sweetheart's hat. Brahms's endearing song is sweetly nostalgic rather than lamenting, a likely reason for his changing the title. The identical first lines of the two verses are set to the same music, and the melodies of the closing phrases of both strophes use the same pitches in different rhythms; but what lies between is so greatly varied and expanded in the second strophe that one hardly recognizes it as akin to the first. Two new phrases are inserted, based on a little dotted-rhythm motif that appeared earlier in the piano; though the first strophe occupies only six measures, the second is stretched to thirteen through text repetition; and a preponderance of subdominant harmony, heretofore almost completely absent, suffuses it with tenderness.

The first two verses of the folkish *Mädchenlied* by Paul von Heyse (1830–1914) describe the spinning rooms where the girls are all preparing something for their trousseaux while the village lads make merry; the remainder of the poem focuses increasingly on the maiden of the title, who reveals in the third verse that she has no one who cares for her, and in the fourth, that she can do nothing but weep. For the first three stanzas Brahms invents a minor-mode melody that consists of three gradually rising two-measure phrases and a fourth phrase that is touchingly extended to three measures by an appoggiatura-like cadence figure as it falls in pitch. Busy sixteenth notes in the accompaniment suggest the turning of the spinning wheels; in the more personal third strophe, their reversed direction, smaller range, and quieter dynamics throw the vocal line into prominence. But the greater emotional intensity of the fourth stanza demands a different treatment. Over an accompaniment of rising arpeggios (often a Brahmsian metaphor for isolation), a new melody is developed from the scalar thirds and fourths that were the principal building blocks of the basic strophe. "What's the use of spinning?" rings out *forte* in the shockingly unexpected key of the raised mediant. "I don't know!" is given three settings of increasing hopelessness, filled with the ache of dissonance. An interlude in falling, detached eighth

notes, like quiet tears, follows each strophe and returns as a postlude to
this haunting portrayal of a desperately lonely girl.

Lucien Stark

VIER ERNSTE GESÄNGE, OPUS 121
Composed 1896; published 1896

1. Denn es gehet dem Menschen [Ecclesiastes 3:19–22]
2. Ich wandte mich und sahe an alle [Ecclesiastes 4:1–3]
3. Tod, o Tod, wie bitter bist du [Ecclesiasticus 41:1–2]
4. Wenn ich mit Menschen- und mit Engelszungen redete [I Corinthians 13: 1–3, 12–13]

As his sixty-third (and last) birthday neared in 1896, Brahms was filled
with somber thoughts. Not only did Clara Schumann, his lifelong con-
fidante, lie near death from the effects of a stroke, but also he had lost
many others of those closest to him in the recent past. On May 7 he
showed the manuscript of a new work, the *Vier ernste Gesänge*, to Max
Kalbeck, his friend and future biographer, describing it as a birthday gift
for himself.

Not surprisingly, the biblical texts are chosen (like those of the *German
Requiem*) to console the bereaved and the burdened. At the same time,
they encapsulate the composer's own earthy, undogmatic spiritual
tenets—that a life well lived is its own reward, that death is certain for all
living things, that compassion is a virtue. The pithy economy of Brahms's
musical language is the perfect counterpart to Luther's sturdy, unadorned German, and their combination speaks with oracular power.
The result is one of the monuments of the song literature.

Compared with Brahms's songs from the 1880s, the *Serious Songs* reveal
melodies that combine recitative and lyricism in a new expressive-
declamatory manner; accompaniments that evoke the orchestra in their
sonorous counterpoint; and construction that is symphonic in concept,
the work seeming to evolve organically from germinal motives.

The principal such basic shape is the chain of descending melodic
thirds that had often served Brahms in the past as a metaphor for death.
It appears most audibly at the beginning of No. 3, where the pitches
B–G–E–C (perhaps not by coincidence, the same pitches that open the
Fourth Symphony) make up both the initial melody and its supporting
harmonies. But in fact, the descending thirds had appeared earlier, in, for

example, the swirling Allegro arpeggios in the accompaniment of No. 1 and the slowly falling broken triad that begins and figures prominently throughout No. 2. Gradually, the motive permeates the entire texture—melodic intervals (whether leaps or scale segments, rising or falling), bass line, harmonic progressions—until, in No. 4, nearly every element seems to derive from the third or its inversion, the sixth.

The fatalistic text of No. 1, Ecclesiastes 3: 19–22, observes that in death, man is no better than the beasts—"as the one dieth, so dieth the other." The setting alternates a dirgelike Andante with a turbulent Allegro ("all are of the dust, and all turn to dust again"). The former is underlaid by a constant tolling of bells; the latter, by an insistent throbbing. Mournful minor keys prevail, though there is a brief brightening to the tonic major at "a man should rejoice in his own works." The final bleak trailing off is punctuated by two stern *forte* chords.

Based on Ecclesiastes 4:1–3, the even more pessimistic second song laments the world's widespread injustices and suggests that the unborn, who have "not seen the evil work that is done under the sun," are better off than either the living or the dead. Brahms's through-composed setting contrasts a touchingly empathetic observation of the tears of the oppressed with suspenseful recurrences of the death-evocative falling thirds in stark, unharmonized octaves. A turn from minor to major at the end of the song seems born more of resignation than hope.

The most pervasive development of the falling-thirds motive as a recognizable entity occurs in the third song, whose text, the apocryphal Ecclesiasticus 41:1–2, contrasts the bitterness of death to one still in his prime with its solace to one who no longer finds joy in life. Graphically and memorably, Brahms draws the equivalent distinction by the simple transformation of falling thirds in minor into rising sixths in major. It is a stunning passage, which has been much analyzed and described—by Schoenberg, among others. Another noteworthy opposition is that of the rhythmic vitality that depicts the man who "hath prosperity in all things" in the first half with the languor that characterizes the "feeble and old" man in the second.

The fourth song seems to stand somewhat apart from the others (Kalbeck asserts that it was sketched earlier for another purpose) because of both its E♭-major cheeriness and its many melodic ascents. The piano introduction announces the fundamental interval of the third as a step-wise movement upward, and the rising sixth appears importantly, notably at the recurring "der Liebe." The text is excerpted from St. Paul's familiar discourse on Christian charity in the thirteenth chapter of I Corinthians. Brahms sets the similarly constructed verses 1–3 as three kindred sections, Andante con moto; the initial "though I" clauses are related musically, as are the added such clauses in verses 2 and 3, the reiterations of "and have not charity," and the three clauses detailing the consequences. Verse 12, "For now we see through a glass, darkly," elicits a soaring Adagio in the otherworldly key of the lowered submediant. The concluding verse 13, "And now abideth faith, hope, charity, these three," becomes a coda that refers to both earlier themes; it can hardly fail to uplift and comfort any listener, however troubled.

Lucien Stark

Brahms with Emmy Weyerman, wife of banker Walter Weyerman and half-sister of Rudolf von der Leyen.

Part Five

VOCAL AND
CHORAL
MUSIC

INTRODUCTION

When we attempt to understand and assess the musical achievements of an earlier era, we sometimes fail to take into account the influence of radical cultural discontinuities on our exercise of judgment. This failure has become particularly marked of late, in the wake of "historically informed" reconstructed performance of so-called early music from before the nineteenth century. It is fascinating to hear and see ensembles play on period instruments and sometimes even in Baroque costume in modern concert venues, but we will never experience Telemann or Handel the way those composers' contemporaries did; indeed, the fascination of such performances lies precisely in the artificiality of the reproduced antiquity and assertion of distance from our own conception of our contemporary context. In some areas of nineteenth-century music as well, as is most vividly illustrated in the tradition of music for vocal ensembles, there is inherent in the genre a genuine distance and strangeness deriving from the disappearance of a whole dimension of social life associated with this music.

Though a strong choral tradition still exists in select universities and communities in England and America, choral singing does not retain the dominant role it once possessed for the public at large in the nineteenth century, especially in German-speaking Europe. It is not surprising that the largest American modern stronghold of choral singing is in the Midwest, where the origins can be traced directly to the massive German-speaking emigration to America before 1900. Amateur choral singing was a dominant component of nineteenth-century German social and cultural life. Few other activities bridged the home and the public sphere so intensely.

Political unification in Germany did not occur until 1871, and was only a partial solution to the recalcitrant issue of how German language and culture could be reconciled with a political structure. In the absence of an inclusive nation-state, German-speaking Europeans before and after 1871 used culture as an explicit form of political expression. The creation of the German Empire denied a large German-speaking population in Europe participation in the ideal of a single unified German cultural entity. For example, the Habsburg Empire possessed many German-speaking communities, not only the Austrian. For even more geographically remote German-speaking communities in South Africa, America, and Russia, the allegiance to things German was maintained in large measure by that curious combination of private and public: the singing group, the Liedertafel and the Singverein. The ideal of cultural affiliation which fed the choral tradition was exemplified in the tenth annual gathering of German singing organizations in 1928, the centenary of the death of Schubert. The conclave took place in Vienna, with a massive parade and numerous marathon concerts, and delegations of singing groups came from all over the world. The significance and vitality of the German vocal-group tradition in the nineteenth century as a pivotal component of musical and political culture cannot be underestimated.

Therefore no composer could ignore the growing demand in the 1840s and 1850s for secular music using two or more voices with piano accompaniment, to be performed in the home and in semi-public venues such as clubrooms and inns. Brahms continued to write for habits of music making which first gained wide popularity in the time of Schubert and continued their expansion through the generation of Schumann and Mendelssohn. From the 1820s on, choral groups for women, for men, and for mixed voices sprang up in every town and city in German-speaking Europe. By the 1860s, there were groups organized not only by region and place but also by guild and vocation. There were choral societies made up of railroad workers, teachers, and so on. These were all secular groups. In Protestant Germany, the popularity of this mode of entertainment was underscored the longstanding tradition of church singing since the days of Luther. Brahms's attachment to the choral tradition was therefore a response to the early Romantic conventions and expectations developed by Schubert and Schumann and also a reflection of his attachment to a vital religious tradition dating back to Schütz, Bach, and Handel. Not only did writing for chorus and vocal groups seem a logical and desirable option for the young Brahms in the 1850s; this genre permitted him to combine his religious commitments and his ambition to make his way as a composer and also to pay homage through music to the history of music. In Brahms, the lure of Romanticism and historicism combine in both the secular and sacred arenas of choral music.

One notable aspect of Brahms's prodigious career is the fact that of all the major composers in the history of music, Brahms was perhaps the only one to have distinguished himself as a choral conductor. As a practicing musician, Brahms's greatest recognition was not as a pianist or orchestral conductor but as a beloved choral conductor. His first appearance as a conductor in 1847 in Winsen an der Lühe was in front of a male choir. In 1859, he created the Hamburger Frauenchor, and his commitment to that organization is witnessed by his composition in the following years of the *Marienlieder, Psalm 13,* and many partsongs and motets. In 1863 he was appointed conductor of the Vienna Singakademie, which helped him as he worked on what would eventually become *Ein deutsches Requiem.* Later in the 1870s he conducted the Singverein, and throughout his life, returned repeatedly to choral music as a source of inspiration and rejuvenation. The result is a unique and distinguished body of work.

Ironically, it is precisely the choral and multiple-voice vocal works that are the least known and appreciated in the music of Brahms in the modern age. All that really remains as part of the conventional repertory is *Ein deutsches Requiem* and to a lesser extent *Schicksalslied* (Song of Destiny). But whether one chooses to listen to the motet *Warum?* or the incomparable *Nänie, Rinaldo,* or the canons for female voices, one finds in this area of Brahms's choral compositional output a treasure trove of miniature and large-scale masterpieces. The reason for their obscurity is not inherent in the music. Rather it rests in the precipitous decline of active participation in amateur singing both at home and in groups. Ear training and sightsinging are no longer skills broadly distributed in the educated population. The remaining vestiges of a once exuberant and inclusive choral tradition are confined for the most part to large-scale amateur performances of such works as Handel's *Messiah*, Bach's *St. Matthew Passion*, and, to a lesser extent, *Ein deutsches Requiem.* Sadly, public interest in choirs as a concert experience has not been sustained during the twentieth century. But from the perspective of Brahms's own aesthetic commitments, choral music was a central and decisive part of musical culture.

16

VOCAL DUETS

3 Duets, for Soprano and Alto, Opus 20
Composed 1858–60; published 1861

1. Weg der Liebe I [Herder: *Stimmen der Völker*]
2. Weg der Liebe II [Herder: *Stimmen der Völker*]
3. Die Meere [trad.]

That the young Brahms would turn to duets as a means of dramatizing the dialogic possibilities of Lieder is not at all exceptional; in his later duets, he makes imaginative use of contrasting voice-characters. However, in the three duets of Op. 20, his first published set of duets (though not his first composed, for *Klosterfräulein,* Op. 61/2, was written in Hamburg as early as 1852), he opts to use the voices singing together in parallel form in all three songs. Yet contrasting perspectives are implied, especially in the first and second duets, written together in 1855 in Göttingen. Both of these are titled *Weg der Liebe,* and are settings of two different parts of Herder's translation of a northern English poem, "Love will find out the way," collected by Thomas Percy in his *Reliques of Ancient English Poetry* (1765). Percy's collection was a seminal text in the late eighteenth century's Romantic fascination with early folk poetry. Herder translated and published Percy's rendition of the poem in 1779 and later in 1807 in his collection, *Stimmen der Völker. Weg der Liebe I* is in E major and marked allegro in 6/8 time; *Weg der Liebe II* is in C major, marked poco adagio, and also in 6/8 time. These duets share the same textual source; both declare in a simple and straightforward manner the power of love to conquer all and find its way through all obstacles. Nevertheless they are quite different in character. The lively, fast-paced themes of the first song contrast sharply to those of the slower, more reflective second song. It is as though instead of expressing contrast through the two voices within the song, Brahms instead places the dialogue between these two related songs.

Die Meere (The Seas), the final duet, composed in Hamburg in 1860, is based on an Italian folk song translated by Wilhelm Müller, and is an Andante in E minor. Both the texts and the settings of Op. 20 point to the influence of Schubert on the young Brahms and specifically the influence of Schubert on Brahms through Schumann. As in some of the more popular of Schubert's songs and duets, there is a disingenuous simplicity about some of these works, the same sense of Schubertian influence that is also apparent in Op. 17, particularly in the use of the horns.

Leon Botstein

4 Duets, for Alto and Baritone, Opus 28
Composed 1860–62; published 1864

1. Die Nonne und der Ritter [Eichendorff]
2. Vor der Tür [Old German]
3. Es rauscht das Wasser [Goethe]
4. Der Jäger und sein Liebchen [Fallersleben]

Though these four duets for alto and baritone represent a more mature and successful approach to the dialogic possibilities of duets than Op. 20, Brahms was more than usually self-deprecating about them. They were written between the fall of 1860 and the winter of 1862, and are dedicated to Amalie Joachim. Brahms maintained a particular affection for Joachim's wife when she and Joachim divorced; indeed, Brahms's sympathy for Amalie over his old friend caused irreparable damage to his relationship with Joachim. In these songs, Brahms uses the contrasting voices as an ironic demonstration of imperfect or misconstrued communication.

The opening duet, *Die Nonne und der Ritter* (The Nun and the Knight), is set to a text for which Brahms had a particular affection. He had marked the Eichendorff poem in a volume that he owned in his adolescence. The text for this affecting piece, in which the nun and the knight at one point sing together without knowing how near they are to each other, is set in an andante tempo in G minor. It opens with the alto declaiming to simple sostenuto piano accompaniment. The baritone enters supported by a somewhat more fluid figuration. The alto then picks up until the middle section, which is faster and begins in C major with the baritone. The alto closes the duet in the original tempo as the piece winds its way back to G minor.

Number 2, marked vivace, is in B major in 3/4 time, with a middle section marked animato. It is based on an Old German text, *Vor der Tür* (Before the Door). Here the baritone takes the lead in the narrative. The duet closes with two voices singing together but really in opposition, for this duet presents the quarrel of lovers. Number 3 is in F major and is set to a text by Goethe. The duet opens with the piano anticipating the opening line, which describes the moving of water. The alto opens the duet and is followed in a more sustained episode by the baritone. The two voices then combine, singing together but each maintaining an independent line. The work closes with a somewhat more extended piano solo. In the last duet, Brahms returns to the subject naturally suggested by the combination of a male and female voice, that of the quarreling lovers. The duet, marked allegro, is set to a text by Heinrich Hoffmann von Fallersleben (1798–1874), from whose collection Brahms probably also took the text for No. 2. In this dialogue between the hunter and his beloved, as the piano keeps the rhythmic pulse moving, the baritone speaks of how he anticipates coming home from the hunt. But the woman sees things somewhat differently, as she would prefer to dance, and seems less optimistic about the consequences of the eager hunter's late night return. The duet is beautifully crafted to show how two people can appear to speak to each other but actually speak past one another, a human circumstance which also fascinated Brahms's great literary contemporary, Theodor Fontane.

Leon Botstein

4 DUETS, FOR SOPRANO AND ALTO, OPUS 61
Composed 1852–74; Published 1874

1. Die Schwestern [Mörike]
2. Klosterfräulein [Kerner]
3. Phänomen [Goethe]
4. Die Boten der Liebe [trad., trans. Wenzig]

Opus 61, which contains four duets for soprano and alto, was completed in January 1874. The last two duets, No. 3 in B major, marked poco andante in 3/4 time, set to a text by Goethe, and No. 4 in D major, marked vivace in 9/8, a fast-paced duet set to a Bohemian folk text, were written in December 1873 and finished in January. Brahms, in order to complete the set of four, turned to earlier works: No. 1 from 1860, an allegretto in 2/4 in G minor, with a text by Eduard Mörike, and No. 2 in A minor, marked andante, set to a text by Justinus Kerner. The duets are all written in a manner that uses both voices together, the lines running parallel, as opposed to an antiphonal use of the voices. Though there has been some discussion of why Brahms in this period does not employ the dialogism he by now had fully developed, the answer is a practical one. Though each of the four had an occasional public performance, as the piano accompaniment and the simultaneous use of both voices indicate, these duets were written for amateur use. The accompaniment is designed to support the voices and there is an unaffected simplicity about these pieces which suggests their utility for amateur resources in the home.

Leon Botstein

5 DUETS, FOR SOPRANO AND ALTO, OPUS 66
Composed 1875; published 1875

1. Klänge I [Groth]
2. Klänge II [Groth]
3. Am Strande [Hölty]
4. Jägerlied [Candidus]
5. Hüt'du dich! [*Des Knaben Wunderhorn*]

As in the case of Op. 61, Brahms wrote the last three duets of Op. 66 near the time of publication, but the first two date from an earlier period. This suggests that Brahms, encouraged by the success of his other works for solo voices and piano, decided to use earlier material, add to it, and publish a coherent group of works. The first duets are based on texts by Klaus Groth, each entitled *Klänge* (Sounds). Both are marked andante; the first opens with the piano in G minor but closes in G major. The second parallels this form and opens in B minor and closes in B major. Both in the accompaniment and in the vocal writing, these duets are somewhat more complex than Op. 61, and there is some more independence in the use of the two voices. Number 3, in E♭ major marked rühig, is based on a text by Hermann Hölty, *Am Strande* (At the Seashore). Number 4, *Jäger-*

lied, (Hunter's Song) marked lebhaft, is set to a text by Karl Candidus. It begins in C major, with the soprano singing alone. She is then answered in C minor by the alto. This question and answer format continues throughout the work; unlike any of the other duets, in this work the voices sing against one another. The last word is given to the alto and appropriately ends in C minor since death, the object of the hunt, is said to be inevitable.

The final duet, set to a text from *Des Knaben Wunderhorn,* is marked lebhaft, with the admonition that it be sung in a manner conveying secrecy and roguishness. The text describes the evils that can befall the unwitting man who is taken in by the beauty of the apparently innocent female. The voices in the duet are whispering warnings. The work is in B♭ major; the middle section is repeated each time with a different verse, and the work closes as it opens, with the piano alone, swiftly and quietly, as if to suggest that such sage and softly uttered advice is as fleeting in its effectiveness as it is charming in its Brahmsian representation.

Opus 66 is particularly interesting because the texts and their settings offer a glimpse into the social conventions of middle-class music making. The subject of love—its sources, its memories, and its dangers—dominates, even in the hunting song, in which the metaphor of hunting is self-evidently used as a surrogate for seduction. The performance of these songs in domestic *soirées* functioned together with conversation and gossip as a primary element of acceptable socializing, both for female groups and mixed company.

Leon Botstein

4 BALLADS AND ROMANCES, OPUS 75
Composed 1877–78; published 1878

1. Edward [Herder: *Volkslieder*]
2. Guter Rat [*Des Knaben Wunderhorn*]
3. So lass uns wandern! [trad., trans. Wenzig]
4. Walpurgisnacht [Alexis]

The neglect of this fine group of settings is due more to practical than to musical reasons. Each of the duets calls for a different combination of voices, in accordance with the demands of the text: alto and tenor, soprano and alto, soprano and tenor, and two sopranos. With the exception of *So lass uns wandern!* (No. 3) these are dialogues rather than true duets, with the protagonists in each case being mother and child. Brahms had originally intended to dedicate the group to his friend Elisabet von Herzogenberg; but, as he told Fritz Simrock, "Numbers 1 and 4 are too horrible, and Numbers 2 and 3 too free, for a lady." When the *Ballads and Romances* were issued by Simrock in 1877 they bore instead an inscription to another of Brahms's close friends, the engraver and photographer Julius Allgeyer, who wrote the biography of their mutual friend Anselm Feuerbach.

Brahms's interest in Herder's translation of the Scottish ballad *Edward* goes back at least to 1854, when it had inspired the first of his four *Ballades,* Op. 10, for solo piano. Although the latter stages of that piece evolve quite freely, the question and answer format of the opening page can be shown to fit the words of the text exactly. Psychologists armed with the knowledge that Brahms had written the piece in the wake of Schumann's suicide attempt, and that the climactic revelation of parricide occurs in a triumphant B♭ major, would no doubt have a field day; though Brahms's continued fascination with the tale some five years after the death of his own father might be harder to explain.

Herder's source for the Scottish text of *Edward* was Bishop Percy's *Reliques of Ancient Poetry,* and in the preface to the translation in his *Volkslieder* of 1779, he described the ballad as: "A Scottish song with the mark of Cain upon it, and seething with unrest. His sword has drunk his father's blood, wherefore his eyes are cast down to the ground. His sin is beyond forgiveness and will pursue him all over the earth. And how the ballad moves, with intervals full of woe, and fury, and deep hidden distress."

Brahms must have known if not Schubert's strophic setting of 1827 (*Eine altschottische Ballade,* D.923), then at least Loewe's famous version, composed in 1818. Loewe's ballad, so deeply admired by Wagner, is of undeniable dramatic power, and its sudden outburst as Edward confesses to his terrible crime is a theatrical coup that Brahms does not attempt to emulate; but the later composer's understanding of the text was surely deeper. Brahms maintains an atmosphere of extreme agitation throughout, with the suppressed excitement of the pianissimo opening a perfect metaphor for conspiratorial whispering. Gradually the tension increases, and the pitch of the voices rises, until, with the confession of parricide, the relentless sixteenth-note movement gives way to chordal writing of symphonic weight. At the end of the setting, Brahms combines both types of material, and as Edward curses his mother the tale falls into place: it is surely she who has instigated the crime.

The two middle numbers of Op. 75 are in much lighter vein, though the father has a rough time of things again in *Guter Rat*, to a text from *Des Knaben Wunderhorn*. Brahms's rhythmic depiction of a trotting horse in the opening pages is altogether charming, as is the chromatic slithering in the piano part of the middle section, where, in a change from E major to G major, the daughter bemoans the fact that she has no money with which to buy clothes to impress the handsome rider who passes by every day. The chromaticism becomes more insistent as she learns that her father has squandered the family assets in gambling. If only she had been born a boy, things would be different—and here the music returns to its starting point, with the sound of the horse replaced by the roll of a military drum.

So lass uns wandern! Op. 75/3 is a Bohemian folk poem which Brahms took from Josef Wenzig's *Westslawischer Märchenschatz*, published in 1857—the source also of the first four in Brahms's set of nine songs, Op. 69. The duet is one of friendship in pastoral surroundings. The young man, afraid of being bewitched by his companion's black eyes, is reassured by her assertion that she has no such designs: did she not give her word underneath that green tree (here the music switches softly from the main key of D major, to B♭ major)? From this point onward, in perfect accord, they can sing in duet as they wander carefree through the countryside. As in so many of Brahms's songs, the accompanimental figuration is generated by the shape of the vocal phrases, so that the setting as a whole has an inevitable organic unity. Also introduced with complete naturalness is the modulation to the supertonic (E minor) for the second phrase, with its mention of those bewitching eyes; and the softly repeated notes in the inner voice of the piano part in the middle section, depicting the crow picking at acorns.

Similar to *Edward* in mood and form is the last of the Op. 75 duets, *Walpurgisnacht*. This, too, was a ballad that had been set by Loewe (Op. 2/3), and again that composer had not been able to resist a sensational dramatic effect at the poem's climax—the frisson-inducing line, "Liebe Mutter, dein Bett war leer in der Nacht" (Dear mother, your bed was empty in the night). The final revelation that the mother is indeed a witch is treated by Loewe in a coda, marked feroce, which quotes the witches' dance from Spohr's *Faust*.

The text of *Walpurgisnacht* was written "on a stormy May 1" by Willibald Alexis, the pseudonym by which the historical novelist Georg Wilhelm Häring is generally known. Brahms replaces the "Liebe Mutter" with which the daughter prefaces each of her observations with the simpler and more effective "Ach Mutter."

Brahms sets Alexis's ballad as a breathless dialogue in which one voice takes over seamlessly from the other, even to the point of occasionally overlapping in their urgency. The syncopated inner voice of the chromatic accompaniment, the sotto voce atmosphere of the exchanges between mother and daughter, the mounting excitement as the music moves inexorably upward from A minor to C minor, C♯ minor, D minor, E♭ minor, and (via a fine enharmonic change during the daughter's observation that the broom went missing during the night) E minor—all this testifies to Brahms's unerring skill at winding up the tension, but also to his enjoyment at handling a ghost story. Following the final exclamation, "Ach Mutter, dein Bett war leer in der Nacht!", Brahms allows the briefest of dramatic silences before the story is clinched with the mother's confession of witchcraft, not only taking the music back to its home key but also providing the climactic highest note of the setting.

Brahms's evident sense of fun in composing the ballad was echoed by Elisabet von Herzogenberg's reaction when he sent it to her:

> I am glad I am still capable of a cold shudder every time I play the duet, although I know beforehand that the mother has flown away up the chimney!... From the very first notes one is in the midst of it. Then the doubling of the voice in the bass at the words "ist heute der erste Mai, liebes Kind," and later (let him who wishes to know the uncanny come and listen to this) how the anxious tones of the daughter "Ach Mutter, was reiten die Hexen," &c., are taken up by the accompaniment as the mother answers, so that the daughter's voice is still in the duet though she herself is silent, and the answer is the inversion of the question! And the wonderful climax at the end, reminding one in a sense of 'Edward'!

Misha Donat

17

VOCAL QUARTETS

3 QUARTETS, OPUS 31
Composed 1859–1863; published 1864

1. Wechsellied zum Tanz [Goethe]
2. Neckereien [trad.]
3. Der Gang zum Liebchen [trad.]

In the period between 1859 and 1891, Brahms wrote seven sets of works, sixty individual numbers, for four solo voices and piano accompaniment. Clearly, Brahms had an affinity for this particular ensemble. In part, they were attractive to Brahms because of the greater complexity and range of sound available to him than offered by duets and solo Lieder. Brahms's twenty duets also suggest his awareness of the ubiquity of domestic music making. But as is evident in the popularity of his *Liebeslieder Walzer*, the vocal-quartet form was distinctly congenial to larger domestic gatherings, convivial salon evenings used as venues for amateur singing and playing. Indeed, in Vienna in 1863–65, when Op. 31 was first heard in public, the salon was in some respects the best venue; there was no modern concert or recital hall on a large scale apart from spaces designed for theater, and the famous Musikverein building had not yet been built. In this sense, these quartets represent a continuation of the kind of musical tradition often associated with Schubert and the Schubertiade. But Vienna had also changed considerably since the death of Schubert. The Ringstrasse was already under construction and a much more extensive amateur middle-class population existed, affording an ample supply of qualified amateurs eager to participate in an evening of quartet singing. The first two numbers of Op. 31, for example, were first performed in an informal evening sponsored by the Singakademie, the choral group of which Brahms was conductor.

Of the three quartets of Op. 31, the first, entitled *Wechsellied zum Tanze* (Alternating Song for the Dance) remains the most enduring and best known. It is written in A♭ major and is based on a dialogue between two dancing couples representing alternative but equally disproportionate attitudes to the activity in which they are engaged. One couple is focused entirely on the dance itself and they are insensible to each other; the others are deeply engrossed with each other and neglectful of the dance. Brahms dramatizes the opposition between two types of moods musically by contrasting them with key changes between C minor with A♭ major. He concludes the quartet by synthesizing the two modes of music, placing minor and major side by side in small units to bring the quartet to a magical close.

Opus 31/1 is the longest of the three quartets. Numbers 2 and 3 are taken from a collection of Moravian and Bohemian folk songs. Number 2, marked allegretto, is in E major and in its depiction of the bantering between lovers, it retains the dialogic form evident in Op. 31/1. Number 3, in E♭ major, develops a more homophonic character. In both of these quartets, as in Op. 31/1, the piano fulfills its role largely as accompaniment, but it is never entirely in a secondary position; rather, Brahms often gives it the lead in the development of the musical ideas, sometimes using it as an ironic counterstatement to the words of the singers.

Leon Botstein

LIEBESLIEDER, 18 WALTZES, OPUS 52
Composed 1869; published 1869 [Daumer]

1. Rede, Mädchen
2. Am Gesteine rauscht die Flut
3. O die Frauen
4. Wie des Abends schöne Röte
5. Die grüne Hopfenranke
6. Ein kleiner, hübscher Vogel
7. Wohl schön bewandt war es
8. Wenn so lind dein Auge mir
9. Am Donaustrande
10. O wie sanft die Quelle
11. Nein, es ist nicht auszukommen
12. Schlosser auf, und mache Schlösser
13. Vögelein durchrauscht die Luft
14. Sieh, wie ist die Welle klar
15. Nachtigall, sie singt so schön
16. Ein dunkeler Schacht ist Liebe
17. Nicht wandle, mein Licht
18. Es bebet das Gesträuche

The eighteen *Liebeslieder Walzer*, Op. 52, for piano duet and vocal quartet, celebrate a predominantly Schubertian heritage. Indeed, together

with the Waltzes for Four-Hand Piano, Op. 39, they play an integral role
in a kind of "Schubert project" that occupied the composer during his
first decade in Vienna. Brahms edited a number of Schubert's unpublished compositions at this time, including, among other works, one
book of *Twelve Ländler* in 1864 (D. 790) and a second of *Twenty Ländler* in
May 1869 (D. 366 and 814). To each he quickly responded with a cycle of
his own making—the Op. 39 Waltzes in January 1869 (see p. 201) and the
Liebeslieder Walzer (marked, tellingly, "Im Ländler-Tempo") in August
1869. Two years later, Brahms considered editing a third group of Schubert dances. Although this project came to nothing, the composer's imagination was once more sparked, and within two years his own *Neue
Liebeslieder*, Op. 65, appeared.

But to return to the first book of *Liebeslieder:* these settings of Eastern
European folk poems in translations by Georg Friedrich Daumer
(1800–1875) are hardly the "trifles" described by their self-effacing composer in a note of August 1869 to his publisher. True, the set begins simply, with "oom-pah-pah" vamping. But this first piece—*Rede, Mädchen*
(Speak, Lass)—rapidly becomes more sophisticated, as Brahms eschews
literal repetition—a hallmark of popular music—in favor of continual
variation. Most striking, perhaps, is the return of the original tune in
free inversion twice later in the piece, with corresponding changes in the
counterpoint of the accompaniment. The first waltz of Op. 52 thus contains within itself the contrast between popular and art music that
Brahms had posed in the last two dances of Op. 39. Throughout the rest
of the work, these opposing forces are played out with a sure hand.

In view of the large number of dances contained within the set, it is not
surprising that Brahms struggled over matters of order and arrangement.
Surviving manuscripts and other documents show that, in some cases,
the question of the dances' sequence, and even of their keys, remained unsettled until it was time to go to press, and that at one time or another
Brahms considered releasing the collection in either two or three separate
books before finally settling on an undivided plan. Still, most adjoining
dances are in closely related keys, and some waltzes share significant harmonic and motivic material. Brahms's arrangements thus yield continuity between adjacent dances, coherence within larger units, and closure
for each complete cycle.

For all its Schubertian background, the cycle reflects a more contemporary source of inspiration as well. From time to time, Brahms drew inspiration from the Waltz King himself, Johann Strauss, Jr. Thus the ninth

number, *Am Donaustrande, da steht ein Haus* (On the Bank of the Danube Is a House), seems indebted to the beloved *Blue Danube* Waltz, not only for its essential imagery but perhaps for certain musical details as well. Years later, Brahms confessed his love for Strauss's masterpiece by inscribing a young woman's autograph-fan with the opening measures of the dance, followed by the remark, "Leider nicht von Brahms" (Unfortunately not by Brahms). On another occasion, he autographed a photograph of Strauss and himself with the same theme set in counterpoint with the beginning of his own Fourth Symphony. And in its own humorous way, of course, the latter case especially reminds us of that same fusion of elements drawn from the realms of popular and art music that form the cycle's very point of departure. (The flavor of Strauss is detectable in more unadulterated form in the little orchestral suite Brahms made in 1870 of several of the *Liebeslieder*—eight from Op. 52, and one published later in the *Neue Liebeslieder,* Op. 65.)

The *Liebeslieder Walzer,* in short, are quintessential Brahms. Though their charm may derive in part from the contrast in which they stand to his work as a whole, their eternal freshness stems from techniques refined in larger forms. As Ernest Newman, the British critic and Wagner's biographer, put it, "Had Brahms never been stretched to the tension of such works as the C Minor Symphony and the Requiem, he could never have relaxed to the charm of the waltzes." This image retells a familiar story—of an uncompromising composer who brought the highest artistic sensibilities to every expression of his music.

David Brodbeck

3 QUARTETS, OPUS 64
Composed 1862–1874; published 1874

1. An die Heimat [Sternau]
2. Der Abend [Schiller]
3. Fragen [Daumer]

Between the *Liebeslieder Walzer* and the *Neue Liebeslieder Walzer* fall the three quartets of Op. 64. Their dates of composition, from 1862 to 1874, explain the greater similarity of at least the first quartet, *An die Heimat* (To the Homeland), to Op. 31 rather than to Op. 52 or Op. 65. Composed in G major and marked bewegt (but not too fast), the quartet also bears some similarity in style to some of Brahms's a cappella choral writing. He uses the four voices both as ensemble and as elements in counterpoint. *An die Heimat* has traditionally been considered the most biographically important quartet of the three; critics have noted a perceptible nostalgia in Brahms's setting of a text by Otto Inkermann, better known by his penname, Sternau. The quartet was written during Brahms's first extended stay in Vienna and suggests his longing for a home that was no longer home, Hamburg.

The second quartet of the set, *Der Abend* (Evening), in G minor (moving to G major) and marked ruhig, differs markedly in its subject matter and tone from the first quartet. Set to a text by Schiller, it employs a classical subject and some ingenious musical features to dramatize the dialogue between Apollo and Thetis. Brahms indulges in some effective if transparent musical metaphor by using the piano accompaniment to simulate the movement of Apollo's horses. Opus 64/2 was written in the summer of 1874, years after No. 1, while Brahms was in Switzerland. The third quartet, titled *Fragen* (Questions), extends the wide contrasts of this opus. It is based on one of Daumer's many translations of Turkish texts. The tenor plays the role of the lover to whom the other three voices direct questions. Brahms's talent for evoking irony is unmistakable in this closing quartet (marked andante con moto and in A major). Despite their eclectic nature, however, all three works share a somewhat choral character, which perhaps explains Brahms's decision to publish them together. The composer's recognition of the similar choral nature of these quartets is indicated in a letter to the publisher Peters: Brahms notes that these numbers could well be performed on occasion by a small chorus.

Leon Botstein

Neue Liebeslieder, 15 Waltzes, Opus 65
Composed 1874; published 1875

1. Verzicht, O Herz, auf Rettung
2. Finstere Schatten der Nacht
3. An jeder Hand die Finger
4. Ihr schwarzen Augen, ihr durft nur winken
5. Wahre, wahre deinen Sohn
6. Rosen steckt mir an die Mutter
7. Vom Gebirge Well' auf Well'
8. Weiche Gräser im Revier

9. Nagen am Herzen
10. Ich kose süss mit der und der
11. Alles, alles in den Wind
12. Schwarzer Wald, dein Schatten
13. Nein, Geliebter, setze dich mir
14. Flammenauge, dunkles Haar
15. Zum Schluss: Nun, ihr Musen, genug!

In September 1875, six years after the publication of the widely popular *Liebeslieder Waltzer,* Op. 52, the *Neue Liebeslieder* appeared in print as Op. 65. Like their predecessors, they are a succession of waltzes scored for four solo voices (SATB) with piano duet, and their love-poem texts, translated from various languages by Georg Friedrich Daumer (1800–1875) and printed in his *Polydora,* are set with seemingly limitless ingenuity within the restrictions of constant 3/4 meter.

But much about these New Love Songs was indeed new:

At Brahms's insistence, the *Liebeslieder*'s perplexing title phrase "voices *ad libitum"* was banned from the *Neue Liebeslieder* so that they would always be performed with the voices (although Simrock later issued a voiceless version for four-hand piano, Op. 65a).

Appended to the waltzes proper is an epilogue, "Zum Schluß," in the form of an interrupted passacaglia in 9/4, *Ruhig.* Its text, the concluding verse of Goethe's elegy *Alexis und Dora,* suggests that only "ye Muses" can relieve the pain inflicted by Love. The six pitches of its ground bass correspond to those of the melody that opens the analogous concluding prayer for the healing of heartache in the *Alto Rhapsody,* Op. 53, also on a Goethe text. The relative seriousness of the words and the formality of their setting combine to lend considerable gravity to the *Neue Liebeslieder.*

Unlike the ordering of the earlier set, which was plagued by lingering indecision, the symmetrical format of the new cycle seems never to have been in question. Its fourteen waltzes fall into two similar groups of seven. Each group begins and ends with a movement for full vocal quartet; enclosed are another quartet and four movements for a solo voice, or, in one case, duet. The last waltz in each group is cast in a form larger than the prevailing simple binary, enhancing its function as a structural marker. The near-relative keys of the first group progress smoothly from A major/minor through D minor and F major to C; those of the second, through E♭ major to G minor/major, and thence through E major back to A. The F major of the epilogue relates to A as lowered submediant, a customary Brahmsian choice to characterize the extramundane; its key thus helps to clarify the peculiar character of this concluding movement—unlike what precedes it but integral to the work as a whole.

The *New Love Songs* have many instances of cyclic recurrence and internal kinship, unifying devices not readily apparent in the Op. 52 cycle. The first sung phrase of No. 1 introduces two important materials—a melodic idea in stepwise quarter notes and a rhythm consisting of a dotted quarter with three eighths; the melodic motive appears prominently in Nos. 1, 3, and 7 (in simultaneous contrary motion), 8 (in successive contrary motion), and 9 (metrically displaced), while the rhythmic motive is featured in Nos. 1, 4, 5, and 10. Because of its strong association with "dark eyes" in No. 4, the appearance of the same rhythm in No. 9, where a girl doubts her ability to resist the lure of love, implies that a pair of eyes is the cause of her wavering. Another such resonance results from the similar passages at "destroyed" in No. 1 and "handsome" in No. 3, hinting that love's potential hazards include physical beauty. Numbers 1 and 2 are not only paired by their poetic imagery (as are Nos. 4 and 5), but much of the musical content of No. 2 is derived from the piano introduction to No. 1. The first halves of Nos. 10 and 11 are based on exactly the same succession of harmonies, though their melodies differ.

The influence of gypsy music, discernible in both works, is markedly stronger in the later cycle, where comparatively harsher emotions predominate; exemplified by the first-movement image of ships shattered on the treacherous sea of love, they include dread, jealousy, vengeance, despair, and lust.

Far more than a mere addendum to the Op. 52 *Liebeslieder,* the *Neue Liebeslieder* constitute an independent, though complementary, work that is completely satisfying in itself, dramatically, emotionally, and structurally.

Lucien Stark

4 QUARTETS, OPUS 92

Composed 1877–84; Published 1884

1. O schöne Nacht [Daumer]   3. Abendlied [Hebbel]
2. Spätherbst [Allmers]   4. Warum? [Goethe]

In 1884, Brahms returned to the vocal quartet form with the four works of Op. 92. The set opens with *O schöne Nacht* (O Lovely Night), marked andante con moto and in E major. This song, a setting a text by Daumer, was originally entitled *Notturno* and was a gift for Elisabet von Herzogenberg. Here Brahms makes use of a wide spectrum of possibility for the four voices, combining solo moments, dialogue, and group singing with consummate agility. As in Op. 64/2, the piano takes on a highly descriptive role and evokes the events of night—starlight, the moon, the nightingale's song. The listener can gather a clear sense of Brahms's keen eye and affection for the landscapes of the Romantic painter Arnold Böcklin. Op. 92/2, *Spätherbst* (Late Autumn; text by Hermann Allmers) is marked andante and is in E minor. Like the stars of Op. 92/1, the autumnal colors of Op. 92/2 receive a vivid realization in music, particularly through the piano accompaniments. The relationship between both of these songs explains why Brahms begins the set with the earlier quartet, composed in 1877. The pairing of E major and E minor emphasizes the contrast in mood and subject matter of the two quartets, taking us from a dreamy, romantic night-thought to a gray image of gloomy closure.

In Op. 92/3, the tonal center changes to F major and we return to another night-thought. *Abendlied* (Evening Song) is marked andante and is set to a poem by Friedrich Hebbel (1813–1863) about the soothing power of sleep. Given the fact that Op. 92/4 is in B♭ major, and therefore tonally related to No. 3, the four quartets of Op. 92 are paired in two halves. The somewhat spiritual and haunting quality of Op. 92/3 is resolved, as it were, by the highly delineated, almost Baroque opening bars of Op. 92/4, in which the piano ascends to the opening exclamation *Warum?* (Why?). The text of No. 4 is based on a poem by Goethe in which the poet explores the power of song to draw the divine closer to the human. Opus 92/4 brings the whole set to a more sprightly and elegant dancelike close, erasing the aggressive sensibility of the opening of this final quartet. The first performance of the set (with the exception of No. 3) took place in 1889 in a concert in Frankfurt. Opus 92/1—clearly a favorite of the composer's—was first performed in its present form in Krefeld in 1885. An earlier version was performed in a private musical evening at the home of Brahms's friend the surgeon Theodor Billroth in 1878.

Leon Botstein

ZIGEUNERLIEDER, OP. 103

Composed 1887; published 1888

1. He, Zigeuner, greife [trans. Conrat]
2. Hochgetürmte Rimaflut
3. Wißt ihr, wann mein Kindchen
4. Lieber Gott, du weißt
5. Brauner Bursche führt zum Tanze
6. Röslein dreie in der Reihe
7. Kommt dir manchmal
8. Horch, der Wind klagt
9. Weit und breit schaut niemand
10. Mond verhüllt sein Angesicht
11. Rote Abendwolken ziehn

The setting of text to music in the form of solo songs, duets, and quartets forms a substantial part of Johannes Brahms's oeuvre, as it does in the cases of Franz Schubert and Hugo Wolf. Although Brahms is better represented in performance today by his symphonies and instrumental chamber works, that he composed and published Lieder throughout his life (in contrast to the occasional attention Felix Mendelssohn and Richard Strauss, for example, gave the medium) speaks to the importance Brahms attached to the vocal genre.

Brahms originally wrote the *Zigeunerlieder* (Gypsy Songs), Op. 103, for vocal quartet and piano, later resetting eight of the eleven songs (published in 1889) for solo voice and piano. He chose the texts, from *25 Ungarische Volkslieder,* an undated Budapest publication containing Hungarian folk songs translated into German by Hugo Conrat, with melodies and accompaniments by Zoltán Nagy, which Brahms discarded. Brahms composed and harmonized the *Zigeunerlieder* anew, in contrast to his claim to have simply arranged pre-existing Hungarian melodies in composing his Hungarian Dances for orchestra.

The poems are short, all but one made up of eight lines or fewer, and are for the most part insubstantial. In keeping with his philosophy that poetic masterpieces are complete in and of themselves but that weaker texts could be reinforced by their musical setting, Brahms expanded and strengthened the form of each of the poems, in some instances choosing one or two lines of text to set as a refrain, in others repeating the entire text two or even three times. His choice of voice, key, harmonic and rhythmic patterns, and use of phrase structure provides an emotional context and artistic point of view for each poem. In keeping with the folk character of the poems, the musical language is simple and direct, with clear, memorable vocal lines and uncomplicated harmonies. The piano accompaniments, also straightforward and unsophisticated, are, however, technically difficult and require proficiency both to merely "cover" the notes and to perform them with the lightness and energy demanded.

Although the *Zigeunerlieder* do not follow a narrative and were not necessarily composed to be performed only as a complete set, the songs do share unifying compositional features. All eleven songs are in duple meter and all but Nos. 7, 8, and 10 are in allegro tempos. Many of the songs begin and/or end with short, sharply punctuated 2-measure cadences, and the vocal lines have a folk-song character, seemingly evolving spontaneously from two or three simple melodic motifs presented at the outset of each song. In Nos. 1, 3, 6, 7, 8, and 11, each line of text is introduced by the solo tenor and "echoed" by the vocal quartet, which declaims the text in a homophonic and syllabic texture. Most of the songs are in strophic or strophic variation form (verses and refrains repeated almost identically). Typical of Brahms's harmonic practice, he sets the key relationships between a majority of the songs at the interval of a third.

The opening song in the opus, *He, Zigeuner* (Hey, Gypsy), exhorts the gypsy to "strike the string" and "play the song of the faithless maiden." Worthy of attention is Brahms's highlighting of the word "bange" (anxious) by ornamenting and lengthening the melodic expression of the word, thus interrupting the previously easy flow of symmetrical phrases and perhaps creating momentary anxiety on the part of the listener. In No. 2, Brahms expresses the surging and roaring of the river waves in the turbulence of the piano part, which is based on syncopated chords alternating between hands and octave leaps in the bass. The writing is *forte* throughout, and the quartet declaims the text emphatically and with authority. Brahms divides the eight-line text in half, asking the quartet and piano to perform an identical repeat of each half. The D-minor song closes, unexpectedly, in the parallel key of D major.

The text of No. 3 speaks from the points of view of a male and a female lover; the first strophe is sung by the solo tenor and the second by the soprano. Both solos open with a four-measure phrase that is followed by an irregular five-measure phrase, drawing our attention and adding poignancy to the answer given to the lover's opening question. Numbers 5 and 6 are notable for their harmonic setting. Between the first phrase and second phrase of No. 5, *Brauner Bursche führt zum Tanze*, Brahms abruptly modulates from D major to F♯ major, the first time in the set that Brahms has moved beyond a simple alternation between tonic and dominant. The harmony of No. 6, *Röslein dreie in der Reihe* (Three Roses in a Row), begins ambiguously, with a G-major chord followed directly by an E-minor chord; it is not until the second half of the song that we feel safely in G major.

The slower andantino tempo of Nos. 7 and 8 is a welcome break from the unremitting vivacity and allegros of Nos. 1–6. Number 7 is through-composed, avoiding repetitions and refrains, the text set to perhaps the most touching and evocative melody found in Op. 103. Especially beautiful is Brahms's setting of the words "Täusch mich nicht, verlass mich nicht . . . lieb du mich, wie ich dich . . ." (Deceive me not, leave me not . . . love me as I love you . . .), in which he uses the motive of a falling fourth or tritone followed by an expressive appoggiatura. The quartet's "answers" to the tenor solo are underscored by ever more expressive piano accompaniments, which include the first example of contrapuntal writing in the songs.

Number 10 is compositionally the most interesting and sophisticated. The piano accompaniment is written in imitation of the cimbalom, a dulcimer-like instrument with strings struck by hammers that is associated with gypsy string ensembles, and becomes a full partner in the melodic expression, initiating each four-measure phrase, which is joined by a duet between soprano and alto or tenor and bass to bring the phrase to a close. The melodic writing is stepwise, in contrast to the predominantly angular melodic motives of the other songs, and the successive duets progressively overlap, blurring the sense of clearly delineated phrases until, at the end, the four voices join together to sing the final two words homophonically.

Brahms returns to the vigor and simplicity of the first two numbers in his setting of the final text, *Rote Abendwolken ziehn* (Rosy Clouds of Evening Drift By). The solo tenor once again introduces a melody built on the same dotted rhythm as the opening song of the set, accompanied by emphatic, syncopated *forte* chords. The song is introduced, interestingly enough, with the familiar two-measure cadence Brahms previously used to end other songs in Op. 103, and closes with piano and vocal quartet together affirming "Und ich träum' bei Tag und Nacht Nur allein von dem süssen Liebchen mein" (And I dreamt, by day and night, only of that sweet love of mine).

Although not the most personal or sophisticated of the songs Brahms wrote in his lifetime, the *Zigeunerlieder* occupy a worthy place in the repertory as a set of eminently accessible, uncomplicated, and exuberant songs about love and loss. Clara Schumann's appraisal could well be our own:

"I am quite delighted with them. How original they are and how full of freshness, charm, and passion."

Nyela Basney

6 QUARTETS, OP. 112
Composed 1888–1891; Published 1891

1. Sehnsucht [Kugler]
2. Nächtens [Kugler]
3. Vier Zigeunerlieder [trans. Conrat]
     i. (Himmel strahlt so helle)
    ii. (Rote Rosenknospen)
   iii. (Brennessel steht an Wegesrand)
    iv. (Liebe Schwalbe)

Many observers have questioned why Brahms chose the particular grouping of the six quartets of Op. 112. As Malcolm MacDonald puts it, the grouping seems "oddly heterogeneous." The first two quartets are set to texts by Franz Kugler, while Nos. 3–6, titled by Brahms *Gypsy Songs*, draw from the same texts as Op. 103 and are based on Hungarian folk songs. Number 1, *Sehnsucht* (Desire), marked andante in F minor, and No. 2, *Nächtens* (In the Night), in D minor and marked unruhig bewegt (restlessly moving), contrast sharply to the four more lighthearted gypsy quartets. Perhaps the explanation for this strange combination rests in the fundamental nature of Brahms's personality. For Brahms, the simple, the unaffecting, and the somewhat naïve often coexist with the intensely introspective, melancholic sensibility of withdrawal and resignation, as if the only answer to the complexities and sufferings of life is the embrace of the simply human. Opus 112 offers the musician and the listener both alternatives as extremes in the spectrum of Brahms's own moods.

Opus 112/1 chronicles the consequences of thwarted desire. Brahms uses the transformative possibilities of counterpoint to depict the voice of the poet in reminiscence. This quartet is a compact and powerful expression of Brahms's own encounter with loneliness. Opus 112/2 ends in D major, but abruptly so, for most of the work is characterized by the unusual rhythmic structure of 5/4, in which groups of 2's and 3's alternate, adding to the sense of discomfort and instability suggested by the tempo marking. Like much of Brahms's later music which deals with the question of death, this quartet suggests his fear that the much awaited sense of peacefulness and resignation associated with oncoming death may be hard to come by. The metaphor of nighttime and slumber as evocative of a peaceful death is not entirely convincing, as the song's self-conscious restlessness makes apparent. Opus 112/1–2 are quintessential works of the late Brahms, but an understanding of the whole of Op. 112 rests in a perception of it as a cycle in which the fragmentary, experimental, and intense qualities of the first two quartets are dispelled by the remaining four. To comprehend Brahms's personality and approach to life, it is important not to separate out the first two quartets, but rather to accept his explicit design in which the folklike quartets, all of which are centered on major keys, primarily D major and F major, should close out the cycle. The simplicity and directness of the last four, and particularly the swift and delicate character of Op. 112/6, are an admonition that the embrace of life without excessive introspection and with modest delight may be the only antidote to the sense of despair, loneliness, and anger derived from reflection and ambition.

Leon Botstein

18

CANONS

13 CANONS, FOR 3–6 FEMALE VOICES, OPUS 113
Composed 1860–67; published 1891

1. Göttlicher Morpheus [Goethe]
2. Grausam erweiset sich Amor an mir [Goethe]
3. Sitzt a schöns Vögerl auf'm Dannabaum [trad.]
4. Schlaf, Kindlein, schlaf [trad.]
5. Wille wille will [trad.]
6. So lange Schönheit wird bestehn [Fallersleben]
7. Wenn die Klänge nahn und fliehen [Eichendorff]
8. Ein Gems auf dem Stein [Eichendorff]
9. Ans Auge des Liebsten [Rückert]
10. Leise Töne der Brust [Rückert]
11. Ich weiss nicht was im Hain die Taube girret [Rückert]
12. Wenn Kummer hätte zu töten Macht [Rückert]
13. Einförmig ist der Liebe Gram [Rückert]

In 1891, Brahms sorted out a great deal of music composed in earlier years that he had left unpublished. Some of the music he destroyed. Opus 113, however, he chose to publish. In this collection of thirteen canons, Nos. 1, 8, 10, and 12, settings of texts by Goethe, Eichendorff, and Rückert, date from the late 1850s and early 1860s. Numbers 2, 11, and 5, also settings of Goethe and Rückert, as well as a folk song, probably also date from around the same period. Numbers 6 and 7 are likely early works but the dates are undetermined. Number 7, a setting of an Eichendorff text, may have been written as late as the mid-1860s. Numbers 9 and 13 were most certainly written later, perhaps as late as the 1880s. The technical complexity of the canon form is somewhat underscored by the use of women's voices alone. Most of the canons are four-part canons; however, Nos. 2, 4, 7, and 12 are in three parts and, appropriately, the last canon is in six parts. The first two settings of Goethe are in E and A minor, and the last two, both to texts by Rückert, are in F♯ minor and A minor.

These canons mirror Brahms's obsession with the formal practices of counterpoint and historical models. During the 1850s, Brahms and Joachim engaged in counterpoint exercises which produced a number of instructive compositions. As young composers, both musicians were eager to command the full repertory of formal compositional techniques associated with the masters of the Renaissance and Baroque. Brahms's return to the medium of the canon late in life has its parallels in the biographies of other composers, such as Schubert, Mozart, and even Bach. In Brahms's case, however, there is another dimension to these works. As a young man, he had worked as a choral conductor in Hamburg and Detmold. Indeed, many of these canons were written for use by the Hamburg Women's Chorus. His resurrecting of the Thirteen Canons therefore also represents a nostalgic act of affection for the composer's early days as a choral conductor.

The canon form, as Brahms and Joachim knew, constituted a fundamental aspect of the study of counterpoint. At the same time, the canon form had a simplicity about it which lent itself to being used as a kind of calling card. Canons in the oeuvre of Mozart, for example, function as a medium for humor and the terse joke. As Christian Martin Schmidt aptly observed, canons were often used as a form of musical aphorism, the sort of short statement one might offer as a greeting, an autograph, or a postcard. Brahms's decision to put together a set of canons late in his career indicates, however, that he believed in the strictly musical virtues of this pithy form. Brahms was uncharacteristically proud of his early achievements, and as if to show both the maintenance and deepening of his understanding of the elements of composition, he rounded out the set with a work of much later vintage.

Finally, there is an element of cultural criticism inherent in Op. 113. The social and political changes witnessed by Brahms from the late 1850s to the early 1890s were deeply disturbing to the composer, who was not a facile adherent to the idea of progress to begin with. He carried with him a more than passing skepticism about the evolution of art and society in his own day. In this sense, Brahms's canons offered to a younger generation a reminder of an aesthetic credo and a discipline that Brahms feared was in sharp decline and in danger of extinction. These canons therefore may have represented an antidote to the kind of superficial, sentimental, expressive compositional fashion characteristic of the late nineteenth century, an ominous comment on the lush, free-form expressiveness indulged in by the young composers under the spell of Wagnerian sonorities. In their mastery of counterpoint technique, these canons are Brahms's way of instructing his young admirers in the virtues of the close study of historical models. Opus 113 perhaps offers an admonition to aspiring composers in a record of how a great composer developed and maintained an allegiance to the fundamental elements of musical composition.

Leon Botstein

19

A CAPPELLA CHORAL MUSIC

MARIENLIEDER, FOR MIXED CHORUS, OPUS 22
Composed 1859; published 1862

1. Der englische Gruß [trad.]
2. Marias Kirchgang
3. Marias Wallfahrt
4. Der Jäger

5. Ruf zur Maria
6. Magdalena
7. Marias Lob

Brahms's *Marienlieder* are linked both with his experience with the Hamburg Women's Chorus and his study of early music, specifically German folk music and polyphonic song. Among the books in his extensive library are the two in which he found his texts: *Deutsche Volkslieder mit ihren Original-Weisen,* by Andreas Kretzschmer and Anton Wilhelm von Zuccalmaglio, which was Brahms's favorite source of folk texts and tunes throughout his life; and Ludwig Uhland's *Alte hoch-, und niederdeutsche Volkslieder,* which includes texts only. Markings in these volumes and others in his library show that Brahms was attracted by examples of the long German tradition of Marian legends. His library also contains his own copies of an assortment of sixteenth-century *Tenorlieder* and polyphonic songs by the later German Renaissance composers Michael Praetorius (?1571–1621) and Johannes Eccard (1553–1611). Among them is one he arranged for the Women's Chorus and liked well enough to perform again in Vienna, in its original version for mixed voices, Eccard's *Uber's Gebirg Maria geht,* the text of which is a folklike exegesis of the Magnificat; some writers feel that this work was the inspiration for Brahms's own Marian-legend pieces.

In early summer 1859, the Women's Chorus held its first formally organized rehearsals, and Nos. 1 and 2 of the *Marienlieder* were among the pieces they sang; Nos. 4, 5, 6, and 7 made their appearance in August and September of the same year. The settings were all for two soprano and two alto parts, a cappella, but when Brahms sent the pieces to his friend Julius Otto Grimm to try with his choir, Grimm complained that the second alto parts were too low. Brahms accordingly suggested that the songs might by sung by two sopranos, alto, and tenor; and in this form he offered them to the publisher P. J. Simrock in September 1860, writing, "The poems are beautiful old folk songs and the music somewhat in the style of old German church and folk songs." (By this time, the seventh song, No. 3, had been added to the set.) Simrock was evidently not interested, and Brahms then offered them, in an arrangement for soprano, alto, tenor, and bass, to Rieter-Biedermann, who published the collection in October 1862.

The style of the seven songs is not so archaic as Brahms's comment to Simrock might suggest; the texts are early, but the music clearly belongs to the nineteenth century, with melodies that are original if fairly simple, harmonies that are generally diatonic, and largely strophic settings.

Der englische Gruß is a verse rendition of the Annunciation, with Gabriel's news and Mary's responses presented in five identical strophes. A sixth stanza receives a new setting as the angels sing a chorus in Mary's praise.

For *Marias Kirchgang*, Brahms may well have used the *Tenorlied* as model and for the final version retained something close to his original setting for women's voices: in six of the eight brief stanzas the melody is in the alto, which is accompanied by two sopranos and tenor. In the story told by the text, Mary wants to reach a church on the other side of a lake; she asks a young boatman to row her across, and he replies that he will, but only if she consents to be his wife. She says she would rather swim, proceeds to do so, and when she reaches the middle of the lake, the church bells ring out—whereupon the young man's heart breaks. In the identically set stanzas, the alto melody is in the Dorian mode, although there are chromatic touches in the accompanying voices; but in the two stanzas that describe the ringing of the bells, the basses join an exuberant major-key display of text-painting.

In *Marias Wallfahrt*, Mary makes a pilgrimage to see the Lord; she finds him bearing a cross and wearing a crown of thorns. Here again there is a contrasting last stanza that contains the moral of the song.

Der Jäger presented Brahms and his publisher with a dilemma that caused several months' delay in publication. The text is another traditional version of the Annunciation dialogue, one in which Gabriel is depicted as a hunter; and Rieter-Biedermann found a portion of it to be obscene (it seems to have disturbed some of the more staid members of the Women's Chorus as well), specifically objecting to the line "Your body will bear a child without any husband." Brahms defended the text on musical grounds; both sides called in outside authorities to try to find a substitute, and they finally managed to agree on a compromise version. The musical result is a charming hunting song, with pairs of identical strophes at beginning and end, and a profusion of atmospheric horn calls in the middle.

The refrain for each of the three identical stanzas of *Ruf zu Maria* is "Pray for us, Mary," and the setting is the only one of the *Marienlieder* in which Brahms unleashed his ability to write chromatic harmony and subtle counterpoint, though they accompany an essentially simple melody.

Magdalena, as the title suggests, is about Mary Magdalene and her visit to the empty tomb on Easter morning; she finds an angel in the tomb and sees Jesus, whom she mistakes for a gardener. The three stanzas are set identically to a somber, almost monotonous melody, doubled in soprano and tenor for the first half and enlivened with imitative counterpoint and touches of chromaticism in the second.

The concluding song, *Marias Lob,* is a generic song of praise in seven identical stanzas; its notable feature is the change from quadruple to triple meter partway through. It provides a triumphant if rather utilitarian conclusion to this collection.

Virginia Hancock

2 MOTETS, FOR FIVE-PART MIXED CHORUS, OPUS 29
Composed 1856–60; published 1864

1. Es ist das Heil uns kommen her [Speratus]
2. Schaffe in mir, Gott, ein rein' Herz [Psalm 51]

By the time Brahms published the motets of Op. 29 in 1864, he had spent a decade studying the forms and styles of sacred music from the past. If the two works in question were not the first products of that labor, they were nevertheless the first to be named Motets. And in many ways, Brahms established with this pair the parameters for his later motets Opp. 74 and 110. All three groups of motets bring together pieces of apparently diverse origin and juxtapose settings of chorale texts with settings of Lutheran biblical texts. Although both works in Op. 29 can be traced to Brahms's counterpoint studies of the 1850s and early 1860s, they stem from different years and arose in reaction to separate compositional issues. Number 2, *Schaffe in mir, Gott, ein rein' Herz* (Create in Me a Pure Heart, O God), was begun as early as 1856, when Brahms sent a five-voice augmentation canon on some portion of Psalm 51:12–14 to his "counterpoint correspondent" Joseph Joachim. Number 1, *Es ist das Heil uns kommen her,* on a chorale by Paul Speratus, probably stems from a later stage in that correspondence, during the spring of 1860, when Brahms and Joachim exchanged various chorale settings.

While the Op. 29 motets share a constructionist approach with many of the items from the counterpoint correspondence that eventually reached a finished form and found their way into publication, Brahms seems to have singled out these two works as specifically German and the motet as a specifically historicist genre. To be sure, any work derived from a counterpoint exercise or based on an archaic form is likely to exhibit historical qualities, but the Op. 29 motets display their historicism more self-consciously, even polemically. Perhaps the distinguishing feature between these motets and Brahms's other sacred music around 1860 is the direct reflection in Op. 29 of his intense interest between 1858 and 1860 in the music of J. S. Bach. Bach served as a symbol of German spiritual and cultural history as well as a potent source of musical inspiration for Brahms. Unlike Mendelssohn, who strove to integrate the spiritual element of Bach's music into his own modern language, Brahms works within and against the background of Bach's Lutheran musical style in the Op. 29 motets, thereby elevating the historicist tone of these works and specifying the German nature of their spirituality. Brahms would rarely recreate that historical reference, but when he did it occurred within the genre of motet, in the two pieces of Op. 74.

Brahms, a North German Protestant, felt a more direct connection to the German motet styles represented by Bach than to the Latin texted *Drei geistliche Chöre,* Op. 37, or the Catholically tinged *Marienlieder,* Op. 22. And while the latter choruses provided Brahms and his Hamburg Women's Chorus with sophisticated harmonic settings in which to indulge their love of German folk song, the motets of Op. 29 serve a more abstract purpose. Notably, no immediate performance was envisaged for these two works when they were completed in the summer of 1860 at Bonn. (By contrast, nearly all of Brahms's other a cappella vocal works from this period can be tied to specific performances with the Detmold, Hamburg, and Vienna choirs that he directed between 1858 and 1864.) These motets are, therefore, conceptual works of art, and they are better able to convey a cultural and artistic message than are the more occasional choral works.

Although none of Brahms's chorale settings from the renewed composition correspondence in the spring of 1860 are preserved, it is nevertheless safe to assume that *Es is das Heil uns kommen her* grew directly out of this demonstrated interest in chorales a few months earlier, either as one of the exercises or as a further development of techniques learned in them. Except perhaps for some overzealous eighth-note motion in the lower voices and some modern-sounding seventh-chord progressions in the final phrase, the four-voice harmonization of the chorale tune that begins the motet is an admirable style-copy of Bach by the twenty-seven-year-old Brahms. Following that Bachian introduction, the rest of the motet consists of generically Baroque five-voice imitation in which the chorale is treated as a long-note *cantus firmus* in Bass 1, with each of its five phrases preceded by motivically derived anticipations in the other four voices. In this way, the motet follows the format of some seventeenth-century chorale motets (although none of Bach's).

The musical allusion to Bach in the opening chorale setting provides the motivic impetus for the counterpoint that ensues. Bach thus stands as a source of music; his stability and timelessness are musically concretized by the stately and (relatively) arhythmic chordal motion of the chorale setting. Throughout the nineteenth century, Bach came more and more to symbolize that which was pure, safe, and unspoiled in German culture against the onslaught of modernism. It would be premature to associate Brahms's musical depiction of Bach here with a later conservative cultural reaction, but it is nevertheless striking that such a strong reference to Bach should be used to set the words "das Heil," which can mean "health" as well as "salvation."

It is useful to note in this light that the same 1860 letters in which Brahms and Joachim discuss their chorale exercises also contain their refinements of the ill-fated *Erklärung* against Franz Liszt, Franz Brendel, and the New German School. Reacting to Brendel's contention in the *Neue Zeitschrift für Musik* that the New Germans continued in the tradition of "Protestant church music up to and including Bach and Handel," which had "long been known as the Old German School," Brahms's declaration ends by condemning and deploring the music of the New German School as "contrary to the innermost essence of music." With its opening evocation of Bach through his most Germanic style—the chorale—Brahms's motet may be heard as a reaction against Brendel's claim to the legacy of older Protestant music, and as Brahms's identification with that which was healthy, pure, and at one with the "essence of music."

The first part of No. 2, *Schaffe in mir, Gott, ein rein' Herz*, was apparently composed by March of 1856, when it was sent as part of the first installment in the composition exchange with Joachim, who acknowledged receipt of a five-voice augmentation canon (of which the first 25 measures in this motet are an example). Working from eighteenth-century counterpoint treatises by Johann Philipp Kirnberger, Johann Mattheson, and Friedrich Wilhelm Marpurg, Brahms set out quickly to master "all possible sorts of canons," including circle canons, double fugues, and other contrapuntal rarities. Contrary to the homogenous *Es ist das Heil uns kommen her*, which was composed in 1860 after Brahms had amassed three years of experience directing choirs, the highly sectionalized *Schaffe in mir, Gott, ein rein' Herz* betrays various layers of composition and charts Brahms's gradually won facility in the choral medium. Moreover, the growing importance of Bach for Brahms's motet style between 1856 and 1860 can be observed within this one piece.

In comparison to the latter three sections of the motet, the opening canon displays a slower, less flexible rhythmic character, marking it as an earlier study work. Brahms is able to fashion undeniably beautiful music from his rigid contrapuntal artifice, but the espressivo, alla breve attempt at an opening bears traces of a modern copy of an eighteenth-century essay in the *stile antico*. Brahms's nineteenth-century harmonic language appears most noticeably at those moments when a canonic voice reaches the end of a phrase—predictably perhaps, for this is where free composition takes over from the rigid canonic underpinnings of the music—as in the floating harmonies above a tonic pedal on G when Bass 2 reaches the word "Herz," or again when the same voice sings "Geist" at the end of this section. The lengthy four-voice fugue in G minor that follows is a more convincing style copy, and the style represented is more clearly Bach's. During 1858, Brahms was immersed in a study of Bach's music. In particular, he prepared the cantata *Ich hatte viel Bekümmernis*, BWV 21, for a performance with his Detmold choir. The results of his efforts can be heard in the angular and chromatic fugal subject that recalls the G-minor choral fugue from the sixth movement of the Bach cantata. Brahms replaces the rising chromatic countersubject of Bach's fugue with a characteristic descending one, like that from the Agnus Dei fugue of the *Missa canonica* on which Brahms worked in June of 1856 (and which would make its way into the opening section of the motet *Warum ist das Licht gegeben dem Mühseligen?*, Op. 74/1, in 1877).

One could point to numerous other echoes of Bach's choral writing in the last two sections of *Schaffe in mir, Gott, ein rein' Herz*. Yet the stronger impression is created by the emergence of Brahms's own modern style against the Bachian background. Brahms's division of his five-voice choir into men's and women's three-voice choruses, for example, evokes a distinctly nineteenth-century predilection for gendered choral timbres—this in spite of the artfully hidden canon at the seventh between the outer voices of each semi-chorus. And although the closing allegro section is based on a pair of believably Baroque melodic figures, the harmonic drive toward the end of the motet (replete with a stretto accelerando) owes more to Beethoven than to Bach. If less polemical than No. 1, Op. 29/2 nevertheless marks Brahms's most successful integration to date of Baroque texture with modern harmonic and motivic writing. And the fact that the modern moments do not stand out uncomfortably from their Bachian stylistic background presages the important role that such techniques would play in Brahms's mature style.

Daniel Beller-McKenna

3 SACRED CHORUSES, FOR WOMEN'S VOICES, OPUS 37
Composed 1859–63; published 1866

1. O bone Jesu
2. Adoramus te, Christe
3. Regina coeli laetare

Brahms scholarship in the later twentieth century repeatedly has stressed the central influence of early music on his style. What is valued in this view of Brahms is not his resuscitation of earlier styles and forms per se, but rather his integration of techniques from the sixteenth through the eighteenth centuries into a nineteenth-century musical language and his role in making the legacy of the past a vital issue in "modern" music. By engaging more directly with music of the distant past, Brahms broke from the Romantic notion of earlier music, in which the supposed purity, simplicity, and piety of Palestrina or the spiritual mysticism of Bach were valued over the worldly artifice of earlier composers (Josquin, Ockeghem, etc.) or the operatically conventionalized church music of the late eighteenth and early nineteenth centuries (Mozart, Haydn, and so on). Against such idealized notions of sacred music, Brahms's thorough study of arcane canonic techniques, as reflected in works like Op. 37, marks a decisive step toward a modernist musical aesthetic.

Whereas his affinity for German music of the past included a pictorial attraction to folk song (as witnessed in the *Marienlieder,* Op. 22), Brahms was led to the study of Latin-based church music by the Schumanns at a time in the mid-1850s when the development of his compositional powers was of the utmost concern to himself and the members of the Schumanns' inner circle. When first he suggested a counterpoint exchange with Clara Schumann in 1855, and later when he carried one out with Joseph Joachim in 1856, Brahms had in mind the mastery of form and technique, not a sentimental religious immersion into the sound of the Catholic past. Numbers 1 and 2 of Op. 37 *(O bone Jesu* and *Adoramus te, Christe)* were composed by September 1859, when Brahms performed them with his Hamburg Women's Chorus, and may well stem from the earlier counterpoint correspondence of 1856. Brahms composed the last number in the set *(Regina coeli)* during his first year in Vienna (1863) for a loosely organized women's chorus there. He was no longer writing counterpoint exercises by this date, having composed the first version of the F-minor Quintet (later Op. 34) with its intricate fugue in the Scherzo third movement, the *Handel* Variations (Op. 24) for piano with their massive concluding fugue, and possibly some portions of *Ein deutsches Requiem* (Op. 45).

Around the same time that Brahms may have begun composing Op. 37/1-2, he was copying out pseudo-Palestrina motets on the same texts, as well as Palestrina's *Missa Papae Marcelli.* But the sound of No. 1, *O bone Jesu,* is far removed from that of his antique models. Any fascination with the mood and color evoked by simple choral style, plagal cadences, and modally inflected melodies is forsaken in the first chorus of Op. 37 for a complex underlying contrapuntal structure that produces an ironically modern harmonic orientation. Brahms wavered over (and eventually decided against) including the Latin inscription, "Canone per arsin et thesin, et per motum contrarium," in the published score. Ultimately, the piece is not strictly canonic according to these rules anyway; the four-voice counterpoint cannot be derived from one voice using this (or any other) resolution, and one can only assume that Brahms's flirtation with the archaic-sounding inscription reflected his interest in the complexity of canonic techniques rather than the spirituality of the Palestrina style. By the same token, Brahms's insistence that the two lower voices be published with alto clefs indicates the academic air he wished to impart.

Without such clues, the complexity of the first chorus is hardly apparent upon first hearing. Unlike many of his early canonic works, the contrapuntal artifice of *O bone Jesu* recedes behind the mainly homorhythmic motion of the four women's voices and the diatonic chords they produce. Rather than hearing the staggered entrances and contrary motion among the parts in the opening measures, the listener is presented with a characteristically mid-nineteenth-century effect: floating harmonies around a diminished chord (E-G-B♭) that resolves to the home key of F major before modulating—through a thoroughly modern passage of mildly chromatic harmonies—to a dominant chord, C major, at the end of the initial phrase of the text *(O bone Jesu, miserere nobis)*. The remainder of the brief piece (eighteen measures) develops this opening material accordingly, never revealing its complex underpinnings or feigning a Gothic modal guise. Brahms even infuses the last line of the text with a bit of Romantic harmonic coloring, introducing a sudden change to the minor mode at the word "sanguine" to capture the sense of the entire phrase: "tu redemisti nos sanguine tuo praetiosissimo" ("you redeem us through your most precious blood").

By contrast, *Adoramus te, Christe* (No.2) displays its canonic structure overtly and presents a melodic and harmonic profile that is unambiguously modal. Brahms considered a Latin inscription for this chorus as well ("[Canone] Resoluzione in 4ta, in 5ta, in 8va"). And here, with some allowance for chromatic alteration in the middle portion of the piece, the four voices follow the instructions, as is made plain by the successively descending entrances in A minor from Soprano 1 through Alto 2 on A, E, D, and A, respectively. The use of staggered entrances leads to a longer, more expansive canon that is twice the length of the first chorus (thirty-six measures). Still more suggestive of the Palestrinian ideal are the carefully crafted, arch-shaped, and step-wise melodies that span no more than an octave in any part. After the canon breaks down with a chromatically prepared cadence at the words "pro nobis," the chorus concludes with a chordal prayer, "Domine, miserere nobis." Here Brahms exchanges one Romantic conception of Renaissance music (strict counterpoint) for another—the pure and simple effect of slow and measured homorhythmic declamation. Although the Romantics were aware and admiring of Palestrinian counterpoint, they were drawn just as strongly to chordal music of the sixteenth century for its simplicity and power of expression. And the chordal conclusion points up the austere contrapuntal artifice of the first twenty-six measures, which emphasize sixteenth-century techniques so strongly as to remove the mystical aura of Palestrina and thereby elevate the modern, historicist quality of this chorus.

Separated from the first two by only a few years, the last chorus nevertheless distinguishes itself as more artistically and self-confidently conceived, reflecting Brahms's progression as a composer of larger and more tightly written works by the early 1860s. *Regina coeli* shares only the use of a canon and its setting for women's voices with the first two choruses. Unlike the homogenous four-voice texture of Nos. 1 and 2, the third chorus in Op. 37 pits a soprano and an alto soloist in canon against the refrain-like "Alleluia" interjections by the S S A A choir. Ironically, while the effect is decidedly less Gothic, the counterpoint between the two soloists provides the strictest canon in the opus: the alto exactly follows the soprano at the third and in inversion. The choral Alleluias evoke the sound of a concertato accompanied canon, implying a later style than the preceding chorus and a less arcane technique than the first. Moreover, the use of a standard duple meter (c) in *Regina coeli* reflects the dancelike eighteenth-century rhythms that pervade this final chorus, after the more strict arsis-thesis motion in the alla breve meter (¢) of *O bone Jesu* and *Adoramus te, Christe*.

The sectionalized refrain process of this piece necessitates a far greater length (seventy-six measures) than in the first two choruses. Brahms thereby creates a sense of progression through the opus (each chorus is roughly twice as long as the previous one) that is balanced by the return in *Regina coeli* to F major, the key of *O bone Jesu*, No. 1. Brahms also produces a progressive effect within the closing number, as the characters of the canonic voices and the chorus become gradually less distinct. In the later choral entrances, the voices become more independent and rhythmically fluid until, by the fourth entrance, Soprano 2 and Alto 2 begin to display pseudo-imitation that prefigures a full-blown double inversion canon among the four choral voices. The solo voices add their own canon to that of the choir to round off the opus with a resounding "Alleluia."

Daniel Beller-McKenna

5 LIEDER, FOR FOUR-PART MEN'S CHORUS, OPUS 41
Composed 1861–62; published 1867

1. Ich schwing mein Horn ins Jammertal [Old German]
2. Freiwillige her! [Lemcke]
3. Geleit [Lemcke]
4. Marschieren (Jetzt hab'ich schon zwei Jahre lang) [Lemcke]
5. Gebt acht! Gebt acht! [Lemcke]

These songs are perhaps Brahms's most neglected works, receiving neither frequent programming by conductors nor serious critical consideration by Brahms scholars. To be sure, Op. 41 has much working against it. First, it is Brahms's only opus for a cappella men's chorus, a medium that is not as popular now as it was in the last century. And, as is true of anomalies in any composer's output, it is hard to determine how these songs fit within the broader development of Brahms's choral style. Moreover, the set contains an odd combination of one demonstrably older piece in an archaic style, *Ich schwing mein Horn ins Jammertal* (No. 1), with four more modern-sounding ones based on militaristic texts from Carl Lemcke's *Lieder und Gedichte* (1861). It is the nature of those texts that leads to the most problematic aspect of the songs' reception history. Men's choirs, for which many such German patriotic songs were composed during the nineteenth century, took on powerful *völkisch* and chauvinistic overtones from the late nineteenth century through World War II, and the sound of period pieces like Op. 41 evokes unpleasant nationalistic associations to modern listeners. Specifically, these are associations we prefer not to draw to Brahms. For whether or not he is seen as a paragon of "absolute" music (a view that is increasingly under attack by Brahms scholars), Brahms is rarely associated with militant German nationalism, an identification that Op. 41 seems to beg. Our well-ingrained view of nineteenth-century German music polarized by Wagner (the nationalistic chauvinist) and Brahms (the composer of universal expression) has not permitted these songs to figure very much into our image of Brahms.

It must be noted that, although the second and fifth pieces in the set (*Freiwillige her!* and *Gebt acht!*) are aggressively chauvinistic and leave no doubt as to how far Brahms's youthful patriotism could lean toward military enthusiasm, the battle to which these texts summon the German *Volk* and *Brüder* is the pre-1848 liberal-democratic unity movement, as the strongly accented "Schwarz, Rot, Gold" (the Tricolor of the liberal movement) in Op. 41/2 makes clear. Max Kalbeck went so far as to suggest that the composer had sought out a Swiss publisher (Rieter-Biedermann) in 1866 so as to avoid any appearance of partisanship during the Austro-Prussian War that year. (Later scholars, however, have pointed out that Brahms settled on the "neutral" Swiss publisher only after German and Viennese publishers had rejected the set in 1865.)

Considering how little Brahms wrote for men's chorus and the fact that he never had such a group to work with, it is impressive that he could easily capture the style of the mid-nineteenth-century men's chorus in Op. 41. Unlike the triple-meter dance rhythms that run through *Twelve Lieder and Romances for Women's Chorus,* Op. 44 (published one year earlier in 1866), songs 2 through 5 of the present set are dominated by duple march rhythms. Even the triple meter of No. 2, *Freiwillige her!* ("Volunteers Come Forth!"), proceeds in forceful dotted rhythms, which combine with the triplet figure of the title-refrain to convey a sense of urgency and anticipation that is lacking in most of Brahms's a cappella choral music and befits instead the call to arms of Lemcke's text. Similarly, the alternation of unison passages with block chords in the more somber *Geleit* (Escort), No. 3, imitates the same device used in numerous *Männerchor* songs of the time. Here, however, within the home key of E$^\flat$ major, subtle shifts of harmony around the pitch D$^\flat$ provide coloristic effects and a more sophisticated aura of melancholy (versus sentimentality) than would be expected in the medium.

In the fifth and final song, *Gebt acht!* (Beware!), a song that rivals No. 2 as the most fervently militaristic in the set, Brahms manages to insert convincingly a passage that he lifted out of his earlier romanticized setting of Ossian's (MacPherson's) *Gesang aus "Fingal,"* from the *Four Songs for Women's Chorus with Harp and Horns,* Op. 17. Whereas in the latter piece an undulation between the dominant harmony and a diminished-seventh chord evokes the passing ghost of the fallen hero Trenar (an archetypal Romantic image of medieval chivalry), in the four strophes of Op. 41/5 the identical musical gesture depicts a world where *Feinde* (enemies) encroach on every side and will use trickery to defeat the *Vaterland*. The musical link between the death of a fictional Nordic warrior and the call to fight to the death for the Fatherland reminds us as modern observers how nineteenth-century German patriotism was fueled by Romantic myths of the Anglo-Saxon past, which in turn helps explain how Brahms was able to set such sentiments so naturally.

The allure of the past is nowhere more strongly felt in Op. 41 than in its first song. Brahms arranged the same setting for his Women's Chorus in Hamburg and a still earlier version for men's voices might have existed. One report that dates the work in his Hamburg youth (around 1848) gains credence through the unusually austere imitation of "early" music displayed here. Not only do the voices move in absolutely like rhythms up until the final extended cadence of each strophe, but the song is set entirely in root-position harmonies. Missing are the trademark intricacies of rhythm and voice-leading that normally mark Brahms's emulation of German styles from the sixteenth and seventeenth centuries. Although the utter simplicity of *Ich schwing mein Horn* might be understood as a character piece that carries parameters of rhythm and harmony to extremes in order to evoke a Gothic aura, it is also possible that this setting predates the intense study of earlier musical styles that Brahms undertook in the 1850s.

It is unclear why Brahms composed no more works for men's chorus after Op. 41. But their absence in his later oeuvre suggest that, for all his satisfaction at seeing the establishment of the *Kaiserreich,* the aggressive tone of Brahms's youthful patriotism receded after the wars of 1866 and 1871. That is not to say that Brahms lost his chauvinism over the years: there are many recorded comments by him concerning the Franco-Prussian War that bear witness to his continued pride over Prussia's military successes. Moreover, Brahms continued to support the major military-political figures in the Reich—Bismarck, Wilhelm I, Wilhelm II. Such strong feelings notwithstanding, Brahms apparently found it either difficult, distasteful, or politically inappropriate to express those attitudes in his art after 1867.

Daniel Beller-McKenna

3 GESÄNGE, FOR SIX-PART CHORUS, OPUS 42
Composed 1859–61; published 1868

1. Abendständchen [Brentano]
2. Vineta [Müller]
3. Darthulas Grabesgesang [Ossian, tr. Herder]

While the histories of these three *Chorlieder* are unknown, they all come from a period in Brahms's life when the course of his career was uncertain, and when he wrote choral pieces for anyone who would sing them. Thus the manuscript of the first belonged for many years to the library of a choir in Altona, a suburb of Hamburg, with which Brahms had an association in 1860–61; the second is found in a version for four women's voices—which may or may not have been the original—in the partbooks of the Hamburg Women's Chorus; the third can be traced with certainty only to an entry he made in his own works list in June 1861. Brahms conducted the first two in a concert of his own works given by the Vienna Singakademie in April 1864. The next year, he made the first of several unsuccessful offers of the entire opus to publishers; it was ultimately accepted by A.F. Cranz of Hamburg and appeared in 1868.

The three pieces in the set share only the number and ranges of voices, S A A T B B—an arrangement that Brahms used here for the first time and clearly found satisfactory because of the number of times he employed it in later works. Otherwise, the contrasts among them could hardly be more striking; they represent three quite different kinds of texts and equally different settings.

The first poem, by Clemens Brentano (1778–1842), is a quintessentially Romantic evocation of the sound of a distant flute heard at night. Its two four-line stanzas receive a varied strophic setting, with nearly all the subtle variation occurring as reharmonization of the second and third lines ("How sweetly it speaks to the heart/through the night which enfolds me"). The six voices appear in shifting combinations—sometimes with the women's and men's voices in close imitation, but at other times in other groupings, and combined so that everyone sings almost all of the time. Triplets and a brief change of meter gently illustrate the words "Brunnen rauschen" (springs murmur) and "zum Herzen spricht" (speaks to the heart). This beautiful song is the first of Brahms's truly great lyric choral pieces, a worthy predecessor to the best of his later works in this vein.

Vineta has long been a favorite of choral groups for its lush setting as well as for its slightly spooky text—the old story of a drowned city—by Wilhelm Müller (better known as the poet of Schubert's great song cycles). He describes the sound of bells tolling from beneath the waters and the reflections of its towers; his heart answers the calling bells, and he feels that angels are calling him into the depths. There is, however, no real narrative and no threat in the poem or its setting; the only hint of trouble, a brief passage ("Out of the heart's utmost depths") in unharmonized octaves—which often stand for death in Brahms's music—is followed only by the news that the bells tell of past happy loves. The six stanzas of the poem are arranged in roughly ternary form, *AABCAB:* the first two are set identically, the third is considerably varied, the unique fourth stanza *(C)* begins with the unharmonized octaves, and the fifth and sixth repeat the music of the first and third. The key is B major (unusual in choral music), the harmonies range widely through chromatic third- and other distantly related keys, and the incessant rhythmic repetition (there are few places where everyone can breathe) all produce an effect of sustained wonder.

Darthulas Grabesgesang is a song of mourning from Ossian (Macpherson) as translated by Johann Gottfried Herder in *Stimmen der Völker in Liedern* (1778-79). By the time Brahms wrote his settings of Ossian (the other is Op. 17/4) Macpherson's forgeries of ancient Scottish poetry had, of course, been thoroughly exposed, but these and other works—the *Edward* Ballade, Op. 10/1, and scattered solo songs and duets—show that Brahms had a fondness for this kind of "Gothic" background. His reaction in this case exhibits a conscious archaism in unisons, parallel octaves, open fifths, an overall modal flavor, and repetitive, funereal rhythms. The dirge for the young and beautiful Darthula is in four stanzas; the first two are set almost identically—some rearrangement of the voices is the only variation—and the third, longer stanza begins the same way: "Never, O never will the sun come awakening to your resting place." The sun is introduced with enharmonic excursions, and at its call—"Awake, Darthula, spring is outdoors!"—the music flowers briefly into the major mode before giving up and sinking back into resignation and grief for the final stanza.

Virginia Hancock

12 LIEDER AND ROMANCES, FOR WOMEN'S CHORUS, OPUS 44

Composed 1859–61; Published 1866

1. Minnelied [Voss]
2. Der Bräutigam [Eichendorff]
3. Barcarole [trad.]
4. Fragen [trad.]
5. Die Müllerin [Chamisso]
6. Die Nonne [Uhland]
7. Nun stehn die Rosen in Blüte [Heyse]
8. Die Berge sind spitz [Heyse]
9. Am Wildbach die Weiden [Heyse]
10. Und gehst du über den Kirchhof [Heyse]
11. Die Braut [Müller]
12. Märznacht [Uhland]

All twelve choruses in Op. 44 were composed for the Hamburg Women's Chorus and can be found among the surviving partbooks of its members. The young Brahms, still finding his choral "voice" when the choir formed around him in 1859, created new repertory by composing simple three- and four-voice settings of folk melodies he had been collecting for more than a decade. Most of the poems in Op. 44 display a Romantic imitation of those same folk lyrics: straightforward strophic verse with regular rhyme schemes, and pictorial expressions of naïve love or noble deeds. As such, this poetry generally accords with the nineteenth-century German definition of the *Romanze,* which is described in Heinrich Koch's *Musikalisches Lexikon* (1802) in part as a song that "related the story of a tragic or amorous incident in lyric verse form" and whose melody consists of "artless, naïve, and peaceful song." Whereas the *Romanze* was understood to be a newly composed work, these characteristics follow those of idealized folk song quite closely. Brahms named five of his opus numbers *Lieder und Romanzen,* ranging from the early simple folk-lyric settings for solo voice of Op. 14 (1860) to the later sophisticated a cappella choruses of Op. 93a. Although there is often little to distinguish such named groups from many that Brahms simply labeled Lieder, Brahms seems to have chosen the title *Lieder und Romanzen* to draw attention to an aura of folklike simplicity.

As was true of many nineteenth-century Germans, Brahms's fascination with folk song stemmed from the revival of the late eighteenth century, dating back to Herder, and the closely related idealization of the past by the Romantics at the turn of the nineteenth century. Early German Romantics, following Herder's lead, saw in the *Volk* of all nations a simple past and pure spirit of culture. Indeed, the ultimate origin of this yearning for the folk past was not German, but rather James Macpherson's fictional British bard Ossian. Accordingly, the only true "folk" lyrics in Op. 44 are German translations from Italian (No. 3, *Barcarole*) and Serbian (No. 4, *Fragen;* Questions).

In Op. 44, Brahms, following the style of his predecessors in the genre of choral Lied (Mendelssohn, Schumann, Loewe, and so on), provides settings for his texts that reflect their cultural distance from the actual folk song they imitate. In fact, the folklike quality of these poems owes as much to their content as their style: nature imagery, intimations of the German Middle Ages, and village scenes abound. Pictorial musical effects mimic similar devices in the poems, as in the *Barcarole* (No. 3), where the horn-call motive of the solo duets evokes the out-of-door setting of the fisher in his boat (and oddly, further teutonicize this German translation of an original Venetian folk song). Similarly, Brahms musically depicts the "gently stirring air" in the third strophe of No. 2, Eichendorff's *Der Bräutigam* (The Bridegroom), through quietly rustling return-figures that pause on a sighlike half-cadence before a favorite Romantic image, *Waldeinsamkeit* (Forest Solitude), closes the stanza. Finally, the dancelike triple rhythms that mark so many of the choruses in Op. 44 are more of a folk caricature than a realistic evocation of folk song.

Brahms's ambivalent use of the piano in the *Lieder und Romanzen* indicated further the middle-class urbanity that underlies the set. The subtitle for Op. 44, "for four-voice women's chorus a cappella or with piano *ad libitum,*" suggests that the inclusion of the keyboard part has little effect on the choruses, and one might expect here merely a doubling role for the piano: aiding the singers but not intruding on their communal voice. In fact, the optional accompaniments transform many of the choruses, adding registral depth, providing textural contrast, punctuating cadences, and creating echo effects. Many of these devices can be observed, for example, in No. 7, *Nun stehn die Rosen in Blüte* (Now the roses are in bloom). After the piano drops down the octave to reinforce the second alto's cadential tones (F♯–B), the repeated B's in the piano echo the iambic rhythm of that cadence, creating poetic (as well as musical) space for the second couplet of each stanza. When in the ensuing phrase Brahms relegates the accompaniment to doubling the two cadences to G major, the relative absence of the piano further sets this phrase off from the rest of the chorus, highlighting its distant tonality from the home key of E major, in which No. 7 begins and ends. Still more integral are the piano echoes toward the beginning of *Die Braut* (No. 11; The Bride), which necessitate a change in meter signature from 3/2 to ¢: the piano interpolations break up the ceaseless flow of the first strain. Again the musical breach is inspired by the recursive poetic ideas in stanzas 1 and 2: "a pity to have dyed it, to have woven it"; "as they steam, as they burn." Thereafter, although the left hand of the piano mostly mirrors the second alto, the right hand's interjections are practically indispensable as they provide the essential leading tones of the harmonies in those measures. Finally, in the last song of the set, *Märznacht* (March Night), the rocking quarter notes of the piano in the right hand and the progressively lower $B\flat$'s of the left hand at the end of the piece add a dimension entirely lacking in the chorus, building anticipation of lovely springtime drawing near ("lieblicher Frühling, du nahst").

Beyond these technicalities, the mere encroachment of the piano on this most communal of genres (secular a cappella choral music) is indicative of middle-class music making in the second half of the nineteenth century. Whereas before 1850, choral singing combined civic participation with musical activity, the home-bound piano began to supplant this experience from the middle of the century on. By individualizing the act of music making, the piano distanced its player from the democratic, choral origins of communal music making. Here, in works that grew directly out of Brahms's early experiences directing a *bürgerlicher* choir, the inclusion of a keyboard part that is essential on the one hand yet optional on the other reflects the transitional role of the instrument at mid-century, and symbolizes Brahms's own ambivalence as an individual artist within musical society, reminding us of his lifelong inability to commit himself to a permanent professional position.

Daniel Beller-McKenna

7 LIEDER, FOR MIXED CHORUS, OPUS 62
Composed 1860–74; Published 1874

1. Rosmarin [*Des Knaben Wunderhorn*]
2. Von alten Liebesliedern [*Des Knaben Wunderhorn*]
3. Waldesnacht [Heyse]
4. Dein Herzlein mild [Heyse]

5. All meine Herzgedanken [Heyse]
6. Es geht ein Wehen [Heyse]
7. Vergangen ist mir Glück und Heil [Old German]

Although the first five songs in this set were composed in 1873–74, when Brahms was director of the Singverein, the chorus of the Gesellschaft der Musikfreunde in Vienna, the last two originated around 1860, when he was conducting in Hamburg. Versions of both for women's voices appear in the partbooks of the Hamburg Women's Chorus, and the manuscript of No. 7 is one of a group of pieces that belonged to the Singakademie of Altona, a suburb of Hamburg; No. 7 also exists in a version for solo voice and piano that was published as Op. 48/6 and in an unpublished version for solo soprano and four-part chorus. (In addition, Brahms wrote a completely different setting of the poem of No. 4 for the Women's Chorus.)

The seven songs share texts of legendary or folk origins. The first two are on texts from *Des Knaben Wunderhorn,* the famous collection published by Arnim and Brentano in 1806–8, while Nos. 3 through 6 are from *Jungbrunnen* (Fountain of Youth), "fairy tales" by one of Brahms's favorite contemporary poets, Paul Heyse (1830–1914). The last is an *altdeutsch* (Old German) text that dates back to the Renaissance. Brahms's setting of No. 7 is also *alt;* it is one of his two imitations of an oversimplified Renaissance style (the other is Op. 41/1)—strophic and completely homophonic, with a melody in the Dorian mode, and triads only in root position.

Perhaps because of their predominantly folk character, all the settings in this collection are strophic, with occasional variations. Number 1, *Rosmarin* (Rosemary), is the old tale of a girl who goes into the garden to gather roses for her wedding garland, but can only find rosemary to wind into a funeral wreath for her dead sweetheart. As with other songs in this set, the simple strophic form belies a wealth of contrapuntal invention and rhythmic complexity, including close imitation between the pairs of women's and men's voices and a change in meter that further confuses an already complex metric situation. *Von alten Liebesliedern* (Old Love Songs), however, is a jolly courting song. In the first stanza, the young lover arrives on his "little horse" and is seen by his sweetheart (divided women's voices); in the second, he greets her (divided men's voices); and in the third and fourth, in identical settings, they dally happily in the garden. The horse's clopping rhythm provides a charmingly naïve refrain to each verse.

Brahms may have been moved to write his three new *Jungbrunnen* songs by the existence of the unpublished *Es geht ein Wehen* (A Wind Blows), the tale of the "wind's bride" whose wailing is heard through the forest as she searches for her lost lover and the peace she will find only in his arms. Her eerie song is reflected in the shifting first-inversion triads in the upper voices in E minor, while divided basses hold a disconcerting G pedal; the texture changes to imitation (and a soaring tenor line) for the meter change in the last two lines of each six-line stanza.

The three new Heyse settings are, in very different ways, among the most inspired of all Brahms's *Chorlieder,* and, like *Rosmarin,* each contains compositional depths that are discoverable on a closer look and that may be related to techniques that Brahms encountered in his study of early music, especially *Tenorlieder* and later German Renaissance choral songs. Number 3, *Waldesnacht* (Forest Night), is a tranquil portrait of the night in three identical strophes. A weary body and restless soul are refreshed and sung to sleep in a texture that seems homophonic but actually contains passages of exact and surprising dissonant imitation. A brief diatonic double canon involving the pairs of women's and men's voices coincides with the word "träumerisch" (dreamy) in the first stanza, while discreet chromaticism underlines the "Qualen" (torments) from which the hearer is freed. Taken all together, though, nothing disturbs the mood of peace that has made this Brahms's most often performed choral song.

Dein Herzlein mild (Thy Tender Heart) is a charming poem in three stanzas that compares the opening to love of an unawakened heart with the morning flowering of a bud. The first two identical stanzas are primarily homophonic, with a brief patch of canonic imitation that temporarily disrupts the sprightly triple meter in overlapping hemiolas. The third stanza begins as the first two did, but at the bud's flowering, the earlier conclusion is expanded by three measures that extend the metric confusion, introduce new harmonic ideas, and show Brahms at his most playful.

The three stanzas of *All meine Herzgedanken* (All of My Thoughts) are set identically, in six parts (Brahms's favorite SAATBB, with groupings SAA and TBB beginning each strophe). The poem is the plaint of someone separated from a lover—whether by distance or by the end of the affair is not clear. There is no specific text-painting here, but there is a re-markable concentration of chromaticism in the brief middle section of each stanza, where the voices enter imitatively in a key distant from the tonic F major, and then magically return to it in a beautiful cadence that promises ultimate reconciliation—God will reunite those who love one another.

Virginia Hancock

2 MOTETS, FOR MIXED CHORUS, OPUS 74
Composed 1856–77; published 1879

1. Warum is das Licht gegeben dem Mühseligen? [biblical]
2. O Heiland, reiß die Himmel auf [anon.]

Each of these motets has its origin in periods of Brahms's career years earlier than their publication in 1878. Number 1, the *Warum* motet, be-gins with the canonic Mass movements (WoO 18) that he composed in 1856 in connection with his studies of counterpoint, while the history of No. 2, *O Heiland,* dates from 1863–64, the season he spent as conductor of the Vienna Singakademie. He had already known the text and melody of the chorale from a collection of old German Catholic songs given to him by a friend in Hamburg, and a reference in that volume led him to the Viennese court library, where he copied the remaining stanzas. Al-though he may have begun composing his own setting at this time, not until 1870 did he tell Max Bruch, who had just published a setting of the Latin hymn *Rorate coeli,* that he himself had made a setting of "the won-derful old melody" with its traditional German text "in motet and vari-ation form." At close to the same time, he asked another friend to return the manuscript of the canonic Mass movements, perhaps with the idea of completing a pair of motets.

Brahms was proud of his selection of texts for the *Warum* motet, which are often compared to those he had used in the *German Requiem.* In the motet, three biblical passages (Job 3:20–23, Lamentations 3:41, and James 5:11) conclude with the first stanza of Luther's German versification of the *Nunc dimittis,* "Mit Fried und Freud ich fahr dahin" (With peace and joy I go there). In the first and longest movement, the initial "Warum" re-curs as a refrain framing the three sections, its repeated question "Why? Why?" underlined by an unresolved leading tone. The first verse of the bleak text, Job's cry, "Why is light given to him that is in misery, and life to one whose heart is troubled?" is set in four parts in D minor to a close reworking of Brahms's canonic Agnus Dei, the dense chromaticism of which is amazingly suited to the German text. A three-note descending figure associated with the word "Mühseligen" becomes the basis of the next section, "Who long for death, but it comes not, and dig for it as for hidden treasure." An ironic gleam of major illuminates the phrase "who almost rejoice and are glad when they attain the grave." The final verse from Job, "And to the man whose path God has hidden from him?" is a triple-meter restatement of the original canonic subject.

In the second movement, "Let us lift up our hearts with our hands to God in heaven," the ascending line in F major that so perfectly illustrates the text comes, in fact, from Brahms's canonic Benedictus, which is reproduced almost exactly in its original four parts, SSAT. After a complete statement, divided basses join in to conclude the movement in six parts. The third movement refers, in a transformation of the canonic Dona nobis pacem, to the happy ones who have the patience of Job. Here the soprano melody is taken from the original canon; the other five parts join in an imitative accompanying tapestry; and the movement ends with a restatement of the end of the previous movement set to the text "for the Lord is merciful." The concluding movement is a four-part setting in Bach-like style of the traditional chorale melody "Mit Fried und Freud ich fahr dahin." Its presence has evoked much discussion about whether Brahms intended the motet as an homage to Bach, or perhaps even as a claim that he was Bach's successor. His own fear that his intent would be read in this way led him to try to withdraw an intended dedication to the noted Bach scholar Philipp Spitta; however, the secret had already been leaked, and in the end Brahms decided to let the dedication stand.

The second motet, a set of five chorale variations, represents Brahms's most direct reaction to his study of German Renaissance and Baroque music, resembling in its structure Bach's Cantata No. 4, *Christ lag in Todesbanden* (Christ Lay in the Bonds of Death), which Brahms had conducted in Detmold in 1858 and performed again in 1873 in Vienna. The first stanza is a straightforward setting of the traditional Dorian melody, which appears in the soprano and is accompanied by imitative counterpoint—including a favorite German Renaissance technique, pre-imitation—in the three lower voices. In the second verse, the soprano continues with the melody, but the speed of the lower voices is doubled, perhaps to depict the image of dew pouring from heaven. The third verse frankly represents its text: the tenor has the melody—like the *Tenorlieder*

Brahms had copied—but it flowers into ornamental triplets as the text speaks of the earth flowering; and references to mountains and valleys receive exuberant leaps and arpeggios. In the slow fourth verse ("Here we suffer greatest need,/ before our eyes stands bitter death,/ ah, come, lead us with a strong hand/ from misery to our Father's land") the melody is in the bass. Pervasive chromaticism and madrigalisms illustrate the text: The upper voices make frequent use of the "sighing figure" common in Baroque music; there is a particularly sharp dissonance on the word *bittre* (which was an alteration by Brahms from the original *ewig*, perhaps for its sound); and the phrase "ah, come, lead us" is presented in a series of entries, each one step higher than the last. The final stanza, a simple statement of praise, is in some ways anticlimactic, but it is also a contrapuntal *tour de force*. Brahms presents a decorated version of the melody in the soprano and in canon in contrary motion in the bass; in the concluding "Amen," the alto and tenor provide a mirror canon of their own. Brahms's friend Franz Wüllner was much struck by this "Amen," writing, "No one else can write the double canon in contrary motion at the end as you do. Writing a double canon isn't so hard; what is hard is to write one that sounds as if it weren't."

The *Warum* motet has been acknowledged by most authorities to be Brahms's greatest achievement in unaccompanied choral music. *O Heiland*, though it has received less attention, is one of his most successful fusions of old and new ideas; he himself considered it worthy of publication beside the *Warum* motet.

Virginia Hancock

LIEDER AND ROMANCES, FOR FOUR-PART MIXED CHORUS, OPUS 93A
Composed 1883–84; published 1884

1. Der bucklichte Fiedler [trad.]
2. Das Mädchen [trad., trans. Kapper]
3. O süsser Mai [Arnim]
4. Fahr wohl, o Vöglein [Rückert]
5. Der Falke [trad., trans. Kapper]
6. Beherzigung [Goethe]

Observing that Brahms had published no other secular a cappella choral music for a decade (that is, since the Seven Lieder, Op. 62, of 1874), it is common to associate the sophisticated style of Op. 93a with the numerous large-scale works that he produced in the interim: three symphonies (Opp. 68, 73, and 90), two concertos (Opp. 77 and 83), two overtures (Opp. 80 and 81), and two large works for chorus and orchestra (Opp. 82 and 89). To be sure, Brahms's mastery of larger forms by the 1870s must have affected his smaller works like these choruses, and one must consider how that influence separates Op. 93a from its earlier and simpler namesake, the *Twelve Lieder and Romances for Women's Chorus*, Op. 44. Moreover, this later set of six choruses almost seems out of place among the more grandiose output around this time.

Yet, the view of Brahms in the 1870s and 1880s as primarily a composer of "large" works speaks more to his contemporaries' long wait for him to direct his attention to "the power and masses of the choir and orchestra" (as Schumann entreated him to do in 1853) and our modern awareness of the role those pieces played in securing his place in the canon, and less to a real shift in interest and emphasis by the composer. During the same period, Brahms published no less than five separate opus numbers for solo voice and one for vocal quartet (Op. 92). Although Brahms had neglected this medium for many years, the *Lieder und Romanzen* form a logical succession to his recent "ballades" and "romances," such as the duets of Op. 75 and the quasi-duets of Op. 84.

What rightly separates Op. 93a from Brahms's earlier secular a cappella choruses is the lack of any immediate performance context for these works. Whereas most of Opp. 44 and 62 were composed while Brahms was directing choirs in Hamburg and Vienna respectively, Brahms had little contact with choral groups in the early 1880s. It is particularly surprising, therefore, that further unlike his previously published secular choral works, which drew extensively on older compositions from his tenure with the Hamburg Women's Chorus, the six choruses in question all were apparently newly composed in the summer of 1883. These are the musical thoughts of an accomplished mind who turns to the a cappella medium out of aesthetic choice rather than professional duty. Indicative in this respect is the first chorus in Op. 93a, *Der bucklichte Fiedler* (The Humpbacked Fiddler). Brahms had set this old Lower Rhenish folk song along with its traditional melody (as given in Brahms's favorite collection, Kretzschmer and Zuccalmaglio's *Deutsche Volkslieder*) for three separate performing media: as an SSA arrangement for the Hamburg women; as an SATB arrangement (for the Vienna Singakademie or Detmold Choir); and finally arranged for solo voice with piano and published as one of his forty-nine German folk songs in 1894. In the *Lieder und Romanzen* of 1883, however, Brahms composes his own melody and creates an entirely new setting for the old text.

Freed from the old minor-mode tune of *Der bucklichte Fiedler,* Brahms constructs a piece that is at once harmonically more sophisticated and full of elegant part-writing, yet pictorializes folk song and "choral" singing more vividly than in the earlier choral Lieder of Opp. 44 and 62. The alternation between unison antecedent and choral consequent in the opening phrase portrays a stereotypical *Tafellied,* while with the open fifths, G–D, D–A, and change to a lilting 3/8 dance meter at the words, "der Geiger strich" (the fiddler bowed), Brahms employs an unusually vivid example of text-painting. As the soprano spins out a flowing melody from a simple three-note motive in a fine example of what Arnold Schoenberg (and more recently Walter Frisch) labeled "developing variation," the bass holds its low G (the note produced by the open lowest string of the fiddle). The result is a series of suavely flowing harmonies above a bass pedal, effortlessly blending the sophisticated and the pictorial. Such integration of the "high" and "low" characterizes Op. 93a and marks it as a new departure in Brahms's choral oeuvre.

Not surprisingly, when the mature Brahms applies himself to the simpler style implied by the title *Lieder und Romanzen,* the result is markedly less naïve than in his youthful efforts (as is already evident in the quasi-duet *Romanzen und Lieder,* Op. 84, of 1882). Inevitably, perhaps, simplicity in these later works turns to nostalgia and sentimentality. These qualities are best expressed in two settings of Romantic poetry from the middle of the set, No. 3, Achim von Arnim's *O süsser Mai* (O Sweet May) and No. 4, Friedrich Rückert's *Fahr wohl, o Vöglein* (Fare Well, Little Bird). In the former, Brahms captures the text's sense of dislocation and isolation by setting off the soprano melody from the remaining three voices, turning what otherwise would be a straightforward chordal setting into one of rich texture, vaguely recalling the complexities of some fifteenth-century German songs Brahms had studied in earlier days. Not only does the top part progress with its own freely expanding phrases in the first and third strains, but below these the rest of the chorus constantly shifts the harmony chromatically downward (B–B♭ in the bass in m. 4; A–A♭ in the tenor two measures later), forcing the soprano to reinterpret its harmonic context with each new phrase and thereby realizing "dislocation" as a tangible musical device. Likewise, in No. 4, the endless chain of separation (wandering bird–falling leaf–parting love) of Rückert's *Fahr wohl* finds its corollary in phrases that are always harmonically directed but never go back to the home key of A♭ major. And just as the figural use of nature metaphors to prefigure the farewell-to-love in the third stanza is too pat here to be mistaken for folk poetry, Brahms's setting uses a harmonic language that is overly refined for the simple strophic form of the piece. Brahms even draws attention to his over-sentimental harmony: the minute decrescendos on each beat emphasize the appoggiaturas of the soprano that never find a full sense of resolution; and even in the closing cadence of the song, this soprano line stalls on C (the third of the tonic A♭ chord, not its root).

The remaining choruses of the set, based on two translations of Serbian folk songs and one Goethe text, are more stark in effect, leading some commentators to attribute their style directly to the instrumental music of this period. Indeed, the strictly homorhythmic chords of the choir against a soprano solo and the grazioso tempo in the Serbian *Das Mädchen* (No. 2) suggest a slow middle movement in a chamber work, and the variation-like form of No. 5, *Der Falke* (The Falcon; also on a Serbian text), owes more to instrumental form than to the subject of the text. That Brahms would react more objectively to the more obscure folk songs in this set (neither narrates its story as plainly as the German "bucklichte Fiedler") shows how deeply imbedded in his basic musical style (vocal and instrumental) were the patterns of speech and tone from folk song.

By the same token, the terse verse of No. 6, Goethe's *Beherzigung* (Reflection), elicits an equally concise canon from Brahms. Goethe's stark division between "feminine" *(weiblich)* timidity and the strength of the "arms of the gods" is played out in a strophic variation; the highly chromatic D-minor canon of the first stanza is transformed in a D-major canon for stanza 2 that gradually sheds all chromatic "bending" to reach an ecstatic climax at the words "Arme der Götter" (arms of the gods) through a fourfold repetition of the high pitch in each voice (A). In comparison with some earlier efforts to manipulate canon to modern effect, the last number of Op. 93a (like the first) points up the fluid mixture of technique and expression in Brahms's later works. Once again, the importance of aesthetic expression over practical composition plays a role. Not that these choruses are any less singable than his earlier secular a cappella works, but the decision to compose in this medium in 1883 is guided by an inner compulsion rather than professional circumstances, and hence the use of a strict compositional technique (like the canon of No. 6) can be put to greater expressive effect.

Daniel Beller-McKenna

5 GESÄNGE, FOR MIXED CHORUS, OPUS 104
Composed 1886–88; published 1890

1. Nachtwache I [Rückert]   4. Verlorene Jugend [trad., trans. Wenzig]
2. Nachtwache II [Rückert]   5. Im Herbst [Groth]
3. Letztes Glück [Kalbeck]

The *Chorlieder* Op. 104, Brahms's last secular works, are the culmination of a development begun more than thirty years earlier with Op. 42.
It is possible that some version of one of the songs, No. 3, was composed
as early as 1877; the poet Max Kalbeck—Brahms's most diligent biographer—had given the composer a manuscript of his "Letztes Glück" in
January 1875, and Brahms told Kalbeck in 1877 that he had set "all sorts
of" things of his (the only other that survives is the song *Nachtwandler*
(Sleepwalker), Op. 86/3). Brahms composed No. 5, *Im Herbst* (In the Autumn), in a first version in A minor in the summer of 1886. After performances by groups conducted by two of his friends, Brahms transposed it
up to C minor and made substantial revisions to the third stanza. All the
pieces were completed sometime before or during the summer of 1888,
and the entire opus was published in October of that year.

The text of the first completed of the songs (albeit in its earlier version),
Im Herbst, by his fellow North German Klaus Groth, is one of the "autumnal" type so often associated with Brahms's later years. In three stanzas, it is a somber depiction of the season of falling leaves, misty days, and
the onset of night, which the poet (not originally) compares with the approach of death; however, a glimmer of hope in the last two lines suggests
that death is not entirely unwelcome. Brahms's setting, the only one in
this opus in the conventional four parts, begins with two identical strophes in C minor; the sustained flow of the compound duple meter comes
to a rest on a bleak open fifth. The third stanza opens with a disconcerting twist into the parallel major and proceeds through a passage of harmonic difficulty—a series of augmented-sixth chords and movements to
distant keys—unlike anything else in Brahms's choral music. The climax
is reached with an outpouring of "the heart's most blissful" tears. (In the
first version of the song, the chromaticism is no less thorny, but it is employed less logically.)

The fourth song, *Verlorene Jugend* (Lost Youth), is a setting in five parts
(divided basses) of a folk text translated "from the Bohemian" by Josef
Wenzig and published in 1830. It compares the heedlessness of youth to

a rushing mountain stream; a stone thrown into the water might be regained, but youth can never be. Brahms's setting of the four stanzas is divided into two closely related parts. The first and third stanzas are both in D minor in a fast tempo, and employ a canon between two of the voices (alto and soprano the first time, first bass and soprano the second) that rushes past like the mountain stream. The second and fourth stanzas are identically set, in D major at a slow tempo, homophonic, and with irregular phrase lengths and frequent pauses, as though the singers were somehow trying to stop time.

Kalbeck's poem "Letztes Glück" (Last Happiness) is yet another autumnal text—the last leaves are falling from the trees, but the unfulfilled heart never quite forgets its last happiness, like a ray of sunshine falling on the late wild rose. Brahms's setting bears a resemblance to his much earlier *Abendständchen* (Evening Serenade), Op. 42/1, in the general mood and the ways in which the six voices are employed. Here, as well as in the pair of *Nachtwache* (Night Watch) settings, Brahms used his characteristic SAATBB combination—a weightier texture than the SSATTB commonly used by Renaissance madrigal composers—but the division into higher and lower groups is used only at the beginning in a double, varied statement of the first lines ("Lifelessly glides leaf upon leaf/ quietly and sadly down from the trees") and again near the end when the same figure appears "as with a last happiness." For the most part, the texture of this setting is rich and full—only "the late wild rose" fades away to a few trailing voices—almost in opposition to the sense of the gloomy poem. Despite its inconsistency, this is one of Brahms's most beautiful and difficult choral songs.

Nachtwache I and *Nachtwache II* are a pair of wonderful settings of poems by Friedrich Rückert. The first text bears only a slight relationship to its title: the soft notes of love are sent out like a breath from one heart to another; but if no open heart is found, "let a night wind bear you back, sighing, to mine." The six parts are consistently deployed in groups of three higher against three lower voices, with a call from each group typically answered by a variant of the same call at a different pitch level. With the phrase "hauchet zitternd hinaus" (whisper forth tremulously), the sound of the language, the chromatic setting, and an extra repetition of the text all reinforce the impression of uncertainty. The last section, beginning with the appearance of the night wind, "sighs" descriptively before the voices unite in a last, falling "zurück, zurück, zurück."

The second *Nachtwache* has been a favorite of singers and audiences since its appearance. One of Brahms's most perceptive and outspoken friends, Elisabet von Herzogenberg, called it "a pearl among the part-songs." Here, the horns of night watchmen sound from the east and answer from the west in falling and rising perfect fourths: "Do they rest? ... They rest." After the horn calls die away, fearful hearts are admonished to listen for the "whispering voices *(flüsternden Stimmen)* of the angels," and to extinguish their lamps in confidence and peace. The six voices build up in gentle sibilants, briefly introduce a new, distant key, and resolve in diatonic confidence to a final glorious cadence. In its brief course, this song encompasses a world of doubt, experience, and hope that was surely possible only for the fully mature Brahms.

Virginia Hancock

Fest- und Gedenksprüche, for Eight-Part Chorus, Opus 109
Composed 1888–89; published 1890

1. Unsere Väter hofften auf dich
2. Wenn ein starker Gewappneter
3. Wo ist ein so herrlich Volk

Shortly before his aborted retirement from composition in 1890, Brahms produced two last groups of sacred choral works, the *Fest- und Gedenksprüche,* Op. 109, and the *Drei Motetten,* Op. 110. These two opus numbers share the normative use of a cappella, eight-voice (double-choir) format, a style in which Brahms had not worked previously. Whereas his interest in polychoral writing may have been sparked by the new edition of Heinrich Schütz's works that began appearing in 1885 (as several scholars have suggested), his reasons for turning to a larger choral format were as much political as musical. For in these works, especially in Op. 109, Brahms uses the historical aura of the Bible and a massive vocal effect to evoke the German nation and to comment upon ominous divisions in the *Kaiserreich* near the end of the century. As in Op. 55, Brahms turned to biblical texts in Op. 109 to articulate his reaction to a political event, the so-called *Drei-Kaiser-Jahr* of 1888. That year witnessed the deaths of the ninety-year-old Emperor Wilhelm I in March and of his successor son Frederick III barely three months later, who was then succeeded by his own son, the twenty-nine-year-old Wilhelm II. Brahms, according to Max Kalbeck, "felt the blow, which befell the royal family and house, the fatherland, and the people, more painfully than many who were closer to the monarch."

After Brahms had composed the *Fest- und Gedenksprüche* (and perhaps the choruses of Op. 110 as well) in May of 1889, he was named an Honorary Freeman *(Ehrenbürger)* of his native city, Hamburg. As thanks, he dedicated Op. 109 to Hamburg's mayor, Carl Petersen, and the works were first performed at the Hamburg industrial trade fair in September of 1889. They were, however, more broadly conceived for the major national holidays of the *Kaiserreich:* the celebration of the Leipzig peasant uprising; the *Sedantag,* celebrating the military victory over France in 1870; and the anniversary of Kaiser Wilhelm's coronation in 1871. Indeed, Brahms originally planned to call the works "German" or "National" festival and commemorative sayings, and dropped the more nationalistic title only at his publisher's suggestion.

Although the historical continuity of the German nation emerges as a central theme of Op. 109, the mythical Volk and the modern political Reich are sometimes separated, other times equated, and constantly made problematic. Whereas before 1848 the Reich was largely anticipated as the ideal embodiment of the Volk, these two entities later represented separate manifestations of the German nation and they came into conflict after 1871. By the time Brahms completed these works in 1889, Volk and Reich practically stood for opposing political allegiances, to Liberalism and late-century Conservatism, respectively. True to his traditional middle-class values, Brahms works against the apparently *völkisch* element in these works by arranging his selected texts so as to place an emphasis on God's law and rule as laid down in the Pentateuch of the Old Testament—a strong rebuke of populist, German-Christian rhetoric from the political Right and a cautious affirmation of the imperial state as the rightful, albeit precarious, realization of the German unity celebrated in Op. 55.

To begin the *Fest- und Gedenksprüche,* Brahms employs polychoral textures that depict separate groups in the most vivid musical terms possible. Choir 2 begins the piece with a unison arpeggio (F–C–A–C) that is immediately embellished by Choir 1 with highly figured four-voice counterpoint. Out of this opening gesture, a pattern emerges in which starkly simple statements by Choir 2 are juxtaposed with and elaborated by a more sophisticated and learned tone in Choir 1. And while simplicity and sophistication would hardly account for all of the potential divisions in German society, they nevertheless imply low and high art, a distinction that could be understood to represent the division between *völkisch* ideology and educated middle-class liberalism. From a number of perspectives, the structure and choral textures in the first of the *Fest- und Gedenksprüche* reflect the unity in the face of diversity that Brahms hoped would hold the Reich together. Two dissimilar groups (that is, Choirs 1 and 2) are pitted against each other, sometimes in stark relief, yet they ultimately flow together at the end of sections in prayerful plagal cadences.

In Op. 109/2, the element of prayer recedes while a direct reference to the Reich surfaces. The opening bars of this chorus are solidly in C major with martial-like rhythms and short, clearly defined motives that project confidence, decisiveness, and uniformity. Unlike most of the previous piece, the choirs here present exactly the same material, enhancing the image of agreement and precision. The image of a "strong man" *(starker Gewappneter)* maintaining order over his palace in No. 2 is often taken as a metaphor for Prince Otto von Bismarck's control of the *Kaiserreich*. Indeed, Brahms was a devoted follower of the Iron Chancellor, and his fears over the future of the German state lay mostly in the strife between the new Kaiser and Bismarck.

Those fears are portrayed both textually and musically in the C-minor middle portion of No. 2. There, Brahms depicts a "divided house" as a "wasteland" through hollow and dissonant tones, and implies "one house falling upon another" through a rushing sequence of cascading keys all the way from C minor to D major within three measures. Brahms also achieves a chaotic effect in these measures by dividing each choir against itself, creating a hyper fragmentation of the choral texture. When the uniform and precise phrasing of the opening section returns, it is as if the "starker Gewappneter" has forcefully restored order and precision to the troubled Reich.

Whereas Op. 109/2 focuses on division, the music of No. 3 in F major depicts union. Unlike the separate groups portrayed at the beginning of No. 1, from which an underlying unity was merely suggested, various combinations of voices at the beginning of No. 3 vividly portray the coming together of separate strands into one integrated whole. Throughout the opening section of the piece, Brahms employs a variety of voice combinations and timbral mixtures that join one or more voices from one choir with voices from the other, thereby helping to blur the distinction of separate groups. The wavelike repetitions of the ascending arpeggio (A–C–F) in these opening bars adds to the fluid effect that draws the listener's attention away from the division between the separate choirs.

Having overcome the urgency of Nos. 1 and 2, Brahms steps back in the middle of Op. 109/3 to offer a basis for the preceding prayers, a reason to believe in their effectiveness. This middle portion, therefore, forms a core of meaning not only to No. 3 but to the whole of the *Fest- und Gedenksprüche*. Brahms appropriately singles out this material within all of Op. 109 through its fine dynamic gradations, rendering this music more contemplative and less festive than that which surrounds it. Another defining feature of this section is its archaic style, signaled by the double canon in Choir 1 at the words "Hüte dich nur und bewahre deine Seele wohl" (Only take heed to thyself, and keep thy soul diligently). The allusion to the music of Schütz, Gabrieli, et al., is basic and generalized but unmistakable. Brahms uses a canon and historical style here to musically depict two aspects of the text from Deuteronomy 4:9—the overt mention of the "history" that we have seen with our own eyes, and the submerged allusion to "laws" in this passage, which is spoken by Moses to the Israelites as he reminds them of their covenant with God in the Ten Commandments.

In the end, Brahms arranged his selected texts to establish historical continuity in the *Fest- und Gedenksprüche; Unsere Väter*, a symbol of the past with which the set begins, finds a corollary in "deine Kindern und Kindeskindern," a symbol of the future with which the set ends. The closing "Amen" provides an ultimate realization of the unity amidst diversity that was expressed at the beginning of the opus. Seven canonic entries arpeggiate every harmony that belongs to the key of F major above a sustained F pedal in Bass 2, thus articulating each individual entity within the tonic key (diversity), while the fundamental pitch of that key is constantly sounding (unity). When the spirit of the *Fest- und Gedenksprüche* is considered in detail, one finds these to be not mere pieces of pomp and nationalistic affirmation, but musical works that reflect Brahms's conflicted attitude toward his own patriotism. Brahms maintained hope in the future of the German nation, so long as the *Volk* were willing to remember their past and follow their own "covenant," which had been realized in the founding of the modern *Kaiserreich*.

Daniel Beller-McKenna

3 Motets, for Four- and Eight-Part Chorus, Opus 110
Composed 1889; published 1890

1. Ich aber bin elend [Psalm 69: 30; Exodus 34: 6–7]
2. Ach, arme Welt [anon.]
3. Wenn wir in höchsten Nöten sein [Eber]

The same impulse that led Brahms to compose the *Fest- und Gedenksprüche*, Op. 109, produced the three motets of Op. 110, two of which are also for double choir. Brahms was as excited by Philipp Spitta's edition of the large choral works of Heinrich Schütz as he had been by the complete works of Bach many years earlier; as each volume appeared, he went through it carefully and noted striking passages, including a number in the polychoral *Psalmen Davids* of 1619 (which appeared in two volumes in 1886 and 1887). Perhaps not coincidentally, he began composition of his own new a cappella works for double choir on sacred texts soon thereafter. The first mention of Op. 110 in the correspondence appears in summer 1889, in the middle of the process of publication of Op. 109, when Brahms told his publisher that he had three additional motets—"better" ones—that he would like to have published at the same time. He also told his friend Franz Wüllner that Wüllner's choir would have "much more fun" with the new pieces. They were first performed in January 1890 by the Hamburg Cäcilienverein under Julius Spengel, and appeared in print later that year.

The text of the first motet is one of a number of excerpts from the Bible that Brahms had copied into a small notebook which also includes the texts of Op. 74/1 and Op. 109. For the second and third, he took texts from a collection of Old German sacred poetry published by Philipp Wackernagel in 1841. All three motets are of a somber character that is in contrast with the patriotic certainties of the *Fest- und Gedenksprüche* and that probably better express Brahms's own feelings at this time of his life.

Ich aber bin elend shares many of the features of the works of Schütz that Brahms had been studying, including responsive psalmody, cross-relations, and unexpected chromatic intervals and dissonance that illustrate the text. The three connected sections of the through-composed motet consist of the two halves of Psalm 69: 30 (v. 29 in the King James version)—"But I am poor and sorrowful; God, your help protect me!"—divided by a longer passage (Exodus 34: 6–7) that praises God's mercy. The intensely chromatic setting of the first section is followed in the second by a litany in which the initial "Herr, Herr Gott" is repeated in the second choir as a constant but always varied response to the first choir's recitation of the Lord's merciful attributes. The final section is a full-voiced affirmation of confidence in that mercy.

The second motet of this group, *Ach, arme Welt* (Ah, Poor World), is for four voices only; it is a mostly homophonic and strophic setting of its text. The first two stanzas are set identically, and slight variations in the third stanza accommodate an additional line (which provides the bass with an opportunity to imitate the melody's striking first figure) and end on a major triad. The melody at the beginning of each verse includes an apparent quotation of the four-note whole-tone scale that begins the traditional melody of the chorale *Es ist genug* (It Is Enough)—one that Brahms had copied and performed not only in its well-known setting by Bach but in an earlier six-voice setting by Johann Rudolf Ahle (1625–1673).

Wenn wir in höchsten Nöten sein (When We Are in Deepest Need) has a chorale text (c.1550) by Paul Eber (1511–1569) and a setting that pairs its four verses in accordance with their contrasting messages. The first and third stanzas, which share a theme of despair and pleading, are set identically and resemble a brief but complex kind of chorale fantasy (it is possible to construct a chorale-like melody that seems to underlie this section but that bears no resemblance to the traditional melody set by Bach). The second stanza, which expresses some hope that God will come to the rescue, opens with massed voices "zusammen ingemein" (together in common), while the fourth is a massively expanded variation of the second. It opens in the same way (but without its obvious reference to the text) and includes many repetitions of the phrase "gehorsam sein nach deinem Wort" (be obedient to thy word). This admonition sounds a note of caution in the otherwise general praise of the last verse and perhaps reflects Brahms's own rather cautious and skeptical view of conventional religious beliefs.

Virginia Hancock

20

ACCOMPANIED CHORAL MUSIC

AVE MARIA, FOR WOMEN'S CHORUS WITH ORCHESTRA OR ORGAN, OPUS 12

Composed 1858; published 1861

SCORING: 2 flutes, 2 oboes, 2 clarinets, 2 bassoons, 2 horns, strings [Text: Luke: 28, 42]

The *Ave Maria*, Op. 12, was composed in September 1858, and was first performed the following year with Brahms's Hamburg Women's Chorus. The text of the *Ave Maria* is from Verses 28 and 42 of the Gospel according to St. Luke. The work is in 6/8 in F major, and has a gentle lyrical cast. It is not clear whether Brahms first composed the work with organ accompaniment or with the orchestral accompaniment he later used in performances in Hamburg and Vienna. Despite the substantial orchestration, Brahms effectively highlights the four-part chorus throughout the work. The orchestral accompaniment is deftly done so that the orchestra blends effortlessly with the voices.

Influences stemming from Brahms's practical experiences and frustrations as a choral conductor during the Detmold years strongly affected his later tenure in Vienna at both the Singakademie and the Singverein. At Detmold, Brahms was often concerned, as he wrote to Joachim, that his own work might be too impractical for the essentially middle-class, moderately sophisticated choristers. Not only did Brahms become familiar at Detmold with the possibilities of vocal ensembles and with the predilections of the influential and significant amateur choral traditions in German-speaking Europe in the nineteenth century, but the experience also fueled his interest in the history of music, particularly sacred music before the Classical era. Brahms's choice of a Latin sacred text for his first choral work has been the subject of much discussion, and Op. 12 has often been compared unfavorably to Op. 13, *Begräbnisgesang,* as a means of demonstrating Brahms's greater ease with German Protestant sources. The inspiration for the *Ave Maria,* however, may have less to do with religion than with images generated by Romantic literature. Hans Michael Beuerle, following Max Kalbeck, has suggested that Brahms was inspired by a scene from E.T.A. Hoffmann's *Kater Murr.* Hoffmann describes a small chorus of girls singing Kapellmeister Kreisler's setting of *Ave Maria.* The title page of Brahms's work contains an oblique reference to this scene. One of the ironies of music history is that this work was the first choral work of Brahms to be published. He was later paid by the same publisher as much for Op. 13 as he was for the D-minor Piano Concerto, Op. 15. As Beurle notes, this fact is an indication of the popularity and economic significance of the choral tradition in nineteenth-century musical life.

Leon Botstein

BEGRÄBNISGESANG, FOR CHORUS AND WINDS, OPUS 13
Composed 1858; published 1861

SCORING: 2 oboes, 2 clarinets, 2 bassoons, 2 horns, 3 trombones, tuba, timpani [Text: Weisse]

In December 1858, Brahms sent Clara Schumann a juxtaposition of recently composed pieces that ought perhaps to have struck biographers as curious, coming as it did two years after the death of Clara's husband: a "Bridal Song" (now lost, though Brahms later quoted from it in his song *Von ewiger Liebe,* Op.43/1); and a "Funeral Song" which, he said, "goes very slowly and is to be sung by the graveside." The association of the matrimonial and the funereal is one that seems to have remained with Brahms. Years later, on the day the Schumanns' daughter Julie married an Italian nobleman, the composer presented Clara with his somber *Alto Rhapsody,* describing it, in ironic reference to his unfulfilled feelings for Julie, as his "bridal song."

In its earliest form, the scoring of the *Begräbnisgesang* (Burial Song) included cellos and basses; but in order to render the piece more suitable

for outdoor performance the stringed instruments were replaced the following year by bass trombone and tuba. Brahms's own title for the work
was *Gesang zum Begräbnis*, but this was altered by the original publisher,
Jakob Rieter-Biedermann, first to *Begräbnisgesang* and then to *Grabgesang*
(Song by the Graveside). In his letter to Clara Schumann enclosing the
piece, Brahms had himself referred casually to it as *Grabgesang*; but now
he felt he could not reconcile himself to the second alteration. He told
Rieter-Biedermann, "It must remain at least *Begräbnisgesang*, not *Grabgesang*. *Gesang zum Begräbnis* is actually best, and that's how it stands in
Winterfeld. We don't sing simply about the grave, but for the burial and
the remembrance of the burial."

Carl von Winterfeld's two seminal studies, *Johannes Gabrieli und sein
Zeitalter* of 1834 and *Der evangelische Kirchengesang und sein Verhältnis zur
Kunst des Tonsatzes* (1843–47) were of central importance to Brahms's research into the music of the past. Nevertheless, the composer was mistaken: Winterfeld refers clearly to the tradition of the *Begräbnisgesang*.

The text of Brahms's work consists of seven strophes by the sixteenth-
century Evangelical writer Michael Weisse. The fact that Brahms had
been studying Winterfeld's book on liturgical song was clearly of relevance to the *Begräbnisgesang*, whose opening measures are so much in the
style of a chorale melody that they have been mistaken for a genuine
chorale ever since—despite the fact that Brahms assured his friend Julius
Otto Grimm that he had made no use of such material.

The somber atmosphere of the *Begräbnisgesang*, with its marking of
Tempo di Marcia funebre, has been seen as a preparation for the mood
of the *German Requiem*; and certainly both the stern nature and the narrow compass of its opening theme provide an anticipation of the Requiem's second movement, "Denn alles Fleisch, es ist wie Gras" (All flesh
is as grass), though there is an even closer parallel with the first of the *Four
Serious Songs*, Op. 121.

Brahms sets the first stanza with utmost simplicity, using only the
starkest of instrumental accompaniments. The opening phrase is intoned first in cantorial style by half of the basses, doubled by bassoons,
and answered by altos, tenors, and the remainder of the basses, with a
single-line accompaniment on the bass trombone and tuba. Only with
the instrumental interlude separating the first two stanzas does Brahms
make use of his full complement of instruments, minus the timpani.
Here, he presents a new melody for solo horn, and a throbbing rhythmic
figure on the bassoons which is to be taken over so effectively by the tim-

pani in the following verse: "Earth he is, and of the earth / And will become earth again / And will arise from the earth again / When God's trombone sounds."

It is with this final line that the sopranos enter for the first time, leading the music to a climax whose forcefulness continues through the third stanza, which is underpinned throughout by a new pulsating rhythmic figure. A return of the previously heard instrumental interlude dissolves seamlessly into the work's central contrasting section in the major. This consolatory middle section, in which Brahms uses a half-chorus, and a smooth accompanimental figure played by the clarinet in triplet eighth-notes does duty for a harp, offers a vision of paradise in which the departed soul lives on. If Brahms's textual underlay is uncharacteristically awkward here (in the opening phrase, "Sein Arbeit, Trübsal und Elend," the first two nouns are curiously mis-stressed), the beauty of the new chorale-like melody is undeniable.

Shortly before composing the *Begräbnisgesang,* Brahms had been conducting the court choir at Detmold in two Bach cantatas, No. 4, *Christ lag in Todesbanden,* and No. 21, *Ich hatte viel Bekümmernis* (I Had Great Sorrow). There can be no doubt that Brahms deliberately recalled the duet for soprano and alto with continuo from Cantata No. 4 in his setting of Michael Weisse's fifth stanza. Bach's two-note phrases thrown from one voice to the next, followed by a long melisma in imitation, are mirrored almost exactly by Brahms. This portion of the *Begräbnisgesang* stands somewhat apart from the remainder: not only does the music for the first time move away from its home tonality of C, in a section that modulates continually, but the "hocketing" voices and the yearning ascending melodic intervals for the sopranos, altos, and clarinets contrast strongly with the surrounding material.

The penultimate stanza returns to the music of the first major-mode section, before the sopranos again fall silent, and a reprise of the work's opening material completes the archlike symmetry of the whole. "Death comes to us in the same way" concludes Michael Weisse; and Brahms's music moves quietly and inevitably toward a unison on the final syllable, while the drum taps out the rhythm of the major-mode middle section, before a closing chord resolves the music in the major, offering a glimpse of comfort.

Misha Donat

4 GESÄNGE, FOR WOMEN'S CHORUS, TWO HORNS, AND HARP, OPUS 17

Composed 1860; published 1862

1. Es tönt ein voller Harfenklang [Ruperti]
2. Lied von Shakespeare (Komm herbei, komm herbei) [Shakespeare; *Twelfth Night*]
3. Der Gärtner [Eichendorff]
4. Gesang aus *Fingal* [Ossian]

These four songs were written in February 1860 in Hamburg and performed in January of the following year by the Women's Chorus of Hamburg, founded by Brahms in 1859. The songs offer a convincing account both of Brahms's engagement with literary Romanticism and his developing confidence with orchestration. The opening text, by the obscure poet Friedrich Ruperti, whose collection of early poems appeared in 1851, sets the tone for the entire collection. With it Brahms is able to justify quite literally the unusual orchestration of the songs—harp and two horns, which constitutes the opening sonority of the first ten bars of the work: Ruperti's poem begins, "Es tönt ein voller Harfenklang" (The rich tones of the harp resound). The horn solo may remind listeners of Brahms's lyrical use of the French horn in other works, particularly the First Symphony, Op. 68, and the Horn Trio, Op. 40. The Romantic quality of this combination of instruments has been much commented upon, but it should also be noted that these works, along with Brahms's other compositions for women's voices from the late 1850s, coincide with his close study of counterpoint and orchestration with Joseph Joachim. When he assumed the directorship of the choir at Detmold, Brahms was initially hesitant to provide complicated repertory, but as his studies led him to Baroque and Renaissance models, he became bolder. The orchestration of Op. 17 represents an effective solution to the particular problems of composing for a chorus of women's voices without male sonorities. How does one find a contrast to register and timbre without detracting from the voices' special quality? In this work, the horns function both as accompaniment and contrast without getting in the way, while the harp provides the rhythmic propulsion often supplied by keyboard instruments.

These songs also indicate the range and subtlety of Brahms's reading habits. Unlike other autodidacts, he ventured on his own beyond established figures, as the choice of Ruperti alongside canonic writers indicates. And it is also revealing that Brahms read texts musically—that is, he chose them not only for the varieties of ordinary meanings that might be evident to readers but also for the music suggested by the words and word orders in terms of tonality, rhythm, and timbre.

The Ruperti song is in C major and is followed by a setting of Schlegel's translation of a song from Shakespeare's *Twelfth Night* (or What You Will) "Komm herbei, komm herbei" (Come away, Death), in E♭ major. A somewhat more brisk piece follows, *Der Gärtner* (The Gardener) by Eichendorff, also in E♭. Having opened the work in C major, Brahms ends it in C minor, the relative minor of E♭ major. This last song is the most ambitious and the longest of the four, and has the most adventurous harmonies. That Brahms reserved the most mysterious sound for Herder's translation of Ossian is not unusual, for this text (taken from MacPherson's *Fingal*) was an almost clichéd emblem of Romantic enthusiasm. Ossian, the Celtic bard who was the fictitious invention of James MacPherson, offered German Romantics a seemingly legitimate competitor to Homer. Goethe's Werther was deeply attached to Ossian, as were Mendelssohn and Schumann.

These works are lyrical and restrained. They show both the simplicity and depth of the young Brahms's interior and his capacity for Romantic self-absorption, particularly at a time when his relationship with Clara Schumann had passed its most intense phase. There is a wistfulness about the songs which makes it even more of a pity that the genre of works for women's choir, particularly with such unusual orchestration, has fallen into obscurity.

Leon Botstein

Psalm 13, for Three-Part Women's Chorus and Organ or Piano, Opus 27

Composed 1859; published 1864

This work was composed for three-part women's chorus with accompaniment by either organ or piano. In a letter to Clara Schumann, Brahms makes reference to a setting of *Psalm 13* for women's chorus and small orchestra. Copyist's parts of an orchestral version still exist, and Brahms performed this work in 1876 in Vienna with organ and orchestra. The only published version, however, is for keyboard accompaniment. The first performance took place with organ accompaniment in

September 1859, with Brahms conducting the Hamburg Women's Chorus. *Psalm 13* has three sections: a slow introduction, a middle Allegro, and a final Allegro non troppo. The work begins in G minor and closes in G major—a progress befitting the text, which opens with a plea to God not to forget the singer, and ends with the expectation of God's grace and help, and the desire to sing to God's glory. The work, as Max Kalbeck puts it, has an almost "conventlike" simplicity to it.

As Malcolm MacDonald suggests, *Psalm 13* is reminiscent of Mendelssohn in the way the setting emphasizes the hopeful sensibilities of the text. In this regard, the work embodies Brahms's complex and often neglected relationship to religion and theology. Brahms's pessimism and melancholy disposition are widely discussed as dominant traits in his personality. If one compares the *Four Serious Songs,* Op. 121, written at the end of his life, to Op. 27, written in the summer of 1859, one can get a sense of the unresolved conflict in Brahms's attitude to faith. His oft-discussed mode of spirituality based in a sense of suffering, replete with continuous tension between faith and the bitter realities of modern life and the historical moment, defines the quintessential character of Brahms and the contemplative, bittersweet qualities of many of his most important works. But there was also the Brahms who copied out German proverbs for Clara Schumann's children in 1855. This selection of proverbs, roughly contemporaneous with the setting of *Psalm 13,* shows how capable the composer was of a more traditional, direct, and trusting Protestant outlook in which grace and redemption are possible.

Although *Psalm 13* has been, comparatively speaking, neglected because it seems not to fit with our image of Brahms as a dour and unsentimental personality, it reflects Brahms's abiding allegiance to a prevailing trust in God. He never lost the conviction that the search for an affirmative approach to the trials and tribulations of life is neither false nor in vain. The comparison to Mendelssohn is therefore apt, for *Psalm 13* approximates Mendelssohn's capacity to reconcile great music and the ethos of affirmation. This work offers a caution against the undifferentiated stereotype of Brahms's beliefs. It should inspire us not to pass over Brahms's apparently simpler and more straightforward works in order to come to terms with the composer's "complex" side. Ironically, in neglecting those translucent works which give voice to Brahms's faith and optimism, one risks the danger of simplifying Brahms by suppressing a decisive element of his character. Our bias toward the artist as a tortured soul, the idealized typology of genres so celebrated at the *fin de siécle,* has led scholars and concertgoers sometimes to explain works such as Psalm 13 away as more occasional pieces. The fact that nearly two decades after its composition, Brahms revived *Psalm 13* and experimented with a variety of accompaniments to it suggests that he did not think Op. 27 a lesser work. Rather, it reminds us of a dimension of Brahms the composer and the man that modern observers have lost the capacity to appreciate easily. In this expression of Brahms's belief in order, goodness, and symmetry, we should resist the conditioned impression that such music is any way superficial. Brahms revered the simplicity of song as a mirror of God's grace and as an eminently legitimate ground for thankfulness.

Leon Botstein

GEISTLICHES LIED, FOR FOUR-PART MIXED CHORUS AND ORGAN OR PIANO, OPUS 30
Composed 1856; published 1864 [Text: Fleming]

Following Schumann's confinement in an asylum in 1854, Brahms helped Clara Schumann organize their large library of early music. He made his own manuscript copies of several pieces of Renaissance polyphony, including two responsories attributed to Palestrina (they have now been accurately assigned to Marc' Antonio Ingegneri); and in February 1855 Brahms proudly told Clara that he "could make canons in all possible artistic forms." The following month he invited her to join him in his contrapuntal studies: "I am really looking forward to one [day] when we shall pass the time, besides taking walks—with counterpoint! We should set each other exercises, the same for each, and then collect and gather them together. Should Joachim come, he must join us. We often discussed wanting to do such studies together. I think it would be wonderfully interesting and amusing."

Brahms must have been aware that nearly ten years earlier Clara Schumann had encouraged her husband to study counterpoint, as a means of calming his mind during a severe bout of depression, and he may well have suggested a similar course of action at this stage in order to divert Clara's attention from Robert Schumann's plight. Clara noted in her diary that she had begun theoretical studies with Brahms, but the plan appears to have made little further progress, and in February 1856, Brahms turned instead to Joachim. The great violinist eagerly agreed to an exchange of contrapuntal studies, and Brahms thought it best to formalize the rules of their correspondence:

> Every Sunday exercises must go back and forth. On one Sunday, for example, you send. On the next I return the exercise with one of my own, and so forth. But whoever misses the day—that is, sends nothing—must send instead one taler which the other can use to buy books!!! Only if instead of an exercise one sends a composition is he excused. Will you join in? Double counterpoint, canons, fugues, preludes, or whatever it may be.

Beginning on March 24, Brahms sent Joachim circular canons, canons based on the subject of Bach's *Art of Fugue*—and, on June 5, two organ fugues (one of them with a prelude), and his *Geistliches Lied*—the last being the only one of these contrapuntal exercises Brahms eventually considered worthy of publication, though revised versions of two "innocent canonic melodies" he sent Joachim on June 22 were included in his *Drei geistliche Chöre*, Op. 37. "I have of course been practicing the organ lately," Brahms told Joachim, "from which these come. No doubt the canon [*Geistliches Lied*] does not especially please you? The interludes are quite terrible? The "Amen" (I mean the word generally) will do; that part pleases me the most."

Although the *Geistliches Lied* met with his approval, Joachim criticized Brahms for paying too little attention to the music's harmonic effect:

> I have nothing at all against the "Amen" at the conclusion; on the contrary, I like it; the organ point must make a holy, devout effect. But there are many harsh places! For example, in the Amen in question, the tenor, which is beautiful in and of itself, clashes all too harshly with the alto and soprano at the place marked! Your ear is so used to rugged harmony in a polyphonic texture of this kind that you rarely think about the voices solely on the basis of their relation to one another—because with you what is proper in that regard is associated equally with what completes it. You can't ask that from a listener, even the most musical one; and since in the end all art is meant to bring pleasure, since that is its most sacred privilege, I ask you to think it over. Often (in all your things) it spoils my unalloyed pleasure, which otherwise they give me as do those of no other living composer.

The form of the *Geistliches Lied,* and the severity of the contrapuntal challenge Brahms set himself, is accurately described by the heading of the autograph score: "Double canon at the ninth." Of the two canons, one unfolds in the soprano and tenor lines, the other in the alto and bass. The text is by the seventeenth-century writer Paul Flemming, and like much of his earlier poetry it has a biblical origin. Here, a free, punning adaptation of verse from the Gospel according to St. John provides a consolatory prayer, and it is difficult not to imagine that Brahms addressed his setting in the first place to Clara Schumann, in her time of adversity.

Lass dich nur nichts dauern	[Let nothing afflict thee
Mit Trauern,	with grief;
Sei stille,	be calm,
Wie Gott es fügt,	as God ordains,
So sei vergnügt	and so shall my will
Mein Wille.	be satisfied.]

That Brahms had Clara's plight in mind is indicated by the material of the organ prelude, and the interludes separating the three verses of Fleming's poem. The prelude, beginning as though in mid-thought, is largely based on a turnlike figure—an anticipation, in inverted form, of the first of the two canons setting the opening line of the text. By the sixth bar of the prelude, this turnlike idea has evolved into an unmistakable quotation of the main theme from the finale of Schumann's Fourth Symphony—the work he once called his "Clara" Symphony.

Brahms sets the poem's three verses to a straightforward ternary design, giving special emphasis in the outer sections to Fleming's shortest line—"Sei stille" and "Steh fest" (be steadfast), respectively—by allowing the material of the two canons momentarily to coincide. The central stanza is differentiated from the remainder of the work not only by its new canonic theme, which presents the turnlike figure in the form in which it had appeared in the opening organ prelude, and its change of key (C minor, as opposed to the E♭ major of the outer sections), but also its texture: four measures for chorus alone, without the support of the organ, provide an entirely fresh sonority.

The concluding "Amen," which caused Joachim so much grief, unfolds throughout its length over a pedal note of E♭ on the organ. Here Brahms abandons his strict canonic writing, in favor of freely imitative voices whose soaring, fervent melodic lines and harmonic suspensions add to the music's intensity. As the work dies away to its peaceful conclusion, a plagal cadence in simple hymn style provides a postscript of touching simplicity.

Misha Donat

EIN DEUTSCHES REQUIEM, FOR SOLOISTS, CHORUS, AND ORCHESTRA, OPUS 45

Composed 1857–68; published 1868

SCORING: piccolo, 2 flutes, 2 oboes, 2 clarinets, 2 bassoons, 4 horns, 2 trumpets, 3 trombones, tuba, timpani, harp, strings

1. Selig sind die da Leid tragen [Matthew 4; Psalm 126:5–6]
2. Denn alles Fleisch [1 Peter 1:24–5; James 7; Isaiah 25:10]
3. Herr, lehre doch mich [Psalm 89:5–8; Wisdom of Solomon 3:1]
4. Wie lieblich sind deine Wohungen [Psalm 74:2–3,5]
5. Ihr habt nun Traurigkeit [John 16:22; Ecclesiasticus 51:35; Isaiah 66:13]
6. Denn wir haben hier [Hebrews 13:14; 1 Corinthians 15: 51–5; Revelation 4:11]
7. Selig sind die Toten [Revelation 14:13]

Ein deutsches Requiem (A German Requiem), Opus 45, was composed over an eleven-year period, and premiered incrementally as it took its final form. The first three sections were essayed unsuccessfully in Vienna late in 1867. The first "complete" performance was given in Bremen on Good Friday of 1868, but what has become the fifth section for soprano solo ("Ihr habt nun Traurigkeit") was added subsequently. Thus the first performance of the final version, in seven parts, took place in Leipzig on February 18, 1869.

The work's incremental origins are interesting for various reasons. As the *Requiem* developed into what would stand as Brahms's largest-scale work, it also developed into his most personal one. It is personal in both its commemorative and confessional aspects.

As a musical act of commemoration, the work's initial motivation, as Max Kalbeck suggested, followed the death of Robert Schumann in 1856. Brahms had apparently planned a work in a single movement, which he had not completed. The *Requiem*'s commemorative work was overtaken in early 1865 by the death of Brahms's mother, Christiane. Brahms's first musical commemoration of his mother appears in the Adagio mesto movement of the Horn Trio, Op. 40, with its quotation from the folk song *Dort in den Weiden steht ein Haus*. It is as a further act of musical mourning for his mother that Brahms returned to the *Requiem* in 1865 and 1866. The addition of the movement for soprano solo makes explicit the maternal aura that had come to surround the piece, emphasizing as well the tone of intimacy that alternates throughout with public solemnity.

The combination of the intimate and the solemn reveals its confessional character as decisively Protestant. The label "German" is thus
to be understood as "North German"—referring to the Protestant na-
tivism of Luther and Bach. Indeed, one astute listener—the surgeon
Theodor Billroth—diagnosed cultural difference as the root of the failure
of the first three movements to please the Viennese: "I like Brahms better every time I meet him," he wrote to a friend. "His *Requiem* is so nobly
spiritual and so Protestant-Bachish that it was difficult to make it go
down here."

None of the traditional liturgical texts of the Catholic Requiem Mass
is used. The Roman Catholic Requiem Mass is prayer for the salvation of
the dead from the terror of damnation by intoning the power of Christ
and the dogma of the Resurrection. Brahms chose his texts from Luther's
Bible—texts used previously by Heinrich Schütz in his *Cantiones sacrae* of
1625 and his *Geistliche Chormusik* of 1648—interspersing selections from
the Hebrew Bible (Psalms, Isaiah, Song of Solomon, Ecclesiastes) and
the Christian (Matthew, Peter, James, John, Hebrews, Corinthians, Revelation). Christ and Resurrection go unmentioned. Rather, the focus is on
death, survival, mourning, and renewal. As the musical enactment of a
ritual of mourning, the *German Requiem* follows the Protestant duality of
privacy and community, with choral writing symbolizing community.
At the same time, the music's dependence on long, arched phrases gives
the solitary listener the sense that the immense musical edifice rises and
subsides with every breath.

The central message of consolation is stated in the first section's opening phrase (Matthew 5:4): "Blessed are they that mourn; for they shall be
comforted." It is repeated often, most clearly in the final section, which
structurally echoes the first and carries the line (Revelation 14:13)
"Blessed are the dead which die in the Lord from henceforth."

But it is, paradoxically, in the fifth section that the theological and
musical discourse of consolation is evinced in its subtlest and simplest.
The soprano, intoning the maternal voice, says, "I will see you again, and
your heart will rejoice," while the choral line states, "I will comfort you as
one is comforted by his mother." There is little doubt that the first-
person voice of the soprano represents the mother—specifically, Brahms's
own mother. The choral voice here would seem to represent music itself,
which claims the capacity to console *as* a mother would. In that word *as*
lies all the difference: between the return of the dead and the memory of
the dead; between magic and memory; between grace and consolation;

between dependence and autonomy. Music's sensuality marks it as the actual sublimation of maternal consolation.

The consolation no longer available from the mother resides now in music alone, now in the inner self alone. Expressed in the *Requiem* through the reminiscent presence of a soprano voice uttering words of literal consolation, the consolation of music is then internalized, in the later works, into patterns of sound alone.

There is also a paternal voice in the *Requiem*. It is personified most explicitly in the baritone solos. This manly voice doesn't console, it calls to action. In the *Requiem*'s sixth section, the baritone solo repeats the call made musically famous by Handel's *Messiah*: "Behold, I tell you a mystery; we shall not sleep, but we shall all be changed, in a moment, in the twinkling of an eye, at the last trumpet." Like its maternal counterpart in the music of consolation, this voice of paternal militancy is sublimated into a purely musical presence. Its musical heir is that aspect of the *Requiem*'s music that is militant and even dogmatic, as in the consistently resurgent timpani. In places such as in the *Requiem*'s second section ("For all flesh is as grass"), at the conclusion of the third section ("The souls of the righteous are in the hand of God"), and in other works, such as the opening measures of Brahms's First Symphony, the timpani resounds with so dogmatic a fervor as to suggest that it is being pounded directly by Martin Luther's fists.

By the time the largest structural arc of the *Requiem* has been traversed—in the seventh section's repetition of the first one's message of consolation—a reconciliation between these maternal and paternal voices has been achieved. At some level, this is the reconciliation between his parents that Brahms could not literally achieve; they had separated in 1864, and he had vainly tried to reunite them.

Mourning involves recovery—particularly the recovery from the self held hostage to the dead. The mourning for a parent is particularly significant psychic work in this regard, as the self has in any case to be molded in the act of separation from the parent. There are at least two parents commemorated in the *German Requiem*: a natural mother and, in Robert Schumann, a musical father. Indeed, Brahms would never lose the sense of himself as a son, the son of at least four parents, including Robert and Clara Schumann, and the son of a North German tradition stretching back to Bach and Schütz. Robert Schumann thus stands as the most immediate musical father in Brahms's vividly present pantheon, intoning the contradictory paternal command at once to create and to obey.

The *Requiem* sets a musical agenda of reconciliation that will inform Brahms's music from this moment on. More than a century of Brahms's listeners have understood, perhaps unconsciously, the meaning and success of this musical discourse of reconciliation. This is the reconciliation of the maternal and the paternal, of the masculine and the feminine, and of the north and the south. It is a cultural achievement as well as a musical one.

The central European *fin de siècle* redounds with analogous, if less successful, discourses of reconciliation. Max Weber, the founder of modern German sociology, a generation younger than Brahms, suffered keenly between the draw of the inward religiosity of his southern German mother and the imperative of rationality and power he absorbed from his Prussian father. Unable in the end to reconcile the polarity, he abandoned any hope for consolation. In the renowned conclusion to his 1920 *The Protestant Ethic and the Spirit of Capitalism,* he describes the modern predicament as an iron cage.

Sigmund Freud confronted similar issues as he pioneered the psychoanalytic theory of the personality in the late 1890s. The mature personality, he began to argue, accrues as childhood desires are necessarily organized into socially functional behavior. With a male bias that remains controversial, Freud suggested that the mother was the first object of desire and the father the first countervailing, disciplining presence. Maturation subsequently involves the internalization—in correct dosages—of the disciplining presence of the father with the appropriate replacement of the mother with another object of desire. What Freud could never work out, in his evolving understanding of human development, was a model for the internalization of the mother. Psychoanalysis thus duplicated the Protestant narrative of the internalization of law and conscience. In the century since Freud developed his argument, psychoanalysis has struggled with great difficulty to develop a discourse of consolation that would be compatible with its central discourse of discovery and truth, rather than one that would in fact constitute a new crime of seduction.

From the foundation of the *Requiem,* Brahms did begin to work through, inarticulately, in music alone, the knotty problem of the co-internalization of law and consolation, of truth and comfort. The deepening harmony of militance and consolation in his developing musical oeuvre points to a notion of the self as an integrator of maternal and paternal resonance. Brahms's musical itinerary points indeed to a resolution—however fleeting or inarticulate—of the cultural codes and anxieties of masculinity and femininity. As listeners—however inarticulate— to this music a century later, do we not also want to draw from it a similar power of reconciliation?

The popularity and significance of Brahms's music resides in its combination of intransigence and lyricism, in how it makes us feel at once inspired and consoled. We may have underestimated both what we want from Brahms and what his music can give us. More than making us feel at times inspired and at times consoled, Brahms is able to weave both of these rhetorics together. It is the harmonization of militance and consolation that is unique in Brahms's music, making it as much a music for our own *fin de siècle* as it was for his.

Michael P. Steinberg

RINALDO, CANTATA FROM GOETHE, FOR TENOR, MEN'S CHORUS, AND ORCHESTRA, OPUS 50

Composed 1863–68; Published 1869

SCORING: piccolo, 2 flutes, 2 oboes, 2 clarinets, 2 bassoons, 2 horns, 2 trumpets, 3 trombones, timpani, strings

Rinaldo is among the largest of Brahms's works for vocal and orchestral forces; only *Ein deutsches Requiem* surpasses it in length and breadth. Conceived early in the summer of 1863 as an entry in a competition sponsored by the Aachen *Liedertafel,* the cantata was not completed until June 1868. Details regarding its genesis are sadly lacking. We can infer from Brahms's correspondence that after a period of intense absorption in the project (though not intense enough to meet the competition's October deadline), his interest waned. Perhaps his attention was also diverted by his new duties as director of Vienna's Singakademie. According to Max Kalbeck, the composition of the final chorus *(Schlusschor)* proved to be a sticking point. In the interim between the cantata's conception and completion, the entire work may have been sketched out in some form, and with a closing chorus quite different from the one we now have: in a letter to Karl Reinthaler of June 1868, Brahms spoke of having finished "a grand new *Schlusschor.*"

For his text, Brahms turned to Goethe, whose *Rinaldo* dates from 1811 and was intended from the start as a dramatic scena for musical setting. Goethe in turn drew upon an episode from Tasso's heroic-allegorical-fantastical epic of the Crusades, *Gerusalemme liberata,* in which the knight Rinaldo is spirited away to the enchanted isle of the sorceress Armida. As Tasso relates this adventure, the knight's comrades set off to retrieve their friend, and, having broken Armida's magical spell, witness the enchantress's vengeful destruction of her luxurious palace and gardens. Goethe picks up the narrative thread at this juncture, but in his poem, Armida's magic is not quite dispelled; it remains a potent and nagging force in the memory of the hapless Rinaldo, who rejoins his fellow knights only after persistent coaxing. The tale had obvious autobiographical resonance for Brahms, whose painful break with the young Agathe von Siebold in 1859 brought to the surface a conflict between love and duty that the composer would also inscribe in another compositional project spanning the 1860s, the *Magelone Romanzen,* Op. 33.

The Viennese premiere of *Rinaldo* on February 28, 1869, with Brahms conducting the Akademischer Gesangverein and Wiener Hofopernorchester, was in many ways a success. Brahms himself was extremely pleased, and the reviewer for Leipzig's *Allgemeine musikalische Zeitung* expressed his admiration for the composer's skillful handling of the voices, his deft orchestration, and the motivic unity of the score. Not every listener, however, was as enthusiastic. Clara Schumann, for instance, doubted whether the new cantata was a worthy successor to the *Requiem.* Reviewing an 1883 performance, Eduard Hanslick found Brahms's musical portrayal of the title character devoid of passion. Nor has posterity been kind to *Rinaldo:* the work is rarely performed today.

In part, *Rinaldo*'s inability to obtain a stronghold in the repertory can be ascribed to the vagaries of reception history. On one hand, the institutional foundation for works such as this—the mixed choral societies and men's choruses that abounded in German-speaking lands during Brahms's day—has simply eroded over time. On the other hand, an informed reaction to Brahms's cantata is predicated not only on an understanding of its text but also on a familiarity with the sixteenth-century epic on which Goethe based his poem. While Brahms may have assumed that his audience knew the earlier text, such an assumption cannot be made today.

Without pretending to say for certain why *Rinaldo* has been shunted to the periphery of the Brahms canon, we might at least sketch the context in which the work came to be written. For some writers, Brahms's contacts between 1862 and 1864 with members of Wagner's circle (Peter Cornelius and Carl Tausig) and with Wagner himself constitute a significant aspect of this context. Hanslick was not alone in drawing a connection between Rinaldo's enthrallment to Armida and Tannhäuser's languishing in the arms of Venus. Later commentators have also noted a Wagnerian quality in the declamatory passages of Rinaldo's arias and in Brahms's situation of the motivic substance in the orchestra during these sections. But if Brahms called himself a "Wagnerian" in a letter of December 29, 1862, to Joachim, he proved to be a highly imperfect one. *Rinaldo* owes just as much to Beethoven's *Fidelio* (especially at the moment when the hero sees his moral degeneration reflected in the diamond shield) and to Schubert's incompletely preserved cantata *Lazarus* as it does to Wagner's romantic operas and music dramas.

Rinaldo should also be viewed against the background of the aesthetic of opera Brahms evolved during his long and unsuccessful search for a suitable operatic subject, a search extending from the late 1860s, when Ivan Turgenev offered him a six-page scenario, through the early 1880s. It is clear from Brahms's letters and comments to friends that the Mozartean number opera represented something of an ideal, and that depth of musical content counted for more than mere theatrical effect. Surprisingly, many of the texts Brahms considered for operatic treatment (for example, Carlo Gozzi's *Love for Three Oranges, King Stag,* and *The Raven*) place supernatural or magical elements in bold relief. This quality likewise hearkens to the textual themes of *Rinaldo*. Indeed, what E.T.A. Hoffmann said of Gozzi's *The Raven* applies just as well to Goethe's dramatic scena: the miraculous happenings in both aim to show how magic is a consequence "of the influence of higher natures on our lives."

Finally, Brahms's attitude toward the musical realization of epic-dramatic texts was decisively shaped by Schumann. Throughout his career, Brahms maintained the highest regard for his mentor's settings of seven scenes from Goethe's *Faust* and his melodramatic treatment of Byron's *Manfred*. In these works (and also in the opera *Genoveva* and the late choral-orchestral ballades on Uhland texts), Schumann's approach was guided above all by two factors: fidelity to the original literary source, and the musical reflection of the text's dramaturgy. Both factors figure prominently in Brahms's *Rinaldo*.

The critic who reviewed the cantata's premiere for the *Allgemeine musikalische Zeitung* emphasized Brahms's unwillingness to alter "even an iota" of Goethe's text. But as noted above, Goethe gave a new slant to *his* poetic source. The struggle between duty to a cause and sensual pleasure in Tasso's poem is enriched, in Goethe's retelling, by a pair of interrelated themes: the notion that memory could be powerful enough to call up the vision of what Baudelaire later called an artificial paradise, and the conviction that the recognition of this vision as a chimera would result in a striking transformation of character. Ultimately, Goethe's poem tells, in a stylized, "classical" language, of the pain wrought by the destruction of an illusion.

Brahms responded sensitively to these themes. His *Rinaldo* reflects the classical tone of the text through a large-scale, symmetrical structure and through the design of the smaller parts comprising the whole. The cantata is framed by two choruses, both in E♭, the first (prefaced by an orchestral introduction) a rousing series of exhortations directed at the hero, the second a boisterous celebration of his return to the Holy Land with his men. Within the frame come two extended arias (amplified with choral interpolations) for the title character. Both of these are in turn grounded in the paradigm for the grand aria established in the late eighteenth and early nineteenth centuries, where an initial recitative gives way to a lyrical *cavatina* and a quicker *cabaletta*, the latter two sections generally falling into *ABA* or similar forms.

Brahms projects the allurements of Armida's artificial paradise through a variety of textual and tonal means. Rinaldo's hallucinatory vision of the enchantress's realm is associated with orchestral colors dominated by the upper winds and at times supported by pizzicato strings. The otherworldliness of this vision is further underscored by the often torturous chromaticism of Rinaldo's vocal lines, and by the fluid modulations by thirds that pervade his arias (the first moves through A♭, E, and C, the second through F♯ minor, A minor, and C minor.) In contrast, Brahms characterizes the "real" world of the knights through mellow brass sonorities, chorale-like or imitative textures, and a predominantly diatonic idiom.

Equally compelling is Brahms's reaction to the intertwined themes of memory and transformation, poetic conceits that find their musical complements in the techniques of motivic recall and transformation. The cantata's principal musical idea, a finely spun-out line presented at the outset, accrues referential specificity only gradually. When heard in conjunction with Rinaldo's opening words, "Ihr ward [wart] so schön" (You were so beautiful), it functions as a sonic metaphor for the image of Armida and her realm preserved in the hero's memory. But when, in the concluding section of his second aria, Rinaldo sees the enchantress as a she-devil and her artificial paradise as a wasteland, his hallucination calls forth a stunning series of transformations of the main musical idea: its initial E♭ major is displaced by C minor, its pastoral tone by frightening orchestral outbursts, and its gentle dips and curves by wrenching chromaticism.

The melodic alterations of the main theme have a counterpart in the harmonic reinterpretations that articulate the moment of dramatic reversal, when Rinaldo views the image of his moral decay as reflected in the diamond shield. Here, a quiet D♭-major fanfare in the trumpets dissolves into an impressionistic haze as it is echoed by trombones and timpani. The auratic quality of the passage is further enhanced by a long-held D♭ fanned out over four octaves in the strings. Rinaldo, however, "misreads" the pedal tone as a C♯, causing the music to shift from the prevailing D♭ tonality to a languid F♯ minor.

This tonal dislocation is an emblem for the pain experienced by the hero as he passes from a dream state to consciousness of the harsh actualities of the real world. Rinaldo's pain persists in varying forms until the end of the work: it can be heard in the plangent strains of his second aria and, soon thereafter, in his minor-mode echoes of the chorus's consoling phrases: "Unglücklicher Reise! Unseliger Wind!" (Unhappy journey! Unfortunate wind!). It persists in the *Schlusschor* by way of Brahms's deliberately equivocal marking: Rinaldo's participation in the final celebration is indicated by a parenthetical *ad lib*. With this simple gesture, the composer underlines a crucial aspect of Goethe's message. The wounds acquired through past misfortunes, he seems to say, are never entirely healed.   *John Daverio*

RHAPSODY, FOR ALTO, MEN'S CHORUS, AND ORCHESTRA, OPUS 53
Composed 1869; published 1870

SCORING: 2 flutes, 2 oboes, 2 clarinets, 2 bassoons, 2 horns, strings [Text: Goethe]

As happens with most artists, some of Brahms's works—by no means all—arose from personal experiences, bad and good. None, however, seemed to emerge so directly and dramatically from his life as the *Rhapsody für Altstimme, Männerchor und Orchester,* generally called the *Alto Rhapsody.*

Its genesis can be traced precisely. On May 11, 1869, soon after his thirty-sixth birthday, Brahms was visiting Clara Schumann in Baden-Baden when she announced that her daughter Julie, then twenty-four, was to be married to an Italian nobleman. Clara was astonished to find Brahms tremendously upset at the news; for days afterward he remained uncommunicative, as if in shock. Her suspicions about the reason were confirmed by their mutual friend, conductor Hermann Levi, to whom Brahms had spilled his feelings: for years Brahms had been nursing an unspoken infatuation for the most beautiful of the Schumann daughters. "Did he really love her?" Clara asked her diary incredulously. "But he has never thought of marrying, and Julie never had any inclination toward him."

Given the old, peculiar but inescapable relationship between Brahms and Clara Schumann, one would expect her to react with outrage to the revelation that Brahms had fallen for her daughter. Instead, Clara appeared to see this passion for the sad spectacle it was, and became unusually kind and solicitous toward him. For his part Brahms, with uncharacteristic lack of common sense, pictured Julie's engagement as a betrayal of himself. Entirely characteristically, he kept his misery largely silent and behaved decently about the wedding, joining in the festivities and giving the couple presents. (By then, he was consoling himself in a flirtation with a young Russian pianist.)

A week after the wedding, Brahms brought the *Alto Rhapsody* to Clara, telling her curtly that it was his "bridal song." He knew she would understand what he meant. She wrote in her journal, "It is long since I remember being so moved by a depth of pain in words and music. . . . This piece seems to me neither more nor less than the expression of his own heart's anguish. If only he would for once speak so tenderly!" To another friend Brahms described the *Rhapsody* as "the epilogue to the *Liebeslieder*," which reveals that those gay and ardent love songs had also been written with Julie Schumann in mind.

The text of the *Rhapsody* is a fragment from Goethe's "Harzreise im Winter," chosen with Brahms's reliable gift for finding poetic texts to express his own feelings. For all the intimacy of the music, it is no less meticulously crafted, hardly less magisterial in tone than he usually was by this point in his career. His anguish permeates the music all the same. It begins in tremolo strings with an agitated dissonance, the colors dark— a striking effect of muted violins and open lower strings, the tonality drifting far from the underlying C minor. The chill of winter seems to pervade the music, but a chill of spirit more than body. "But who is that standing apart?" the alto intones, like a woman addressing the solitary Brahms. She continues in a mournful recitative:

Aber abseits, wer ist's?	His steps recede into the bushes,
Ins Gebüsch verliert sich sein Pfad. . . .	The thickets close behind him. . . .
Die Öde verschlingt ihn.	The barren waste swallows him up.

An aria follows the recitative—almost a true operatic aria and perhaps the finest of its kind that Brahms ever wrote:

Ach, wer heilet die Schmerzen	Ah, who can heal the pains of one
Des, dem Balsam zu Gift ward?	For whom balm has become poison,
Der sich menschenhaß	And who sucked hatred of mankind
Aus der Fülle der Liebe trank?	From the abundance of love?

After the misanthropic bleakness of those lines, set to music dark and wandering in both tonality and rhythm (much two-against-three, neither settled), there is a pause. Then a prayer breaks out in the men's choir, beginning in unambiguous C major, direct and heartfelt as a hymn. The alto soloist soars above the men:

Ist auf deinem Psalter,	If in your psaltery,
Vater der Liebe, ein Ton	Father of Love, there is a tone
Seinem Ohre vernehmlich	Which his ear can discern,
So erquicke sein Herz!	Refresh his heart!
Öffne den umwölkten Blick	Open to his clouded gaze
Über die tausend Quellen	The thousand springs
Neben dem Durstenden	Alongside him as he thirsts
In der Wüste.	In the wilderness.

Those words express Brahms's feelings and his purpose in the work. The psaltery of the end, the harp of God's succor that Goethe invoked, was for the poet simply a metaphor. For Brahms the composer, the harp stands for the healing power of music, and so stands for the *Alto Rhapsody* itself.

Brahms's connection to this text, however, goes beyond that. Given his considerable knowledge of German history and literature, he may have known that for Goethe, the journey to the Harz Mountains came at a turning point—away from his youth toward a more mature vision of his life and work. Certainly Brahms knew about the acquaintance of the poet's who had inspired the text. It was a youth who had fallen into depression under the spell of Goethe's novel *The Sorrows of Young Werther,* about a man who kills himself for love of a friend's betrothed. In the wrenching years of Robert Schumann's decline and death in the asylum, when Brahms fell headlong in love with Clara Schumann, he had identified himself intensely with the suffering figure of Werther.

The *Rhapsody* was premiered in Jena on March 3, 1870, by the contralto Pauline Viardot-Garcia and the Akademischer Gesangverein. The piece represents a turning point in Brahms's life, as "Harzreise im Winter" had been for Goethe. Even though it is a short piece—thirteen minutes—with it, Brahms returned not only to the top of his form as a composer for the first time since *Ein deutsches Requiem*, but returned to joy in his creativity after a fallow period. He wrote his publisher Simrock that he considered the *Rhapsody* the best thing he had done.

The piece also represents Brahms's melancholy acceptance that at age thirty-six all he had was his art. In that sense too it is his bridal song, his final embrace of solitude after years of yearning for wife, home, and family (and at the same time fleeing every opportunity to gain them). Whatever succor and redemption from misanthropy and despair he might find in life, he would find henceforth in music. There would be more flirtations with women and fantasies of marriage here and there, but none really serious.

So the *Rhapsody* can stand as another of Brahms's farewells to love, and appears to have been that in his own mind. It is significant that he does not end the piece with Goethe's "Wüste," but rather backs up in the poem to end with the possibility (though not certainty) of consolation: "Refresh his heart!" It concludes with the familiar IV-I *Amen* cadence. Yet the word "Wüste" would be conspicuous in Brahms's letters in the next years; it refers to desert, wilderness, wasteland. And in choral works of the coming years, the sense of wasteland and inexorable human fate would overpower the song of hope that ends the *Alto Rhapsody*.

Jan Swafford

SCHICKSALSLIED, FOR CHORUS AND ORCHESTRA, OPUS 54
Composed 1868–71; published 1871

SCORING: 2 flutes, 2 oboes, 2 clarinets, 2 horns, 2 trumpets, 3 trombones, timpani, strings [Text: Hölderlin]

In May 1870, Brahms wrote his friend Julius Otto Grimm that he had finished "a second piece in the manner of" the *Alto Rhapsody*, Op. 53, meaning a medium-length work for chorus and orchestra. The inception of the piece went back two years, to a visit with the family of composer and conductor Albert Dietrich. At Brahms's request, the Dietrichs and friends had taken a sightseeing trip to the great Wilhelmshaven, a naval port, during which Brahms excused himself and vanished. Later, Dietrich saw him sitting on the beach writing music. He was sketching a setting of Friedrich Hölderlin's *Hyperions Schicksalslied*, which he had read at Dietrich's earlier that day. Given the regularity of his habits, especially the rigid regime of composing alone from dawn to early afternoon, the idea of Brahms hurrying away from friends to compose was unusual, an indication of how much the verses had seized him.

The orchestral introduction of the *Schicksalslied* is a singular moment in his music, ethereal and dreamlike, with an underlying timpani impulse that in Brahms tends to be associated with the idea of fate (other examples are the *Begräbnisgesang*, the "All flesh is as grass" movement of *Ein deutsches Requiem*, and the introduction to the First Symphony). The $E\flat$-major introduction forms one of his most yearning, piercing, *moll-Dur* stretches—his characteristic mingling of minor and major. Even the opening major chords sound minor, with their scoring in low strings and flutes, the violins muted. Brahms never achieved a more subtle orchestral texture, more expressive in its very sound. The introduction rises to a peak of longing, then sinks for the entrance of the altos declaiming Hölderlin's vision of the unreachable bliss of the gods:

Ihr wandelt droben im Licht	You walk up there in the Light
Auf wiechem Boden, selige Genien!	Upon soft ground, blessed Genii!
Glänzende Götterlüfte	Gleaming divine breezes
Rühren Euch leicht	Touch you gently,
Wie die Finger der Künsterlin	As the fingers of the woman musician
Heilige Saiten.	Touch sacred strings.

After the full choir enters, the verses unfold like a hymn. Then, after an echo of the introduction, which draws a line under the evocation of the gods, the middle section plummets to earth and human fate:

Doch uns ist gegeben	But it is our lot
Auf keiner Stätte zu ruhn;	To find rest nowhere;
Es schwinden, es fallen	Suffering mankind
Die leidenden Menschen	Wastes away, falls
Blindlings von einer	Blindly from one
Stunde zur andern,	Hour to the next,

Wie Wasser von Klippe	Like water hurled from crag
Zu Klippe geworfen,	To crag,
Jahrlang ins Ungewisse hinab.	Down into endless uncertainty.

The music here is the most violent possible in Brahms's musical language, climaxing on frenzied cries of "Blindly! . . . Endlessly!" He repeats the verse, the second time wrenching the music up from C minor to D minor, rendering the voices more shrill and intense. The end of the section sinks to an exhausted whisper: "Down into endless uncertainty."

Then comes a gesture recalling the *Alto Rhapsody*. Brahms did not want to end the piece, as Hölderlin's verses conclude, with an unequivocal gesture of uncertainty and despair—not quite. The obvious thing to do (as he had done in the *Rhapsody*) was to back up, to repeat the opening stanza with the opening music, as if the work again turned its gaze to the heavens. In fact, Brahms sketched that approach but found it was not sitting well, for reasons perhaps musical, perhaps personal. So he visited the adviser he most trusted at that point, the conductor Hermann Levi, and together they went through the piece.

Levi advised Brahms to leave out the chorus entirely at the end and let the uncanny music of the opening have the last word. Brahms did so, though with gnawing uncertainty. Even after the piece was printed he wrote to his friend Karl Reinthaler, "I had already gone as far as writing something for the chorus, but it didn't work out. It may turn out to be a miscarried experiment, but such grafting would only result in nonsense." Besides leaving the chorus tacet for the entire last section, Brahms reorchestrated the first phrases (winds taking the earlier string music) and changed the opening key of E♮ to C major—an uncommon example for those days of a piece ending in a key different from its start. Brahms conducted the premiere, with Levi's orchestra and choir, in Karlsruhe on October 18, 1871.

There remains the question of what he finally meant by the wordless ending of the *Schicksalslied*, however it took shape. The more apparent answer is the kind of stoic agnostic reassurance that pervades *Ein deutsches Requiem*. But ending in a new tonality—in the time's terms the "wrong" key—is a wrenching gesture for all the quietness of the end. Tovey wrote of the "ruthless beauty" of that ending, with the drums whispering the Brahmsian fate motive. For Brahms, fate was always an ominous thought. "Because this vision rouses our longing," Tovey adds, does not mean "it is an answer to our doubts and fears." With the ending in a new key, Brahms denies us a true resolution, a return home.

So if he would not exactly end the *Schicksalslied* on a note of despair, neither could he bring himself to finish it with hope and consolation like the *Requiem* or the *Alto Rhapsody.* He finished with music alone, its "ruthless beauty" the only solace he now knew. In October, acknowledging his fee for the piece from his publisher Simrock, Brahms wrote with *Moll-Dur* irony, "Here's the receipt for my heart's blood, also my thanks for the purchase of the poor little piece of soul."

Jan Swafford

TRIUMPHLIED, FOR EIGHT-PART CHORUS AND ORCHESTRA, OPUS 55

Composed 1870–71; published 1872

SCORING: 2 flutes, 2 oboes, 2 clarinets, 2 bassoons, contrabassoon, 4 horns, 3 trumpets, 3 trombones, tuba, timpani, strings

MOVEMENTS: 1. Lebhaft und feierlich; 2. Mässig belebt; 3. Lebhaft [Text: Revelation 19]

Brahms composed this "German *Te Deum*" in 1870–71 during the patriotic fervor of the Prussian military victory over France and the subsequent establishment of a long-awaited *Kaiserreich* under Prince Wilhelm I of Prussia. Like *Ein deutsches Requiem,* the *Triumphlied* is a multimovement setting of biblical texts for chorus, soloist, and orchestra, and the two works form a distinct pair in Brahms's sacred music. Brahms drew the text of the *Triumphlied* from Revelation, Chapter 19, the principal apocalyptic book of the Bible. By choosing this text source to celebrate the apocalyptic turn of events of 1871, Brahms connected Op. 55 to a central vein of German thought since the French Revolution. Infused with a new religious enthusiasm in the early decades of the century and coupled with a generation of Romantic thinkers who were steeped (and often trained) in theology, Germans came to anticipate the arrival of a unified German nation along biblical, apocalyptic lines. In the aftermath of the French reign of terror and Napoleon's conquest of Europe around the turn of the century, the re-establishment of a German Reich was anticipated as a Messianic arrival. All of these events fit perfectly within the eschatological framework of apocalyptic writing in the Bible. According to such thinking at that time, the State was the ultimate and positive manifestation of the new Kingdom.

If the *Requiem* subtly represents an individually centered Germanic mode of expression, the *Triumphlied* is its public counterpart, bringing any nationalistic undertones in the earlier work completely to the surface. A gradual emergence of the public voice can be traced through the works for chorus and orchestra with which Brahms occupied himself from the beginning of the Op. 45 in 1868 to the completion of Op. 55 in 1872. In between, the *Alto Rhapsody,* Op. 53 (1869), once more displays an individual perspective epitomized by the solo voice, while the *Schicksalslied,* Op. 54, is decidedly communal and (much more than his sacred works per se) "universal" in expression. Perhaps it is the blatant expression of what can only be sensed in the *Requiem* that has consigned the *Triumphlied* to second-class status among Brahms's works. For despite the disfavor into which the *Triumphlied* has fallen in this century, the work was very well received and continued to be performed regularly during Brahms's lifetime, often in the presence and to the great satisfaction of its composer. Most observers, including those in the Brahms circle, recognized Op. 55 as a sister work to Op. 45, as a *Deutsches Te Deum* to match *Ein deutsches Requiem.* The fact that Brahms premiered the first movement (at that point the only one completed) on Good Friday, April 7, 1871, in the Bremen Cathedral along with the first complete, seven-movement performance of the *Requiem* there, was certain to draw a parallel between the two works. Moreover, this concert, consisting of Brahms's *Requiem* and what at that time was labeled "Sacred Song of Triumph," was held "in memory of those who fell in the war," a designation that automatically linked the two pieces and cemented their national significance. The reactions of critics to Op. 55 are especially interesting in this respect. In addition to lauding the work's musical characteristics, they frequently cite it as an example of "Christian" art, a positive counterpart to Op. 45, while barely mentioning its relevance to current political events. Our modern understanding of the *Triumphlied* strictly as an "occasional" piece needs to be tempered by its initial reception as a primarily religious work.

There is no evidence to suggest that Brahms pre-selected or pondered the text of the *Triumphlied* as he had for the *Requiem,* and as he would for all of his later biblical settings. Rather, it is likely that the passages from Revelation 19 were compiled spontaneously following the beginning of the Franco-Prussian War. Thus this work began as a reflexive act of patriotism and exposes Brahms's core affinity to the political and military agenda of Bismarck's Germany. At the center of this jubilant three-movement work in D major for double chorus and large orchestra, God is especially praised and thanked for establishing the Kingdom: "Denn der allmächtige Gott hat das Reich eingenommen" (v. 6). Although divided into three movements, Op. 55 proceeds essentially as one continuous thread. Each movement begins with distinctive dotted march rhythms displaying a relatively animated character (I. Lebhaft und feierlich; II. Mässig belebt; III. Lebhaft), and the music never strays far from the central key of D major for very long—even the second movement in G major (a closely related key to D) contains a lengthy lebhaft middle portion in D major. Brahms fills these celebratory parameters with massive choral effects. Even when fugato sections are introduced, they inevitably lead to repetition of the fugal text in full homorhythmic declamation by the combined choirs. Completely absent here are the intimations of polyphonic, a cappella choral style that surface in nearly all of Brahms's other works for mixed chorus and orchestra (at no point do the voices actually sing without accompaniment). Rather, the two choirs express their scriptural text in a relatively objective and uncharacteristically blunt manner.

In Op. 55, then, Brahms produces not only the massive sounds one would expect in a national celebratory work of art but also an aura of populist democracy that nineteenth-century commentators commonly associated with Handel's oratorios (in direct comparison to the more individualistic utterances of Bach). And by extension, the choral writing in the *Triumphlied* sounds more Beethovenian than any other Brahms choral work, a similarity that probably is owing to the earlier composer's own high esteem for Handel. Although the Beethovenian sound of Op. 55 is not grounded in quotation or allusion per se, the acceleration into the animato closing section in the D-major first movement, with its strong syncopations and resounding unison A's, illustrates its affinity with the D-major conclusion of Beethoven's Ninth Symphony. Likewise, in the middle of the *Triumphlied*'s third movement, the ascending diminished-chord arpeggios at the words "and he trampled the winepress of almighty God's fierce wrath" evoke the "sprech leise" passage in the Prisoners' Chorus from Act I of *Fidelio*.

As with works like Beethoven's choral symphony and opera, Brahms's *Triumphlied* probably requires the visceral effect of a live performance to be fairly judged and appreciated. Given the work's disfavor in this century, however, relatively few listeners have had such an opportunity, a circumstance that merely accentuates the work's poor reputation, deserved or not.

Daniel Beller-McKenna

NÄNIE, FOR CHORUS AND ORCHESTRA, OPUS 82
Composed 1880–81; published 1881

SCORING: 2 flutes, 2 oboes, 2 clarinets, 2 bassoons, 2 horns, 3 trombones, timpani, harp, strings [Text: Schiller]

After a nine-year period given to instrumental composition, with *Nänie* Brahms once again took up the genre of middle-length works for chorus and orchestra that he had perfected with the *Alto Rhapsody,* Op. 53, *Schicksalslied,* Op. 54, and *Triumphlied,* Op. 55. The inception of *Nänie* came from three interwoven inspirations. His old painter friend Anselm Feuerbach died in January 1880, after a frustrated career. In June of that year, the celebrated surgeon Theodor Billroth, another close friend, asked Brahms to arrange something of his own that would be suitable someday for the surgeon's funeral—but since Billroth was not religious, he hoped for nothing overly pious. Brahms replied that he would keep it in mind, and that may have given more impetus to the idea of non-Christian funeral music. Finally, the gifted composer and Brahms acquaintance Hermann Götz, who died young in 1876, had set the Schiller verses that Brahms eventually chose for his own work. As Karl Geiringer notes, Götz's setting has musical echoes in Brahms's version.

Even when he was working from profound feelings of his own, it was characteristic of Brahms to couch his musical response in a more universal form. *Nänie* is funeral music inspired by the deaths of friends, but it is not service music for a specific funeral. Rather, it is abstracted funeral music, and a larger statement about death and commemoration than one man's mourning for a particular friend.

Yet everything about the music recalls Anselm Feuerbach's art and the sympathies that drew Brahms to pursue a friendship with that arrogant and sophisticated genius. He first met the artist in 1876, and came to admire him more than any painter alive. Feuerbach had developed a somber neo-Classical style, his subjects usually taken from Greek mythology or Italian literature. Brahms saw Feuerbach as representing virtues to which he himself also aspired: clarity, restraint, subtle lyricism, respect for tradition, an aesthetic that exalts form over color.

With his canny sensitivity to political climates, Brahms had advised the painter against taking a teaching position at the Vienna Imperial Academy in 1873. He knew the city was dazzled by the bright trivialities of the painter Hans Makart, and would have little patience for Feuerbach's muted neo-Classicism. With his usual defiance, Feuerbach did go to Vienna intending to conquer the city, and Brahms's worst fears were realized. The Viennese critics and public savagely attacked the painter, shattering his mental and physical health and, for a time, turning him against Brahms. Yet with extraordinary patience, Brahms kept up his attentions. When the painter finally left the city in defeat in 1876, Brahms turned up to give him a fur coat for the trip. Feuerbach died four years later.

In May 1881, Brahms traveled to Pressbaum near Vienna to begin his accustomed summer composing sojourn in the country. He brought with him in progress the Second Piano Concerto and *Nänie*. For help in finding a text for his tribute to Feuerbach, he had appealed to the extraordinary musical amateur Elisabet von Herzogenberg, who at that time was a trusted adviser. In the end he settled on the Schiller by himself, but what he was looking for can be found in his appeal to Elisabet: "Won't you try to find me some words? ... The ones in the Bible are not heathen enough for me. I've bought the Koran, but can't find anything there either."

Though Brahms, an agnostic permeated by German Protestantism, had set Scripture often and would again, for this purpose he wanted something to recall the ancient world that Feuerbach had portrayed. Schiller's verses were the ideal solution, a recreation of the ancient funeral dirge called *noenia,* sung by parents on the death of a child. (In keeping with that, Brahms dedicated the piece to the painter's stepmother, who indeed embraced it as her funeral song.) The verses are an evocation of the pagan and Classical world, a dirge at once tragic and serene, whose opening words resound unforgettably in memory of a painter who was dramatically handsome but prickly and proud in nature, who lived a difficult and fractious life painting serene canvases:

> Auch das Schöne muß sterben, das Menschen und Götter bezwinget!
>   Nicht die eherne Brust rührt es des stygischen Zeus ...
> Siehe, da weinen die Götter, es weinen die Göttinnen alle,
>   Denn das Schöne vergeht, daß das Vollkommene stirbt.
>
> Even the beautiful must die! That which conquers men and gods
>   Does not touch the brazen heart of Stygian Zeus. ...
> See! Then the gods weep, all the goddesses weep
>   Because the beautiful perishes, because perfection dies.

Though like most of Brahms's texts it spoke deeply to his own life, his setting is far from the resignation of *Ein deutsches Requiem,* the personal anguish of the *Alto Rhapsody,* the threatening despair of *Schicksalslied.* After a lyrical, wind-dominated orchestral introduction, he breaks the verse into an overall *ABA* structure and sets Schiller's hexameters to exquisite melodies in richly woven counterpoint: a ceremonial dance before the grave, a tonal analogy to the quiet gravity of Feuerbach's art, and one of the highest examples of what has been called Brahms's "sublime" style. Maybe no one but Brahms, with his unshakable reserve masking a feeling soul, could have set "Even the beautiful must die!" to a gently lilting, D-major soprano melody that captures the sorrow of death and transcends it in the singing. The beginning already embodies the closing words: "Even to be a song of lament on a loved one's lips is glorious." At the same time, the very proclamation of "perfection dies," from the hand of a composer who aspired to the highest perfection in art, marks a stage in Brahms's spiritual journey from the hope and consolation of *Ein deutsches Requiem* of 1868 to *Gesang der Parzen*, Op. 89, of 1882, and its stark portrayal of the gods' indifference. The sense of fate weighed on Brahms more and more through the years of his greatest triumphs.

Brahms conducted the premiere of *Nänie* in Zürich on December 6, 1881. *Jan Swafford*

GESANG DER PARZEN, FOR SIX-PART CHORUS AND ORCHESTRA, OPUS 89
Composed 1882; published 1883

SCORING: 2 flutes, 2 oboes, 2 clarinets, 2 bassoons, contrabassoon, 4 horns, 2 trumpets, 3 trombones, tuba, timpani, strings [Text: Goethe]

The ten years between the *Schicksalslied*, Op. 54, and *Triumphlied*, Op. 55, of 1871, and Brahms's next choral-orchestral works, *Nänie*, Op. 82, and *Gesang der Parzen*, Op. 89, completed in 1881–82, saw a period of largely instrumental composition. These choral works therefore frame a period of historic creative outpouring in "abstract" instrumental forms, and in their texts and treatment they reveal the spiritual journey of a composer who by nature was given to revealing as little as possible of himself—and that generally hidden in jokes, in oblique observations in his letters, and in his music.

Brahms composed *Gesang der Parzen* (Song of the Fates) during his sojourn at Bad Ischl in 1882, the same summer he completed the C-major Piano Trio, Op. 87, and the F-major String Quintet, Op. 88. The *Parzen's* theme of fate had shadowed several earlier works, but in them hope always had the final word. *Ein deutsches Requiem* ends with the word "selig" (blessed). The picture of a misanthropic separation from the world in the *Alto Rhapsody* ends nonetheless with a prayer, "Refresh his heart!" The *Schicksalslied* concludes more equivocally with an orchestral postlude, but still ends in wordless peace. In *Nänie,* the gods weep at the death of beauty. Now, in *Gesang der Parzen,* there is no prayer, no resolution either in its harmonies or in the implications of its verse, and now the gods are distant and indifferent.

The text is a song from Goethe's *Iphigenia auf Tauris,* which Brahms had heard recently at Vienna's Burgtheater:

Es fürchte die Götter	Let the race of man
Das Menschengeschlecht!	Fear the gods!
Sie halten die Herrschaft	They hold the power
In ewigen Händen,	In eternal hands
Und können sie brauchen	And they use it
Wies ihnen gefällt.	As they please.
Der fürchte sie doppelt,	Let that man fear them doubly
Den je sie erheben! ...	Whom once they exalted! ...
Es wenden die Herrscher	The rulers turn away
Ihr segnendes Auge	Their blessing-granting eyes
Von ganzen Geschlechtern,	From entire generations,
Und meiden, im Enkel	And refuse to recognize in the grandson
Die ehmals geliebten	His ancestor's quietly speaking features,
Still redenden Züge	Which once they loved.
So sangen die Parzen;	Thus sang the Fates;
Es horcht der Verbannte	In caverns of night
In nächtlichen Höhlen,	The exile, an old man,
Der Alte, die Lieder,	Remembers his children
Denkt Kinder und Enkel	And grandchildren
Und schüttelt das Haupt.	And shakes his head.

Thus sang Brahms, a man once called the Messiah of music by Robert Schumann, exalted by fate, now nearing fifty and watching his generation fall to pieces. In a way, from the composer's standpoint *Gesang der Parzen* is work of what a later age would call middle-age crisis: I'm getting old, music is going to the dogs, I have no children, nobody will remember me when I'm gone. But the chaos Brahms felt gathering around him was quite real, and he saw it with prophetic clarity. Vienna and its empire were collapsing toward the social and spiritual malaise caught in the term *fin de siècle,* and what social critic Karl Kraus would call the "Staging-ground for World Destruction." When the anti-Semitic Christian Democratic party got its leader Karl Lueger elected mayor of Vienna in 1895, Brahms barked to a dinner party, "Didn't I tell you years ago that it was going to happen? You laughed at me then and everybody else did too. Now it's here, and with it also the priests' economic system [socialism]. If there were an 'Anti-clerical Party'—that would make sense. But anti-Semitism is madness!"

Brahms despaired not only for the future of society and of music in general but for the future of his own work. In Germany and especially in Austria, the liberal, art-loving bourgeois public, for whom Brahms mainly composed, was under mounting attack from reactionary and anti-Semitic forces. Now Brahms approached his age with his personal gods—Bach, Mozart, Haydn, Schubert, Beethoven, and others—all in the past, the gods in the heavens withdrawn, his public under assault, and the fruits of his own labors, for all their value, still short of the perfection for which he had hoped.

All these elements contributed to the atmosphere of *Gesang der Parzen.* At the same time, once again Brahms bound up his personal feelings into an impersonal statement of impeccable craftsmanship.

The searing introduction that begins *Gesang der Parzen* might be called a brutal echo of the elevated Handelian tone of the *Triumphlied.* In that sense, perhaps here Brahms is deliberately taking back the *Triumphlied*'s forthright exaltation of empire. It is significant that the patriotic work is in D major, the *Parzen* in D minor. Brahms generally called it *Parzenlied* for short: the "Song of Triumph," then its negation, "Song of the Fates."

The opening harmonies are among the most unsettled Brahms ever created, not touching the central tonality of D until the third measure, and there equivocally. One hears hardly a firm harmonic resolution in the entire piece. (Brahms's more advanced harmony has been called "centripetal": he tends to obscure a key or keys that are nonetheless still there, and the music sooner or later condenses into that underlying tonal center. This is in contrast to Wagner's looser, "centrifugal" harmony that is more likely to drift from its starting point with little looking back.)

In contrast to the *ABA* tendencies of other choral works, the *Parzenlied* is rondo-like, with two major-key episodes for contrast, and a coda; it is less contrapuntal and more declamatory than *Nänie* from the previous year. Brahms wrote most of his choral music in four parts; this has

six, in order to create antiphonal effects and weighty textures in the direction of the eight-part antiphonal chorus of the *Triumphlied.* The leading theme on "Es fürchte die Götter das Menschengeschlect!" (Let the
race of men fear the gods!) is an inexorable dactylic chant recalling
episodes in Brahms's music going back to the last of the songs of Op. 17:
what has been called his "bardic" style. Usually it is associated with pri-
mal violence from myth and folk song.

Many found the harmonic turmoil of the opening shocking, among
them Theodor Billroth, who wrote to Brahms, "You will, of course, have
your conscious and unconscious grounds . . . to emphasize these abnor-
mal hardnesses . . . but our modern ears are sometimes pained by it."
Brahms replied patiently as usual to his admired friend, explaining that
there was nothing unconscious about it: "Think back for a moment to
the minor chord [in the third measure]. Think of how the modulation
from then on would be without any effect, and also quite restless, as if
one were searching for something, unless one had heard this progression before and very much emphasized!"

He means that the dissonant and unsettled are keys to this work, and
to begin with stability would have created the wrong impression. Clara
Schumann understood that immediately: "Words fail me to tell you of
the joy I have had from the piece—the gloomy beauty of its harmonies.
The progression in the second measure, of which Billroth speaks . . . is
precisely what stirs me most."

For all its quietness, the elegiac coda of the piece is perhaps its most despairing gesture, a drifting through indefinite tonal centers on a bass
line of descending major sixths, to end on a bleak open fifth of D–A.
Anton Webern seized on this coda as prophetic of the atonal school of
Schoenberg, Berg, and himself: "Its really remarkable harmonies take it
far away from tonality! . . . The chromatic path has begun!" For Brahms,
the musical metaphor of the end was not a hopeful one imagining a new
path, but the end of an old and beautiful path, in the caverns of night.
With *Gesang der Parzen,* he declared the bonds between men and gods to
be shattered—and he meant the gods both cosmic and musical.

If it had been only his personal despair that the piece reflected, Brahms
might not have allowed himself such self-indulgence; he was far from
the sort of artists who harp incessantly on their troubles in their work.
The bitter breakup of Joseph Joachim's marriage had shaken him. Surely
he was thinking of Clara Schumann, too: aging, much in pain, a son and
a daughter dead in ten years, another son mad and another broken by

drugs. Beyond those concerns, he thought about the state of music, to his mind with a few streaks of hope like Antonin Dvořák, but with no one in sight who seemed to possess the kind of mastery and depth that he did, poor as those were in relation to the gods'. And he looked with a shudder at the state of his adopted country. In 1883, just after he finished *Gesang der Parzen,* Brahms wrote to Fritz Simrock, "In a city and a land where everything not rolls but tumbles downhill, you can't expect music to fare better. Really, it's a pity and a crying shame, not only for music but for the whole beautiful land and the beautiful, marvelous people. I still think catastrophe is coming."   *Jan Swafford*

Tafellied for Six-Part Mixed Chorus and Piano, Opus 93b
Composed 1884; published 1885 [Text: Eichendorff]

This work was composed in the summer of 1884 and is set to a text by Eichendorff. In both 1884 and 1885 Brahms spent the summer in Mürzzuschlag, a year-round resort noted for its many beautiful walks. Brahms had copied out Eichendorff's poem, entitled "Dank der Damen" (Thanks to the Ladies), in the 1860s. *Tafellied* (Table Song) is in six parts, for mixed choir and piano, and is in B♭ major. It is dedicated to the Concert Society of Krefeld in recognition of the Society's fiftieth anniversary. This was the same group that in January of 1883 had impressed Brahms with its performance of a very different work, the *Gesang der Parzen,* Op. 89, also scored for six-part chorus. *Tafellied* is in the best tradition of German drinking songs: set in a gracious fluid tempo, it is structured as a lively dialogue between women's and men's voices. They eventually unite for the final verse. As Max Kalbeck points out, it has all the requisite contrast in rhythm and fanfare suggestive of the nineteenth-century's slogan of "wine, women, and song." In this work we encounter Brahms at his most sociable, cheerful, and lighthearted, celebrating without irony or pretension the accepted rituals of socializing among men and women that he enjoyed until the end of his life. *Tafellied* also points to Brahm's appreciation for the popular music of his time and the conviviality it evoked.   *Leon Botstein*

The last photograph of Brahms, taken at the home of the Von Miller zu Aichholz family, December 11, 1896. Standing from left: pianist and pedagogue Julius Epstein, the Russian musicologist Eusebius Mandyczewski, the cellist Robert Hausmann, Henrietta Hemalo, Dr. Passini, violinist Emmanuel Wirth, Carl Halir. Seated: Fraulein von Miller zu Aichholz, the music critic Eduard Hanslick, Brahms, Frau Passini, and the violinist Joseph Joachim.

Part Six

BRAHMS
MISCELLANY

21

WORKS WITHOUT OPUS NUMBERS

In addition to the works already discussed, which carry opus designations, Brahms produced a miscellany of works, many of which were published during his lifetime. This essay focuses on some of the highlights of this extensive corpus. Among the best known are the orchestrations of the Hungarian Dances, WoO 1. These appeared first in the form of works for piano four-hands in the late 1860s. Versions for a single pianist were published in the 1870s. Of the total set of twenty-one dances, three (Nos. 1,3,10) were orchestrated by Brahms and published in 1874. In 1880, Nos. 17–21 were orchestrated and published in 1881 by none other than Antonín Dvořák. Many of the dances proved extremely popular, particularly those that were orchestrated.

Perhaps equally important are the seven volumes of *Deutsche Volkslieder,* WoO 33, which appeared in 1894. Brahms also brought out a set of fifteen *Kindervolkslieder,* WoO 31, published in 1858. Brahms chose not to assign opus numbers to these works, in part because of a desire to underscore the difference between composed works and those designed primarily to document the folk sensibility and idiom. The debt revealed in so many of his numbered works to nineteenth-century folk traditions should not be underestimated. Neither should the absence of an opus number deter us from a recognition of the quality of this music, much of which is very familiar to listeners. Heinrich Schenker once made the observation that in music, as opposed to the other arts, complexity is not necessarily a virtue. One of the hardest achievements is to come up with a great musical idea that appears uncannily naïve and simple. Schenker's views echo those of Brahms, whose admiration for Dvořák rested primarily on the latter's prolific and startlingly natural gift for melody.

Likewise, the skill required to adapt or write accompaniments for folk songs should not be underestimated. Many listeners are familiar with settings of well-known Christmas carols, the vulgarity and bowdlerization of which obliterate any shred of the original charm and beauty of the carols. The nineteenth-century German public was inundated with numerous editions of folk songs with piano accompaniment designed for domestic use for both children and adults. The evolution of a German cultural nationalism in the first half of the nineteenth century, which inspired the work of the Grimm brothers and Clemens Brentano, led to the publication of several important compendia of German folk songs.

Brahms was highly critical of these compendia and therefore decided in 1894 to publish his own edition of folk songs. Unlike some of his fellow composers who were interested in folk music, Brahms was extremely restrained in his use of piano accompaniments and was thus able to infuse a compelling elegance and grace into his versions and harmonizations. That disciplined and delightful economy became his trademark in his folk arrangements. The last volume of WoO 33 is written for solo voice, piano, and four-part chorus. The fingerprints of a great composer are discernible in every setting.

The WoO 31, the children's songs, share these virtues, as does WoO 32, the twenty-eight German folk songs written in 1858 and published posthumously in 1926. In 1864, when Brahms was conductor of the Singakademie, he arranged fourteen songs for four-part chorus, and these were published that same year. In the 1920s, when a good deal of Brahms's music was rediscovered and published, scholars were not entirely surprised to find that Brahms, who was notoriously fastidious about preserving the music he regarded as good enough for publication, had composed twelve more settings for four-part chorus, WoO 35. These German folk-song arrangements were published in 1926 and 1927.

The extent of Brahms's patriotic enthusiasm for highly romanticized and idealized cultural nationalism as manifested in these folk-song arrangements can be gathered from the sheer volume of works of this sort in his total output. Brahms's intense engagement with issues of primary sources, his polemical and sharply critical attitudes to other editions, and his affection for folk material is especially apparent in WoO 36, eight German folk songs for three- and four-part chorus, written for the Hamburg Women's Chorus. Ironically, these were published first in America by Edwin Kalmus in 1938, the year of *Kristallnacht* and the *An-*

schluss. Kalmus was a member of the Jewish family of music publishers from Vienna who emigrated to New York in the 1920s. This set of eight turned out to be the tip of the proverbial iceberg. In 1964 and 1968, WoO 37 and 38 were published, containing sixteen and twenty German folk songs, respectively, for three- and four-part women's chorus.

Another important work is the Scherzo WoO 2 in C minor from the so-called *F-A-E* Sonata for violin and piano. This work, written in 1853 and published in 1906 posthumously, was dedicated to Joseph Joachim. Brahms's rhythmically powerful and wholly original movement represents the high point of the *F-A-E* Sonata collaboration and has remained in the violin repertory. The other movements were composed by Albert Dietrich (first movement) and Robert Schumann (second and fourth movements). The *F-A-E* Sonata marks the pinnacle of intensity of Brahms's encounter with Schumann and his circle. The title of the sonata refers to the group's motto, *frei aber einsam* (free but alone).

Brahms also created a significant number of works without opus consisting of arrangements and versions of works by other composers. He wrote six magnificent orchestrations of Schubert songs for voice and orchestra. *An schwager Kronos,* D. 369; *Gruppe aus dem Tartarus,* D. 583; and *Geheimnis,* D. 719, are remarkable, as is the setting of *Memnon,* D. 541 and *Greisen Gesang* (Song of the Old), D. 778. Brahms also arranged the Chaconne from the D-minor Partita and the Presto from the G-minor Sonata for violin by Bach, as well as a rondo by Weber and an étude by Chopin, in a volume entitled *Five Studies for Piano,* published in 1869 and 1878. Among the many piano arrangements of music by other composers, we should note his versions of three of Joseph Joachim's overtures, *Hamlet,* Op. 4, *Demetrius,* Op. 6, and *Henry IV,* Op. 7. Brahms was convinced that Joachim possessed substantial talent as a composer, but the close association between the two men in the 1850s proved detrimental to Joachim's compositional aspirations. He was overwhelmed by the superiority of Brahms's talent. Later in life Brahms encouraged Joachim to reconsider the work of his youth. As part of their collaboration in the 1850s, Brahms made piano reductions of Joachim's music. He also made a fine four-hand arrangement of Robert Schumann's Op. 47, the Piano Quartet in E♭ Major, as well as piano arrangements of Schubert's *Ländler,* D. 366 and 814.

The other works without opus include a series of exercises for piano, chorale preludes, fugues, sarabandes, gigues. These are all for piano; some are arrangements of music by others, but many are acts of imitative composition. Brahms reveals his close study of historical models and his engagement early in his career with the possibilities of continuing as a concert pianist. Brahms made arrangements for piano four-hands of many of his own works.

Not surprisingly, there are a host of pieces without opus for voices, including vocal quartets with piano and a cappella pieces. Also extant are some works for organ, cadenzas for a Bach Concerto (BWV 1052), for the Beethoven Piano Concerto No. 4, Op. 58, and for the piano concertos of Mozart, K. 453, 466, and 491. There are also a host of canons for voices, some of which were published in Brahms's lifetime, and others published posthumously. Of the solo songs without opus, perhaps the most interesting are the five *Shakespeare* settings WoO 22 (texts based on the Schlegel translation of *Hamlet*), written in 1873 and published in 1935. They were written for the wife of the leading male stage actor of Vienna, Joseph Lewinsky. Writing for the Lewinskys would be comparable today to writing for our most important film and theater stars; Vienna possessed an influential and alluring theater world with personalities that were adored by their audiences. Lewinsky was the most lionized of the actors of Vienna, and counted among his greatest admirers Johannes Brahms. Writing on November 21, 1862, the sagacious Clara Schumann wrote to Brahms, "I could have predicted your enthusiasm for Lewinsky. Haven't I always told you he is a genius?"

CHRONOLOGY

1833 Johannes Brahms is born on May 7 in Hamburg to Johann Jakob Brahms and Johanna Henrike Christian Nissen.

Felix Mendelssohn, Symphony No. 4 *(Italian)*
Robert Schumann, *Paganini Studies,* 2nd set
Frederic Chopin, Etudes Op. 10
Alexander Borodin is born.

1834 Hector Berlioz, *Harold en Italie*
Schumann, *Symphonic Etudes*

1835 Johannes's brother Fritz is born.

Schumann, *Carnaval*
Gaetano Donizetti, *Lucia di Lammermoor*
Vincenzo Bellini dies.
Camille Saint-Saëns is born.

1836 Schumann, Fantasy in C
Mikhail Glinka, *A Life for the Tsar*
Mendelssohn, *St. Paul*
Giacomo Meyerbeer, *Les Huguenots*

1837 The Brahms family moves from Specksgang 24 to Ulricastraße 38.

Berlioz, *Grande Messe des morts*
Chopin, Etudes Op. 25
Schumann, *Davidsbündlertänze*

1838 Berlioz, *Benvenuto Cellini*
Schumann, *Kreisleriana*
Georges Bizet is born.
Max Bruch is born.

1839 Brahms attends Heinrich Friedrich Voss's Privatschule. He begins music lessons with his father.

Chopin, 24 Preludes.
Mendelssohn conducts the first performance of Schubert's *"Great"* Symphony in C.
Modest Musorgsky is born.

1840 Schumann, *Frauenliebe und -leben.*
Schumann and Clara Wieck are married.
Donizetti, *La Fille du régiment*
Nicolò Paganini dies.
Peter Ilyich Tchaikovsky is born.

1841 Brahms begins piano lessons with Otto F. W. Cossel.

Schumann, Symphony No. 1 (*Spring*)
Gioachino Rossini, *Stabat mater*
Emmanuel Chabrier is born.
Antónin Dvořák is born.
Giovanni Sgambati is born.

1842 The Brahms family moves to Dammerthorvall 29. Cossel moves into the rooms at Ulricastraße.

Mendelssohn, *Scottish* Symphony
Glinka, *Ruslan and Lyudmila*
Albert Lortzing, *Der Wildschütz*
Meyerbeer is named general musical director of Royal Opera House, Berlin.
New York Philharmonic is founded.
Richard Wagner, *Rienzi*
The polka becomes fashionable.
Boito is born.
Luigi Cherubini dies.
Jules Massenet is born.

1843 Brahms makes his first public appearance as a pianist at a private benefit concert. He begins advanced study with Eduard Marxsen.

Donizetti, *Don Pasquale*
Wagner, *Der fliegende Holländer*
Mendelssohn, music to *A Midsummer Night's Dream*
Schumann, *Das Paradies und die Peri*
Edvard Grieg is born.
Hans Richter is born.

1844 Brahms attends secondary school. He plays his own composition—a piano sonata (lost)—for Luise Japtha.

Guiseppe Verdi, *Ernani*
Pablo Sarasate is born.

1845 Mendelssohn, Violin Concerto
Lortzing, *Undine*
Wagner, *Tannhäuser*
Gabriel Fauré is born.

1846 Brahms continues studies with Marxsen while playing for money in Hamburg taverns.

Berlioz, *La Damnation de Faust*
Clara Schumann, Piano Trio
Robert Schumann, Symphony No. 2
Lortzing, *Der Waffenschmied*
Mendelssohn, *Elijah*

1847 Brahms conducts male-voice choir at Winsen an der Lühe, where he summers to improve his health. His first public concert occurs on Nov. 20.

Franz Liszt, *Magyar Dállok*
Friedrich von Flotow, *Martha*
Verdi, *Macbeth*
Mendelssohn dies.

1848 Brahms hears Joseph Joachim perform the Beethoven Violin Concerto. Brahms gives his first solo concert.

Donizetti dies.
Sir Hubert Parry is born.

1849 Brahms gives his second solo concert. He takes on some pupils.
Phantasie über einem beliebter Walzer (lost)

Liszt, *Totentanz; Tasso*
Berlioz, *Te Deum*
Meyerbeer, *Le Prophète*
Otto Nicolai, *The Merry Wives of Windsor*
Wagner flees to Zürich after participating in the Dresden uprising.
Chopin dies.

1850 Brahms meets Eduard Reményi, but neglects to meet the Schumanns when they visit Hamburg.

Bach Gesellschaft is founded.
Schumann, *Genoveva*; Symphony No. 3 (*Rhenish*); Cello Concerto
Wagner, *Lohengrin*

1851 Brahms writes a few pieces of chamber music, some of which are performed in a concert with Gade.

Scherzo in E♭ Minor, Op. 4; Duet for cello and piano (lost)

Verdi, *Rigoletto*
Liszt, *Hungarian* Rhapsodies
Charles Gounod, *Sappho*
Vincent D'Indy is born.
Lortzing dies.

1852   Piano Sonata Op. 2; String Quartet in B♭ Major (lost); Violin Sonata in A Minor (lost).
Bach Gesellschaft, Vol. I published.
Schumann, *Manfred*

1853   On tour with Reményi, Brahms meets Joachim and spends the summer with him at Göttingen. He then meets the Schumanns in Düsseldorf.
F-A-E Sonata; Piano Sonatas Opp. 1 and 5; *Gesänge* Opp. 3, 6, and 7
Schumann writes an article on Brahms in the *Neue Zeitschrift für Musik*.
Liszt, Piano Sonata in B Minor
Clara Schumann, *Variations on a Theme by Robert Schumann*

1854   Brahms meets von Bülow. He composes a number of small piano pieces.
He begins work on a D-minor symphony (lost).
He visits Clara Schumann extensively.
Trio Op. 8; *Schumann* Variations, Op. 9; Ballades, Op. 10
Robert Schumann tries to drown himself and is committed to Endenich Sanatorium.
Hanslick, *On the Beautiful in Music*
Liszt, *Les Préludes*
Wagner, *Das Rheingold*
Berlioz, *l'Enfance du Christ*
Humperdinck is born.

1855   Brahms tours with Clara Schumann and Joachim. His Piano Trio Op. 8 is premiered in New York.
Quartet in C♯ Minor (lost); Prelude and Aria (lost)
Wagner conducts in London.

1856   Brahms meets Rubinstein and Julius Stockhausen.
He begins counterpoint studies with Joachim.
Brahms attempts another symphony, which later becomes the First Piano Concerto.
He visits Detmold.
Early version of Piano Quartet Op. 60; *Geistliches Lied,* Op. 30; Variations Op. 21
Schumann dies.

Liszt, *Dante* Symphony
Wagner, *Die Walküre*

1857 Brahms acquires an appointment at Detmold conducting and teaching piano to Princess Friederike.

Hans von Bülow marries Cosima Liszt.
Liszt, *Faust* Symphony
Edward Elgar is born.
Glinka dies.

1858 Brahms becomes attached to Agathe von Siebold.
First *Hungarian* Dances; Ave Maria *Op. 12; Lieder und Romanzen* Op. 14; Duets Op. 20
Joachim, Violin Concerto, the "Hungarian"
Offenbach, *Orphée*
Handel Gesellschafti founded.
Charles Barry designs the third Covent Garden opera house.
Giacomo Puccini is born.

1859 Brahms breaks off his engagement to Agathe von Siebold.
He forms the Hamburger Frauenchor.
Premieres: First Piano Concerto, First Serenade.
Begräbnisgesang, Op. 13; Serenade in A, Op. 16; String Sextet Op. 18; *Gedichte* Op. 19; *Marienlieder,* Op. 22; Psalm 13, Op. 27

Verdi, *Un Ballo in Maschera*
Gounod, *Faust*
Louis Spohr dies.

1860 Brahms leaves Detmold and returns to Hamburg.
He meets Fritz Simrock.
Serenade in D (final version), Op. 11; Partsongs, Opp. 17, 42; Motets, Op. 29; 12 *Lieder und Romanzen,* Op. 44

Franz von Suppé, *Das Pensionat*
Gustav Mahler is born.
Ignace Paderewski is born.
Hugo Wolf is born.

1861 *Schumann* Variations, Op. 23; *Handel* Variations, Op. 24
Quartet No. 1, Op. 25.

Tannhäuser scandal occurs in Paris.

1862 Brahms begins C-minor Symphony, Op. 68.
He meets Hanslick and Tausig.
Quartet No. 2, Op. 26; Duets Op. 28; Quartets Op. 31; Partsongs Opp., 41, 62; Motets Op. 74; Adagio for cello and piano (lost).

Berlioz, *Béatrice et Bénédict*
Verdi, *La Forza del Destino*
Claude Debussy is born.

1863   Brahms becomes the conductor of Vienna Singakademie. *Paganini* Variations, Op. 35

Bizet, *Les Pêcheurs de perles*
Berlioz, *Les Troyens*
Felix Weingartner is born.
Pietro Mascagni is born.

1864   Brahms conducts Bach's *Christmas* Oratorio in Vienna.
He resigns from the Vienna Singakademie.
Lieder und Gesänge Op. 32; Quintet in F Minor, Op. 34; Sextet No. 2, Op. 36

Anton Bruckner, Symphony No. 0 *(Die Nullte)*
Offenbach, *La belle Hélène*
Meyerbeer dies.
Richard Strauss is born.

1865   Brahms's mother dies.
Brahms meets Hermann Levi.
Magalone Romanzen, Op. 33; Cello Sonata No. 1, Op. 38; 16 Waltzes, Op. 39
Horn Trio, Op. 40

Liszt, *Missa choralis*
Wagner, *Tristan und Isolde*
Schubert's *Unfinished* Symphony is first performed.
Paul Dukas is born.
Alexander Glazunov is born.
Jan Sibelius is born.

1866   Brahms meets Billroth in Switzerland.
String Sextet Op. 36; *Lieder und Gesänge* Opp. 46, 47, 48, 49, 57, 58, 59

Bruckner, Symphony No. 1; Mass in E Minor.
Liszt, *Christus*
Bedřich Smetana, *The Bartered Bride*
Ferrucio Busoni is born.

1867   Brahms embarks on a concert tour of Austria with Joachim.
The first three movements of *Ein deutsches Requiem* are performed in Vienna.

Gounod, *Roméo et Juliette*
Strauss, *The Blue Danube* Waltz

Verdi, *Don Carlos*
Arturo Toscanini is born.

1868 Brahms travels to Copenhagen with Stockhausen.
Gesänge Op. 43; String Quartets Op. 51
Premiere of *Ein deutsches Requiem,* Op. 45, in Bremen.

Grieg, Piano Concerto.
Wagner, *Die Meistersinger von Nürnberg.*
Tchaikovsky, Symphony No. 1
Rossini dies.
Max von Schillings is born.

1869 Brahms tours Budapest with Stockhausen.
He settles permanently in Vienna.
Rinaldo, Op. 50; *Liebeslieder Walzer,* Op. 52; Duets Op. 61; Quartets
Op. 64; Hungarian Dances

Joachim becomes director of the Berlin Hochschule.
Bruch, Violin Concerto
Wagner, *Das Rheingold*
Berlioz dies.
Hans Pfitzner is born
Siegfried Wagner is born.

1870 *Alto Rhapsody,* Op. 53

Tchaikovsky, *Romeo and Juliet* Overture
Wagner, *Die Walküre*
Wagner marries Cosima von Bülow.

1871 Brahms moves to Karlsgasse 4 in Vienna, his home for the rest of his life.
Schicksalslied, Op. 54; *Triumphlied,* Op. 55

Verdi, *Aida*
Saint-Saëns, *Le Rouet d'Omphale*
Albert Hall, London, is opened.

1872 Brahms's father dies.
Brahms becomes director of Gesellschaft der Musikfreunde.
He meets Nietzsche.

Bruckner, Symphony No. 2
Bizet, *L'Arlésienne*
Tchaikovsky, Symphony No. 2
Alexander Scriabin is born.

1873 String Quartets Nos. 1 and 2, Op. 51; *Haydn* Variations, Op 56; Hungarian Dances Nos. 1, 3, 10 orchestrated.

Dvořák Symphony No. 3

Enrico Caruso is born.
Feodor Chaliapin is born.
Max Reger is born.
Sergei Rachmaninoff is born.

1874 Brahms meets Elisabet von Herzogenberg and Philipp Spitta.
Neue Liebeslieder Walzer, Op. 65; *Lieder und Gesänge* Opp. 63, 69, 70, 77, 72, 84, 85, 86, 91, 94

Musorgsky, *Boris Godunov*
Verdi, Requiem
Smetana, *Ma Vlast*
Strauss, *Die Fledermaus*
Gustav Holst is born.
Arnold Schoenberg is born.

1875 Brahms resigns from the Gesellschaft.
He meets Dvořák.
He returns Wagner's MS of *Tannhäuser.*
He begins work on the First Symphony.
Quartet No. 3, Op. 60; Duets Op. 66

Bizet, *Carmen*
Bizet dies.
Goldmark, *Die Königin von Saba*
Tchaikovsky, Piano Concerto No. 1
Brüll, *Das goldene Kreuz*
Maurice Ravel is born.

1876 Symphony No. 1, Op. 68; String Quartet No. 3, Op. 67

Tchaikovsky, *Swan Lake*
Bruckner, Symphony No. 5
The first complete Ring Cycle is performed at Bayreuth.
Pablo Casals is born.
Bruno Walter is born.
Ermanno Wolf-Ferrari is born.

1877 Symphony No. 2, Op. 73

Saint-Saëns, *Samson et Dalila*
Bruckner, Symphony No. 3
Dvořák, *Symphonic Variations*
Ernst von Dohnányi is born.

1878 Brahms encounters Hugo Wolf.
4 Balladen und Romanzen, Op. 75; *Klavierstücke,* Op. 76; Violin Concerto, Op. 77; *5 Romanzen und Lieder* Op. 84; Quartets Op. 92

Tchaikovsky, Violin Concerto; Symphony No. 4
Dvořák, Slavonic Dances Op. 46
Gilbert and Sullivan, *H.M.S. Pinafore*

1879   Brahms is awarded an honorary doctorate by Breslau University.
G-major Violin Sonata, Op. 78; Rhapsodies, Op. 79; *Academic Festival* Overture, Op. 80.
Wagner attacks Brahms in "Über das Dichten und Komponieren."

Cesar Franck, Piano Quintet
Tchaikovsky, *Eugene Onegin*

1880   Brahms meets Brüll and Johann Strauss, Jr.
He argues with Joachim over Joachim's divorce.
Books 3 and 4 of Hungarian Dances published; *Tragic* Overture, Op. 81; Overture in F Major (lost); Trio in E♭ (lost).

Mahler, *Das klagende Lied*
Dvořák Symphony No. 6
Hans Rott, Symphony in E.
Gilbert and Sullivan, *Pirates of Penzance*
Spitta, *Johann Sebastian Bach*
Ernst Bloch is born.
Offenbach dies.

1881   Completes *Nänie*, Op. 82, in memory of Anselm Feuerbach.
Piano Concerto No. 2, Op. 83

Offenbach, *Les Contes d'Hoffmann*
Bruckner, Symphony No. 6
Fauré, *Ballade*
Béla Bartók is born.
Musorgsky dies.

1882   Completes C-major Piano Trio, Op. 87
F-major String Quintet, Op. 88; *Gesang der Parzen*, Op. 89

Wagner, *Parsifal*
Hugo Riemann, *Musiklexicon*
Tchaikovsky, *1812* Overture
Rimsky-Korsakov, *The Snow Maiden*
Debussy, *Le Printemps*
The Berlin Philharmonic is founded.
Igor Stravinsky is born.

1883   Brahms meets and forms close relationship to Hermine Spies.
Symphony No. 3, Op. 90; 6 *Lieder und Romanzen*, Op. 93

Bruckner, Symphony No. 7
Dvořák, *Scherzo capriccioso*

Chabrier, *España*
Delibes, *Lakmé*
Metropolitan Opera, New York opens.
Wagner dies.
Anton Webern is born.

1884   Brahms begins a friendship with Fellinger family.
       He starts composing the Fourth Symphony.
       Tafellied Op. 93; *Lieder* Op. 95

       Franck, *Les Djinns*
       Bruckner, *Te Deum*
       Massenet, *Manon*
       Mahler, *Lieder eines fahrenden Gesellen*
       Viktor Nessler, *Der Trompeter von Säckingen*
       Spitta begins Schütz edition.

1885   Brahms meets Richard Strauss.
       He conducts the premiere of the Fourth Symphony with von Bülow's
       Meiningen Orchestra.
       Lieder Opp. 96, 97; Symphony No. 4, Op. 98.

       Dvořák, Symphony No. 7
       Franck, *Symphonic Variations*
       Liszt, *Bagatelle without Tonality*
       Gilbert and Sullivan, *The Mikado*
       Strauss, *The Gypsy Baron*
       Alban Berg is born.
       Anna Pavlova is born.

1886   Brahms is elected honorary president of Wiener Tonkünstlerverein.
       Cello Sonata No. 2, Op. 99; Violin Sonata No. 2, Op. 100; Piano Trio
       No. 3, Op. 101; *Lieder* Opp. 105, 106

       Fauré, Requiem
       Franck, Violin Sonata
       Goldmark, *Merlin*
       Liszt dies.
       Wilhelm Fürtwangler is born.

1887   *Zigeunerlieder* Op. 103; Double Concerto Op. 102; Quartets Op. 112

       Bruckner, Symphony No. 8
       Verdi, *Otello*
       Strauss, *Aus Italien*
       Borodin dies.

1888   Brahms meets Grieg, Tchaikovsky, and Martucci.
       Violin Sonata No. 3, Op. 108; Partsongs Op. 104

Eduard Marxsen dies.
Tchaikovsky, Symphony No. 5
Rimsky-Korsakov, *Sheherazade*
Mahler becomes musical director of the Budapest Opera.
Irving Berlin is born.

1889 Dvořák Symphony No. 8
Mahler, Symphony No. 1
Strauss, *Don Juan*

1890 Brahms meets Alice Barbi.
String Quintet No. 2, Op. 111

Busoni, *Konzertstück*
Strauss, *Tod und Verklärung*
Wolf, *Spanisches Liederbuch*
Mascagni, *Cavalleria Rusticana*
Tchaikovsky, *Queen of Spades*
Franck dies.

1891 Brahms writes his will, the "Ischl Testament."
He goes to Meiningen and hears Richard Mühlfeld. As a result, he composes the Clarinet Trio, Op. 114, and the Clarinet Quintet, Op. 115.
7 Fantasias, Op. 116

Rachmaninoff, Piano Concerto No. 1
Wolf, *Italienisches Liederbuch*

1892 Brahms's sister Elise dies.
Elisabet von Herzogenberg dies.
3 Intermezzos, Op. 117; Piano Piece in C Minor (lost)

Dvořák, *Te Deum*

Dvořák becomes director of National Conservatory, New York.
Leoncavallo, *I Pagliacci*
Tchaikovsky, *The Nutcracker*

1893 Hermine Spies dies.
6 Piano Pieces, Op. 118; 4 Piano Pieces, Op. 119.

Dvořák, Symphony No. 9
Tchaikovsky, Symphony No. 6
Verdi, *Falstaff*
Sibelius, *Karelia* Suite, Op. 10
Puccini, *Manon Lescaut*
Cole Porter is born.
Tchaikovsky dies.
Gounod dies.

1894 Brahms refuses conductorship of the Hamburg Philharmonic.
       Clarinet Sonatas Nos. 1 and 2, Op. 120; *Deutsche Volkslieder* in seven
       volumes

       Sibelius, *Finlandia*
       Debussy, *L'Après-midi d'un faune*
       Massenet, *Thaïs*
       Billroth, von Bülow, and Spitta, all close friends of Brahms, die.
       Anton Rubinstein dies.

1895 Brahms attends Meiningen Festival of "Three B's."

       Dvořák, Cello Concerto
       Mahler, Symphony No. 2
       Puccini, *La Bohème*
       Rachmaninoff, Symphony No. 1
       Strauss, *Till Eulenspiegel's Merry Pranks*
       Oscar Hammerstein is born.
       Paul Hindemith is born.

1896 Clara Schumann dies.
       Vier ernste Gesänge, Op. 121.

       Choral Preludes
       Mahler, Symphony No. 3
       Reger, Suite for Organ
       Strauss, *Also Sprach Zarathustra*
       Alexander Zemlinsky, Clarinet Trio
       Edward MacDowell, *Indian Suite*
       Giordano, *Andrea Chenier*
       Bruckner dies.

1897 Brahms makes his last public appearance at a performance of Symphony
       No. 4, conducted by Hans Richter.
       Brahms dies of liver cancer, April 3.
       Mahler becomes conductor of the Vienna Opera.
       D'Indy, *Fervaal.*
       Erich Wolfgang von Korngold is born.

SELECTED BIBLIOGRAPHY

Antonicek, Susanne, and Otto Biba. *Brahms-Kongress Wien 1983*. Tutzing: H. Schneider, 1988.

Avins, Styra. *Johannes Brahms: Life and Letters*. New York: Oxford University Press, 1997.

Bell, Craig. *The Lieder of Brahms*. Darley: Grain-Aig Press, 1979.

Botstein, Leon. "Brahms and His Audience: The Later Viennese Years, 1875–1897," in *The Cambridge Companion to Brahms,* ed. Michael Musgrave. Cambridge: Cambridge University Press, 1998.

———. "Brahms the Performer, Editor, and Collector," in *Guide to the BBC Proms*. London: BBC Radio Publications, 1997.

———. "Johannes und Clara," *Gewandhausmagazin* 9 (Fall 1995).

———. "Brahms and Nineteenth-Century Painting," *19th Century Music* 14 (1990): 154–68.

———. "Time and Memory: Concert Life, Science, and Music in Brahms's Vienna," in *Brahms and His World,* ed. Walter Frisch. Princeton: Princeton University Press, 1990.

Bozarth, George. *The Brahms-Keller Correspondence*. Lincoln: University of Nebraska Press, 1996.

———, ed. *Brahms Studies: Analytical and Historical Perspectives*. Oxford: Clarendon Press, 1990.

Brinkmann, Reinhold. *Johannes Brahms, Die zweite Symphonie: Späte Idylle*. Munich, 1990. Tr. Peter Palmer as *Late Idyll: The Second Symphony of Johannes Brahms*. Cambridge, Mass.: Harvard University Press, 1995.

Brodbeck, David, ed. *Brahms Studies,* vol. 1. Lincoln: University of Nebraska Press, 1994.

———. *Brahms: Symphony No. 1*. Cambridge: Cambridge University Press, 1997.

———. "Brahms," in *The Nineteenth-Century Symphony,* ed. D. Kern Holoman. New York: Schirmer Books, 1996.

Brown, A. Peter. "Brahms's Third Symphony and the New German School," *Journal of Musicology* 2 (1983): 434–52.

Burkholder, J. Peter. "Brahms and Twentieth-Century Classical Music," *19th Century Music* 8 (1984): 75–83.

Clapham, John. "Dvořák's Relations with Brahms and Hanslick," *Musical Quarterly,* 57 (1971):241–54.

Dahlhaus, Carl. *Nineteenth-Century Music.* Tr. J. Bradford Robinson. Berkeley: University of California Press, 1989.

Epstein, David. *Beyond Orpheus.* Cambridge: MIT Press, 1979.

Evans, Edwin. *Historical, Descriptive & Analytical Account of the Entire Works of Johannes Brahms.* 4 vols. London: W. Reeves, 1912–38.

Fink, Robert. "Desire, Repression, and Brahms's First Symphony," *Repercussions* 2 (1993): 75–103.

Floros, Constantin, et al, eds. *Johannes Brahms: Eine Ausstellung.* Hamburg: Deutsche Bank, 1981.

Forner, Johannes. *Johannes Brahms in Leipzig.* Leipzig: Peters, 1987.

Frisch, Walter. *Brahms: The Four Symphonies.* New York: Schirmer Books, 1996.

———, ed. *Brahms and His World.* Princeton: Princeton University Press, 1990.

———. *Brahms and the Principle of Developing Variation.* Berkeley: University of California Press, 1984.

Gál, Hans. *Johannes Brahms: His Work and Personality.* London: Weidenfeld and Nicolson, 1963.

Geiringer, Karl. *Brahms: His Life and Work,* 2d ed. London, 1963; reprinted New York: Da Capo Press, 1982.

Groth, Klaus. "Erinnerungen an J. Brahms," *Gegenwart,* 1987.

Hancock, Virginia. *Brahms's Choral Compositions and His Library of Early Music.* Ann Arbor: UMI Research Press, 1983.

Harrison, Julius. *Brahms and His Four Symphonies.* London, 1939, reprinted New York: Da Capo Press, 1971.

Harrison, Max. *The Lieder of Brahms.* New York: Praeger Publications, 1972.

Heuberger, Richard. *Erinnerungen an Johannes Brahms.* Tutzing: H. Schneider, 1971.

Hofmann, Kurt. *Johannes Brahms und Hamburg.* Reinbek: Dialog Verlag, 1986.

Holmes, Peter. *Brahms: His Life and Work.* Southborough: Hippocrene, 1984.

Horstmann, Angelika. *Untersuchungen zur Brahms-Rezeption der Jahre 1860–1880.* Hamburg: K. D. Wagner, 1986.

Jacobsen, Christiane. *Das Verhältnis von Sprache und Musik in Liedern von Johannes Brahms.* Hamburg: K. D. Wagner, 1975.

Jacobson, Bernard. *The Music of Johannes Brahms.* London: Tantivy Press, 1977.

James, Burnett. *Brahms: A Critical Study.* New York: Praeger, 1972.

Jenner, Gustav. *Johannes Brahms als Mensch, Lehrer und Künstler.* Marburg: N.G. Elwert, 1905.

Kalbeck, Max. *Johannes Brahms*. 4 vols. Vienna, 1904–14; reprinted Tutzing: H. Schneider, 1974.

Keys, Ivor. *Johannes Brahms*. Portland, Or.: Amadeus Press, 1989.

Knapp, Raymond. *Brahms and the Challenge of the Symphony*. Stuyvesant, N.Y.: Pendragon Press, 1996.

——. "Brahms's Revisions Revisisted," *Musical Times* 129 (1988): 584–88.

Kross, Siegfried. *Johannes Brahms: Versuch einer kritischen Dokumentar-Biographie*. 2 vols. Bonn: Bouvier, 1997.

Küntzel, Hans. *Brahms in Göttingen*. Göttingen: Herodot, 1985.

Leyen, Rudolf von der. *Johannes Brahms als Mensch und Freund*. Düsseldorf: K. R. Langewiesche, 1905.

Litzmann, Berthold, ed. *Letters of Clara Schumann and Johannes Brahms 1853–1896*. New York, 1927; reprinted New York: Vienna House, 1973.

Mackelmann, Michael. *Johannes Brahms: IV. Symphonie e-Moll op. 98*. Munich: W. Fink, 1991.

McClary, Susan. "Narrative Agendas in 'Absolute' Music: Identity and Difference in Brahms's Third Symphony," in *Musicology and Difference*, ed. Ruth Solie. Berkeley: University of California Press, 1993.

McCorkle, Margit L., and Donald M. *Johannes Brahms, thematisch-bibliographisches Werkverzeichnis*. Munich: G. Henle, 1984.

MacDonald, Malcolm. *Brahms*. New York: Schirmer Books, 1990.

May, Florence. *The Life of Brahms*. 2d ed. 2 vols. London, Reeves, 1948; reprinted St. Clair Shores, Mich.: Scholarly Press, 1977.

Musgrave, Michael. ed. *The Cambridge Companion to Brahms*. Cambridge: Cambridge University Press, 1998.

——. *A Brahms Reader*. New Haven: Yale University Press, 1998.

——. *Brahms: A German Requiem*. Cambridge: Cambridge University Press, 1996.

——. *The Music of Brahms*. London: Routledge and Kegan Paul, 1985.

Neunzig, Hans. *Johannes Brahms in Selbstzeugnissen und Bilddokumenten*. Reinbek: Rowohlt, 1973.

Ophüls, Gustav. *Erinnerungen an Johannes Brahms*. Berlin: Deutsche Brahms-Gesellschaft, 1923; reissued Ebenhausen-bei-München: Langeweische-Brandt, 1983.

——. *Brahms-Texte*. Ebenhausen-bei-München: Langeweische-Brandt, 1983.

Notley, Margaret. "Brahms as Liberal: Genre, Style, and Politics in Late Nineteenth-Century Vienna," *19th Century Music* 17 (1993): 107–23.

Platt, Heather. "Jenner versus Wolf: The Critical Reception of Brahms's Songs," *Journal of Musicology* 13 (1995), 377–403.

Pleasants, Henry, tr. and ed. *Hanslick's Music Criticisms*. New York: 1950; reprinted New York: Dover, 1988.

Reimann, Heinrich. *Johannes Brahms*. 3d ed. Berlin: Harmonie, 1903.

Sams, Eric. *Brahms Songs*. Seattle: University of Washington Press, 1972.

——. "Brahms and his Clara Themes," *Musical Times* 112 (1971): 432–44.

Schaefer, Hansjürgen. *Johannes Brahms: Ein Führer durch Leben und Werk.* Berlin: Henschel, 1997.

Schoenberg, Arnold. "Brahms the Progressive," in his *Style and Idea: Selected Writings,* ed. Leonard Stein. London: Faber & Faber, 1975.

Schorske, Carl. *Fin-de-Siècle Vienna: Politics and Culture.* New York: Knopf, 1979.

Schubert, Giselher, "Themes and Double Themes: The Problem of the Symphonic in Brahms," *19th Century Music* 18 (1994): 10–23.

Schumann, Robert. *On Music and Musicians,* ed. Konrad Wolff. Tr. Paul Rosenfeld. New York: Norton, 1969.

Sisman, Elaine. "Brahms and the Variation Canon," in *19th Century Music,* 14 (1990): 132–53.

Spitta, Philipp. *Zur Musik: Sechzehn Aufsätze.* Berlin: Gebrüder Paetel, 1892.

Stark, Lucien. *A Guide to the Solo Songs of Johannes Brahms.* Bloomington: Indiana University Press, 1995.

Swafford, Jan. *Johannes Brahms: A Biography.* New York: Knopf, 1998.

Tovey, Donald F. *Essays in Musical Analysis,* vol. 1: *Symphonies.* London: Oxford University Press, 1935.

Weber, Horst. "Melancholia: Versuch über Brahms' Vierte, in *Neue Musik und Tradition: Festschrift für Rudolf Stephan zum 65. Geburtstag,* ed. Josef Kuckartz et al. Laaber: Laaber-Verlag, 1990.

Zemlinsky, Alexander von. "Brahms und die neuere Generation: Persönliche Erinnerungen," in *Musikblätter des Anbruchs* 3 (March 1922): 69–70.

CONTRIBUTORS

Nyela Basney has conducted numerous orchestras, including the American Symphony Orchestra, the Shreveport Symphony, and the Rochester Philharmonic. She is currently a faculty member of Vassar College.

Michael Beckerman is professor of music at the University of California, Santa Barbara. He has written essays and articles on Brahms, Mozart, Sullivan, and Czech topics. He is the author of *Janáček as Theorist* and the editor of *Dvořák and His World* and *Janáček and Czech Music*. He contributes to the *New York Times* and provides commentary for PBS's Live from Lincoln Center.

Daniel Beller-McKenna is assistant professor of music history at the University of New Hampshire. He has published several articles on Brahms's sacred music and is currently writing a book on Brahms and German nationalism.

Leon Botstein is music director of the American Symphony Orchestra, as well as Leon Levy Professor of the Humanities and president of Bard College, Annandale-on-Hudson, New York. The author of numerous articles on nineteenth-century music and culture, he is the editor of *The Musical Quarterly* and is a contributor to the forthcoming new edition of the *New Grove Dictionary of Music and Musicians*. Among his recordings are Brahms's Serenade No. 1, the music of Joseph Joachim, Bruckner's Symphony No. 5 [Schalk version], Dohnanyi's D-minor Symphony, and Bruch's *Odysseus*.

George S. Bozarth, professor of music at the University of Washington, is executive director of the American Brahms Society. His most recent book is *The Brahms-Keller Correspondence*. He has also edited *Brahms Studies: Analytical and Historical Perspectives* and has written numerous articles on Brahms documents and manuscripts, Brahms's pianos, and the relation of poetry to Brahms's vocal and instrumental music.

REINHOLD BRINKMANN, the James Edward Ditson Professor of Music at Harvard University, is most recently the author of *Late Idyll*, a study of Brahms's Second Symphony. Since 1996, he has also been Honorarprofessor at Humboldt University in Berlin. He has published extensively on music history and aesthetics from the eighteenth through the twentieth centuries. He is currently preparing a study on the early history of Beethoven's *Eroica* Symphony, and is collecting material for a book on music and German racist ideology.

DAVID BRODBECK is associate professor and chair of the department of music at the University of Pittsburgh. He is the author of *Brahms: Symphony No. 1* and numerous essays on the music of Schubert, Mendelssohn, and Brahms. In addition, he has prepared critical editions of works by Mendelssohn. President of the American Brahms Society from 1995 to 1997, he also edits its *Brahms Studies* series.

TODD CROW is professor of music at Vassar College. He is musical director of the Mt. Desert Festival of Chamber Music in Northeast Harbor, Maine, editor of the volume *Bartók Studies*, and a pianist who is heard in the major halls of New York, London, and elsewhere. He has recorded frequently for BBC Radio, and his performances can be heard on several record labels.

JOHN DAVERIO, professor and chair of the musicology department at Boston University School for the Arts, is the author of *Nineteenth-Century Music and the German Romantic Ideology, Robert Schumann: Herald of a "New Poetic Age,"* and articles on the music of Schumann, Brahms, and Wagner. He is currently president of the board of directors of the American Brahms Society.

MISHA DONAT has contributed to many of the leading journals in England, including the *Musical Times, Tempo,* the *BBC Magazine, The Listener,* the *London Review of Books,* and the *Times Literary Supplement.* He has taught in the U.S. at U.C.L.A. and Vassar College and in England at Durham University and the Dartington Summer School of Music. For more than twenty-five years he was a senior producer in the music department of BBC Radio.

DAVID EPSTEIN, professor of music at M.I.T., is a composer and conductor who has written extensively on theoretical questions of structure and timing in music, especially as they pertain to performance, often focusing on the music of Brahms. He has been on the board of directors of the American Brahms Society since 1983.

WALTER FRISCH is professor of music at Columbia University and past president of the American Brahms Society. His publications include *Brahms and the Principle of Developing Variation* and most recently *Brahms: The Four Symphonies,* as well as the edited collection *Brahms and His World.*

CHRISTOPHER H. GIBBS has taught at Columbia University and Haverford College, and is currently assistant professor of music at the State University of New

York at Buffalo. He was the musicological director for the final three years of the acclaimed *Schubertiade* at the 92nd Street YM–YWHA in New York City. His articles have appeared in many scholarly journals and in several anthologies. He is editor of the *Cambridge Companion to Schubert* and is now writing a biography of Schubert.

VIRGINIA HANCOCK, professor of music at Reed College in Portland, Oregon, holds degrees in chemistry from Reed and from Harvard University and a doctorate in music history from the University of Oregon. She is the author of *Brahms's Choral Compositions and His Library of Early Music* as well as a number of articles on the subject of the composer's study and performance of Renaissance and Baroque music, his own choral compositions, and his songs.

TIMOTHY L. JACKSON, musicologist and music theorist, has published extensively on Bruckner, Tchaikovsky, Richard Strauss, and other late-nineteenth- and twentieth-century composers, and co-edited *Bruckner Studies*.

RAYMOND KNAPP, associate professor in musicology at U.C.L.A., has published and lectured on a variety of musical repertories ranging from the fourteenth century to our own, although his principal interests remain in the eighteenth and nineteenth centuries. He is the author of the recent *Brahms and the Challenge of the Symphony*.

KLAUS KROPFINGER, a distinguished musicologist residing in Berlin, is the author of *Wagner and Beethoven: Richard Wagner's Reception of Beethoven* and numerous articles on Brahms and nineteenth-century music.

MARK MANDARANO is assistant conductor of the American Symphony Orchestra, the American Russian Youth Orchestra, and the Westchester Philharmonic. He is also director of the Festival Orchestra and Chorus of the Hoff-Barthelson Music School in Scarsdale, New York. He serves as an adjunct assistant professor of music history and theory at Bard College.

ROBERT P. MORGAN is professor of music at Yale University and writes frequently on nineteenth- and twentieth-century music and aesthetics. He is the author of *Twentieth-Century Music* and the editor of *The Twentieth Century*, part of the revised edition of *Strunk's Source Readings in Music History*.

MICHAEL MUSGRAVE is professor emeritus of music at Goldsmiths College, University of London, and works as an independent scholar in New York City. Among his recent books are *The Music of Brahms*, *The Musical Life of the Crystal Palace*, and *Brahms: A German Requiem*; forthcoming are *A Brahms Reader*, *The Cambridge Companion to Brahms*, new editions of the *Liebeslieder* and *Neue Liebeslieder* Waltzes and the Serenades for Orchestra, all by Brahms.

MARGARET NOTLEY has published articles about Brahms, Schubert, Bruckner, Beethoven, and Viennese musical life in *19th Century Music*, the *Journal of the Amer-*

ican Musicological Society, and various anthologies. She is editor of the *American Brahms Society Newsletter.* With the benefit of several national grants, she is preparing a book about late Brahms.

KAREN PAINTER received her doctorate from Columbia University, where she was the editor of *Current Musicology.* She has served on the faculty at Dartmouth College and now teaches in the music department at Harvard University. She is completing a book on the ideology of the symphony in Austro-German thought and culture from 1900 to 1945.

HEATHER PLATT is assistant professor of music at Ball State University. Her articles on Brahms's Lieder have appeared in numerous journals and collections, including *Intégral* and *The Journal of Musicology.* Her dissertation on the Lieder received the inaugural Karl Geiringer Award for Dissertation Research from the American Brahms Society and the Barry S. Brook Dissertation Award. Her other areas of research include eighteenth-century orchestral music and the operas of Alban Berg.

ELAINE SISMAN is professor of music at Columbia University. The author of *Haydn and the Classical Variation* and *Mozart: the "Jupiter" Symphony,* she also edited *Haydn and His World* for the Bard Music Festival. She is a member of the board of directors of the American Brahms Society, as well as an editor of *Beethoven Forum,* associate editor of *19th Century Music,* and a member of the editorial board of the *Journal of the American Musicological Society.*

LUCIEN STARK is emeritus professor and former chair of the piano faculty at the University of Kentucky. A widely respected exponent of the music of Brahms, he is the author of *A Guide to the Solo Songs of Johannes Brahms* and the forthcoming *Brahms's Vocal Duets and Quartets with Piano.*

MICHAEL P. STEINBERG, associate professor and director of graduate studies in history at Cornell University, also serves as associate editor of *The Musical Quarterly.* He is the author of *The Meaning of the Salzburg Festival: Austria as Theater and Ideology, 1890–1938* and is completing a book on the role of music in the development of modern subjectivity.

JAN SWAFFORD is a composer and writer living in Cambridge, Massachusetts. His music, which has been published, recorded, and performed in the U.S. and abroad, has won awards including an N.E.A. Composers Fellowship. His books include *Charles Ives: A Life with Music,* which received the 1997 PEN New England Award and a nomination for the National Book Critics Circle Award, and *Johannes Brahms: A Biography.*

R. LARRY TODD is professor of music and chair of the music department at Duke University. He has written extensively about nineteenth-century German music, especially the music of Mendelssohn, and is currently writing a new biography of that composer.

Laurence Wallach is a pianist, musicologist, and composer who lives in Great Barrington, Massachusetts, and heads the music program at Simon's Rock, Bard College. He has published articles on Charles Ives in *The Musical Quarterly, Current Musicology,* and elsewhere. He has received several "Meet the Composer" grants in New York State, won a competition for composers sponsored by the New School of Music in Cambridge, and created the score for *Songs from the Heart,* a television film about Edith Wharton.

Richard Wilson, composer-in-residence with the American Symphony Orchestra and Mellon Professor of Music at Vassar College, is a native of Cleveland and a graduate of Harvard College. He is the composer of some seventy works, including two symphonies and an opera, *Æthelred the Unready.*

INDEX

Note: **Boldface** numbers indicate principal discussion of the referenced works;
numbers in *italics* indicate photographs.